Library Service

...raries

6.9

RZ

Y 5 99

...Road
...ertford Road
Enfield
...992-710580

06. MAY

10.-8.93   APP N°   (B) 11/97   F 9/02

NO
RENEWAL   TO   Bush Hill Pk. Library
                   35 Agricola Place
16. NOV   Enfield EN1 1DW

LASER   24. APR 9   081-367 4917   1-7 APR 2004

due 23/11/93   11. APR. 96   P 5798

+a.   (E) S. 6. 9... (M)   (R2) 4/05

APP NO   ...Library
60/31975   (RZ)   ...Road
                    ...367...

Please remember that this item will attract overdue charges if not
returned by the latest date stamped above. You may renew it by
personal call, telephone or by post quoting the bar code number and
your personal number. I hope you enjoy all of your library services.

Peter Herring, Head of Arts and Libraries

30459297

18. APR 96

30126 00981241 0

Saraband:
The memoirs of E.L. Mascall

Dedication

To Those Whose Names
Do Not Occur
Herein

Saraband:

The memoirs of E.L. Mascall

A well-written Life is almost as rare as a well-spent one.
— Thomas Carlyle

First published in 1992

Gracewing
Fowler Wright Books
Southern Ave, Leominster
Herefordshire HR6 0QF

Gracewing Books are distributed

In New Zealand
Catholic Supplies Ltd
80 Adelaide Rd
Wellington
New Zealand

In Australia
Charles Paine Pty
8 Ferris Street
North Parramatta
NSW 2151 Australia

In Canada by
Novalis
P.O. Box 990
Outremont H2V 457
Canada

In U.S.A.
Morehouse Publishing
P.O. Box 1321
Harrisburg
PA 17105
U.S.A.

Typesetting by Action Typesetting Limited, Gloucester
Printed by Bookcraft Ltd., Bath, England.

ISBN 0 85244 222 X

Table of Contents

Foreword

Truly that clerk is crippled and maimed to his disablement in
many ways who is entirely ignorant of the art of writing.
— Richard de Bury, *Philobiblion*, ch. vi.

There is a story of an elderly man who was asked how he spent
his retirement. 'Well,' he replied, 'I have breakfast in bed every
morning and read *The Times*. And when I get to the obituaries,
if I don't find my name among them, I get up.' I retired officially
fourteen years ago. I do not have breakfast in bed, but I do read
The Times each day. I have not so far found my name among
the obituaries, though I nearly did a year ago, but I suppose one
should bear in mind the possibility that this is an indication of
insignificance rather than of survival.

The suggestion that one should write one's memoirs raises some
serious questions. Has one's life been stocked with enough exciting
incidents or one's mind with enough brilliant and creative ideas to
warrant their recording? Can one's overall contributions to scholarship claim a more distinguished verdict from posterity than that
which the examiners awarded to a candidate for the Ph. D. degree
when they reported: 'Mr X's thesis contains much that is profound
and much that is original. Unfortunately, what is profound is not
original, and what is original is not profound.'? Failing that,
has one that magic touch of phrase and epithet that turns the dullest
mud into dazzling gold; am I one of that favoured brotherhood
who can endow a journey on the Underground from Bond Street
to Oxford Circus with all the poetry of the Golden Road to
Samarkand? In any case, at what stage of life's journey should
the recording process be undertaken? The only Admiral of the
Fleet I have ever met published his autobiography when he was
in his sixties, and a fine work it was, with a picture of the
sailing ship in which he went to sea as a cadet; but, as he lived to

vii

be a hundred, it covered little more than half of his adult life. *Nel mezzo del cammin di nostra vita* – but who can tell when that has been reached? If one waits too long, death may intervene and the work remain unwritten; few can be able to imitate the distinguished academic lady whose book was entitled *My First Hundred Years*. What, in my case, is the justification for a retired professor in holy orders recording his reminiscences at the age of eighty-six?

Certainly, it is not that I have had a life packed with thrilling adventures and hairbreath escapes; nor have I been present at the turning points of history or been involved in decisions affecting the destinies of nations. T. E. Lawrence and Winston Churchill have nothing to fear from me. Even in the academic and eccles-iastical worlds I have rarely been much more than a spectator on the touch-line; *quorum pars minima fui* is the most that I can say. Nevertheless, from what is admittedly a worm's eye view, I have known some interesting people and witnessed some interesting events. To the adjective 'interesting' one might frequently add 'amusing'. Much of my story is no doubt trivial and the incidents ephemeral and my own share in it only that of the idle singer of an empty day. However, I have been fortunate in seeing a number of noteworthy persons, institutions and events from unusual and revealing angles and I have done my best to recall my observations. I hope that some of them at least have been worth recording.

Qui s'excuse s'accuse, and here I must make three self-accusations. First, although I have done my best to be accurate, this is not a serious work of historical research. I am not one of those who can give the impression of having kept up a carefully written and detailed diary from their infancy onwards. From 1940 I have a practically complete set of pocket-diaries containing my engagements; in a few places they are now illegible and in others, even to me, unintelligible. I have made ample use of printed matter and documents, where obtainable, and have sometimes been able to check my own memories with those of my contemporaries, though death has taken many of these in recent years; this task would have been easier if I had been writing ten years ago. I have had to rely a great deal on my memory and I am very conscious that it is not infallible. Cambridge colleges in the eighteenth century (that notoriously lax period), when certifying that their candidates had fulfilled all the requirements for a degree, used to protect themselves from perjury by inserting the saving clause 'although not entirely according to the form of the statute'. I should like to protect my own recollections by a similar qualification. I have done my best to be accurate, but my tradition has not had, for example, the special safeguards, natural and supernatural, enjoyed by the writers of the Gospels. I therefore solemnly declare that my narrative is as accurate as I can make it, *licet non omnino secundum formam statuti*.

Secondly, I have tried not to make mention, except briefly and incidentally, of persons who are still alive. This does not mean that I feel free to say whatever I like about those who are no longer with us in the body, relying on the fact that they can neither knock my block off nor sue me in the courts. As a Christian, I believe that they still exist as men and women created by God and redeemed by Christ and are entitled to truth and charity. But I also know that quite accurate references to quirks of temperament and oddities of behaviour which presumably can do no harm to those who are occupied with far more important matters beyond the grave may cause pain and embarrassment to those who are still in this vale of tears. So, for example, I have suppressed my memories of a very successful college tutor, devoted to his pupils and beloved by them, who was the subject of almost weekly anecdotes in Oxford after the Second World War. Only in the last two chapters have I found it necessary, in the interests of my narrative, to dispense myself from this self-denying ordinance, and I have tried to do this in a way that will give neither pain nor offence.

Thirdly, I must mention another reason for the non-occurrence of names in this book. There are persons whom I hold in deep affection and to whom I am indebted in many ways, who, as far as their characters and virtues are concerned, are more worthy of admiration than many whose more spectacular qualities have earned their admission. Merely to say that

> Along the cool sequestered vale of life
> They kept the noiseless tenor of their way

would be far too negative; some of them were furnaces of supernatural charity. But there is nothing that I know how to say about them that would interest those who were not fortunate enough to know them. Their names are written in the Book of Life, which is far more important than the present volume. But I have dedicated this volume to them, as a mark of indebtedness and gratitude.

Finally, I must refer to a problem to which it will become all too obvious that I have not found an answer. Should my plan be — to use a fashionable jargon — synchronic or diachronic? That is to say, should I rigidly follow the canon laid down by the King of Hearts – 'Begin at the beginning, and go on till you come to the end; then stop' – or, when some particular person, movement or institution has first appeared in my story, should I ramble off into whatever I have to say about him, her or it, regardless of where this may take me, before returning to the point that I had reached when the digression began? It will be plain to the reader that I have made little resistance to the temptation to digress, but I would claim some justification from the fact that I have been writing a memoir and not an autobiography. Now a biography is about the person whose biography it is, and an *auto*biography is about its author. 'How foolish of Montaigne to set out to paint himself', reflected Pascal; and how foolish it would be of me to write all about myself. I have certainly not kept myself entirely out of my story. Even a bundle needs some string to tie it together, as the philosopher Hume found to his undoing; though some of my readers may think there is rather too much string and too little bundle. But, to repeat the distinction, a memoir is not an autobiography; it is about what the author remembers, and it may be hoped that he will remember something other than himself. So the digressions, however clumsily handled, are part of the sort of book this is; and I should not be surprised if they are the most interesting part. But I hope the fairly ample dates which I have provided will do something to help the adherents of the King of Hearts.

Chapter One
Ancestry and Infancy
(- ? - 1905 – 1910)

'You come of the Lord Adam and the Lady Eve', said Aslan,
'And that is both honour enough to erect the head of the
poorest beggar, and shame enough to bow the shoulders of
the greatest emperor on earth. Be content.'
            – C. S. Lewis, *Prince Caspian*, ch. xv.

As a child I had a receptive and retentive mind, but I cannot
claim, as did the brother of one of my friends, to have once felt
a slap on the chest and simultaneously heard a delighted voice
announcing 'It's a boy!' The earliest *impression* of which in fact I
am conscious is of being peacefully crooned to sleep by my mother
to the background accompaniment of waves tumbling and washing
on a shingly shore. In contrast, the earliest *episode* of which I have
any recollection was traumatic; it is of being taken for a walk by a
small girl slightly my senior, getting completely lost, being found
exhausted and asleep by the local Boy Scouts, and being restored to
my distracted relatives, who only too reasonably feared that we had
fallen into the sea or into one of the refuse-pits of the neighbouring
chemical works. I was three years old at the time. The place was
Shoreham Beach in Sussex, later to be adveritised and vulgarised
as Bungalow Town, and my maternal grandmother had one of the
earliest bungalows on it. My mother and I were staying with her
while my father was away on a business appointment for a year in
India. The bungalow was called 'The Anchorage' and basically consisted of two superanuated railway-coach bodies; these were cheap
to buy and, being extremely robustly constructed, were able to resist
the south-west gales in a way totally beyond the power of more
conventional but flimsier building materials. And what gales some
of those were! I remember on a later occasion walking along the
length of the beach after one of the worst storms on record, when
a number of bungalows had been washed away to sea and many

1

others reduced to wreckage; 'The Anchorage' had just survived. I visited the Beach many times during my childhood and youth, either to stay with my grandmother or in other bungalows which my parents rented, and I saw the successive introduction of the amenities of civilisation. To begin with, there was no metalled road, no piped gas, electricity or water, no drainage and no footbridge. 'Sanitation' was coped with by a horse-drawn vehicle which made nocturnal, and later less agreeable diurnal, visitations. Water was, I think, supplied by another vehicle but we relied chiefly on the rain, of which there was usually plenty. To cross from the town to the beach involved either a long trudge round by the Norfolk Bridge and then along the shingle (one developed a peculiar rolling gait for this) or else the extraction of a reluctant ferryman from a pub to row one across the Adur. The latter alternative could be intimidating, especially on a dark and dirty night and at low tide, when, having landed from the boat, one trusted to Providence to keep one's feet safely on the 'hard' and out of the river mud. I do not remember hearing of anyone meeting his death by this unpleasant form of suffocation, but I should be surprised if it never happened. Anyone who spent a winter on Shoreham Beach in the old days was in a good position to understand the petitions in the Psalms for the guidance of one's footsteps in a literal and not only a figurative sense.

In fine weather the Beach could, of course, be a very delightful place, as was realised by those who developed it between the Wars. But it could never become a popular resort on the model of Blackpool or Brighton. It always retained a number of perm-anent residents, even if the needier of them tended to let their bungalows in the summer and retire to less eligible localities inland. It suffered badly during, or rather after, World War Two, when the troops from overseas, who had taken the place of the civilian population to protect it from Hitler's anticipated but abortive invasion, celebrated their departure by a vandalistic spree which left it looking like a battlefield. But it was and is an interesting place, not least from its unique historical and geographical aspect. Shoreham, with its harbour protected by a fold of the Downs just within the mouth of the River Adur, had been one of the most important seaports on the south coast. Unfortunately towards the end of the Middle Ages it was pro-gressively ruined by the famous eastward drift in the channel, which finally built up a shingle barrier three miles in length extending from the former river mouth to Portslade. This effectively cut off access to the harbour, which now is represented by fields lying between Old and

New Shoreham churches. Commercial salvation came, however, in the sixteenth and seventeenth centuries, when the river broke through the barrier about one third of the way along. This left to the east a cul-de-sac which became the new Harbour, while the strip of shingle to the west, roughly a mile long, became what is now Shoreham Beach and the scene of my earliest memories.

I must resist the temptation to write about Shoreham at length and will simply refer any interested reader to the admirable volume [1] written in the nineteen-twenties by the postmaster on the Beach. He was one of those gifted amateur local historians whom our country is so successful in producing. Although my earliest memories are of Shoreham, it was in London that my parents were married and settled and I was born. According to family tradition, they first met in the unconventional setting of a railway train, in which they were both passengers but which my mother realised after it had started was going to a destination other than that for which she had purchased a ticket. My father, moved by the spectacle of beauty in distress, not only took it upon himself to conduct her safely to the town, and indeed to the house, where she was expected, but also called shortly afterwards to express the hope that she had taken no harm from her alarming experience. One version of the story exonerates my father from any unwarranted and ungentlemanly intrusion upon a solitary and unprotected young lady – which would in any case have been altogether inconsistent with his rigidly Victorian code of behaviour – by adding that he was the unintentional spurce of her misinformation in the first place and was anxious, if not indeed under a moral obligation, to minimise its effects. Be that as it may, this chance encounter initiated a romance which culminated in wedding-bells at Old St Pancras' Church on August 2nd 1899 and led in due course to my own appearance *in hac lacrymarum valle*.

Dorothy L. Sayers has written that 'between the bishops who assure us that the family is the one and only seed-bed of all the virtues, and the psychiatrists who warn us that it is a hotbed of all the vices, we hardly know how to advise any child to enter upon the hazard of existence.'[2] It was therefore perhaps well for me that I was spared the ante-natal attention of both groups of experts and that my birth-certificate simply testifies on the word of my father, who is omniously described as 'the informant', that I opened my eyes upon this world on December 12th 1905 as the son of John Richard Strutt Mascall, commercial traveller, of 2 Earlsthorpe Road, Sydenham, and Susan Lilian Mascall, formerly Grundy, and that the event in question took place at the parental residence. It was, of course, the usual custom in those days for infants to undergo the exacting but common place experience of birth at home, and I appear to have come through it successfully, though my mother told me, years later, that the hastily summoned nurse was greeted with the information (which she was unwilling to credit) that the baby had 'already arrived'. My parents' only other child, John Richard Claude, had already died in early infancy, and this no doubt largely accounts for the anxious solicitude with which my childhood and adolescence were surrounded. It is only right that I should bear witness to the long years of self-denial which they imposed on themselves in order that I should enjoy advantages of which they themselves had been deprived. As I look back I am deeply conscious of my failure during their lifetime to recognise adequately the debt which I owe to them.

I see, on consulting the atlas, that Earlsthorpe Road, which still exists, is one of a cluster of streets of which the remainder bear the names of Kingsthorpe, Queensthorpe, Princethorpe, Dukesthorpe and Bishopsthorpe; they appear to descend no further in the social scale. This nomenclature suggests some veneration for nobility and indeed for regality, though it may be too much to suggest that the residents of Bishopsthorpe Road enjoyed lower status or paid lower rents than their exalted neighbours of Kingsthorpe. In any case, viscounts and barons were unrepresented and, although in the Royal Borough of Kensington and Chelsea the inhabitants of Earls Court can look down their noses at their humbler fellow-citizens two stations nearer the sunset on the District Line, there are in Sydenham no Baronsthorpians to wilt beneath the pitying glances of their episcopal eponyms. More to the point perhaps is my parents' belief, which was probably fully justified, that if the wind was in the north we in Sydenham could hear the bells of Bow Church in the City. This I have always felt frustrating, since, without ascertaining the precise moment of my birth and the meteorological conditions then pertaining (and this I have never succeeded in doing), it is impossible to discover whether I am a cockney or not. I hope that I am; and my early manifested ability to acquire the relevant linguistic skills in spite of parental discouragement would seem to support the hypothesis, but I have never been quite sure. On the other hand, Sydenham, besides being in the recently established County of London, was – as it still is – undoubtedly in the geographical county of Kent and is well to the west of the Medway; and this makes me quite certainly a Kentish Man as distinct from one of the Men of Kent, many of whom, it is alleged (though I do not credit this, for they include most of my direct ancestors), are born with tails for their alleged complicity in the murder of the great Archbishop.

At this point I suppose I shall be expected to say something about my family, although I am far from emulating Disraeli's aristocrat who thanked Providence every day that his family was not unworthy of him[3] and although, in view of Lord Melbourne's warning 'Who the devil knows who anybody's father is?', the persistence of the 'Y' chromosome in the male-line may not be of invariable dynastic significance.

The name 'Mascall' (and may I inform any American readers that the stress falls on the first syllable), of which 'Maskell' appears to be merely a spelling variant, is etymologically identical with the much commoner name 'Marshall'. The Frankish-Latin word *mariscalcus*, whose literal meaning was simply 'horse-servant', had, not surprisingly, a wide range of applications in the Middle Ages and could designate anyone from a farrier or a groom up to a commander of cavalry or a high officer of state. 'Mascall' is a fairly immediate contraction of it, 'Marshal' or 'Marshall' only slightly more remote, through the French intermediary *maréchal*. To this day the Earl Marshal is, of course, the head of the College of Arms, which administers whatever remains of chivalry; the more recently devised rank of Air Marshal suggests the extension of marshalship to the oversight of the Pegasine species. All through the Middle Ages documentary mention of Mascalls occurs, chiefly in Durham, Yorkshire, Sussex and Kent; Robert Mascall, a Carmelite friar, who held what must have been the exacting office of confessor to King Henry IV, became Bishop of Hereford in 1404. As far as I know, the northern and southern Mascalls have no relationship except common descent from Adam, but the Sussex and Kent Mascalls were clearly prosperous, prolific and locally influential; and, although few if any of them are to be found there today, their names are still to be found in a number of place- and house-names and their memorials in the churches. Mascalls and Little Mascalls at Paddock Wood, and Mount Mascall and Vale Mascall near Bexley, all in Kent, are examples, but quite the most interesting to my knowledge is to be found in Sussex. Just to the east of the village of Lindfield is East Mascalls, a fine two-storied timbered house. In 1904 E. V. Lucas, in his *Highways and Byways in Sussex*, described it as a ruin and F. L. Griggs's illustration certainly showed it as such; but even then it was said to have been 'taken in hand' and it now appears well restored and cared for.[4] In 1550 the estate was sold away from the family but, in an attempt forty years later (which was in fact unsuccessful) to recover it on the alleged grounds of an entail, a pedigree was produced which showed it to have been in the possession of John le Marescall in 1341; his son appears to have preferred the spelling Mascall and in that form it continues without a break. An interesting ornament of the family, though he left no local memorial, was Leonard Mascall, an ingenious and possibly eccentric character of Tudor times. He died and was buried in 1589 at Farnham Royal in Bukinghamshire but he lived for many years at Plumpton Place, a moated house four miles to the north-west of Lewes, and wrote a number of books on horticulture and agriculture. Fuller, in the *Worthies*, describes him, on his own word, as having introduced into England both carp and pippins, 'the one, well cook'd, delicious, the other cordial and restorative.' He also coloured apples by injecting pigments, loosened them from the tree by hot fumes of brimstone and had a simple means of killing ants. But when I saw the house it was badly dilapidated and was indeed a rural slum; and no trace of memorial of Leonard was to be seen.

From the ample surviving records it is clear that for many centuries the Mascalls of Sussex and Kent were solid and successful people, well rooted in the countryside, prudently managing and from time to time extending, their property and marrying into other families of similar and occasionally slightly superior station. But none of them seem to have shown either desire or aptitude to get involved in the religious or political upheavals of their times. But where did they come from in the first place, whatever in this context 'the first place' means? Here is the story as I received it, and I repeat it without comment or affidavit.

In the eleventh century Geoffrey de Bec Crispin, of the family of le Mareschall of Valance in France, owned the fief of Venoix in Normandy. He must have crossed the Channel with the Conqueror, since he is mentioned in Domesday Book. He left two co-heiresses, who married two of their cousins, Gilbert and Robert, who were in fact brothers. Robert, who held certain lands by grant of the conqueror, was the ancestor of the Mascalls of Lindfield. Gilbert became Sheriff of Surrey and Sussex, and a third brother, William Fitz Norman, was the domesday owner of Combes in Sussex and the ancestor of the baronial family of Kilpec. Gilbert's grandson, John, became Sheriff of Sussex as did also the heir, another William, who entered into royal service, made a judicious marriage, became Earl of Pembroke and was one of the leading figured of Magna Carta. (The romantic story of the curse laid upon the family by the Bishop of Fernes in Ireland, as a result of which all William's five sons died without issue, makes interesting reading but is not strictly relevant to the present purpose.) From his brother, John, are descended the Mascalls of Maresfield.

I shall now skip a number of centuries to come to my own direct forebears, who come clearly into view as Men of Kent in the seventeenth century. In 1664 John Mascall, an attorney of Ashford, married Mary Hunt of Canterbury. Their union was blessed with a son, also baptised John, in the same year. (A second marriage produced the ancestor of Robert Mascall, of the 'great house' in Ashford, who became Deputy Lieutenant of Kent and Sussex and died in 1815.) In 1702 this second John begot a third John, and he in turn begot in 1738 a fourth, who died in 1802. All lived in Ashford, all were attorneys, and the last one was Lord Warden of Winchelsea, one of the famous seven Cinque Ports. There were thus four generations of John Mascalls carrying on for a century and a half a respectable and presumably reasonably remunerative legal business in this quiet Kentish country town. Then there came a break, and the commitment of the senior line of the Mascalls to the profession of the Law became (how I do not know, but one can surmise that the background of European politics had something to do with it) an equally strong commitment to the profession of arms and in particular to that small but very special and distinguished body the Royal Marines. Certainly this change cannot have been motivated by any financial considerations, for the attorneys were obviously doing quite well for themselves, while the Marines were a small force in which promotion was extremely slow; I have been told that one member of my family was still a First Lieutenant awaiting his Captaincy when his son had just been promoted from Second Lieutenant to First.[5] Whatever the reason, the son of the fourth of the Attorneys, born in 1760 and, needless to say, another John, acquired a commission in the Royal Marines. A beautifully printed morroco-bound Marine List of 1819, which was given to my father by an uncle in 1885, records John Mascall as having received his captaincy in 1812 and been reduced to half pay in 1814. He died in 1819 and is buried at Kingston, Kent. Had he, I wonder, broken with his father, and what happened to the family business anyhow? The second son, Edward Charles, showed similar martial ambitions to his elder brother's, although he was less successful. Having become a midshipman in the Navy, he had to leave on account of bad sight and was refused a commission in the Marines for the same reason. The remaining son, Foley, was said to have emigrated to the West Indies and to have done well there. I have myself two interesting mementoes of Captain John Mascall, my great-great-grandfather. One is a rather inferior portrait in oils, showing him in his scarlet uniform; it used to have, hanging over it, a small red ensign, which puzzled observers who did not know that the red ensign was originally not the insignia of the merchant navy but of one of the three squadrons into which the Royal Navy was divided until 1864. The other is a small water-colour painting of a forlornlooking hulk, flying the union flag and the white ensign and with a variety of garments hung up to dry from lines strung between the vestigial masts. Its origin is explained by the following attached note in my grandfather's writing:

> In the reign of George the Third in September 1799 lay moored some few Prison ships containing French prisoners of war, this one named as under, done by one of their number. The figure represented on the Port side of the Quarter deck is First Lieutenant John Mascall of the Royal Marines, serving on board. His Majesty's Ship, 'Vigilant'. 1799.

The figure referred to, shown from the waist upwards, is about three millimetres high, but a black top hat and a red coat are plainly visible. A family tradition holds that my ancestor had performed some kindness for the French prisoner, possibly communicating with his relatives, and that this little picture was a token of gratitude. We like to believe that he was at the Battle of Trafalgar in 1805, though probably not on the *Victory*.

Captain John introduced an element of variety into the monotony of Christian names by having his eldest son baptised John Richards, and John Richards have recurred ever since. This John Richard performed the remarkable feat of becoming not merely a captain but a major; he died in 1867. I have one delightful memento of him, not actually his own work but that of his schoolmaster and presumably presented to him as a parting gift to a satisfactory pupil. It is a quite exquisitely executed example of penmanship with a quill, so perfectly and minutely done that viewers always take it to be a copper engraving, not least because of the delightfully depicted tiny flies with which the dominie ornamented his moral and pedantic text. The latter runs as follows, and it was no doubt felt to be highly appropriate for the son of an officer in his Majesty's forces who, it was hoped, would follow in his father's footsteps:

COMMAND OF HAND
Fabricius was not to be Bribed by the Gold of Pyrrhus, nor daunted by his Elephants. For neither the Charms of the One

nor the Frightfulness of the other, should shake a Spirit that is truly devoted to the Honour & Interest of his Country a glorious Example.

This was authenticated by my grandfather on the back of the frame in these words:

This was done by Mr Hand, my Father Major Mascall's School Master, at Seal (I think) near Sevenoaks, Kent, now about 100 years old.
Jno. R. Mascall

3rd Jan. 1889.

And the future major was in fact given the rank of Second Lieutenant in 1808.

His son, my grandfather, the second John Richard, was born in 1833. He became Second Lieutenant in 1854 and First Lieutenant automatically a year later. Twelve years later he obtained his captaincy and two years after that – in 1869 – he was placed on half pay, when a drastic 'reduction' of the Marines took place. After expeditions to the West Indies and the Baltic during his first four years his service seems to have been entirely at home. Clearly after the Crimean War the nineteenth century must have been a dull and depressing time for ambitious officers in Her Majesty's Royal Marines. I have in my possession the two lieutenancy commissions addressed by the great Queen to her trusty and well beloved John Richard Mascall, and above the printed name 'Victoria' with which they begin there is the actual signature of the Sovereign herself. I can only suppose that it was her practice at that time to sign personally the commissions of all her officers, as my family certainly had no personal contact with the Royal Family, and that the number of such commissions was small enough to make that possible.

My grandfather married three times, and I must stress that the first two marriages were terminated by death and not by divorce. As far as I know, we had no scandals of any kind in the family throughout the century, though I have seen a letter suggesting that the will in which a local member of the family left his property to a lady described as 'my wife X' might be disputed on the grounds that at the time of their wedding 'it was well-known' in the place where they resided that she was already married to another living person and therefore had never legally been the wife of the testator at all. This assertion of notorious connivance at bigamy in respectable naval and military circles in the mid-nineteenth century somewhat surprised me, but I could find no traces of its following-up and I feel pretty sure that it was groundless.

My grandfather's first marriage was to Catherine, the daughter of a certain Judge Strutt of Georgetown, Demerara. There were three children, my aunts Florence and Ada and my father, John Richard Strutt. The second marriage produced one child, George Percival Yorke, my uncle Percy. The third marriage, entered on in old age to the widowed daughter of a naval captain, was childless. My grandfather died in 1906, when I was less than a year old, so I have no recollection of him, nor of his widow, who died less than a month later.

By the eighteen-seventies and eighties a century of loyal service in the Royal Marines had exhausted whatever fortunes the family ever had and by the time of his death in the Lewisham Union Infirmary my grandfather was evidently in considerable poverty. There had been no question of my father going into the Marines. He had been found a place in the Royal Naval School at New Cross in Kent, a very reputable institution which alas no longer exists; it owed its foundation to the Sailor King William IV in his concern for the families of his less prosperous officers. On leaving school my father obtained a junior post in a commercial firm, and he continued in similar appointments, either in business corporations or under government, until he retired on a very inadequate pension a few years before the Second World War. He was thoroughly conscientious and reliable but by worldly standards unsuccessful and disappointed. Very occasionally he was financially at ease, though never anywhere near to opulence; sometimes he was desperately hard up. Only as I look back can I understand something of the anxiety and deprivation which he and my mother had to face unassisted; and these were not lessened by the façade of sufficiency which in those days the middle class felt obliged to maintain in order to conceal its basic and growing insecurity. It was his constant and overriding concern that I should have better opportunities in life than he had had. He died in 1940 at Parkstone in Dorset.

Very different from my father, both in temperament and in appearance, was his younger half-brother, George Percival Yorke Mascall. A tall, dark, flamboyant extrovert, my uncle Percy had a remarkable resemblance to King Alfonso XIII of Spain. By his own account, he had a most unsatisfactory early upbringing. At the age of ten he ran away from school at Blackheath and evaded search by police and relatives for no less than four years, during which time he lived on his wits in London. Finally captured at the age of fourteen, he was taken by his father to the Admiralty and enlisted in the Royal Marines as a bugler. Another four years enabled him at eighteen to become a full private and for the next seventeen years he worked his way steadily up through every rank to colour sergeant. Clearly he had found his vocation in the family career, though his progress was not without its hazards. He survived, as sergeant, the threat of a court matiral on the ridiculous charge of deliberately failing to recognise an officer on a dark and stormy night. Less serious, and possibly less authentic, was an alleged incident when, finding himself ashore with a party of friends, he obtained free entertainment in an expensive and exclusive restaurant as the King of Spain 'travelling incognito', and narrowly escaped exposure when the manager, forgetting the warning, instructed the orchestra to play the Spanish national anthem. He became in fact a senior non-commissioned officer and, shortly before World War One, he was lent, as was then a common practice in peace time, to be chief of police in the West-Indian island of St Lucia. By that time he had, through marriage with a Roman Catholic lady, himself become a Roman Catholic, though a remarkably uninstructed one, and I remember him and his wife and their four children staying with us at Upper Norwood on their way out to the Caribbean.

With the coming of War he was brought back and immediately given a commission. He was sent with the Royal Naval Division on the disastrous Gallipoli expedition and there contracted lung trouble, which led to his being invalided out of the forces. He had thus became the Mascall of the fourth generation to be an officer in the Royal Marines; this was a record shared by only one other family. On the coming of peace, perhaps with racial memories of Leonard Mascall of near-by Plumpton, he decided to take up fruit farming and went to be trained at government expense on a small farm near Ditchling, to the north of the South Downs. His eldest Son, John, had died in the West Indies, but the second, Reginald, went to the Jesuit school Beaumont College near Windsor, and the two daughters to the school of the Sacred Heart Sisters at Brighton. I once spent a holiday with them at their cottage called Beanacre on the slope of the Downs, and Reggie and I enjoyed ourselves together, unsuccessfully chasing rabbits with the aid, or more accurately the company, of his small fox terrier. However, Uncle Percy's enthusiasm for fruit waned before he got to the point of acquiring a farm of his own. What he did purchase was a poultry-farm near Chelmsford in Essex, and this was to all appearance a success, until he decided instead to sell, first flowers and then silk stockings, in the West End of London. Finally he set up his elder daughter in a hat-shop. This brought him to the metropolis and he and my Aunt Florrie set up house together in the Finchley Road, with an ex-Marine as butler. Stockings, however, did not go too well, and Uncle Percy next moved into tobacco, selling through the post his own guaranteed Marine brand, soaked in naval spirit and bearing the appropriate name 'Rummy'. This, unfortunately, produced trouble with the excise authorities, and the spirit had to be replaced by a non-alcoholic substitute of similar flavour. I lost touch with him during the later inter-war period and still more during World War Two, though I gathered he had taken up farming in East and/or South Africa and was, at any rate for some time, conducting the sale of Rummy from somewhere in that continent. I saw him once again, after the War in 1960, when he was living, visibly aged, in a boarding house congenially situated at the garrison town of Chatham. His son Reggie obtained a commission in the Marines during the War, thus raising our score to five. Reggie's ship was sunk and he floated about in the Mediterranean for a long time before he was rescued. He survived to receive the Distinguished Service Cross. He returned to civilian life and died of cancer in early middle age. I saw him and the priest who ministered to him before he died, and was impressed immensely by the simple faith with which he approached his death; his last days were spent in almost constant prayer. He left two sons, John Richard and David, both of whom had a spell in the Marines themselves. This brings the family score up to six generations, which must surely constitute an unchallenged record. I received an invitation to the marriage of the former as I was beginning to write this book. So for good or ill the continuance of the Mascalls seems assured.

I cannot leave mention of the family without reference to one remarkable figure of positively Dickensian type. Reginald John Mascall Stedman was through his mother (or, as he would probably have preferred to say, by distaff kinship), a grandson of the aforesaid Major John Richard Mascall. He was by profession a solicitor, and he had lived and practised and managed to bring up a family of several children (I cannot imagine how) in the same tiny house in Rochester High Street which he and his wife Amy had occupied throughout their married life. He had become such a permanent and well-known local monument that his writing paper bore as its heading the one word 'Rochester', and one felt it would have been an insult to add the name of the street and, still more, the number of the house. He was the doyen of the legal and medical professions of the city and had for many years held the important office of coroner; I remember him indiscreetly telling my father and me in a loud voice on the platform of the railway station the verdict that he was going to bring in at an inquest which was to be held the following day. He was an old-fashioned high-churchman and a Jacobite, though in practice loyal to the established Hanoverian dynasty. On the appropriate occasions he would appear with oak-apple leaf in his button-hole and slap himself on the chest while uttering seditious sentiments about Bonny Prince Charlie. He was intensely proud of his Mascall descent, distaff and not spear though it was. He and his quiet little wife came to stay with us once or twice at Hove and he was an impressive figure on the promenade in an old-fashioned morning coat and a panama hat. Once when my father and I went to see him at Rochester, he took us into the little front room that had served him all his professional life as his office; piles of dust-covered documents carefully bound with tape lined the walls. When we came out into the passage he carefully locked the door of the office and hung up the key on a nail at eye-level, while remarking on the importance of security. He always spoke in formal old-fashioned language, well studded with legal terms. 'I wonder, Cousin John,' I can hear him saying to my father, 'whether perchance you may recall the name of one Tráfalgar[6] Brattle, formerly resident in this city?' My father replied that he thought he remembered *his* father mentioning such a person. 'Ah,' said Cousin Reggie, 'poor fellow, poor fellow; he was struck by a bomb in an air-raid and he passed away.' This was soon after World War One; but early in World War Two Cousin Reggie wrote me a letter which I only wish I had preserved. It was to tell me that the railings surrounding the grave of a female forebear (I think it was my great-grand-mother) were threatened with being melted down for ammunition, but that, in response to a movement initiated by him for their preservation, they would be spared if members of the family would pay for their rehabilitation, as they were in a vary dilapidated condition. It was a splendid letter full of legal terms, and the lady in question was repeatedly referred to as the 'deceased' and as her husband's 'relict'. I couldn't really have cared less about the railings, but I could not resist Cousin Reggie's appeal to my *pietas* and I duly contributed my share. I presume the railings were saved, but I do not think I heard any more about them. Pedantic as he was, Cousin Reggie was excellent company and there was even a family tradition of certain harmless frivolity in the past, when he was alleged to have been a great admirer of the ladies of the local theatre. He was nevertheless a monument of family and professional responsibility and I can still see his short but dignified figure inhaling the air on Brighton front with a bundle of legal documents projecting from his breast-pocket.

I have recorded my father's ancestry in the conventional way, tracing it from past to present and in the male line; my mother's, so far as it is known to me, I shall trace in the opposite direction and almost entirely through females. This does not indicate sudden conversion from male chauvinism to women's lib. in the course of writing this work; it is entirely due to the way in which the events arrange themselves in my recollection and, still more, to their exiguous nature. For I cannot lay claim to the distinction of Seize Quartiers carefully recorded or investigated, even were I satisfied with less exacting evidence than would be demanded by the Earl Marshal and his heraldic subordinates.[7] My mother's father held what must have been, at least for his family, the extremely pleasant position of estate manager to the Earl of Darnley at Cobham Hall in Kent, and she and her sister and three brothers were brought up on the estate in a large ivy-clad house named The Mount, which appears to have been demolished since that time. The Earl was, from all accounts a benevolent but severe figure of feudal dimensions, compared with whom Sir Leicester Dedlock would have been some way to the political left. He rarely failed to attend and vote in the House of Lords, where his sole speech was alleged to have consisted of the single sentence 'Shut that damned window!' When the Earl or the Countess drove through the village of Cobham the poor men at their gates (all of whom were tenants and employees of the Hall) did due homage, and at election-time the whole population were conveyed in wagons to register their suffrages. The Earl was of course patron of the living, but, although he had appointed the Vicar, he was unable to remove him, and, having quarrelled with him, found himself under the painful necessity of driving to a neighbouring village for divine worship every Sunday. The Vicar in question, the Reverend A. H. Berger, had been ordained as curate of West Ham in 1860. He became incumbent of Cobham in 1876 and was still listed in Crockford as holding the living in 1931, by which time Cobham was no longer the quiet village of my mother's childhood and had become a growing dormitory centre. He was a cleric of strict evangelical views and, on finding the schoolchildren singing the lyric 'Goosey goosey gander', with the scandalous line 'There I met an old man who wouldn't say his prayers', emended the offending words to 'There I met an old man breaking up the chairs', thus preserving the religious character of elderly adults at the cost of unintelligibility. The chief claim of the Earl's family upon more than local fame was provided by the Honourable Ivo Bligh, who earned undying glory in cricketing circles for bringing back the 'Ashes' from Australia in the 1880s. Like many ancient families the Darnleys have fallen from their former high estate, largely through a succession of short tenures of the title and property, with the consequent depredations of death duties; a number of pieces were sold off, in one case for the laying out of a golf course, and I imagine that on each occasion there must have been indications of considerable angular momentum inside the tomb of my mother's Earl. I found the Hall open to the public one day in the sixties and was amazed by the magnificence of both the building and its contents; most of it is now, I believe, an educational institution and only one wing is occupied by the family.

My mother's father was neither a Kentish Man nor a Man of Kent, nor was her mother the female equivalent, and I presume that it was the prospect of an attractive job that had brought him from the midlands to the south-east. It must have been when his family was just getting grown up that the calamity occurred which cut off their connection with Cobham and the Darnleys. He was thrown from his horse and killed, leaving a widow and five children, and very little else. I shall say something about his widow later on; she was the only one of my grandparents of whom I have any recollection and she lived to be just on ninety.

My mother had three brothers, all of whom as young men emigrated to Canada, but only the youngest settled there permanently; the second, my uncle Frank, the only one of whom I saw very much, was an ideal uncle from a child's point of view and I loved and admired him immensely. He had a fund of the most splendid stories about the exploits, almost entirely illicit and clandestine, perpetrated by himself and his brothers at Cobham in the company of another juvenile delinquent named Benny Baker (how strange it is that a name should stick in the mind after all these years), which were tremendously enthralling to a nephew in the London suburbs who had neither the opportunity nor the courage to indulge in organised wrong-doing. He combined great ingenuity of invention with total inability to exploit it gainfully; he had designed, so he told me, the first machine for selling postage-stamps but he could not convince the authorities that it was not cheaper to sell stamps over the counter. He made me a number of toys, for which I was duly grateful. From a conventional standpoint his only personal success was, surprisingly, in the Army, and then only in time of war. He had — this was of course before I was born — obtained a commission in the Royal Engineers during the Boer War and had been signals-officer to Lord Roberts.

Signals in those days were mainly a matter of running out miles of wire for telephones and morse, though in the climate of South Africa a great deal of use was made of heliographs, which had among other advantages that of being highly directional, like, though less than, the modern laser. It was possible for different units on hills surrounding a besieged town to communicate with each other by flashing messages in morse unknown to the beleagred forces below. One reminiscence of my uncle's was of Lord Roberts and General Cronje, both of whom were godly bible-reading warriors, waging verbal warfare in slack periods by heliographing against each other appropriate and bloodthirsty texts from the Old Testament, so that some nasty insinuation from, say, Jeremiah might be countered a few moments later by an effectual back-hander from II Kings. When, decades later, in South Africa itself, I read Rayne Kruger's history of the campaign[8] I was struck by the detailed closeness of my uncle's accounts of incidents, such as Cronje's surrender at Paardeberg, at which he was present. Uncle Frank was, in fact, a superb story-teller, and I can still feel my agonised suspense, as a patriotic young Briton, when he concluded one day's instalment of the saga with the British forces simultaneously besieged in Mafeking, Kimberley and Ladysmith. (And of course there was Baden Powell, the founder of the Scout movement and the great hero of contemporary boyhood.) To his disappointment, my uncle's active service in the First World War was brief and left him permanently disabled. He settled down, however, fairly rapidly to a life of contented partial activity and we remained on terms of great affection. As a young man he had had a number of innocent but inconclusive romances, through which, as a small boy, I received acceptable gifts from honorary and ephemeral aunts, and he then seemed to have moved into a contented and permanent bachelorhood. It was thus an astonishment to us all when, on the verge of old age, he married an Irish Roman Catholic lady whom he had known for many years. They were extremely happy, and their happiness was assisted by the fact that they shared a remarkable unconsciousness of the passage of time. I went to see them regularly in their house off the front at Hove and by taking care to arrive at least an hour after the appointed time avoided making an inconveniently early appearance. He is buried near his mother in the cemetery at Shoreham-by-Sea.

Of my mother's other two brothers I saw very little, but her sister, who, like my mother, had been very beautiful young woman,

I saw fairly frequently. She married a Scotsman, a civil engineer in the employment of the Admiralty. He worked his way up from imperial outposts as far-flung as Ascension and St Helena, to become Super-intendent Civil Engineer in Portsmouth Dockyard, via places as varied as Simonstown, Malta and Rosyth. When he and his family came back from South Africa they brought as presents for my parents an ostrich's egg, tastefully painted with a view of Table Mountain, which I still treasure and which appears to be quite indestructible, and also a stuffed porcupine-fish or tetradont, a fearsome monster, like a foot-ball studied with spikes, which my parents hung on a standard lamp in their drawing room. It was in fact one of my earliest memories and I was quite surprised to discover later on that there were families whose standard lamp lacked this particular embellishment. When it came into my possession it continued to hang on the lamp from which I transferred it to just outside the door of my study, and visitors some-times told me that it provoked disturbing (but they were kind enough to add, unrealised) speculations about what they would find on the other side. Finally it succumbed to natural decay and I regretfully had to discard it. My aunt and her husband and children were in Malta for almost exactly the period of World War One, during which they were virtually cut off from the outside world. When after the armistice they returned to England and stayed for some time with my grandmother, their clothes, which had continued to be made by Maltese tailors and dressmakers after the fashions of 1914, caused some surprise and amusement. For clothes-styles, like other more important things, had changed a good deal during the tragic four years.

My grandmother came from the midlands, as I have said, and from Staffordshire to be precise. She was a very affectionate and kindly person, thoroughly domesticated, unintellectual and conven-tional, and I was for some reason her favourite grandchild. She could always produce the appropriate aphorism for any occasion. One must not be noisy on Sunday because 'it was God's holy day'. One went to a party with the reminder to be 'merry and wise'. Catastrophes were 'sent to try us', and arguments were defused with the advice 'Let us waive the point'. All her relations were farmers named Pratt, Blake or Allen, and where she met her husband William Grundy I never found out. At the age of four I was taken by my mother for a holiday, which I found delightful, with my grandmother's brother George Pratt. Great-uncle George was an efficient and successful farmer, whose establishment, Seale Fields, was highly up-to-date by contemporary standards, which did not exclude the location of the privy (a remarkable structure with two full-sized seats and a small one set in a row) at the end of a winding path. I found the drive to church, where Uncle George was warden, quite terrifying; the two seats, placed back to back, were perched above the single axle, and the two backward-facing occupants were always liable to be precipitated straight into the road, a hazard intensified by the fact that Uncle George used to received young horses to be 'broken-in' and that the animal between the shafts on any occasion was likely to be still under instruction. Children notice odd things and I was much intrigued by the fact that Uncle George's breeches had the pockets located in the front and not, like pedestrian trousers, at the sides. And I felt tremendously flattered because while his wife and daughter and my mother had jam with their bread-and-butter at tea time, I was allowed to share his Patum Peperium. 'The Gentleman's Relish', he would read from the label, 'This is the food for us men, not women's stuff.'

Only a mile or two away was the farm from which both Uncle George and my grandmother had − I can only say − escaped, presided over by my great-grandmother, Mrs Pratt. When many years later I read Stella Gibbon's novel *Cold Comfort Farm* I never found any difficulty in accepting it all as authentic. I had seen, and smelt, it all as a small boy, at Clifton Campville. We approached it on foot up a winding lane, where I was reduced to tears by swarms of the most bloated and vindictive flies, which tormented my tender skin. In contrast to the healthy animal scents of Seale Fields, Clifton Campville was enshrouded by a miasma of simple and unmitigated sewage, the source of which was evident when one sloshed across the farmyard. My great-grandmother Mrs Pratt was the presiding figure of the establishment and was a worthy counterpart to Miss Gibbon's Aunt Ada Doom. When her husband had died I have no idea, nor of how many children she had had, except that it must have been at least five, for in addition to Uncle George and my grandmother, Susan Anne, both of whom had got away, there were three others who had been held captive in order to run the farm and who were kept in adolescent bondage, Aunt Clara, Uncle Joseph and Uncle Arthur; all must have been in their sixties when I met them. Uncle Joseph was suspected of hidden depths of wickedness, on account of a tendency to arrive back rather late from Ashby-de-la-Zouche (the Local *ville lumière*) on market-day; in a general atmosphere of gloom he alone showed signs of cheerfulness breaking through. He conducted me round the farm and imparted to me much, and possibly not all entirely accurate, information; I remember that he introduced me to a shaggy individual who was outstandingly malodorous even by Clifton Campville standards and who he informed me was my uncle Ebenezer (or it may have been Ezekiel, I am not sure). We had a massive tea, seated round a long table over which Great-Grandma Pratt presided; facing her at the far end of the room there was a remarkable pianoforte with a very short keyboard but a very high pleated satin front. I was seated between the two uncles, and Uncle Joseph, with whom I had now established an excellent relationship, was tickling my ribs and doing his best to ensure that I should be not only seen but also heard. However, the lynx-eyed matriarch observed precisely what was going on. 'Joseph!' she thundered down the table, 'I shan't blame the child, Joseph, I shan't blame the child!' We both collapsed into perforated silence, but I have often wondered what happened to Uncle Joseph after the meal; was his pocket-money stopped, or was he kept in next market-day? I am glad to think that I met my great-grandmother; her lifetime must have included the entire reigns of Queen Victoria and King Edward VII. It has been pleasant to tell the grandchildren of my cousin Peggy that I once saw their great-great-great-grandmother. I believe the old lady lived to be nearly a hundred, but longevity seemed to be endemic in Staffordshire in those days. I was taken to tea with a very aged Mr Allen, who was partially paralysed and who, people said, 'kept his foot in a box'; this to my immature mind suggested that the affected limb was detached from his body and stored when not in use on the mantelpiece. I found this somewhat alarming, but I was slightly disappointed as well as reassured on discovering the less sensational truth of the matter.

I think my mother and I stayed twice at Seale Fields, but it may have been only once. Crossing London from Victoria to St Pancras on top of a station horse-bus for one of our visits we heard the newsboys crying the demise of Edward VII, which fixes this date as May 6th 1910. I have a vivid visual image of the placards bearing the words

DEATH
OF THE
KING

but this must, I think, be the result of a later retrospective imagination. We were normally kept well up to date with family news from Staffordshire by the letters of Uncle George's daughter Ethel ('Cousin Effie' to me). She was a voluminous and racy correspondent, whose sole contribution to economy in writing materials consisted in 'crossing' her manuscript with a second pagefull of writing at right angles to the first. This increased a problem of hermeneutics which independently existed through her tendency to omit the subjects of verbs, thus frequently leaving the reader in doubt as to whom a sentence was about. She was an accomplished retailer of gossip, which was usually indicated by the attachment of ', they say' or ', X says' to the end of a statement.[10] She could rise to heights of passionate oratory, as when describing the intrigues and iniquities of the 'other side' in a rural-council election. She could also revealingly depict the scandals and indiscretions of a closely integrated social community. When a well-connected young woman gave birth to an unauthorised baby and refused to disclose the identity of the father, Cousin Effie reported in detail the speculations of the various schools of thought and the ultimate general adoption of the theory placing the responsibility on 'young Mr Y', based upon the testimony of an aged woman that the unwelcome infant was the living image of 'old Mr Y' when himself a child. I am sorry that Cousin Effie's letters have perished; they might have been quite useful social documents.

Before leaving this early period of my life, I should like to say something about the way in which children were dressed. Whatever may be said about the progress or retrogression of Western society in other respects during my lifetime, there can be no doubt that children are now clothed far more sensibly than they were. There were three particular forms of torture to which small boys (I can say nothing about small girls; they must speak for themselves) were subjected in my childhood. The first was the chafing of one's thighs by the edges of one's shorts in cold weather; the second was the cutting of one's flesh by garters made of narrow elastic and by chin-bands of the same material. The third – and this applied only when one was dressed in one's Sunday best – was the infliction of unlined kid gloves; these were quite inadequate as a protection against the cold, both because they were extremely thin and because they fitted tightly to the skin; furthermore, because of this skin-fitting character, they had to be massaged on to the hands finger-by-finger in a way which was unpleasant and indeed painful. One might just possibly be allowed to wear long black stockings in winter and thus eliminate the first of these three horrors, but these were looked upon as rather effeminate and sissy, and not really the thing for the young of a nation of Empire-builders. What no one seemed to think of was allowing small boys to wear trousers, with the single exception when they were part of a sailor-suit. But sailor-suits merit a paragraph to themselves.

I do not know precisely when, nor even why, the custom

established itself of putting children into nautical uniform, or into the upper portion of it. It applied to girls as well as to boys, and any idea that it was an expression of pride in Britain's glorious naval history — a permanent juvenile celebration of the Rule Britannia — seems to be discounted by the fact that it was not limited to our own imperial race. (Between the World Wars there was an epigram to the effect that Hungary was a Kingdom without a king, that its Regent was an admiral, that it had no navy, but that its schoolgirls wore naval uniform.) I was put into it at a very tender age, when I had masses of golden curls and, as it was still the custom for very small children to wear petticoats regardless of their sex, it was not uncommon for kind-hearted strangers to stop us in the street and say to my mother 'Isn't she a pretty little girl?', thus provoking me to furious and tearful protests. The accompanying correct headwear was a sailor's broad-brimmed straw hat and its band was usually inscribed with the patriotic legend 'H.M.S. Victory'. Shortly before the War I was given an officer's peaked cap and the overcoat with gilt buttons that went with it, but, with my knowledge of the ranks and uniforms of His Majesty's forces, I was unhappy about the sartorial solecism.

I have run far ahead of my story, but where childhood memories are involved it is futile to attempt exact chronology or even to be sure of getting events in the right order. And I have nobody now by whose recollections I can check my own. Apart from Shoreham, we lived in various south-London suburbs — Balham, Brixton and Mitcham stick in my mind — but it is only with Upper Norwood that I really emerge from the realm of myth into that of history.

Notes

1. *The Story of Shoreham*, by Henry Cheale.
2. *The Comedy of Dante Alighieri the Florentine*, vol. II, p. 30.
3. *Lothair*, ch. i.
4. Most of this family history is derived from the research of Mr F. H. Mascall, a distant cousin, engaged in mining operations in Chile, who visited my father in 1920 and left with him a large amount of interesting material, collected over a number of years. I have not been able to check the information but it is clearly the result of much careful and conscientious work, provided with abundant references, mainly done in 1904 and added to in 1908 and 1916.
5. In the Marines, as also in the Artillery, the Engineers and the Navy, commissions were not obtained by Purchase. The Marines, though a very distinguished corps, were not at all aristocratic.

6. Accent on the first syllable, of course.
7. I cannot forget the awful warning of the successful American business-man who employed a professional genealogist to investigate his ancestry. All that the expert could discover was that his employer's grandfather had been executed in Sing-Sing. However, being both tactful and ingenious, he reported simply that the unfortunate convict had 'occupied the chair of applied electricity in one of our largest national institutions'.
8. *Good-bye Dolly Gray.*
9. This idiom has, of course, since become common on news-headlines, like this, reported to me from Chicago: 'Wife hews mate with axe, justified says Judge'.

Chapter Two

School Days:
Belvedere and Latymer

Paulatim, ergo certe
– Motto of Latymer Upper School

A boy may be a good mathematician, but cannot be a philosopher or physicist.
– Aristotle, *Nichomachaean Ethics*, VI.8.

It was, I think, in 1910 that my parents and I moved to Upper Norwood, only a mile or so from the Crystal Palace, and it is from our time in that pleasant suburb that my recollections have some kind of ordered and coherent shape. I have always been glad that my vivid childhood memories include those years before the First World War, for, even in the trivial details of daily life – and these are, after all, what a child chiefly remembers – Britain before 1914 and Britain after 1918 were two different worlds. Pre-war and Wartime London as they appeared through the eyes of a middle-class child have been evocatively depicted, though from a more opulent stratum of the middle class than ours, by Mr Osbert Lancaster in his delightful book *All Done from Memory*, which still, in the phrase of an Italian visitor, fills me with nostalgic reminds. It was above all else a London in which an enormous lot was always going on in the streets. There were piano-organs, street-singers, German bands, muffin-men with trays on their heads covered with green cloths, lavender-women with their haunting melody 'If you buy it once you'll buy it twice; it'll make your clothes smell very ni-ice', and on rare occasions fascinating onion-men from Brittany who tended to sit down and weep on the doorstep if you refused their wares. Although the internal-combustion engine had put the taxi-cab (as the taximeter-cabriolet was now commonly called) on the streets and other types of horseless carriage were fast displacing the horse-drawn variety, hansoms and four-wheelers could still be found and indeed most of the household deliveries were made by horse-drawn vehicles. The daily arrival of the two-wheeled milk-float, with its one or two churns and its standing driver, from the former of which the latter decanted into unhygienic pewter cans their unpasteurised and unsterilised contents, was one eagerly anticipated joy; another was the visit of the postman in his strangely shaped shako and with his characteristic double knock. Just occasionally a telegraph-boy came on a bicycle and produced an orange-coloured envelope from his pouch; his approach would always cause some apprehension, for telegrams were less often bringers of good news than of bad. Very few people in those days had telephones, and they weren't much use if you had, as very few of your friends had them either. In emergencies, as readers of Sherlock Holmes will know, you fell back on the 'wire', though at sixpence for twelve words it was expensive compared with the penny letter or the halfpenny postcard.

On the subject of horses it is worth recording that their steel shoes, combined with the fact that many streets were cobbled, disprove any notion that large cities were quiet places in the pre-petrol era. In the wealthier districts you would sometimes see the roadway carpeted with straw to lessen the sufferings of some indisposed plutocrat. Some of the horses were of course magnificent specimens, especially those that drew the dust-carts and the brewers' drays. If they caused a good deal of organic pollution, there was always the thriving if unofficial industry conducted by small boys who rushed out from the kerbs with shovels and buckets, and it is a moot point whether the scent of gasoline is less offensive than that of equine excrement. I must add that, to my regret, I was never taken for a ride in a hansom; I know that we considered them dangerous physically as they were liable to overturn, and I suspect there was a suggestion of moral danger about them too. Was there not a verse about 'a handsome woman in a handsom cab'? However, by the time that I reached the age of moral peril hansoms had become extinct.

In the pre-War period the economic condition of the middle class had already become serious, or at any rate that of the section of the middle class to which we belonged. It might, I suppose, have been described as the middle-middle class and was quite distinct from the lower-middle class, which included shopkeepers. Readers of the Grossmiths' *Diary of a Nobody* will recognise an intermediate stratum, which might be described as 'lower middle-middle' or 'upper-lower middle', in the Pooters, but that book was published in 1892 when the middle-middle class, like all other British social classes except the lower or 'working' class, was stable and, within its limits, prosperous. By 1910 the middle-class was under serious strain but was determined to keep up appearances. This involved among my parents and their friends a great deal of real heroism but also, I am sorry to record, what is less commendable, a great deal of hypocrisy. Still in 1910 the ladies had their at-home days and each family kept at least one domestic servant; though my impression is that by 1914 at-home days had declined and ladies would often utter the euphemistic apology 'I am afraid we are at the moment without a maid'. Having the front flight of steps whitened each day was a necessary mark of status, even if it was furtively whitened before daybreak by the mistress of the house; to have a tiled doorstep which merely needed washing down was a sign of slovenliness and social indiference. Nobody ever admitted to being in any kind of financial tightness or anxiety, though it was clear that almost everyone was; but money, like religion, sex and incurable illness, was never talked about. I wish I could think that this was due to a Franciscan lack of concern with material possessions; I am afraid it was more often due to a fear that your friends would drop you if they thought you had not plenty, or at least enough, of them.

The house which my father rented was of the single-fronted semi-basement terrace type with small gardens at front and back and was quite adequate for our needs. After a year or so we moved to a slightly larger corner house across the road, which to my childish scale of distances seemed palatial. We saw very little of any of our neighbours, whom I think we considered socially inferior; Palace Square was on the down-grade and already many of the houses contained more than a single household. But we saw a great deal of my grand-mother, who had bought a house next to our later one, and we formed a close friendship with our previous next-door neighbours, the Baker Beales. Of their four children the eldest was a girl a year younger than myself; the other three, who included a pair of very rumbustious twins, were boys. Isabel and I became inseparable playmates and she allowed me to dominate her with admirable patience; I still remember with shame reducing her to tears by the selfishness with which I insisted on appropriating all the most impressive wooden bricks when we were building houses together. There was a sensational and alarming episode when the Beale family were quarantined with suspected diphtheria; I simply cannot remember whether the suspicion turned out to be justified, but I remember the administration of anti-toxin, which was just coming into use. Nor in those days diphtheria was one of the real killers and the tracheotomy scars on the necks of survivors were a common sight in the streets. Shortly before the War the Beales moved to Shoreham Beach, which they had come to know from renting my grandmother's bungalow for a holiday. I still saw them from time to time, often when I went on holidays to Shoreham myself; and I still have an elegant silver-knobbed ebony walking-stick bearing my initials, which Isabel gave me for my twenty-first birthday. But I lost touch with the family soon after that and have only once seen any of them since.

Mention of my selfishness impels me in honesty to record that at the period in question I must have been a very horrid little boy. I was treated by my parents with very great indulgence, which was no doubt largely due to the fact that I was not physically robust and that before my birth they had lost one child in infancy; so, although I was not literally what my Vicar later on was to describe as 'that monstrosity an only child', I had virtually both the advantages and the disadvantages of that status. I had a violent temper and, when thwarted, would give way to fits of stamping and screaming, from which I was calmed down only by being warned of the example of an unidentified but allegedly authentic small boy whose tantrums resulted in his feet falling off, so that for the rest of his life he had to make shift with artificial ones. I later learnt to control the more sensational manifestations of inner frustration and took refuge in sulks rather than in outbursts. This was less disturbing to my elders and kept me out of the hands of the police, but I cannot think that it indicated any real improvement in my character. When, however, my female playmate was superseded by two boys slightly older than myself, one of whom was as self-centred as I was and slightly more obstinate in addition, I began to accept the fact that the only alternative to dwelling in a very shruken universe was to be neither the centre nor the apex of it. I think, therefore, that I became less aggressive and more withdrawn as childhood progressed to adolescence.

Self-analysis is always a hazardous activity and after over sixty years its retrospective performance can be ridiculous. There is, however, no doubt that I was what was described as a 'difficult' child, though there are two points on which, without withdrawing the plea of Guilty, I might plead a measure of extenuation. The first is that, largely owing to my strict upbringing, I had a very strong ethical sense, rather stronger in fact than it was in some of those who had instilled it into me; and, like most well-brought-up

children, I did not distinguish clearly between the realms of morality
and convention. Now, two of the moral principles which I had
been taught were that you must not drop your aitches[1] and that,
at tea time, you must have two slices of bread-and-butter before
embarking upon the cake. I therefore felt impelled, regardless of
the consequences, to denounce two of my mother's guests for
violation of these fundamental moral principles and resisted all
attempts to silence me as a disobedient child who refused to be
seen and not heard. I must insist, with my hand on my heart,
that my obstreperousness was due not to self-assertion but to a
sheer respect for truth and a conviction of the duty to witness to
it, the very stuff, in fact, of which martyrs are made. I only
wish that I had manifested equal courage throughout my life. 'But,
mummy, I *saw* it; she *has* only had one slice of bread-and-butter.'
Furthermore, I was sharply conscious of the fact, to whose consequences parents and pedagogues are not always sufficiently
sensitive, that they too often represent themselves not only as
the accredited teachers of morality but also as the paradigms
of the virtues which they commend. In any case, that I was
sometimes willing to endorse the judgement passed on me by adult
authority was shown by the fact that I disturbed the composure
of my elders by remarking, towards the end of one particularly
turbulent afternoon, 'I shall be very glad to see the back of myself
to-night.'

My second plea in extenuation is that I developed very early,
if only in a rudimentary form, the basic logical instincts and
questionings out of which my subsequent brief career as a mathematician developed, and that attempts to make my elders see
what I was worrying about were often doomed to frustration. The
logical impropriety of saying '£1.6s.8d. per cent' when you meant
'$1\frac{1}{3}$ per cent', the puzzling fact that if you were given the sides
of a right-angled triangle the hypotenuse was fixed for you[2], the
difference between 'think' meaning 'hold as probable' and 'think'
meaning 'hold as certain'[3], these were present to my mind at the
age of seven or eight, though they did not seem to worry my
contemporaries. On the other hand, it cannot have been until I
was about fifteen that I discovered for myself the cosmological
argument for the existence of God. I cannot remember ever having,
like Dorothy L. Sayers, 'the astounding moment when the realisation broke in upon my infant mind that every other person
in the world was 'I' to himself or herself as I was I to myself';
perhaps, little egoist that I was, I had had that conviction from
the womb! Evidently I was, in those early years, more of a logician

than a metaphysician, though I hope I did something to restore the balance later on.

What education, then, was offered to the middle class in Upper Norwood in those dear, dim, distant days? Half way up the hill, Belvedere Road, a certain Mr Boland ran a preparatory school for boys which specialised in producing future Alleynians. But lower down there was an establishment under the direction of a formidable lady with the improbable name of F. E. Smith, and it was to this that I was confided. Its title and description ran, on the prospectus, as follows:

BELVEDERE COLLEGE
SELECT ACADEMY FOR THE DAUGHTERS OF GENTLEMEN
Kindergarten for Little Girls and Boys

And a supplementary rubric informed the cautious parent: 'Tradesmen's Children not Admitted'.[4] That this was no empty threat is shown by the one serious crisis that took place during my time at the College as one of the little girls and boys in the Kindergarten department. This occurred when a monster of juvenile depravity called Martin (I forget his surname), who was constantly in trouble for minor offences (he would kick his partners' shins in the dancing class and I was once shocked to overhear one of the mistresses describe him to a colleague as a 'friend'), was proved to have circulated a report that another pupil named Peter Pringle was the son of Mr Pringle who owned a large and flourishing ironmongery shop on Westow Hill. To nip this calumny in the bud the culprit was made to recant his heresy before the assembled community and it was explained to us that Peter's father, so far from engaging in trade, held a very important appointment in the City of London, to which he travelled each day. I suspect also that it must have been Martin who was responsible for our conviction that the sour countenance and snappy manner of the least popular of the teaching staff was due to her having been 'crossed in love', a description which strongly impressed us though I doubt whether any of us had the least notion of its meaning. The staff as a whole were kind and competent and commanded our affection, with the exception of the black-clad and corseted Principal, of whom we all stood in awe. I can still, after sixty-five years hear the accents with which Miss Smith's enquiry 'And why, pray, did you ...?' struck terror into the hearts of the guilty or suspected.

The fees were high, as befitted an establishment which was sensitive about its social status, but my parents, in view of our poverty-genteel condition and our freedom from any taint of tradesmanship, were granted a considerable reduction. I am pretty sure that this was true about a good many others, though it was not the kind of thing that one would have talked about. I have just discovered my bill for the winter term of 1915 – my last term, as I left before Christmas that year. It amounted to £2.19s.0d., and included such 'extras' as Class Singing 5s.0d., Drill 5s., Games 3s.6d. and Kindergarten Materials 3s.6d. I imagine the last item was in connection with 'Geography with Sand', an enjoyable occupation for which we stood round a large tray and in which rivers and lakes were represented by strips of tin-foil; my report declares that I was 'Very Good' at it. I had presumably dropped dancing by this time; I never much liked it. I was at one time the only boy in the class, though I was later joined by the criminal Martin. My dancing costume I vividly remember as consisting of a light-blue knitted-silk jersey, black velvet knickers, short white socks, patent-leather pumps with silk bows – and, of course, white cotton gloves. We learnt French from a real French lady, though later from a Belgian refugee, and if the accent of the latter was Walloon rather than Parisian I do not suppose that mattered at our early stage. The teaching was thorough and disciplined and by present-day standards no doubt antediluvian. At the risk of permanent injury to our infant psyches we learnt a great deal by heart, but we did not find this unpleasant, as it comes much more easily at an early age than it does later. We learnt to spell, to parse and to do long division; I think I was even initiated into the mysteries of practice and square roots. We memorised the Sovereigns from the Norman Conquest onwards, the capes of England and Wales and the counties and capitals of Great Britain (though only those south of the border were allowed to have rivers). The spelling has stayed with me to this day, though I can no longer rely on getting beyond Stephen-1135 and Durham-Durham-on-the-Wear. Now, with our universities supplied with students many of whom, though ornamented with A-Level English, are unable to express themselves intelligibly on paper or to explain the difference between an adjective and an adverb, I am inclined to think that there may be something to be said for the pedagogical techniques of Belvedere College, Upper Norwood. Self-expression – to which I was far too prone – was given legitimised exercise as Elocution; possibly by some prophetic intuition, I was once assigned a recitation beginning 'I, a very learn'd professor, keep a school for little boys ...'! My participation in the Drama involved even less than a 'walking-on' part, inasmuch as it was limited to standing rigid (and sniffing miserably, as I had a bad cold and had been forbidden on grounds of military and aesthetic propriety to use a handkerchief) as one of the soldiers by the throne of the Queen in the College's production of the trial scene of *Alice in Wonderland*. This was at an ambitious concert in the Anerley Town Hall, and it was perhaps a faint indication of the tremors already affecting the social fabric that even the more expensive tickets were unable to make a more categorical requirement than 'Evening Dress *Preferred*'! My father got his 'tails' out of their moth-balls for the occasion and I remember his irritation on finding that some of the moths must have belonged to a resistent strain. Last flash in the pan as it was of a passing era, Belvedere College with all its unrealities and absurdities gave me the basic disciplines of an education and it is only right that I should acknowledge my debt to its Principal, Miss F. E. Smith, and her assistants.

From those years at Norwood various memories have survived the passage of time. My father, like Mr Pringle the Non-ironmonger, went up to the City every weekday and had worn as a matter of course a morning coat and silk hat, taking a spare collar and cuffs with him in hot weather. When the War got under way however, all the starch was needed for explosives, and stiff collars and shirts were the first sartorial casualties, rapidly followed by others; it was, a long time before he got reconciled to wearing a soft collar. I was always expected to say my prayers at night, but we rarely went to church. When we did, my father took me to St Paul's, Hamlet Road, where I had been baptised; the Vicar was a formidable old man, Canon Ranscombe, who preached thunderous sermons, largely, I was told (though I don't remember them at all) about the iniquitous goings-on at St John's, Auckland Road, the only Anglo-Catholic church in the neighbourhood. Somebody, I cannot think who, did in fact once take me to St John's, where, in those days, they had on Sundays full choral matins followed by Sung Eucharist. It must have been matins to which I went, but I remember nothing about the service. All that I recall were the enormously long hymn-board (it displayed the numbers for both services, in black and red respectively) and the great gilded cross which hung from the roof. This cross − it had no figure upon it and was made, of all materials, of cork − was a real rock of offence in the neighbourhood as a symbol of the enormities of St John's. On the rare occasions on which religion was touched on at my mother's tea-parties the opinion was expressed that it would serve 'those people' right if it fell on them and crushed them;

indeed I felt vaguely apprehensive of this fate on my solitary visit. I had, I must add, a tendency, if permitted, to conduct a form of worship of my own composition in the drawing room on a Sunday evening; and for this I wore, stole-wise, the embroidered runner from the keyboard of the piano. At this time, the attitude of my parents to religion was, I think, that characteristic of the middle class in general; they approved of it, they identified it with British morality, they thought churchgoing was good for children, soldiers, convicts and such like but felt no special need of it for themselves. Though they were ready to indulge in it occasionally for a special reason, and they thought that the British social fabric was so thoroughly permeated with religious and moral principles that, provided you preserved its official and external profession, there was nothing more that you needed to do about it.[5] I think my parents detected in me an early interest in religious matters − it was nothing more than that − which led them to wonder whether I might be led, as my father would have said, to 'go in for the Church' and that they did not view the possibility with enthusiasm; years later, when my vocation to the priesthood had become clear, they had themselves become devout Catholic churchpeople and gave me every encouragement and assistance.

It may be that, like the sundial, my childhood memory has recorded only the pleasant hours − *Horas non numero nisi serenas* − but my recollections of Norwood are very happy ones. We frequently went to the gardens of the Crystal Palace, for which we had season tickets; the great stone prehistoric monsters were a never-failing source of delight. There were also some splendid side-shows, the joy-wheel, the water-chute, the cake-walk, the ghost-train and many others, and even if one was too timid to go on some of them − and I was a very timid child − one could always get a vicarious thrill by watching other victims.

There were also the early cinematographs but they were not much encouraged; the flickering might be bad for one's eyes and the people who went to them might be verminous. Even going shopping with my mother on Westow Hill had its delights; there was the lovely Penny Bazaar, which sold innumerable games all based on the formal principle of throwing a die and going x places forward but embodying endless variety of material content, so that in one of them you might be travelling across the African Continent and in another winning the Derby or making your fortune on the Stock Market.[6] There were also, for a penny each, quantities of toys, stamped out of metal and almost always 'Made in Germany'; they were cleverly designed, but they had sharp edges and the lugs which held their parts together could jag you; furthermore the points might be poisonous, so your elders said, and you were strictly forbidden to put them in your mouth. I have often felt envious of modern children, with their plastic models which reproduce in three dimensions all the details that in my childhood could be represented only by superficial outlines, but I wonder whether this envy is justified. The child's imagination is wonderfully vigorous and I suspect that the modern toys often appeal to adults more than to children; I have been taken by a small boy to see his 'Butlin's racer' which he had made for himself out of bits of cardboard and the like without any sense of lack of realism. But this, as the older novelists would say to excuse their padding, is a digression. Two or three times I saw an aeroplane, and once, when the *Daily Mail* had organised a round-Britain air race, my father took me to see what we could from somewhere on the North Downs – and we saw precisely nothing. One Sunday morning he took me to St Paul's Cathedral and we sat in the south transept; the service was interrupted by suffragettes, and my father, who had no sympathy with feminists, went to see if he could help to throw them out. He could not have been gone for more than a few minutes, but I can remember still the sense of lostness that I felt at being left alone in that vast building surrounded by strangers, some of whom, for all I knew, might be suffragettes themselves! My mother, in contrast, felt a lurking sympathy for Mrs Pankhurst but she never approved of extreme measures or went further than wearing a purple skirt, and even that, like the hobble skirt which she also acquired to my father's disapproval (was it perhaps the same one, a purple hobble?), may have signified fashion rather than politics.

Two events of national and world significance impressed themselves on me in 1912 for singular, diverse and in themselves trivial reasons. The first was the sinking of the *Titanic* on its maiden voyage by an iceberg in the Atlantic; the second was the death of Captain Scott and his companions in the Antarctic. Both have been described frequently and at length; but why should they have specially affected a child of six? Well, first, it was my mother's custom, as of many British housewives, to read the *Daily Mirror*, which in those days was very different from what it has become, though even then it relied largely on its pictures for its appeal. (It was said that Alfred Harmsworth, having started the *Daily Mail* for people who could not think, then started the *Daily Mirror* for those who could not read.) A prominent place in the *Mirror* for many years was occupied by the daily cartoon of W. K. Haselden, and, although (or perhaps because) its point was frequently lost on me, its images were sufficiently familiar for me to seize on it eagerly and pore over it intently. Now on the day when the loss of the *Titanic* became known, the *Mirror* appeared in mourning *and without Haselden's cartoon*. To one small reader this was like a violation of the laws of nature; nothing could have brought home so forcibly the magnitude of the tragedy. I think I should have been less surprised that morning if the sun had risen in the west. I wonder whether adults always recognise the extent to which children identify the invariable with the necessary. Certainly it was the absence of Haselden's cartoon that brought home to me the sense of horror with which the loss of the allegedly unsinkable *Titanic* had smitten the British people in those complacent days. And the death of Scott and his companions – ? Simply that one of those companions was Lieutenant Bower and it happened that his sister was one of the mistresses at Belvedere College. As soon as the news of the calamitous ending of Scott's expedition arrived Miss Bower left for Rome, where her mother was living, to give her comfort and support. Subsequent events after 1914 have put in the shade the sagas of Antarctic exploration, but at the time, with the episode of Oates's heroic and unavailing attempt to save the lives of his friends at the cost of his own, the story of the Scott expedition was one of the sublimest records of British endurance. To have been involved, remotely and vicariously, in such an epic was, for an obscure and snobbish academy for the daughters of gentlemen with its associated kindergarten for little girls and boys, an unforgettable honour. So at least we felt, and let those mock who can afford to do so.

My fundamental belief in these halcyon pre-War days – a belief which I shared with my parents and their friends – might be now described (though it would not have been so described then) as unreflective demythologised British-Israelism. Not only was England top nation but it always would be, and right-thinking foreigners recognised this and indeed rejoiced in it. This was indeed what the Reformation had really been about. For a Briton's word was his bond, England had always scrupulously honoured her obligations and so, to the great benefit of mankind, she had never been defeated in war or her territory invaded. (1066 was a long time ago and anyhow we were hardly English before William arrived from Normandy; and the American War of Independence was never mentioned.) 'Foreigners' did not mean persons who were in a country other than their own but simply those who were not British, so that France or Germany was a country almost entirely inhabited by foreigners. If this seems an impossible attitude for anyone to hold it must be remembered that to the great bulk of British people foreigners were known only by hearsay as strange beings whom the twenty-mile gulf of the English Channel made virtually as remote as Martians. Apart from the picturesque and exotic German-bandsman, the Italian ice-cream-merchant (whose wares I was not allowed to buy because it was believed that 'he kept them under his bed') and the Breton onion-man, I think the only foreigner I had seen before the War was the lady who taught me French at Belvedere College. When in 1914 waves of refugees appeared English people found it difficult to know what to make of 'them Belgiums'.

Even in England itself there were tremors in the social fabric, though I was hardly allowed to know about them. I think I heard about strikes, though I don't think they meant anything to me. There were wicked people called 'liberals' and even worse ones called 'radicals', though the only radical that I met was a kind old gentleman who lodged with my grandmother and who lent me copies of a paper containing exciting stories and bearing the unsubversive title of *The Union Jack*. These were, I think, mildly disapproved of, but as sensational rather than as politically undesirable. But lurking in the background there was of course a demonic figure named Lloyd George, who was set on the destruction of civilisation. Later on, with the assistance of two lesser heroes called Horatio Bottomley and Pemberton Billing, he was mysteriously transformed into an angel of light and became the saviour of our country; but that was later on, during the War.

Even in those days I was an omnivorous reader, too young as yet for the *Magnet* and the *Gem* and even for the *Boys' Own Paper*: those were to come later. I fell deeply under the spell of *Comic Cuts* and its imitators, as much for the brilliance of their coloured illustrations as for their literary contents, They were discouraged parentally, as the characters depicted in them used language that, while morally inoffensive, was regrettably 'Common', and many middleclass parents welcomed the appearance of the *Rainbow*, which, while presenting the same general appearance, was open to no such objections. It was a splendid paper of its kind, and I eagerly devoured the adventures of Tiger Tim and his friends at Mrs Hippo's school and cut out and assembled the ingenious peepshows and other models which it gave away from time to time. Every week I conscientiously purchased the current issue of *Tales for Little People* and I proudly wore the badge that denoted that I had become a member of the League of its supporters. I read with avidity story-books handed down by my mother which reflected the social outlook of the Earl and Countess of Darnley in her girlhood.

One story which I recall with special appreciation was about a small boy, the son of a peer, who had been warned by his noble father not to paddle in the sea because of the danger of catching cold. Unfortunately he had also been told by the butler that it was impossible to catch cold from sea-water. He therefore disobeyed his father, went into the sea, was carried away by a sudden storm and was drowned. The moral, as I remember it, was not so much that one ought not to disobey one's parents as that it was imprudent to engage in conversation with one's social inferiors. I was also given *Little Lord Fauntleroy*, but, possibly because the illustrations depicted him in the kind of clothing I had to wear on Sundays, I could not get on with it. Though personally a very timid child, I liked more exciting material, and revelled in the stories of the Brothers Grimm. These, if I dip into them now, seem to me to be absolutely horrific (think, for example of *Marienkind*, the tale of the young queen who was burnt to death on the unjust suspicion of having eaten her own babies!) and might have been expected to reduce any normally sensitive child to nightmares and screaming fits, but I cannot recall that they produced any other reaction in me and my friends than one of absorbing interest. Mr Arthur Mee's *Children's Encyclopaedia*, with its monthly continuation as the *Children's Magazine* and its final growth into adolescence under the ingenious title of *My Magazine* ('edited', as it proclaimed, 'by Arthur *Mee*') made use of all the recent developments in photolithography to seduce the inquisitive child into a process of painless and indeed enjoyable self-education, against an inoffensive but unquestioned background of progress, patriotism and undogmatic protestantism. A great joy was the discovery of several early bound volumes of the *Strand Magazine*, including the first volume (1891) which contained the first of the Sherlock Holmes stories. I think it must have been a little later that I relished the full savour of His Majesty the King of Bohemia, the Red-Headed League and the Man with the Twisted Lip, but the feature that I remember with particular interest was one entitled 'Portraits of Celebrities at Different Times in their Lives': my impression is that the celebrities chosen for inclusion were almost entirely either royal (mainly continental, and of these there were of course in those days a very large number) or else theatrical. Of a similar, and roughly contemporary, feature in a periodical called the *Picture Magazine* Mr Osbert Lancaster, in *All Done from Memory*, has recorded his own delight, and has in addition provided his own pictured recollections, which I would give a great deal to be able to imitate, of the original portraits, of, in his words, 'so many extraordinary countenances adorned with immense moustaches, upstanding in the style of Potsdam or down sweeping in the style of Vienna, some fish-eyed, some monocled, some vacant, some indignant but all self-conscious'. But in my innocence I was puzzled by the fact that, while beneath each portrait there was printed the age of its subject at the time when it was taken, there was an invariable exception with the final portrait when that subject was a lady, in which case there was simply the uninformative caption 'Present Day'. I also revelled in a copy of *Scouting for Boys* which somehow came into my hands, and, although, in spite of the debt which I owed to the Movement for my rescue by the Shoreham troop at the age of three, I had no intention of ever joining it myself (there was in any case a faint suggestion that it wasn't quite meant for 'people like us'), I knew that improving manual almost by heart. Finally, there was a heavy bound volume of the *Illustrated London News* for 1851, the year of the Great Exhibition, which I found quite fascinating. The illustrations, needless to say, were woodcuts and uncoloured, but there was a superb frontispiece which unfolded to give a full-length view of the Crystal Palace in its original form and location in Hyde Park. When, in 1911, the Palace, in its second site less than a mile from my home, became the setting for the now forgotten Festival of Empire history was felt to be repeating itself. But now the exhibition could no longer be confined within Sir Joseph Paxton's great glass-house; pavilions devoted to the various dominions were erected all over the palace grounds and a delightful electric tramway, specially constructed for the purpose, transported the visitor symbolically through that realm on which in those days the sun never set.

Then came Sarajevo and all that followed it, and the site of the Festival, transformed *more nautico* into H.M.S. Crystal Palace, became a naval station and swarmed with sailors of all ranks, though we were still allowed inside. The wave of patriotic fervour which swept through the nation at the outbreak of the War did not leave Belvedere College unaffected and a noticeably martial element appeared in our activities. I became quite an authority on the rank-badges of the armed forces and on the flags and national anthems of the allied powers; I can still sing most of the Marseillaise and bits of the Brabançonne, and I caused some embarrassment to one of my teachers by pointing out that what Miss Smith had supplied to us for one of our symbolic exercises was not, as she had asserted, a French flag but a Russian one. I had always enjoyed playing with lead soldiers, but now I felt more realism was called for and I organised several of my friends into an ephemeral corps with the impressive title of 'Mascall's Young Defenders and Palace Square Bodyguard'. My uncle Percy, recalled from the West Indies and now a commissioned officer in the Royal Marines, brought his wife and children (now reduced in number to three, since, to their great sorrow, their elder son John had died in the tropics) to stay with us for a time; he himself became a member of the disastrous Dardanelles expedition which was Winston Churchill's most famous failure, and brought back with him a large tin of toffee which turned out to be inedible owing to the presence of foreign matter in the form of sand. (What trivial details a child remembers!) Another wartime visitor from overseas was my mother's brother Claude who had emigrated to Canada years before, engaged in a number of enterprises including lumberjacking in British Columbia and now reappeared as a sergeant in the Canadian Mounted Rifles. His brother, my uncle Frank, who had served under Lord Roberts in the Boer War, easily acquired a captaincy in the Royal Engineers and moved into the Royal Corps of Signals when that more specialised body was formed. In France he was badly gassed at the beginning of the Battle of the Somme, was invalided out after a long period of treatment and convalescence and remained much of an invalid for the rest of his life.

In 1915, when the romantic optimism of the War's first phase had passed into the grim reality of submarine warfare and the trenches, my parents decided to move to a pleasantly situated flat overlooking Ravenscourt Park in the Borough of Hammersmith. The reason was that I had now outgrown the educational advantages offered by the kindergarten department of Belvedere College and my father had heard very good reports of Latymer Upper School, which occupied a cramped but stragegic position between King Street and the River Thames. In the long run this choice turned out to have been an extremely good one from my point of view, and the last six of my eight years at Latymer, which culminated in my securing an open scholarship at Pembroke College, Cambridge, were both happy and fruitful, but the first two, for a nervous and sheltered child of eleven who had been acclimatised to the prim gentility of Belvedere College, were nothing less than a nightmare. Outside classes there was an almost total lack of discipline and organisation, though I suppose conditions were mild compared with those in some of the tougher schools of the present day. I do not think any masters were ever physically assaulted by their pupils or that anybody suffered permanent bodily harm. But there was a great deal of bullying, and in the lower forms it was virtually impossible for a boy whose attributes were scholarly rather than muscular to feel at ease and free from fear. My chief concern for my first two years was to avoid being noticed and, in view of my subsequent career, it is a revealing indication of my state of mind that one of my reports in Mathematics reads 'Very weak: fails in applying the simplest rules'. It is only fair to state that some of the most efficient members of the staff were away in the Forces and that the Headmaster's refusal to engage any women teachers resulted in one or two of the temporary members being very peculiar people indeed. Something, however, needs to be said about the Latymer foundation itself.

Edward Latymer was born in 1557 or 1558 and died in 1627. His father was Dean of Peterborough and he was educated at St John's College, Cambridge; he later became Clerk to the Court of Wards and Liveries and was obviously a man of substance. Like other wealthy men of the period he left an endowment to educate the young and clothe the aged, in his case eight poor boys and six poor men. The endowment, being in the form of land in the present Borough of Hammersmith and Fulham, steadily increased in value and the first school to educate the Latymer boys together was built in 1756; it was superseded by a new building in the Hammersmith Road in 1863 and this continued to function for a century. However, the assumption by the State of responsibility for elementary education in 1870 released the main funds of the Latymer Trustees for other purposes and the result was the opening of the Upper School as a place of secondary education in 1895. The building, which subsequently received many piecemeal additions, must be unique among school buildings for its combination of extreme ugliness with almost unworkable inconvenience; the best that Mr R. C. Davies could find to say for it in the history of the School which he wrote in 1967[7] was the remark of the rich man when told that wealth does not always bring happiness: 'No, but it enables one to be miserable in comfort.' One consequence of this history is that, while Latymer, like many other schools of similar type, goes back to the testamentary benevolence of a seventeenth-century business man, its present existence and the buildings which it occupies are less than ninety years old. It opened with 106 boys; when I entered there were 700 and there are now 1100, so it is one of the larger day-schools in the country. And, after the successive stages of Aided and Direct-Grant, Latymer now survives with the controversial status of an independent institution. It may be interesting to note that in 1921 the fees were still £2.15s.0d per term, inclusive of books and everything else;[8] but I was very soon given a scholarship to cover these and so, I think, was almost everyone else. Belvedere College was certainly more expensive than Latymer!

The outstanding reputation which this humble institution rapidly acquired was chiefly the achievement of the first Headmaster, the Reverend Charles James Smith; he was still in office when I went there and indeed did not retire until 1921.

'Tubby' − the nickname was almost inevitable − was a thick-set shaggy-grey-bearded cleric, always clad in a black clerical frock-coat and trousers and crowned outdoors with a broad low-brimmed hat of the type that was known as the 'gentle shepherd'. He was a Hammersmith boy of lowly origins and had himself been a pupil at the old Latymer School; he once told some of us that he used to eat his lunch in the fields round Hammersmith Broadway. After training to be a teacher at St Mark's College, Chelsea, he obtained a headmastership in Cambridge and this gave him the opportunity of becoming a non-collegiate member of the University and in due course of obtaining a degree. He returned to be Vice-Principal of his old College and was thence appointed to Latymer. He was a headmaster of the old type. Mr Davies wrote of him:

> Although at heart he was a kindly man, boys regarded him, if not with fear, with tremendous awe. He was intolerant of slackness of any form in work or conduct and did not hesitate to administer corporal punishment when he thought it salutary ... He made it clear to boys that the object of coming to school was to learn and that, if they did not work, there were many boys who were quite ready to fill their vacated place.

This is perfectly true, but I would add that, if we regarded him with awe, we also took it for granted that a headmaster ought to be awe-inspiring and we did not resent this. He had an amazing knowledge of the details of every boy in the school and on the rare occasions when I came into actual contact with him I found him understanding, sympathetic and helpful. He was a man of tremendous but tranquil force of personality and if in some respects the school was like a bear-garden this did not worry him, as he had no doubt whatever who was in ultimate control. Few schools of the size can have been run with so little organisation. But this did mean that, when he retired in 1921 after twenty-six years' service, drastic reorganisation – indeed organisation – was needed.

Determined as he was on his appointment to a small and new-born institution to create for it a reputation for scholarship of the highest level, Tubby very wisely decided to concentrate on an important but limited range of subjects. Therefore he built upon a good general foundation of the basic disciplines a sixth and seventh form entirely restricted to mathematics and physical science, with some slight concession to the arts in the form of history and literature. Science itself was simply physics and chemistry; in the eyes of Latymer biological science did not exist. The result of this policy of concentration in a limited field was spectacular, especially in the prestigious area of Cambridge mathematics. Without any Cambridge mathematician on the staff, Latymer produced a regular sequence of wranglers and fellows of colleges (one of whom ended as Astronomer Royal) to which no other school could offer a parallel. Tubby's justified confidence in his ability to keep things under his control led him cheerfully to assemble a staff of brilliant eccentrics whose idiosyncrasies would have daunted a lesser man. By us boys, who had no standard of comparison by which to judge, it was taken as a matter of course that schoolmasters were like that, but I realised on looking back in later years that, while the masters at Latymer in my time were on the whole a very attractive, conscientious and competent set of men, who obtained and deserved their pupils' respect and gratitude, all of them were individualists and not a few were oddities of a high order. I shall come back to some of them shortly.

The general ethos of the school might be described as one of unaggressive and tolerant Protestant patriotism, of which the ritual and ceremonial expression was the assembly of the whole school for the saluting of the Union Jack on Empire Day. The Cadet Corps (which I somehow avoided joining) was much in evidence, and an address was given by the local M.P. (a Conservative lawyer named Sir William Bull); and I am almost sure that the choir sang 'Land of Hope and Glory'. What I am quite sure is that we all had to sing an Empire Day Song whose extreme vacuity of content and abysmal literary inferiority combine to entitle it not to be forgotten. The first verse posed a natural, though excessively worded, question:

What is the meaning of Empire Day?
Why do the cannon roar?
Why does the trumpet's martial bray

Echo from shore to shore?
etc

And then we roared in chorus the uninformative reply:

On our nation's scroll of glory
Are the deeds of valour told.
There is writ the story
Of our heroes bold in the days of old.
So, to keep their deeds before us,
Every year we homage pay
To our flag so proud that has never bowed –
And (*fortissimo*) THAT'S THE MEANING OF EMPIRE DAY!

Tubby was succeeded as Headmaster by the senior English and History master, the Reverend Edmund Dale, D. Lit. To follow so long established and dominant a personality as Tubby would not have been easy for anyone, and to appoint to a school so heavily weighted on the scientific side someone who knew little about science and who had moreover for thirteen years been on equal terms with those who now came beneath his sceptre was a daring decision for the Governing Body to make. The Science Seventh had some difficulty in keeping straight faces when the new Headmaster described the Wheatstone Bridge as a great engineering triumph. There was a rather more serious problem when, in his laudable respect for mathematics, he instituted a system by which every achievement of every boy throughout his school career should be given a numerical mark and his final degree of excellence determined by the grand total so accumulated. As everyone expected, the system proved to be unworkable, chiefly on account of the impossibility of estimating the relative numerical value of, say, scoring a goal in a junior house-match and coming second in geography three years later in a form examination. There were other problems too; when the Head had decreed that in each subject the average mark *in each form* was to be a standard x per cent (I forget what the value of x was), one of the mathematics masters had great difficulty in explaining to him why it was that the A forms did not appear to be doing any better than the B and C. But it would be wrong to suppose that the 'Old Man' (as we privately called him) was not in the main a success. He brought about a much needed element of order and discipline. He expanded and developed the prefect system, which had previously been little more than a means of conferring titular distinction on athletes. He introduced a division of the School into Houses, named after the ancient residences of the Borough, and, although this could not have the significance in a day-school that it can among boarders, it produced a healthy element of structure and competition which diminished the tendency of a growing society to become amorphous. He also persuaded the masters, most of whom by this time were graduates, to wear their gowns in class. As I left in 1924, most of the developments which took place in his term of office fall outside the scope of this book. I must, however, briefly mention the literary and dramatic society which, with his warm encouragement, was set up by his successor on the Arts side, Mr Fred Skinner, for it included in its membership most of the senior boys on both sides of the School and I was one of its most active supporters. It was called the Gild, and adopted the nomenclature and the general organisation of one of the trade guilds of the Middle Ages. It was tremendous fun and I remember especially a costume reading of *Macbeth*, in which a live cat, which had been specially obtained (no doubt, as Mr Crummles would have said, at tremendous expense) for the witches' scene, took fright when the curtain rose and leapt out into the front row of the audience with all its claws extended, to the temporary interruption of the production. My own Gild triumph came when, after I had left, I was asked to return and supervise the production of a comic opera of which I had written the libretto and which had previously only been read in secret. Its location was a school and it had some harmless but topical allusions. The extremes to which we went in the costume and make-up to meet the demands of authority that there should be nothing that could be interpreted as reflecting upon the actual headmaster were so excessive as almost to amount to a caricature by negative implication.

On one thing, in our drama, the Old Man was adamant: there must be no female participation. He was indeed almost morbidly sensitive to the dangers of any association with the gentler sex, and not least to the perils offered by the existence, less than half a mile away, of the sister institution of the Godolphin and Latymer Girls' School,[9] to which naturally the sisters of many of our own boys belonged. More than once, 'expulsion' (and he had a memorably dramatic way of uttering the word) was announced as the penalty awaiting any boy seen walking with a girl in the street. I do not remember any instance arising and I imagine that the crime in question must have been driven underground. (The story that a boy had narrowly escaped the extreme penalty for walking with his sister must, I think, have been apocryphal.) Latymer was nevertheless a totally male society, though, surprisingly, the first breach in the sex-barrier was made by the Old Man himself, when he introduced a lady secretary. Tubby would never have done this, and, in any case, he wrote his letters himself. Now however, I must return to the eccentrics.

Quite the most pyrotechnic of these was the Reverend Douglas Frederick Kennedy Kennedy-Bell. He was not one of Tubby Smith's originals but came during the War in 1916 and stayed until 1921. Most schoolmasters tend to develop a vocabulary largely of their own through their need of a supply of epithet of a highly emphatic type which are nevertheless suitable for the ears of the young. In Kennedy's case, however, this almost amounted to the invention of a new language. Thus he almost always addressed one in the third person, as 'little boy' or 'small youth', while a genuinely third person would be designated as 'Tommy Jones'. Furthermore his sentences were noteworthy for an extreme and characteristic exaggeration in their idioms. Thus, if two boys were detected in confidential conversation in class, Kennedy would shriek across the room: 'Small youth will kindly cease to embrace Tommy Jones like a long-lost brother and will remove himself to the utmost confines of the habitable universe, ten million cubic miles away!' If one was insufficiently audible, he would exclaim: 'Can't hear, can't hear! Vainly striving to catch expiring groans of little boy clearly in last stages of consumption!' If on the other hand we pressed too closely upon him, he would hurl our books on the floor with anguished cries of 'Breathing space! Breathing space!' His lessons were entertaining and we got a good deal of pleasure out of 'doing Kennedy' for the amusement of those of our friends who did not attend them; but I cannot say that we really enjoyed them, for his punishments were severe and rather quixotic. Nor, in spite of the vigour which he put into them, were they really profitable, for he never established a genuine *rapport* with his class. There was a story, which I believe to be true, that on one occasion, wishing to escape early from a tedious school function, he made a surreptitious descent from a window into the cycle shed and fell straight into the arms of detectives who, unknown to him, had been stationed there. Tubby, who had strong views about evasion of duties, refused to come and identify the suspected thief in the disguise of a clergyman until the function was ended. Kennedy was active outside school as well as inside. He was a strong public supporter of the political campaign of Mrs Dacre Fox in Richmond, Surrey. And he wrote three articles in the *Sunday Pictorial* which created quite a stir at the time; they were entitled 'Why men don't go to church', 'Why women do go to church' and 'Why children are sent to church', and we were amused that the first one was published with the author's photograph immediately by the title.

Another clerical character on the staff, and this time a vintage Latymerian, was the Reverend Robert ('Beaky') Palmer. He was appointed by Tubby in 1906 and lived to be ninety. He had a bird-like appearance and a high-pitched nasal voice, which one assumed to be cockney but which was I believe, Cambridgeshire. He was popular, in spite of the invariable cheerfulness with which he would distribute punishments. 'Let me see, old chap', he would say to a boy on the morning of a half-holiday, 'you've got detention this afternoon, haven't you?' 'No, sir', might be the reply. 'Oh yes, you have', Beaky would chuckle, 'I've just given it to you.' He would take evening prayers in the absence of the Headmaster and the hymn would be either 'Holy Father, cheer our way' or 'As now the sun's declining ray'. With typical schoolboy humour someone wrote the lines:

> Beaky Palmer had no sense;
> He wrote a hymn for eighteen pence.
> The only words that he could say
> Were 'Holy Father, cheer our way.'

If he caught sight during prayers of a boy who was doubled up in conversation he would interrupt our devotions with with a resonant and triumphant cry: 'I say, I say! Boy there become a Mahommedan! Completely lorst to view!' If a boy was ten minutes late in the morning he would receive the greeting 'Good evening, you're too early for this afternoon's lesson.' Then with a change of tone: 'Go away! We don't want you, we don't want you.' But, as R.C. Davies records, his tongue, so caustic, was yet strangely inoffensive.

Then there was E. D. Martin ('Scrubby'), a thick-set military figure, with a close-clipped moustache and a limp, who not only commanded the Cadet Corps but also conducted his classes with a similar parade-ground efficiency: 'Open desks! As you were; boy opened desk with the wrong hand! Open desks! Remove Shakespeare! Open Shakespeare!' His reading of *Twelfth Night*, interspersing the text with instructions for annotations, detracted somewhat from the beauty of the verse, but perhaps in the Fourth Form we were not much concerned with that in any case. 'If music be the food of love play on. Give me excess of it that surfeiting underline surfeiting write vomiting in the margin the appetite may sicken and so die ...' Scrubby loved a well-rounded period and I can hear him rolling the following sentence round his mouth in the Geography lesson: 'The rotation of the earth upon its axis and its constant parallelism – its constant parallelism – account for the varying length of day and night and the phenomena of the seasons – the phenomena of the seasons.' But he was a sympathetic and kindly person, and he once sent my father some information about our family that he had discovered in the course of his reading. After he retired I went to see him at Worthing and we had a delightful tea-party together.

But far and away the most remarkable man on the staff, and the one to whom I owe the largest personal debt, was the senior mathematics and science master, Granville Morton Grace. He was always known, at least to the boys, as 'Cod', from his strikingly fishlike profile. (For this reason another physics master who came while I was at the School was known as 'Hake', although there was nothing piscine about him; so strong is the power of analogy.) In view of the tremendous reputation that he built up for the School in mathematics at Cambridge, it is amazing that Cod was not primarily a mathematician at all but an experimental physicist with a flair for technology, and that his mathematical grounding was non-Cambridge and pre-twentieth century.[10] He had been producing his results for twenty years before a top-level mathematical specialist was added to the staff in the person of Mr F. Jackson. Cod's great quality was capacity to inspire enthusiasm and to evoke interest; even the humblest member of one of his classes was made to feel part of a living enterprise in which new discoveries were being made and new inventions devised. He was active – some of his colleagues would have said unscrupulous – in canvassing the brighter boys when they reached the crucial point of specialisation and persuading them that they had better choose Science rather than Arts, then physics rather than chemistry, and then concentrate on mathematics as the primary weapon of the modern physicist. Not, indeed, that he was in the least degree a mere theorist. He always expressed the greatest contempt for 'arm-chair philosophers' and would often repeat the aphorism 'Physics, beware metaphysics'. He had a characteristic clipped way of speaking and a habit, which we mercilessly parodied, of referring to himself as 'one' rather than as 'I'. He was unconcerned and impatient with the logical subtleties of the rigid pure mathematicians. We used to sing a ditty in private which ran:

> Now Mr Grace he is content
> With a simple-definition-of-a-differential-coefficient:
> It's what you have to multiply
> The differential dx by
> In order to get the d of y;
> With a fal, lal, lal etc.

In fact, the phrase 'by in order to get' (or, as he pronounced it, 'by in order to *git*') was held by him to be the essential factor in definitions of physical quantities, and, as he was an assiduos patron of auctions of scientific apparatus, we used to hold that, in the modified spelling 'Buy in order to get', this was really his heraldic motto.

This leads me to mention that, as a background to the modern equipment of the physics laboratory, which was itself of almost university standard, Cod had acquired for the School a number of pieces of apparatus of historic interest. We always looked forward to his return from the auction-rooms, in anticipation of treasure trove with which we might be allowed to experiment; I remember particularly trying (not entirely successfully) to determine Verdet's constant for the rotation of the plane of polarisation of light by barium-glass, with an instrument which had belonged to Sylvanus P. Thompson. There was also an antique set-up for measuring the thermal conductivity of an iron bar about four feet long, which we reluctantly had to abandon on discovering that one end of it would need to be heated day and night for something like a week in order to acquire a state of thermal equilibrium – or so at least we were led to believe. The more valuable or more recondite items were housed in a small and stuffy subterranean laboratory which gave those of us who had the privilege of working in it some sense of familiarity with the arcana of the universe akin to that of Lord Gifford deep beneath the ground in Scott's *Marmion*. In his own house close to the School, where he lived with his wife and three rosy-cheeked young daughters, Cod had his own workroom containing several fine lathes which he would allow pupils of approved industry and reliability to operate. There was really no trouble which he would not expend on a pupil whom he felt was able and willing to profit by it. This was, however, characteristic of the team which Tubby Smith had assembled and which he so brilliantly held together.

Holding them together can have been no easy task, for, however loyal and devoted they were to their pupils, even their pupils
had no difficulty in discerning that they did not get on at all
well with one another. In particular, relations between Cod in the
Physics department and his scientific colleague George Francis, who
was responsible for Chemistry, were at times on the verge of open
war. I suspect that this was partly due to Cod's ruthless canvassing
methods, but, whatever the cause, it was assisted by his openly
expressed contempt for Chemistry as such. He would describe it
as 'a smelly [pronounced 'smilly'] business', and once when his
own lecture was interrupted by a loud explosion, accompanied
by a vivid flash, from the neighbouring chemistry department, he
merely remarked in a gently pitying tone 'Oo, another of those
bangs'. George was himself an extremely able teacher, with an
elaborately systematic method which I at least (for I had to take
subsidiary Chemistry) never fully fathomed. By the time one had
underlined passages in a large text-book and more passages in
a smaller text-book and summarised both in a note-book there
seemed to be little time for anything else. He had a tremendous
enthusiasm for his subject, but its effect was lessened by the furious
indignation which burst out upon anyone who did not altogether
share it. I still remember how he scarified a small boy who, at a
time when there was an acute shortage of iron for the manufacture
of munitions of war, admitted to a lack of interest in the chemistry
of the blast-furnace.

The cause of the hostility between Cod and George was something of a mystery. It was believed by their pupils that originally
George had taught physics and Cod had taught chemistry, that
they were complete failures until they exchanged their subjects and
that they never forgave each other in consequence; this ingenious
theory, improbable in itself, is completely disproved by the records.
Of the feud itself there is, however, no doubt, and, if memory is
reliable, it reached its finest hour when Cod, in whose department
the electrical rectifying plant was located, cut off the direct-current
supply from the chemistry side. Cod had one great advantage in
that he never lost his temper, while George, who had always
been extremely excitable, developed, after a bicycle accident in
which he suffered a concussion that was nearly fatal, an almost
uncontrollable irascibility.

Not all the masters were as colourful as those I have mentioned,
and there were several to whom I owe a great deal of whom there
is not much to say except that they took an interest in their pupils
and taught them well, which is after all what they were there to do.

There was for example Horace Clewley, under whom I not only learnt to read French with enthusiasm and even to pronounce it with something approaching accuracy but who even inspired me to translate French poetry, if not into English poetry at least into English verse. There was Clement Ayres, who, having undertaken to take a class in subsidiary English, which had a syllabus of lunatic dimensions extending from Chaucer to Thomas Hardy, not only got us through the exam but kindled in some of us scientists an enthusiasm for great literature which we never lost. There were Fred Skinner and R. C. ('Archie') Davies with the Guild, in which that enthusiasm found practical expression. No doubt there were others to whom my debt is as great but on whom in my mind more than half a century later oblivion hath blindly scattered her poppy.

After the initial nightmare period, which must have lasted for nearly two years, my life at Latymer became increasingly enjoyable. I had little difficulty in avoiding organised games, which I hated; while the War was still on, problems of staff and equipment caused evasion to be readily connived at. Later on when my academic ability became more evident I was wisely encouraged to concentrate on the things that I could do rather than on those that I could not. I did in fact, when I was in the seventh form, become very keen on Lawn tennis, which I played extremely badly but with great enjoyment; this was assisted by the fact that Cod skilfully transformed the masters' tennis club, of which he had been secretary, into a club for the senior boys. (It was said that he had terminated a dispute with his fellow members of the earlier organisation and its existence simultaneously, by the drastic but simple expedient of confiscating all the tennis-balls; however improbable this may sound it would not have been out of character.) However, our sense of loyalty was strong and we of the intelligentsia took considerable pride in the School's notable athletic record provided we were not expected to contribute actively to it. Our closeness to the River stimulated a keen interest in the Oxford-and-Cambridge boat-race, in which most of us supported the light blues. The Old Man used to invite the prefects to view it from his house, which overlooked the course, but as long as my parents continued to live in Hammersmith we used to have our own party, for which we would arrange a largish group of friends to make the long trek over Hammersmith Bridge to take up a position on the Surrey side, finally returning to our flat for lunch or tea.

I am sorry if I disappoint my readers by saying that, as far as I can remember, we do not seem to have been obsessed by sex, though I think some of us might have been saved a good deal of anxiety and perplexity by some straightforward factual information. I can think of a small number of boys who specialised in humour of the lavatorial type, but they were tolerated rather than admired; anything much more than that was either uncommon or I failed to observe it, or else I have simply forgotten it. In the seventh form we argued interminably about almost everything else; literature, science, politics and – quite a lot about philosophy and religion. I discovered the cosmological argument for myself at about the age of sixteen, but I do not give myself any credit for that, as it has come naturally to almost all the human race except where it has been artificially conditioned away by a secularist environment or a positivist technique. Our contacts with the opposite sex were minimal and, in the context of the School, non-existent. But one occasionally met the sisters of one's friends if one went to their homes and even the Old Man's edicts could not prevent that.

My interest in mathematics came to life quite instantaneously during a lesson when I was in the fourth form. I had never previously been free of a conviction that mathematics so-called was a rag-bag of miscellaneous and uncoördinated stuff without logical coherence or shape (I would not of course have expressed by misgivings in those words!). In particular I could not see, and no one had ever tried to tell me, what algebra and geometry had in common that justified including them in the same discipline. On the day of enlightenment it was revealed to me that, in Cartesian co-ordinates, a straight line was represented by a linear equation. There the link was made; it was only later on that I was told that other equations represented other lines, that quadratic equations for example represented conic sections, but that did not matter. *Ce n'est que le premier pas* ... From that moment on my fate as a mathematician was determined. There were other notions that puzzled me. That of an 'unknown' was one; how could you represent a number by a number by a symbol when you didn't know what it was? That of a 'variable' was another; how could you represent a number by a single symbol when it wasn't one number but a whole range of numbers? But that could bide its time; the Rubicon had been crossed, and I was ready for the day several years later when Cod would clothe these logical dry bones with physical flesh in a lesson on electrostatics and so complete my mathematical conversion. If this account appears implausible and indeed riduculous I cannot help it, but that is how it happened. R. C. Davies wrote of 'Edgar Coyle with his beautiful voice that earned him so many evening engagements that he frequently set his form some work and spent the afternoon asleep', but it was well for me that he was awake one afternoon in 1917, for he set me on the path that culminated ten years later in a First Class in the Cambridge Mathematics Tripos.

I have said virtually nothing about my religious development during my schooldays and indeed the School had virtually nothing to do with it. In Tubby Smith's time religious concern was limited to prayers at morning and evening assembly and a scripture period each week which was devoted to a rigidly textual study of the sacred text until one got into the fifth form; I remember 'doing' I Samuel in the third form and the Acts of the Apostles in the fourth. What lay behind this was presumably the view, for which there is a lot to be said, that in a day-school the religion of the pupils was primarily the concern of the clergy of the parishes where they lived. There was great concern for the freedom of Jewish boys to be absent on the occasions of their own religious observances, but when some Christian boys pressed for an analogous extension of the principle they were unsuccessful, apparently on the grounds that the School was a 'Christian school'. (Some years later, Dr Dale managed to secure the appointment of an Anglican chaplain, who held confirmation classes and Communion services, and to convert an empty room into what was oddly called the Chantry Chapel, through a rather questionable view about the services to learning of the medieval chantry priests; but this was after my time.) My own religious awakening led me to a stronghold of evangelical respectability near my home, St Mary's, Stamford Brook, where the Holy Table was devoid of candlesticks and even of a cross until one was presented by the local M.P., who had a tendency to make such gifts to churches in his constituency. Some indication of the churchmanship is given by the discussions that animated the congregation when somebody offered to present a banner – for outdoor and strictly utilitarian use. Any possibility of superstition was excluded by having nothing on the banner but the simple inscription 'St Mary's Church' – though I have sometimes meditated on the tremendous theological content that those words could have if taken seriously; but the real problem arose over the ornament at the top of the staff. A large gilded cross was doctrinally offensive, a spearhead was too warlike, a fleur-de-lys would suggest the Boy Scouts and there was some objection, I forget what, to a knob. The final solution was in fact a cross, but it must be very small and inconspicuous and, of course, ungilded.

The Vicar was a very saintly elderly bachelor. The Curate, by whom I was prepared for confirmation, was a perfect replica of the curate of fiction; he was more easily shocked than almost anyone I have ever met, and my mother, who was herself always careful in her speech, was specially unfortunate in earning his rebukes. 'Oh, Mrs Mascall, nothing is ever past *praying for.*' 'Oh, Mrs Mascall, not enough to make the *angels* weep.' Of my confirmation instructions I have only two recollections. One was of a quite sound exposition of the need of interpreting the Ten Commandments in a positive sense. The other was of a warning never to enter a 'high' church, which was defined as one where there were candles on the Holy Table. Whether it was because of the difficulty of knowing from purely external observation whether a place of worship conformed to this criterion or not, I must confess that I soon began to gravitate towards churches of the unsound type and that my degeneration, though slow, was progressive. That it was not more rapid was, I think, due to four main causes. The first was that I was convinced at the start simply that Protestantism was true and that Catholicism was false, and it took me a long time to revise this conviction. The second was that I was equally convinced that Catholicism was foreign while Protestantism was basically English, and patriotism was a very obstinate element in the Mascall tradition. Thirdly, I had somehow acquired the notion, which may have been derived from early experiences of services to which I had been taken, that religion was meant to be unpleasant, so that the fact that Catholic worship was more enjoyable than Protestant seemed to be a positive argument against it; it was years before I could enjoy a Catholic service without experiencing a *frisson* of guilt. And fourthly, the curate of St Mary's and his wife had taken the next flat to ours and I was therefore under continuous inquisitorial observation. I can remember the sense of profound relief with which I heard that he had been appointed to a rich living in the West Country of which the retiring incumbent, a fine old Trollopian cleric in a shooting-jacket who used to come and stay with him at intervals, had inherited the patronage. St Peter's, Hammersmith; St Nicholas', Chiswick (the only medieval church in the neighbourhood and a pleasant half-mile's walk on a Sunday morning); and, very occasionally, Holy Innocents', Hammersmith, represented gradations on my pilgrimage. A break of several months in my studies, which we spent at Brighton to clear up a spot which was believed to have developed on my lung, gave me the opportunity of exploring the ecclesial riches of that hot-bed of Anglo-Catholicism. St Bartholomew's in particular, with its great red and green marble baldachino (a visitor once remarked that he expected to see a maharajah ride out from behind it on an elephant at any moment), its soaring roof, higher than that of any English cathedral and alleged to be the second highest in Europe, and its Byzantine marble pulpit and baptistery of proportionate dimensions, helped me to appreciate that imitation Gothic was not the only possible modern setting for Christian liturgy. For the last part of my health-cure we moved to a bungalow on Shoreham Beach, and there I learnt to serve Mass in the Church of the Good Shepherd, a tiny rough-cast sanctuary which in all respects except its religion was as great a contrast to St Bart's as could be imagined; it was in the care of a devoted and physically delicate priest named Gerald Engelbach. I returned for my last year at Latymer fully restored in health and fully convinced that that the Church of England was Catholic and not Protestant, though I was uneasy about certain extreme and un-English developments which were alleged to have appeared in some undisciplined quarters, especially in the notoriously antinomian diocese of London. It must have been about this time that I acquired a secondhand copy of Walter Walsh's *Secret History of the Oxford Movement*, a work which, like other exposures of subterranean vice, by imparting to the innocent reader information of which he was previously ignorant was as likely to encourage the atrocities which were its concern as to assist in their suppression. Mr Walsh's account of how microscopic examination revealed a mysterious iron object to be the celibate ring of the Society of the Holy Cross is worthy of the best traditions of spy fiction. It was however perhaps unfortunate that many of the enormities which he denounced as clandestine in the late eighteen-nineties had lost much of their secrecy by the early nineteen-twenties. For these were the years of the great Anglo-Catholic Congresses, and whatever those were they were not clandestine or, in the popular sense, apologetic.

Notes

1. How strong this was among the middle class is evident in an episode in G. K. Chesterton's *Autobiography*, in which he got his own way by uttering the awful threat to drop the aspirate from the word 'hat'.
2. I had never heard of Pythagoras or of the word 'hypotenuse'. But I had a vague idea of bending the paper to make the hypotenuse conform, so I had perhaps an inchoate intuition of non-Euclidean geometry.
3. I had Isabel almost in tears for saying 'but I *did* think it was so' about something of which I forced her to admit she had been uncertain. What a little prig I was!

4. How different this from the famous reply of the great High Master, Walker, of St Paul's to the question whether he was careful about the social standing of the boys at his school: 'Madam, so long as your son behaves himself and the fees are paid, no questions will be asked about his social standing'!
5. My maternal grandmother's public worship consisted entirely of going to a Watch-night Service on New Year's Eve and I remember her disappointment on arriving at St Paul's to find that one had not been arranged.
6. Philosophers may be interested in this example of the Aristotelian doctrine of form and matter.
7. *Latymer Upper School (1895–1967).* (Privately published.) The standard work on Edward Latymer is *The History of Edward Latymer and his Foundations* by Wm. Wheatley, 2nd ed. 1953. (Cambridge U.P. for Latymer Upper School).
8. The fees, according to Whittaker's Almanack for 1980, are now £1155 per annum.
9. This had been opened in 1905, with the assistance of the Latymer Foundation, in buildings formerly occupied by the Godolphin School for Boys, an institution which declined and died as a result of the migration of St Paul's School from the City to Hammersmith in 1885 and the opening of Latymer Upper in 1895.
10. He was a B. A. of Lampeter, a B. A. of Jesus College, Oxford, and a B. Sc. of London. Presumably his origins were Welsh, but his highly characteristic manner of speech did not suggest this.

Chapter Three

Cambridge in the nineteen-twenties

(1924–1928)

It seems just as wrong to accept merely plausible arguments from a mathematician as to require demonstrations from a rhetorician.

– Aristotle, *Nichomachaean Ethics*, I.

In October 1924 I went up to Pembroke College, Cambridge, with an open scholarship in Mathematics. I had originally intended to try for Jesus College, on which Latymerian mathematicians had recently tended to concentrate and where the mathematics fellow, Leopold Alexander Pars, was himself an old Latymerian. However, Pembroke had just decided to award its scholarships for this and future years not by the established mechanism of special examinations held by groups of colleges, for which the candidates had to come and sit in Cambridge, but on the results of the Higher Certificate Examinations taken in the various schools. Both my fellow-Latymerian David Murray, whose subject was chemistry, and myself were offered scholarships in this way, and it would obviously have been pointless and foolish to refuse. I learnt much later that the other colleges were furious at what they considered an unscrupulous attempt to skim the milk before them; it was said that the Head of one prestigious institution jumped on the issue of *The Times* which contained the announcement of the outrage and committed it to the combination-room fire while uttering appropriate anathemas upon the Master and Fellows of Pembroke. I believe that Pembroke in fact abandoned the experiment later, through doubts whether scholarships awarded only to those at schools which took certain examinations could properly be described as 'open'. If this is so, my academic career began under something of a moral cloud and my subsequent honours rooted in dishonour stood, but I knew nothing about this at the time. 1927 and 1928 were certainly years of notable success for Pembroke in the triposes, and 1924 came to be referred to in the College as the *annus mirabilis*. But this was perhaps pitching things rather high, and there could be more than one reason for it.

Pembroke was one of the oldest colleges in the University and under the title of 'the hall or house of Valence-Marie' it was founded in 1347 by Mary de StPol in memory of her husband Aymer de Valence, Earl of Pembroke, who was, by partly female descent, great-grandson of the William Marshal of Magna-Carta fame, whose name has already occurred in this work; I did not, however, think it worth while to try to establish foundress' kin. I must not attempt to give here a history of the College, which was apostrophised by Queen Elizabeth I in the unforgotten, though hardly memorable, words *O Domus antiqua et religiosa!* That was done admirably in 1936 in the volume written by Aubrey Attwater and completed after his death by Sir Sydney Roberts. I will however mention that in the sixteenth century Pembroke nurtured no less than four noteworthy Calvinistically-inclined ecclesiastics in the persons of John Bradford, Nicholas Ridley, Edmund Grindal and John Whitgift. A century later, it housed the mellower figures of Lancelot Andrewes and Matthew Wren. Wren, whose succession of bishoprics included that of Ely, provided the College at his own expense with a new chapel and employed as its architect his young nephew Christopher, whose first work it was and who later enjoyed a wider fame. His chapel still stands, extended by George Gilbert Scott. The College treasures a mitre and pastoral staff which were carried at his funeral, and admirers of the catholicity of the Caroline divines have maintained that the state of the lining was so decayed that little could be deduced from it. The mitre itself is a very heavy inflexible structure of solid silver and I find it difficult to suppose that anyone could have actually worn it for more than the briefest period, if at all. I wonder whether, like one of our present bishops, Dr Wren simply had it carried before him. In the literary field far and away the most famous sons of Pembroke were the poets Edmund Spenser and Thomas Gray. In politics the younger Pitt. The College treasures a letter from the Tutor's 'most faithful and most obedient humble servant, Chatham' which opens with the portentous and ringing annoucement 'Apprehensions of gout, about this season, forbid my undertaking a journey to Cambridge with my son.' In nineteenth-century science Pembroke can claim John Couch Adams, the co-discoverer of the planet

Neptune, and the great mathematical physicist Sir George Gabriel Stokes, though truth impels one to admit that the former was imported from St John's. And now, to skip over a third of a century, S. C. Roberts could write in 1936 that 'in the years since the [First World] war Pembroke has given to the world bishops, judges, governors of provinces, members of parliament, university professors, captains of English cricket and football, and the leader of the last two Everest expeditions'. I will conclude this very selective catalogue with the names of two Pembroke men roughly contemporary with myself who achieved high distinction in public life, R. A. ('Rab') Butler, later Lord Butler of Saffron Walden, who nearly became Prime Minister and did become Master of Trinity, and P. J. ('Bob', later Sir Pierson) Dixon, who, after a brilliant diplomatic career which included being British Representative at the United Nations and Ambassador at Paris, died suddenly in 1965.

It is merely trite to say that Cambridge in 1924 was very different from Cambridge today. The proctors patrolled the streets at night with their 'bulldogs' and fined anyone *in statu pupillari* who was not wearing (carrying was not enough) both cap and gown 6s.8d. for undergraduates and 13s.4d. for B.A.s. Gate-fines were imposed if we came in late at night and more serious measures taken if this happened too late or too often. An *exeat* was needed to be away for the night and, in theory at least, an *absit* for the greater part of the day. Later on I was struck by the contrast between the formidable array of rotating spiked wheels, barbed railings and walls topped with broken bottles with which Cambridge colleges have tended to protect themselves and the much milder fortifications of the Oxford colleges. This may be due to a more tolerant attitude of Oxford to the practice of climbing in, but is also, I suspect, to a belief at Cambridge that the easiest way to trap offenders is to leave one or two easily observable gaps in an elsewhere impregnable perimeter. This might form the basis of an interesting study in comparative university criminology and, indeed, psychology, but I shall not develop it here.

In our first year we had to dine in hall at six o'clock every evening; in our later years there were successive relaxations. Most of us got our own breakfast and lunch, as the college kitchen was beyond our means. As we had no gas or electric rings (though the electric light was oddly charged for as 'gas') we used primus stoves, which were inefficient and alarming, though I never heard of one actually exploding. Cooking in one's rooms was prohibited, though it was tolerated provided it was not too ambitious or odorous. ('These is gentlemen's rooms, sir, not cook'ouses', one of my friends was reminded.) After some initial experiements with a frying pan, which were less than fully successful, I settled down to the popular lunch of bread, cheese (usually gorgonzola) and jam (usually strawberry). At tea-time one ate very large Chelsea buns, which were drenched in syrup and stuffed with currants, and a variety of rich cakes which went under the generic name of 'deadlies'; these made up for the deficiencies of the impending dinner in hall. And if one had a meeting in one's rooms after dinner, it was absolutely *de rigueur* to provide chocolate biscuits with the coffee and cigarettes. Nobody at that time had heard of lung-cancer, but many of us preferred the manly pipe to the effeminate cigarette and had on our mantelpieces porcelain tobacco-jars adorned with our college arms, which were known as 'freshers' delights'. One's rooms were looked after by a bed-maker or 'bedder', who was assisted by another lady called a 'help' (the 'h', unlike the lady herself, was usually silent), and it was one of the features of Cambridge life that one was woken up in the morning by the high-pitched voices of the bedder and her help, raised in altercation. A good bedder was a treasure and, when in my second year I moved into a quiet set of rooms over the Dean and next to the Chapel, I had the best bedder in college, the admirable Mrs Overton.

Chapel, at least once on Sunday, was still compulsory at Pembroke in my time. There was Holy Communion at 8 a.m., a very plain Sung Eucharist at 10 a.m. and a rather formal Morning Prayer at 11 a.m. The easiest service for the godless was Evensong, which was wedged in between second and third hall; I went to it once and thought it dreadful. At the collection the worshippers came up one by one in order of seniority and placed their offerings in the recesses of a heavy and ornate silver dish which the officiating minister held out at the communion-step with his eyes tactfully directed somewhere in the direction of the constellation of the Great Bear; I remember profanely reflecting that if they were really hard up they would have sold the dish instead of collecting our humble shillings and sixpences.

The college garden was large and delightful, but was banned to junior members on the insistence of a small number of the older fellows who hardly ever used it; only once in my four years was I invited into it. There was in fact nowhere in college in the open air where it was legitimate for an undergraduate to sit and read or talk, though there was a small patch of grass in a remote corner where one was unlikely to be observed by one's elders. Typical of the official attitude was the episode of the plus-fours, which deserves to be recorded. Most of the time that I was up the most popular form of nether apparel was this particular garment, which originated, as its name suggests, on the golf-course and was favoured by the Prince of Wales. Pembrochian authority however considered it excessively informal and decreed that at dinner trousers were to be worn. (This may seem paradoxical, as one imagines that a century or so earlier trousers had been frowned upon and knee-breeches held *obligatory*.) The practice then arose, among men who were in lodgings, of keeping an old pair of trousers in the rooms of a friend in college, pulling these on over the improper garment before dinner and removing them after. All went well until, one warm and fine evening, one of the senior fellows who had left hall early was scandalised to behold a large proportion of the undergraduate population sitting round the court removing the less mentionable portion of their clothing. After this the ordinance against plus-fours was either rescinded or quietly allowed to lapse. Strange as it may seem, although we occasionally grumbled mildly at some of the less rational disciplines which we were under, I do not think we had any real sense of grievance. But then most of us felt we were very lucky to have got to the University at all and did not, like many students today, apparently feel that we had conferred a favour on the community by condescending to be educated at someone else's expense. My time at Cambridge was on the whole extremely happy, although it was difficult, even at one of the less expensive colleges, to make both ends meet on my scholarship and the grant which I received from the London County Council; it would in fact have been impossible had my parents not supported me in the vacations.

The only game which I played was tennis, of my former abysmally low quality, but I took interest and pride in the College's achievements on the river. I engaged in interminable arguments on every subject under the sun, either formally in the College debating society or with my friends in their rooms or on walks in the country. My social life was lived almost entirely with other scholars from schools of the same type as my own, for Pembroke, though not positively unfriendly, was certainly cliquish; but I certainly never felt lonely. There was a brief but drastic interruption in my second year with the General Strike of May 1926. Needless to say, Pembroke almost unanimously sided with the Government and, without actual compulsion (which would in any case have been impossible), gave us every encouragement to offer our services. I found myself living for a week in a factory in Whitechapel, as part of an improvised police force which, fortunately for everyone concerned, never had to take any action. My own section was under a notably tough law don from another college who was alleged (and I could believe it) to have once run a revolution in South America, and we were marched through the streets partly to impress the populace and partly to take baths in the Tower of London. This is not one of the episodes in my life in which retrospectively I have taken much satisfaction, but it was sincere at the time.

Academically I had a bad set-back at the end of my first year, when I got only second-class honours in the First Part of the Mathematical Tripos. This was looked upon quite seriously, as, in contrast with Part Two, Part One was considered to be fairly elementary and was commonly taken by physicists as well as by mathematical specialists. However, my tutor was able to persuade his colleagues that I had been concentrating upon the more important, and to me much more interesting, advanced work, and there was certainly a good deal of truth in this. I must honestly admit that I had found Cambridge such a fascinating place and the freedom from close supervision so welcome that I had simply let the time slip by without proper attention to its passage. Anyhow, I had learnt the lesson and retrieved my reputation in the intercollegiate examination (the so-called 'Mays') a year later when I also got a First in the Final of the London B.Sc.; and finally, in Part Two at the end of my third year, I obtained a First Class as a Wrangler, with a distinction (the 'B-star') in the optional Schedule B.[2] As a result I was given a Foundress Scholarship for a fourth year.

The actual process of sitting the examination for Part Two was without doubt by far the severest nervous and intellectual ordeal that I have ever had to undergo. In most subjects – and I say this in no disparaging spirit – a candidate who has mastered his material and is in good health at the time of the examination has not a great deal to fear and, unless he succumbs to panic, the chief strain which he is under at the time of the actual examination is that of recalling, manipulating and expressing on paper knowledge which he has already got under his command; the real work has been already done. In mathematics, on the other hand, the crucial part of the work has to be done in the examination-room; the candidate is confronted with problems most of which he has never seen before, and everything will turn upon the vigour and elasticity of his mind at that particular time. A bad headache or even a cold in the head can be disastrous. In my time the compulsory Schedule A was taken at the end of one's third year in six three-hour papers on the Monday, Tuesday and Wednesday of one particular week, and the optional and specialised Schedule B in six further papers on the corresponding days the week after, thus comprising two three-day periods of torture with four days of intermission between.

In Schedule B each question-paper was a booklet of something like forty questions without any obvious arrangement, so that one had to spend some time searching through it to find a question that one could even understand; it was assumed that one good answer on each paper would be rewarded with a distinction. This was specialisation with a vengeance. I believe my own distinction was largely due to my success in discovering inductively the meaning that presumably would have to be given to a symbol which the examiners had omitted to identify. I spent the later part of these ten days in a kind of stupor, and after the last paper I went into the Botanical Gardens, lay on my back under a tree and, without in any normal sense going to sleep, simply lost all sense of space and time for some unrecorded period. It was several weeks before I could be relied on to remember trivial social duties and engagements. As far as I know, I suffered no permanent mental harm from taking the Tripos, but perhaps my friends are in a better position than I to judge. I can certainly think of few more drastic intellectual exercises. We, of course, had no college nurses to soothe us with tranquillisers or psychiatrists to palliate our shortcomings. Nevertheless, to have spent several years in grappling with the concepts and methods of mathematics, pure and applied, is in itself of inestimable value in forming habits of clear and exact thought, whether one is going to be a professional mathematician or not; nor in my experience has it a narrowing tendency. There are, of course, notorious exceptions, but my observation is that mathematicians tend if anything rather more than other specialists to have interests outside their own subjects. Having myself moved later on into another realm of research, I have often found myself wishing that some of the theologians whose works I have had to read had been subjected to as rigorous a training. Conscious as I am of my weaknesses in never having had an academic theological training, I have never regretted as a theologian the training that I had as a mathematician. When I have heard Oxonians enthusing about the tremendous intellectual discipline of the Greats School, I have sometimes dared to remind them of another place where people speak of the tremendous intellectual discipline of the Mathematical Tripos.

An undergraduate's opportunities of getting to know the dons of his college are more or less limited to those in his own subject and those who have some special interest which he shares. The Master of Pembroke, William Sheldon Hadley, was respected and genial, and I found him very friendly on the few occasions when we met. The Senior Tutor[3], John Cuthbert Lawson, was a formidable and austere Scot, whom one met, unless one was one of his pupils, only if one had committed one of the more serious college crimes. Being far too timid for these, I cannot remember that we ever spoke, though I think we must, as I was the senior scholar of my year. He had been a naval officer in the War and engaged in various unauthorised as well as authorised activities in Crete; his fascinating book *Tales of Aegean Intrigue* reveals a side of his character which we never saw. Henry Comber, 'the Old Man' to those who knew him, was a gigantic figure who was an enthusiast for soccer and, surprisingly, bred canaries in his rooms. Sir Ellis Minns, who discoursed most interestingly to me about the Slavonic alphabets when I once sat next to him at dinner, was a quite amazing polymath. He was Professor of Classical Archaeology and I sat enthralled at a popular lecture in which he demonstrated, with an instrument of his own invention, how the Babylonians wrote in cuneiform on clay tablets. He was also an expert on Slavonic and was the author of the leading English book on Russian icons. Nobody knew how many languages he wrote and spoke; it was alleged that he taught himself Georgian in a fortnight so that the Foreign Office could reply to a letter in that language from the newly established republic in the Caucasus. He said, however, that his wife would not let him learn Chinese, as so many of the people who tried committed suicide! I should nevertheless be very much surprised if he had not managed to pick up a good deal of Chinese surreptitiously!

My own Tutor, Supervisor and for eight of my nine undergraduate terms, Director of Studies, George Birtwistle ('Bertie' to us, 'George' to his colleagues), was something, but only something, of a character. He was tall, willowy, nervous and dyspeptic, almost always wearing a very light-coloured suit and a very loosely fitting collar, with a bow-tie which looked like the ribbon from a box of chocolates. He was one of the last people in Cambridge to teach both the pure and the applied side of the Mathematical Tripos. He had settled in happily and unambitiously as a fellow, with a charming set of rooms in college and a charming house in Newnham Terrace, where his delicate health was ministered to by his devoted wife. He had produced no original research that I know of, but had kept well in the forefront of applied mathematics in the fashionable areas of Relativity Theory and Quantum Mechanics, and his books *The Quantum Theory of the Atom* and *The New Quantum Mechanics*, though now of course outmoded, were uniquely useful in their time. My copy of the former, inscribed to me by the author 'in recognition of [my] success', is still one of my treasures. Once a week two of us would go to him for supervision in college; he sat between us with his back to the fire, and would strike innumerable matches, of which few would reach his pipe but which he would project with infallible accuracy under his arm into the coal-fire behind him. Once a term we were expected to go to tea on a Sunday with Mrs Birtwistle; Bertie, who because of his nerves had his tea alone in the study, would join us shortly before we left. Towards the end of my time, when I had become one of his more favoured pupils, I would go more frequently and was admitted to the study, where he and I would have tea together in semi-darkness relieved only by a green-shaded oil lamp and he would give me the latest news about quantum research. He was in fact extremely kind to me and I became very fond of him. The signs of my forthcoming divergence from mathematics would have saddened him. But he died rather suddenly in 1929; and very soon afterwards his wife, who had little left to live for without him, tragically followed him.

However, the Pembroke don to whom I owe most, not only while I was up at the University but for many years after, was the Dean, Harold Edward Wynn. Edward, as he was always known, became Dean three years before I came up; he was then in his early thirties. Of our association in the Oratory of the Good Shepherd I shall write later. To me as a freshman he was just the most wonderfully friendly, humorous, devout and naturally Catholic priest, who made no secret of his convictions but happily conformed to the liturgical prescriptions of the Prayer Book of 1661. He was always 'at home' on Sunday evenings to anyone who liked to drop in (and a great many people did) and on most other evenings as well. He was in fact one of a small group of college chaplains after the First World War who deliberately decided to put pastoral work even before theological research as their priority in the University. Many years later he remarked to me that, in view of the uninspiring bleakness of Anglican academic theology, he wondered whether they had been altogether wise. While agreeing about the deplorable condition into which Anglican theology has drifted in recent years, I am sure that in his case the decision was a wise one. For Edward, though he was a competent historical scholar (and he had an unrealised ambition to write a book on the Avignon Papacy) and was a man of very high general intelligence, was above all a superb pastoral priest. To give one example, it was a matter of common knowledge that he heard more confessions of both senior and junior members of the University than any other Anglican priest. I made my first confession to him during my second year and this was needless to say one of the great landmarks in my life. He did not, in his earlier years at Pembroke, have an altogether easy time from all his colleagues. To take one instance, his determination, in which he was ultimately successful, to get compulsory chapel abolished met with strong opposition, especially from some of those who rarely or never came to chapel themselves. In the end, however, his sheer holiness and pastoral dedication won through.[4] F. I. G. Rawlings, who was a freshman at Pembroke in 1922 and later became the scientific expert at the National Gallery, records that Edward once said, 'One cannot expect anything to happen until about 2 a.m. when somebody comes to one's rooms to talk about their soul.'

When in 1935 the College suffered a calamitous series of deaths among its fellows, it was obvious that Edward was the inevitable person to be (senior) Tutor and, in spite of misgivings whether he could make it a genuinely pastoral office, he accepted and found to his relief that he could. In 1951 he became Bishop of Ely and had to face the demands both of a university community and of one of the most depressing of rural dioceses. The former presented no special new problems, but the spiritual desolation of the latter came as a dreadful revelation to him. The loneliness of the remoter parishes appalled him in its effect on the clergy; he told me of one parish where the incumbent had given up writing altogether, even his own signature. In another, when he suggested that the people ought to contribute to the incumbent's stipend, the churchwarden protested: 'Help to pay for our parson? Why we might as well be Methodists and have done with it!' And a third − a worse case − where his suggestion that a proposed course of action was contrary to the teaching of Christ evoked the reply: 'Yes, and that's just where he was wrong; look where it got him!' The central administration of the Church frankly bored him; he felt he had no special flair for it and he was worried about some of the things that the bureaucrats were doing to the Church. He once said to me, before a meeting of the Church Assembly, pointing to a gaitered figure who was dashing into a door: 'Look at that man! Nothing can be as important as what he thinks he's doing.' These recollections however belong to a later time, and I must return to Pembroke in the twenties, where I belonged to one of those many generations of Pembroke men who remembered Edward Wynn as the genial dispenser of endless cups of tea and coffee, the brilliant raconteur and mimic (his imitations of Searle and Gwatkin were famous), and above all as the dedicated priest and pastor. He died as Bishop of Ely in 1956.[5]

The only other fellow of Pembroke in Holy Orders was the Lady Margaret's Professor of Divinity, the Reverend Doctor James Franklin Bethune-Baker. (He pronounced the first half of his surname as spelt, in order, we believed, to upset those knowalls who presumed it would rhyme with 'Eton'.) He was a bearded figure of lugubrious appearance and a peculiar measured diction, in which the habit of placing a slow sneering emphasis upon certain words could give even the most trivial remarks the impression of a carefully constructed insult. As he was apparently an extremely generous man, I can only suppose that what seemed to be deliberately offensive must have been his idea of gentle and good-humoured raillery, but it certainly could be very off-putting. He was one of the leaders of English Modernism in theology.

In my first term one of my fellow-freshmen remarked to me after a sermon of Edward Wynn's that that modernist fellow was a good preacher. When I explained that the preacher was in fact by no means a modernist, he replied, 'Well, we've only got two parsons here and I know that one of them's a modernist; and it couldn't be that old man with the beard'! In spite of his insistence on remodelling theology to bring it into line with the theory of evolution, the 'Bath Bun' (as we called him) strongly stood for orthodoxy in the early church, and his textbook *The Early History of Christian Doctrine* has been used as a balanced and lucid manual of an orthodox traditional type almost to the present day. He had been Dean from 1891 to 1906 and, having failed to be re-elected to that office in the latter year, ostensibly on theological grounds, he refused for the remaining forty-five years of his life ever to preach again in the chapel. I had a characteristic conversation with him at the end of my final year, when I told him that I was about to go down. 'You are go-ing to be or-dained, are you not?' he enquired. 'No,' I replied, 'I am going to be a schoolmaster', for that was then my intention. 'Oh, I see. But you are inter-ested, are you not, in *religion*?' Feeling rather foolish, I replied that I supposed I was, or something to that effect. 'Oh, that is very inter-esting', he went on, seeing that I had fallen into the trap, 'I knew that you were inter-ested in sacra-ments and serv-ing and *that kind of thing*, but I did not know whether you were interested in *religion*.' Edward told me of a typical riposte of which he himself was the victim shortly after becoming Dean. B.B. walked out of chapel during one of Edward's sermons, and Edward, deciding to take the bull by the horns, said to him shortly afterwards, 'I'm sorry, Professor, that my sermon upset you this morning.' 'Oh, my dear Wynn,' came the reply, 'nothing that you could say would have *any-effect-upon-me*, but I must ask you to instruct your *myrmidons* that, if they persist in leaving the cha-pel window open immediately over my stall, not even the pleasure of *listening-to-your-oratory* will induce me to remain and contract pneumonia – if you don't mind my saying so, my dear Wynn.' He had for many years refused to take the D.D. himself on the grounds that bishops who were Cambridge graduates were entitled to the degree automatically, whereas if you were wearing a B.D. hood people knew it meant something. When doctorates *jure dignitatis* were abolished he took his own D.D. It was said, and I can believe it, that it was more exacting to be a fellow-examiner with him in the Theological Tripos than to be one of the candidates, such was his severity with his colleagues' questions. He was, I suppose, more influential than anyone else in maintaining in Cambridge theology that minute concern with details of scholarship which made it at once so conscientious and so uninspiring. Like so many of the British modernists he showed that excessive deference to what they believe to be necessitated by the scientific revolution which is common among non-scientists who are afraid of being left behind in a scientific age. In his case it took the form of an obsession with the idea of evolution which could become at times naively uncritical. Thus he could write:

It is just in this history of Man's progress that we find God manifested, and using personal terms as we must, a plan or purpose being worked out – a scheme of things through all the ages that have been and are to be, through different races and individuals in them at different times, and of course at present especially through the Nordic race.[6]

And this was written in 1927, nine years after the First World War! Or this, from him who in his *Early History of Christian Doctrine* had championed Nicaea and Chalcedon:

We must absolutely jettison the traditional doctrine that [Jesus'] personality was not human, but divine. To our modern categories of thought such a statement is a denial of the doctrine of the Incarnation. There is for us no such thing as human nature apart from human personality; the distinction that he was Man but not 'a' man, while it has deep religious value, has ceased to be tenable.[7]

'The Myth of God Incarnate' – that is, the view that God

Incarnate is a myth – would seem to have started at Pembroke when I was an undergraduate.

One final anecdote, which was told me by one of B.B.'s colleagues and which seems to be the only case where one of his darts became a boomerang. During the Second World War, when rationing was at its height, a visitor asked him, 'Have you dined often in college this term, Professor?' 'I have come in to din-ner twice every week,' came the measured reply, 'but I have failed to *dine* once. The food that is provided in this col-lege would be difficult to parallel in one of the *cheaper eating-houses* in the *lower parts* of this city.' The Bursar was present and there were all the signs of an imminent explosion, when the Master, Montagu Butler, whose experience in governing an Indian province had made him skilful in handling awkward situations, nipped in adroitly. 'Would any other fellow', he enquired, 'like to contribute his experiences of cheap eating-houses in the lower parts of Cambridge?' B.B., to do him justice, took his discomfiture in good part. 'Very good, Master,' he said, 'very good.'

One of the most colourful figures in Pembroke in my time was neither a don nor an undergraduate but the kitchen manager, Alfred Chapman. 'Chappie' had served the College all his working life, having originally lived in as a boy on the top floor of Ivy Court. His career was nearly ended prematurely when a bucketful of slops which he was projecting from an upper window over the garden-wall into the shrubbery on the other side fell short into the intervening passage on to the Master, who was proceeding to chapel in surplice and hood. 'Absolutely disgraceful, yer know; absolutely disgusting, yer know. Shan't smell sweet, not if yer hang me on Coe Fen for a fortnight, yer know', was the reported comment of the Master, C. E. Searle. 'Had ter 'ide me away for a fortnight, they did', was the culprit's own reminiscence, in his engaging Cambridge-cockney accent. Having gradually worked his way up to the key position in the College's material welfare, he became adept in handling dons and undergraduates alike. To be confronted by a delegation from the Junior Parlour was a familiar experience for him and he dealt with it by a uniform technique. 'Now, gentlemen, I can see what it is, you've got a complinte. We shan't get anywhere if we lose our tempers; you've got your point of view and I've got mine. We must try to understand one another.' The delegation would sit down, a bottle of port would be produced and, after half an hour the delegation would return and report that Chappie was doing a splendid job under very difficult circumstances. And, apart from a few minor changes, things would

go on as before. Chappie once explained to me that the high price
of our meals was due to the size of the breakage account, which
he attributed to the fact that every plate went through 'nineteen
distinct processes' between being placed on the table one evening
and being placed on it the next. This was true, but it depended on
how you defined a 'process'; picking up the plate was one, and
carrying it across the hall was another. He was never one to rebel
against the dispensations of providence. To a complaint about the
inefficiency of one of his subordinates he replied, 'Ah, sir, you
know, 'e can't 'elp it. It's just that nothing ever goes right with
'im. If 'e was to fall into the river and get drowned, 'is body'd
float up stream.' His conversation was nicely adjusted to person
and circumstance. He would commiserate with the clergy with the
reflection, 'Well, sir, you know, no crahn without its crawss.' After
Dr Hadley's death, he reflected: ''E was a good man, the Master;
'e wouldn't 'ave nothing to fear on the Great Day. You know, sir,
my father used to say to me, "Alfred," 'e'd say, "always live a
good, clean life, always tell the truth, don't do nothing dishonest;
and then, when the Great White Throne is set, and there's them
as did right on one side and them as did wrong on the other, well,
it's your two chances to their one."' He was devoted to the College
and remembered it in his will.

In my third year I became Secretary, and in my fourth year
President, of the Quintic Society, which, as its name might suggest,
was a mathematical society covering five of the men's colleges and,
as its name would not suggest, made the audacious innovation of
extending its ambit to the feminine foundation of Newnham. This
brought me into contact with such eminent persons as Sir Arthur
Eddington, Sir Joseph Larmor and Dr Paul Kapitza. Eddington,
who was a shy and modest Quaker, was the leading authority
in Cambridge on the evolution of the stars; he also achieved
wide popularity as the most lucid and readable expositor to the
general public of the difficult but intriguing ideas of the Theory
of Relativity, which at this time had just made their sensational
impact on the outside world. While still at school I had devoured
his book *Space, Time and Gravitation*. No one then could have
guessed that towards the end of his life he would produce a work
on fundamental cosmological theory of such extreme obscurity that
no one has ever claimed really to understand it. Larmor, who gave
the impression of being much older than he actually was, had done
great work on electrical theory at the turn of the century; now he
was simply lecturing very vaguely on a subject described equally
vaguely as 'Electricity' to a handful of people late on Saturday

afternoon. George Birtwistle had assured me that I should find ten minutes of each lecture made attendance well worth while, and he was correct. 'I want you to think of a gas,' Larmor began, making dots at random with chalk on the blackboard, 'a whole lot of molecules, all here and there, all buzzing about, all higgledy-piggledy – like this.' 'I seem rather to have disgressed,' he reflected after one long ramble down a by-path, 'but after all the main thing is to be concise.' Kapitza was a man of many eccentricities and the subject of many stories; he left Cambridge somewhat abruptly for the Soviet Union and refused to return; and, as nobody was willing to continue his experiments on high magnetic fields, his apparatus ultimately followed him. I was once at a meeting of the Physical Colloquium at which Kapitza, who was in the chair, suddenly rose to his feet, announced in his strong Slavonic accent 'Declare meeting closed' and walked out; but the meeting went on as before. The most famous Cambridge scientist at this time was undoubtedly the Master of Trinity, Sir Joseph James Thomson, to whom the discovery of the electron is generally ascribed; I never met him but I once heard him lecture. He had a disconcerting habit of pulling his teeth into position by a sharp muscular contraction resembling a smile; this could lead the uninstructed into responding with a polite but, in the circumstances, inappropriate titter. There were many stories about his absent-mindedness, but they are well-known and need not be repeated. I often saw him on his afternoon walk through the fields towards Trumpington; he would trail a walking-stick behind himself with both hands, giving the impression that it propelled him by electricity drawn from the earth. One had the feeling that if one dared to lift it up gently he would come to an abrupt stop, but I resisted the temptation.

In my last year I attended a course by a distinguished mathematical lecturer whose behaviour was giving rise to some anxiety in the University, as he was, not for the first time, going out of his mind. Though a ruthless critic of established authority, he was a generous champion of those he believed to be its victims and was a kindly and encouraging teacher; I will refer to him simply as Dr B. One of the first symptoms of his malady to appear in his lectures was a speedy change in their division from roughly fifty minutes on Electric Waves and five minutes on the private lives of the fellows of Trinity (not perhaps unexpected from a very self-conscious Johnian) to almost the precisely opposite proportions. Though himself a Fellow of the Royal Society, he vehemently denounced that eminent institution for its alleged identification with the high table of Trinity. On one occasion, desiring information on some remote point in geometry – I think it was the number of regular solids in space of seven dimensions – he forcibly dragged Professor Baker in from a neighbouring lecture-room, introduced him to the class and put the question to him. 'I haven't the slightest idea', Baker replied, detached himself from Dr B's grasp and fled. Dr B turned to the class in triumph. 'Gentleman,' he said, 'you have seen a very rare phenomenon. You have seen a fellow of Trinity admitting that there is something he does not know.' Dr B spoke with particular feeling about the scurvy treatment which he held that the mathematical recluse Oliver Heaviside had received from the establishment, and whose claims to recognition he had himself vindicated; he exhibited to us with pride the diploma which Heaviside had been given by the University of Kiel and which he had bequeathed to Dr B. When an undergraduate magazine, reviewing the lectures of prominent dons, criticised George Birtwistle for inaudibility, Dr B tried to persuade me to call upon the Editor, accompanied by the Captains of the Pembroke Boat and Boxing Clubs, to beat him up. When I told Bertie that I had no intention of manifesting my loyalty to him in this way he was obviously relieved, but I felt that I fell in Dr B's estimation for my poltroonery. Some of the stories that circulated about Dr B were obviously false or distorted, as, for example, that he was discovered under the Vice-Chancellor's dining-table drawing up a petition or that he was seen on self-assigned point-duty regulating the traffic. On the other hand, I believe it is true that, when the Dean of St John's emerged in a dressing-gown from the dons' toilet facilities on one occasion, he found himself ceremoniously introduced by Dr B to a group of undergraduates with whom the latter was chatting and that when the disconcerted cleric indignantly gathered his garment round him and turned on his heel, he heard Dr B's voice repeating the introduction with an addition: 'Gentlemen, the Dean of St John's – from the rear.' Finally, it was said, when two medical friends called to see him on the urgent representations of his colleagues, he received them most courteously and conversed for a long time with every appearance of complete rationality, until finally, having lured them to the top of the house on the pretext of showing them the view, he shoved them into an attic, locked the door and left them with the triumphant cry, 'Certify me now if you dare, damn you!' Which, the story alleged, they did.

Apart from Edward Wynn there were no clerics in Cambridge whom I knew at all intimately, as I was not reading theology. I did however make some contacts outside my own college when I became Secretary of the Confraternity of the Holy Trinity. S. T. C., as it was commonly called (the initials stood for *Sanctae Trinitatis Confraternitas* and had not then been adopted by Standard Telephones and Cables), was a devotional society which had been formed in 1867 on the model of an earlier Brotherhood of the Holy Trinity at Oxford and was of a definitely but cautiously Catholic type; it had never outgrown its early archaic and insular flavour. Most of its members were undergraduates and many were aspirants to the priesthood. Its President in my time was the Dean of King's, Eric Milner-White. He was a man who combined considerable skill and influence in many practical matters with an aesthetic and romantic side which was almost totally unrelated to reality. King's had been notorious for many years, as the Cambridge college most marked by a cynical and atheistic aestheticism. Eric seemed convinced however, on the strength of its splendid chapel and its world-renowned choir, that it was the hive of a fervent seventeenth-century Anglican piety. When he later became Dean of York Minster, Edward Wynn told me a characteristic story of how he and Wilfred Knox (who must have been the least aesthetic priest who ever lived) were vetting the preface which Eric had written to a volume in reply to the apologia of a very influential mission-preacher who had become a Roman Catholic. '"Now that Father Vernon has removed his chamber from among us ...?"', Eric began. 'You can't possibly say that', Edward interrupted. 'Why not?' protested Eric. 'Of course you can't ', Edward insisted. 'But what else can I say?' enquired the baffled author. '"Now that Father Vernon has *left us*"', Wilfred interposed. 'Oh no,' said Eric, deeply shocked, 'I couldn't *possibly* say *that*.' He had acquired the reputation of being a great liturgical expert, but I think he knew very little about either the history or the theology of liturgy. He produced several manuals of prayer and was much in demand as a writer of collects for special occasions. But, beautiful as these undoubtedly are, they have always seemed to me to be badly lacking in strength and drive.

A much respected figure in church circles was the Reverend Charles George Griffinhoofe, whom we irreverently but more accurately knew as the Griffinclaw. He was a dignified and courteous man of middle stature and wore an old-fashioned tail-coat of a peculiar clerical cut. He had retired from a country rectory in 1918 and lived in Regent Street, where he did some coaching. His almost invariable form of address was 'My dear sir', uttered in deferential and ceremonious tones. On the day when Dr E. W. Barnes's appointment to the see of Birmingham was announced, a friend, meeting him in the street, asked him, 'Have you seen *The Times* this morning, Mr Griffinhoofe?' He had; and, shaking his head sadly, simply replied, 'Oh my dear sir, my dear sir.' Then, after a pause, he repeated even more tragically, 'Oh my dear sir, my dear sir.' And turning on his heel he slowly retraced his steps. He was a loyal churchman of a rigidly Tractarian type, and was frequent in attendance at meetings of S. T. C. Once, when an enthusiastic undergraduate tried to enlist his support for the Student Christian Movement on the grounds that it was a world-wide fellowship of Christians, he replied, in his habitual well-bred diction, 'I was undah the impression that I had already become a membah of a-ah – world-wide fellowship of Christians. I refer to my-ah-baptism, wherein I was made a membah of Christ, the child of God and an inheritah of the Kingdom of Heaven.' He was a scholar in his way, and his works ranged from *Wintering in Egypt* (1894) to *Celebrated Cambridge Men* (1910).

More striking to the eye and more formidable intellectually was the great authority on canon law, Edmund Gough de Salis Wood. His name had become indissolubly linked with that of an equally striking Oxonian, of similar churchmanship and even greater intellectual achievement, sixteen years his academic junior, in the quip asserting that

> The heathen in his blindness
> Bows down to Wood and Stone.

Wood had been 11th Senior Optime in the Tripos of 1864 and had been Vicar of St Clement's, Cambridge, since 1885. His deeply bent figure could be seen shuffling through the streets wearing a B. D. gown and a top hat; for he was technically non-resident and there was an ancient rule, which I think nobody but Wood in fact observed, that non-residents should wear that headgear instead of the usual academic 'square'. He was a rigid adherent to the exact letter of the 1661 Book of Common Prayer and held that any deviation from it was a grave sin. So, I gathered (for I never went to St Clement's for a service), his normal Sunday worship consisted of Morning Prayer, Litany in procession and Holy Communion. Furthermore, the standard that he set for his acolytes was so inhumanly demanding that as time went on the only person who satisfied it was one of his own contemporaries; so the procession in which the Litany was sung consisted of the two old gentlemen tottering round the church together. He was nevertheless tremendously respected and, although he was virtually boycotted by the authorities of both Church and University, was a great spiritual force. Edward Wynn told me that, when he and Eric Milner-White were going to be army chaplains in the First World War, they were persuaded against their own judgment to consult Wood about the pastoral problems with which they would be confronted and were astonished to receive from him instruction that turned out to be of the utmost relevance. He sat in Convocation for many years as a proctor for the clergy of the Ely diocese. His uncompromising churchmanship and his abrasive manner of giving it verbal expression had not endeared him to authority either in Church or in University and, apart from an honorary canonry of Ely, conferred on him surprisingly by Bishop Chase in 1911, he had received no official recognition of any kind until he was invited in extreme old age to give a prestigious course of lectures in the university pulpit. The subject was connected, I forget in what precise respect, with canon law, and the size of the audience at the first lecture was an indication of the width of the respect which he commanded. The performance, unfortunately, was pathetic; he muddled his manuscript, repeated himself and lost the thread of his argument. He was a great survival from a past age and there were many stories about him. He had promised the Bishop, presumably Woodford, not to wear the eucharistic vestments but, it was said, adopted them immediately after the Bishop's death. 'Oh Vicar', a scandalised lady parishioner protested, 'How could you do this, and his dear Lordship not yet cold?' 'He knows better now' was all the reply she received. When courteously invited to give the Diocesan Conference the benefit of his great erudition on the subject of the ministry of women, he simply barked out 'Women are incapable of receiving the character of holy orders' and refused to say anything more.

I have mentioned already that, in consequence of my success in Part Two of the Tripos, I was given a scholarship for a fouth year. The intention behind this was that I should begin research on quantum theory for the Ph. D. degree and while doing this should obtain an academic post. It did not however work out that way. For one thing, academic posts in those days were much less plentiful than they later became; during the year only two appeared, one in Cambridge and the other in a provincial university, and neither of them fell to me. Secondly, my supervisor, who was an extremely eminent applied mathematician in another college, was almost incapable of remembering an appointment; on the very few occasions when I managed to see him he threw out a few general suggestions and rushed away. The fact was that he was much involved with people who were far more advanced in research than I was; he had really no idea how to launch a beginner. He was, incidentally, one of the worst lecturers I have known; he muttered haltingly in a dimly lighted room while making illegible chalk-marks on a greasy blackboard, was frequently unable to read his own notes and had a habit, which did not inspire confidence, of blowing the dust off the pages as he turned them. But I cannot just blame others for my own lack of success. It rapidly became plain to me that there is a great difference between being capable of getting a good degree in mathematics and having a flair for making original contributions to the subject. A suspicion was also beginning to form itself at the back of my mind, that while the intellectual formation that the Mathematical Tripos had given me and the knowledge of modern scientific developments that had accompanied it had not in any way been a waste of time – and had been an essential part of the preparation for my ultimate vocation – that vocation, so far as its academic content was concerned, would lie rather in the field of philosophy and in particular in that part or aspect of philosophy which borders upon theology. I did not at this time see this as included in a vocation to the priesthood and I have always felt the suggestion that any serious concern with religion ought to issue in ordination as little less than an insult to the laity. What I began to envisage myself as ultimately producing, whether officially or in my spare time, was not, as I had once hoped, a series of important contributions to Relativity or Quantum Theory, or even the long-desired and still unachieved Unified Field Theory. Rather it was a comprehensive and reasonably well-informed work on the relations between Christian Theology and Natural Science.

That ambition never left me entirely, though it got pushed into the background for nearly thirty years, and a lot of water was to flow under a good many bridges before it received concrete form in my Bampton Lectures at Oxford in 1956. I was encouraged in this by the Master of Corpus Christi College, the formidable Will Spens, himself both a science don and a convinced Anglo-Catholic, to whom Edward Wynn introduced me. He treated me very kindly and, although later on I came to differ from him on a number of points, both on the nature of scientific theory and, more importantly, on the status of Christian Dogma, he wrote to me enthusiastically on the appearance of my Bamptons and asked me to stay with him at Ely, where he was by then retired.[8] In 1928 however, my immediate problem was to find a way of earning a living, and I felt that, if I was not to assist in the diffusion of knowledge as a don, I might at least hope to do something in this line as a school-master. With this in view, I applied for and obtained a post as Senior Mathematics Master at an ancient, though by no means famous, day-school in the midlands and so began what I may truthfully say were, next to my first two years as a small boy at Latymer, the unhappiest years of my life. At this point however I must draw breath and say something about the way my religious understanding had developed during my four years at Cambridge.

Notes

1. At Oxford, traditionally, the rooms were looked after by men, who were known as 'scouts'; at Cambridge the male servants, called 'gyps', had other duties. But nowadays, in both universities, the traditional patterns have changed a great deal, with altered social and economic conditions.

2. For purely historical reasons, the three classes in Part Two of the Maths Tripos are called Wranglers, Senior Optimes and Junior Optimes respectively. Many years ago the lists ceased to be arranged in order of merit, although the title 'Senior Wrangler' continued to exist in an altered form. I gathered unofficially that my place was roughly thirteenth, which was satisfactory but not spectacular.

3. A tutor at Cambridge, is not, as such, involved in teaching, but in undergraduate organisation and discipline. An undergraduate's work is the concern of his Director of Studies and his actual teaching is done by his Supervisor. But any or all of these functions may be, and usually are, combined in the same person. George Birtwistle was all three for me.

4. Surprisingly, Bethune-Baker (of whom, more below) had unsuccessfully pressed for the abolition of compulsory chapel in 1892. See article by M. B. Dewey in *Pembroke College Annual Gazette*, 1979, p. 13.

5. I may be allowed to reproduce the following squib, which I circulated privately on Edward's elevation to the episcopate:

> What though the icy breezes
>   Sweep over Ely's isle?
> What though, whene'er it freezes,
>   The place is simply vile?
> All good established voices
>   Unite in tuneful din,
> And every heart rejoices
>   In worthy Bishop Wynn.
>
> But Pembroke's halls are smitten,
>   The fellows' heads are bowed,

The scholars weep in silence,
    The porters wail aloud.
The Master finishes his port,
    And, moving slowly bedward,
His voice re-echoes round the court:
    'My Edward! Oh my Edward!'

For Harold Edward Wynn, D.D.,
    By royal nomination,
Capitular election and
    The grace of consecration,
Adorned with mitre, ring and staff,
    Now reigns, supremely, freely,
Not only in the C. of E.,
    But in the See of Ely.

I have never seen any public mention of Edward's extraordinary facial resemblance to Pope Pius X, whose only other resemblance was, I think, in his deep pastoral sense.

6. *The Way of Modernism* (C.U.P. 1927), p. 79. 2. ibid., p. 93.
7. ibid., p93
8. Spens was in national politics an unyielding conservative in university affairs was adroit and astute to the fury of his opponents, though I think T. E. B. Howarth is unfair in saying (*Cambridge Between Two Wars*, p. 37) that he 'combined a Disraelian pragmatism with many of the attributes of Warwick the Kingmaker'. In the Second World War he was in his element as Area Commisioner; this would, in the event of invasion, have made him virtual Dictator over the Eastern part of England. He wrote on apologetics and eucharistic theology. He never quite succeeded in making Corpus the model liberal Catholic stronghold that he had hoped, but Edwyn Clement Hoskyns, who was Dean of Corpus for many years, produced, a stream of brilliant disciples, among whom were Francis Noel Davey and Arthur Michael Ramsey. Hoskyns was a dynamic and prophetic exponent of Biblical theology and a critical admirer of Karl Barth. His outlook was never acceptable to the ruling modernist caucus and on his early death in 1937 they did their best to eradicate his influence. Not until 1950 did Ramsey receive an academic appointment at Cambridge – and then as Regius Professor.

Chapter Four
Retrospect on Cambridge and Elsewhere
(1924–1937)

It is better to be vaguely right than precisely wrong.
— Wildon Carr

The time spent at a university (assuming that one has been lucky enough to go to one) is bound to be formative in many ways and I have no intention of indulging in platitudes on this topic. When I came up in 1924 I had been a regular communicant for several years and had effectively detached myself from St Mary's, Stamford Brook, without having found a stable spiritual home elsewhere, though I was quite clear in what direction that home would lie. One of the advantages of intellectual precocity was that I had got through a period of doubt about the basic truths of religion and of Christianity well before my confirmation. With the aid of the local public library I had tackled the challenges of determinism and evolution; very superficially no doubt, but nevertheless I had tackled them. What I had now to get clear was where I stood in Christendom, or, more precisely, where in Christendom I could find the beliefs and practices that Christianity, as I now understood it, involved. I had no desire to leave the Church of England and I had discovered that there were churches within it where what I was looking for was to be found; but I also knew that most of the bishops strongly disapproved of it, except in its most unoffending and harmless form, as had their predecessors for a century. On the other hand the story of the Catholic Movement was a stirring one, from its beginnings in Oxford of the 1830s, with the great names of Pusey and Keble, and its later triumphs in the slums and the mission-field, and if the lofty ones in Church and state discountenanced and even tried to suppress it — well, the

76

young can find a certain attraction in shocking their elders. I read
with great excitement Baring-Gould's *Church Revival* and got my
contemporary thrills from the *Church Times*, which was not then,
as it has become since, all things to all men, but was the defiant
organ of a movement which rejoiced in being persecuted and was
confident of victory.

Religious activity was booming in many ways. The Lambeth
Conference of 1920 had issued its famous Appeal to All Christian
People. The Church Assembly of the Church of England came
into existence the same year. 'Copec' (the Conference on Politics,
Economics and Citizenship) met in 1924. The controversy over
prayer-book revision was a subject of animated argument all the
time that I was up. The rejection of the revised book by the House
of Commons in 1927 and again in 1928 came at the end of my
time; some Anglo-Catholics saw it as an outrageous insult to the
Church's inherent right to determine its own forms of worship,
others as a mysterious deliverance of the Church by God from a
liturgical monstrosity, but subsequent reflection made it clear that
the real weakness of the whole process had been that its explicit
purpose had been not to provide the Church with as worthy a
liturgy as possible but to prevent the Anglo-Catholic clergy from
breaking the law. But the great events of the 1920s for the rank and
file of Anglo-Catholics were the Congresses of increasing size and
importance of 1920, 1923, 1927 and 1930, with their culmination in
the great Centenary Congress of 1933, when Pontifical High Mass
was celebrated in the White City Stadium. I was still too much on
the fringe to take part in the first two (in 1920 I was only fourteen
and still trying hard to be satisfied with St Mary's, Stamford Brook)
but I read everything that I could about them. The intellectual
quality of the addresses that were delivered to the sweating ranks
of the faithful those two summers in the Albert Hall was indeed
formidable; for it had been deliberately decided to refute the view,
wishfully cherished in some quarters, that the Catholic Movement
was nothing but a combination of frivolity and aestheticism. But
neither could the opposite accusation be made that it was merely a
fad of pedants and professors; and the concluding speech in 1923,
made by the great Bishop of Zanzibar, Frank Weston, with its call
to dedication, sacrifice and discipline, has been quoted ever since
and is as relevant today – perhaps more relevant – than it ever
was. This is not the point at which to discuss the subsequent history
of the Movement and to assess its triumphs and failures. There was
of course silliness to be found, but those who have held that Britain
would have been ready to embrace a sober English catholicism of

the type depicted in Percy Dearmer's *Parson's Handbook* had the
pitch not been queered by the baroque excesses of those who have
been described as the Playboys of the Western Church are, I am
sure, as far from the truth as was Archbishop Davidson with his
firm conviction that the English people as a whole had a deep
and sincere veneration for the Established Church although most
of them never came near it. The chief weakness of the Catholic
Movement was, I believe, the assumption that all churchpeople had
imbibed with their mother's milk, or at any rate, learnt at their
mother's knee, ninetenths of the Catholic religion without knowing
what it was, and that all that was needed to turn them into fully
informed Catholics was to add a few admittedly very important
extras concerning confession, the real presence, prayers for the
dead and the veneration of the saints. It was just not understood
that, while there is (or, rather, was) a vast common area of belief
that is common to Catholicism and that vaguely delineated attitude
that the average Englishman referred to when he described himself
as a Protestant, Catholicism is a view of reality and a way of life
that form an integrated and coherent whole. That the Incarnation
of the Eternal Word is not a past episode but a continuing reality,
that God has taken *our* nature so that we might be taken into *his*,
that nature is really transformed by grace and not merely adorned
by it — such pervasive and orientating essentials of Catholicism
seem to have been simply taken for granted by our scholars. The
consequence being that, instead of penetrating the Church as a
whole, they have been first ignored, then forgotten, and finally
treated as irrelevant. Today we have arrived at a situation in
which, when both the Trinity and the Incarnation are denied by
prominent members of the clergy, the accredited guardians of the
Faith, while adopting the ornaments of Catholicism and expressing
approval of the achievements of the Catholic Movement, cannot
be persuaded that the preservation of the basic truths of the Faith
is sufficiently important to justify their intervention. Many of the
parish clergy are sensitive to the situation; and they feel badly let
down not only by the bishops but by the scholars.

In retrospect, I think that the Congresses mark almost the last
moment at which there was real *rapport* between the pastoral clergy
and the theologians, and even then it had begun to weaken. In the
previous century, of course, the pastoral clergy and the theologians
were largely identical. With some notable exceptions — and these
were mainly in the realm of critical and historical rather than in
strictly theological study — the universities were not centres of
living and creative theological thought. Cathedral canonries were

not very much more productive, but it is remarkable how much good scholarship came out of country parishes. This was due in part to material reasons; financial, and until 1882 matrimonial, considerations often made an incumbency more attractive than a college fellowship, whereas today the pressure is all the other way. No doubt scholarly clerics could sometimes be remote from their flocks; *Punch*'s preacher saying to his congregation of yokels, 'Aha, I know what you are thinking; you will say to me "Sabellianism!"' had his counterparts in real life. Nevertheless I cannot think that the present situation, in which the parish clergy are too busy to be theologians and the professional theologians are mostly unconcerned with the Church's pastoral and evangelistic work, is good for either party or for the Church at large. However, to return to the 1920s, most Anglican scholars on the Catholic wing who were conscious of a responsibility for the actual situation of the Church felt called to concentrate on apologetics rather than upon systematic theology. The characteristic expression of their outlook was the symposium *Essays Catholic and Critical*, which appeared under the editorship of E. G. Selwyn in 1926; it was repeatedly reprinted and acquired almost the status of a manifesto. Its apologetic concern was revealed in the first sentence of the Preface as 'a common desire to attempt a fresh exposition and defence of the Catholic faith'; 'defence' we notice, no mention of attack. Futhermore the apologetics seemed to be directed, whether deliberately or not, specially towards the university senior common and combination rooms. The writers' primary concern appeared to be to convince their colleagues that they could honestly adopt and practise the Christian religion while making only the minimum of change in their modes of thought and behaviour. To suggest that the acceptance of Christianity might involve in the first place a radically new outlook on the world and man, that Christian belief might have specific and far-reaching intellectual and practical consequences, would have seemed illiberal and imprudent. There were of course tactical advantages in beating one's opponent at his own game and many of the Anglo-Catholic scholars of the 1920s became very skilful in playing it. I was not the only one of their admiring and grateful disciples who came later on, without losing either our gratitude or our admiration for them personally, to feel that the successes had been won at too high a price and that what really needed questioning was the game itself or at any rate the rules by which it was played. Why this was not recognised at the time is not altogether easy to see. Partly it was that any appearance of authoritarianism raised the spectre of Rome, and in those very pre-Vatican-II days that was a terrifying spectre indeed. The Modernist upheaval in the Roman Communion was fresh in the memory of many; and Englishmen, with their strong sense of justice, felt an indignation for the shocking treatment that the modernists had received which predisposed them in favour of the liberal attitude of the modernists to religious truth generally. Partly the notorious English pragmatism had its influence. As long as the things that Catholics liked doing could be justified, it did not matter – and indeed it might help in keeping the bishops mollified – if it was clear that the grounds on which they were advocated were such as Catholics in neither East nor West (especially West) had ever held before. It was in aid of this attitude that about 1933 a theory was propounded about something called 'Northern Catholicism', which was alleged to have characterised the northern countries of Europe down the centuries and to have sober, restrained and unsuperstitious in contrast to the vulgar and semi-pagan religion of the Mediterranean shores. A volume of essays entitled *Northern Catholicism*, with the sub-title 'Centenary Studies in the Oxford and Parallel Movements', was published in its alleged support. However, although the distinguished contributors produced much fascinating and important material on a variety of topics covered by the sub-title, it contains little that directly supports its avowed thesis. The attempt to argue that thesis which was made in a brilliant *tour de force* by one of the editors, N. P. Williams, who had recently become Lady Margaret Professor at Oxford, received amusing and damaging dismantling in two articles in the periodical *Laudate* by Dom Gregory Dix of Nashdom Abbey.[1] But this belongs to a rather later period.

An event which turned out to be of lasting importance to me in a number of ways took place in the Christmas vacation of 1927, when I was invited to attend the Second Anglo-Russian Student Conference organised by the Student Christian Movement. Like many Anglicans I had acquired an interest, not unmixed with a certain romantic curiosity, in the Eastern Orthodox Church as the great non-papal Christian communion which antedated our Western schisms and prided itself on its immutability. I had been present, as a very minor but thrilled and excited member of the congregation, in Westminster Abbey on 29 June 1925 at the Sung Eucharist in celebration of the sixteenth centenary of the First Ecumenical Council, that of Nicaea. It had indeed been an impressive occasion; two Greek patriarchs were present, two exiled Russian metropolitans, and many representatives of other branches of the Orthodox Church, to say nothing of twenty Anglican archbishops and bishops. Archbishop Randall Davidson preached a sermon in which he gave dramatic expression to the historic and symbolic character of the occasion while avoiding any reference to the lack of representation of the largest of all the Christian communions. It was in fact, in these post-First-World-War years easy to convince oneself that Anglican-Orthodox union would soon be achieved and that Rome was both incorrigible and unimportant. I remember that splendid old pastor Bishop Hough of Woolwich telling some of us one evening in Edward Wynn's rooms that we would be in full communion with the Orthodox in five or ten years. Of course some remarkable contacts and démarches had occurred on the official level, largely through the serpentine expertise of that amazing character Canon John Albert Douglas. But the Student Conferences, and the Fellowship of St Alban and St Sergius to which they gave birth, had a different function, with its own strengths and weaknesses. They brought together for several days a number of English students, mainly Anglicans, and of Orthodox students, predominantly Russian exiles, to worship, study and confer under the leadership of some senior people. That so interdenominational a body as the Student Christian Movement should sponsor and organise so apparently sectional an undertaking is explained by the empirical fact that the Russian Exile S.C.M. was virtually an Orthodox organisation, and this in turn by the fact that Russian exiles, if they were Christians, were almost always Orthodox. (Later on, the Fellowship, having outgrown its kindly nursing by the S.C.M. and its own student youthfulness, got entirely on its own feet; it celebrated its fiftieth birthday in 1977.)

It is no exaggeration to say that this conference opened up to me a new world of Christian thought, worship and spirituality, which subsequent experience over a great many years has deepened, enriched and, since it was inevitably in some respects partial and unbalanced, has corrected, but of which nothing has dimmed the impression that I then received. I have subsequently shared in Orthodox worship under a vast variety of conditions, linguistic, ceremonial and climatic, but the setting in which I first experienced it, having trudged through the darkness of the snow-bound streets of St Albans to the small and intimate chapel of the diocesan retreat-house, where bearded hierophants were celebrating an unfamiliar and mysterious rite, in clouds of incense and the archaic Slavonic tongue, seemed highly appropriate at the time to one whose notions of Russia and of Orthodoxy largely consisted of Siberian snow and rejection of the Pope. Grotesque and distorted as that first impression was, I was conscious that I had met something that was to play a very great part in my future development. Both for the personal friendships to which they led and for the realm of theological understanding and spiritual experience which they disclosed, I have since come to reckon those few days at the end of 1927 as one of the turning-points of my life. Little did I suspect that from 1929 to 1936 I should be chairman of the Fellowship's Executive Committee, that in 1934 I should edit a book of essays by its members or that from 1937 to 1946 I should be the editor of its journal. For many years the driving-force of the Fellowship was its Secretary, Dr Nicholas Zernov, who added to an unexampled power of awakening and holding enthusiasm a gift for popular instruction which is embodied in his printed works. On the Anglican side the Fellowship has had contacts of one kind or another with most of the leading pastors and theologians, the careers of many of whom can be traced in its journal *Sobornost'*;[2] Lord Ramsey of Canterbury was one of its most loyal supporters. Fr Walter Frere, C. R., who became Bishop of Truro, and was a profound though idiosyncratic liturgical scholar, was President for many years. At St Albans I had my one and only conversation with Charles Gore, who was then in his middle-seventies but looked much older. The venerable prophet (who was once somewhat ambiguously described by Bethune-Baker as 'one of the noblest and most persuasive exponents of some convictions that all Christians share, and the most competent apologist of lost theological causes that I know'[3]) was standing in the Cathedral gazing at the roof. He lowered his head, caught my respectful eye and said, in his unforgettably gruff voice, '*What a wonderful building!*' 'Yes, isn't it?' I replied uncontroversially, and the conversation concluded.

The Orthodox members of the Conference came mainly from the very impressive Institute of St Sergius in the Rue de Crimée in Paris. It had been founded to train priests and maintain theological research under the conditions of the Russian exile. The ordinands were, as one would have expected, for the most part both older and more mature than the average Anglican ordinand and the latter must have seemed very callow to them, though they were too polite to say so. Some of the leading theologians and philosophers were very impressive people indeed. Many were converts from Marxism or other forms of unbelief and their background was as unlike that of the typical English academic theologian as can be imagined. Dr Zernov's book *The Russian Religious Renaissance of the Twentieth Century*[4] gives an excellent account of the intellectual and social milieu from which they came. The most striking on first acquaintance was Fr Sergius Bulgakov, the Rector of the Institute and a voluminous writer on dogmatic and philosophical theology. I have heard various people described as 'leonine', but in his case it was exact; he really had a head like a lion. He had abandoned Marxism early in the century but became a priest only just after the Revolution in 1918. He had a tremendous personal influence over individuals and indeed became, if not a *guru*, something of a *staretz*. He elaborated some very idiosyncratic doctrines about the divine Wisdom, which brought criticism even from some of his fellow exiles and provoked a formal condemnation by the Moscow partriarchate in 1935. To those of us however, who were making our first acquaintance with Orthodoxy and who were predisposed as loyal Anglicans to accept anything that was clearly untainted with the rationalism of Rome, the mystagogic streak in Fr Sergius seemed very authentic. It was only later that some of us recognised that what we had taken to be the profound expression of the inherent orthodoxy of Holy Russia (*anima Russica naturaliter orthodoxa*) owed quite as much to Hegelian idealism and something to Jacob Boehme. One Russian who saw this but did his best not to give an appearance of divisiveness was George Florovsky, then, like so many Orthodox theologians, a layman but later a priest; he was a deeply-versed patristic scholar, which Bulgakov was not. In later years he took to dressing as a Greek, rather than as a Russian, he priest, to show in which direction he thought true Orthodoxy lay.[5]

There can, however, be no doubt about the brilliance of the scholars who clustered round the Institute of St Sergius in the 1920s and 1930s. Many of them were laymen, such as G. P. Fedotov, A. V. Kartashev, V. V. Weidlé and L. A. Zander, thus carrying on the example of Khomyakov and Solovyev, and the most celebrated of these was Nicholas Berdyaev, with Nicholas Arseniev running a close second. Berdyaev, many of whose books were translated into English, was understandably felt by many of the Orthodox to be of somewhat dubious orthodoxy, whether spelt with a small or a large 'O'; his doctrine of freedom and creativity as antecedent to God, and his extreme anti-intellectualism which made rational discussion with him practically impossible, set him very much apart from the main stream of Orthodox thought. But he had a considerable following, especially among those for whom turgidity of style and inconsistency of argument are attractive rather than deterrent. He had a remarkable facial resemblance to the traditional portraits of Shakespeare, but was afflicted by an unfortunate tic which caused his tongue to shoot out at frequent intervals like that of a lizard catching flies. He never in fact had very much personal contact with the Fellowship.[6] Arseniev, on the other hand, was a frequent participant. He was short-sighted, warm-hearted and excitable and one could hardly fail to be attracted by him. He was tremendously learned, bubbling over with enthusiasm and impossible to control. His book *Mysticism and the Eastern Church*[7] is anything but a systematic presentation of its alleged topic and is from most points of view a thoroughly badly written work, but, with its insistence upon the glorification of the world by the incarnation, crucifixion and resurrection of the Son of God, it brought to life for many Western Christians a central truth of the Faith that the West has only too often allowed to fall into obscurity but which Orthodox spirituality and liturgy have continuously maintained. One example of Arseniev's disarming irrepressibility at a later gathering remains in my mind. I was in the chair, an extremely full programme had been arranged and Arseniev was not expected. But he turned up all the same, and begged to be allowed to make some very important remarks which he promised would not exceed five minutes. Fearing the worst, I weakly gave way, and after he had been prophesying for twenty minutes I attempted to interrupt him. He swung round on me in indignation. 'You cannot stop me now,' he cried, 'it would be blasphemy!'[8]

Not all the Orthodox whom I met at St Albans were theologians. Dr Vladimir Korentchevsky, for example, was a biologist whose speciality was gerontology, the study of human ageing. He was living and working in London, and with him and his wife and two daughters I formed a lasting friendship which provided me, among other things, in due course with a half-Russian godson. Most of the Russian participants came from Paris or even farther afield and I met them much less frequently. Subsequent Conferences and Summer-Schools of the Fellowship took place in a variety of places, High Leigh in Hertforshire, Broadstairs in Kent and Abingdon in Berkshire being the most notable. It played its part in providing many of the Anglican priests who belonged to it with Russian Orthodox wives. At this point I must remind myself that I am writing my own memoirs and not a history of the Fellowship, and that although the Fellowship and those to whom it introduced me will recur from time to time the point which I have reached is the end of my Cambridge career in the summer of 1928. I must, however, say something about the only one of my school friends with whom I maintained an unbroken and continuous friendship through my Cambridge days and afterwards until his death in 1965, Christopher Douglas Waddams.

Christopher's father was a master at Latymer, but I was never actually taught by him as he was away in the Army during the years of the First World War. Christopher himself was a year senior to me by birth but two years senior academically, and although this separated us almost completely in our earlier days at school we became close friends in our later days at Latymer for two reasons. One was that we were both mathematicians and the other was that we were both emerging from the churchmanship of St Mary's, Stamford Brook, and feeling our ways to a more Catholic Anglicanism. We thrashed out our joint position in the course of a number of walks together through the West-London streets or while engaging in sightseeing expeditions. Christopher had two brothers and a sister, all younger than himself; both his parents came of very large families engaged in elementary and secondary education, so his cousins were innumerable. I was amused, when invited to a family celebration at his parents', to see a constant procession of married couples with children coming up the garden path of whose identity Christopher himself did not seem altogether certain. He was short, red-haired, vivacious and hospitable, but basically shy, and he had, I gathered, been in early childhood excessively and painfully so. Some people said he was humourless and he sometimes said that he was himself, but I think in fact that, like others of whom that has been said, he often saw the point of a joke before other people, but did not think it was a very good one and had dismissed it from his mind before they had got round to it.

He could indeed tell a very good story himself. One, which he related with great effect, was of an incident on Christmas Eve when he was in an Underground train on the way to his parents, when he rescued an intoxicated reveller who was in imminent peril of falling out of an open door (these were the days before automatic doors) and settled him in the seat next to his own. The reveller departed, with some assistance and with expressions of gratitude, at West Kensington and his place was taken by a person of severe and puritanical aspect. This new neighbour turned to Christopher and said in tones of indignation, 'Disgraceful behaviour, sir, quite disgraceful! What would the ladies have thought if he'd fallen out on the line?' The suggestion of a code of social behaviour according to which falling out on the line was an act which a perfect gentleman would perform only in exclusively male company could reduce Christopher to tears of speechless laughter when he referred to it. Not that his own moral code was in any way lax, either in speech or in conduct; and he became known, at a time when rowing men were notoriously foul-mouthed, as the Jesus-College cox who, when he ran his boat into the bank at Grassy Corner, merely said 'Oh, bother!' In childhood he had had an extremely serious mastoid infection and it was said that the operation which was performed as a last resort had invariably resulted in either death or insanity for the patient; as Christopher survived to take a triple first at Cambridge and obtain a fellowship, he was presumably the first person to undergo it successfully. He went up to Jesus College, Cambridge, with a mathematical scholarship in 1922, two years ahead of me, and became a Wrangler with a B-star in Part Two of the Tripos in 1925. By this time, however, he was convinced of his vocation to the priesthood ('I don't know what's happening to our mathematicians,' Cod lamented when I dropped in at Latymer one day, 'X has gone out of his mind and Waddams is going to be ordained'; what he would have said when I came to the same decision in 1931 I cannot imagine), so, instead of going on with mathematics, he took part of the Theological Tripos in Philosophy of Religion, and got another First, before going to Ely Theological College for a year. He was ordained deacon by Bishop Garbett of Southwark to Christ Church, Clapham, a depressing South-London parish, in 1928 and was priested the following year. Almost at once he was snatched away to be Chaplain and teach mathematics at St Catherine's College, Cambridge, where he remained for the rest of his life. He became Tutor in 1946 and Senior Tutor in 1957 and had no desire for higher office. He was a very good teacher, though his handwriting was appalling, and was efficient and conscientious in his college duties. But he never produced the work on theology and philosophy that was once hoped for and expected; his whole literary output was confined to a few articles and reviews. For the fact was that, as soon as he became a priest, his heart was no longer in either mathematics or philosophy, though he remained proficient in both; it was, as was that of Edward Wynn and some other Cambridge chaplains, in his pastoral vocation, as many generations of former undergraduates could testify. We often stayed with each other or travelled together, and when he died of cancer in his early sixties in August 1965, I had lost my closest friend. And, at the risk of disappointing those who like to explore the murkier regions of the human soul, let me say categorically that, devoted as we were to each other, there was nothing in our relationship that was in the least degree erotic.[9]

My visits to St Catherine's as Christopher's guest became so frequent that I became more familiar with the S.C.R. of that college than with that of my own, especially in view of the extraordinary mortality which struck the fellows of Pembroke soon after I went down; at one time Edward Wynn was, I think, my sole remaining personal link. The society of St Catherine's was small and friendly, and it was delightful and amusing to see how Christopher's sheer goodness overcame whatever disquietude his antecedents – Ely and Christ Church, Clapham – had raised in some minds. His great friend was the geographer Alfred Steers, with whom until middle-age intervened he used to go running in the afternoons; and the contrasted figures of tall dark Alfred and little red-haired Christopher making for Coe Fen together in singlet and shorts each afternoon raised some kindly smiles. There was the correct quota of 'characters', such as the melancholy and depressing 'Malaria' Jones, so called not from his valetudinarianism, notorious as that was, but from his distinguished researches into the medical aspects of the decline of the Roman Empire. There was the eminent and extraverted mycologist Newman, whose highly entertaining stories usually ended with one of the standard colophons 'There was I puffin' a big cigar' and 'Couldn't see me for dust and small stones'. 'Haw, Waddams,' he once announced, 'Saw a gentleman of your profession down at the docks today, black as the ace of spades; nothing to be seen in the dark but false teeth and a clerical collar.' There was Henry John Chaytor, a low-church clergyman with a large grey moustache, heavy thick-soled boots and a gruff unceremonious equanimity, who, after an unspectacular academic career at Oxford in the eighteen-nineties and a successful professional career as a schoolmaster in the early decades of the present century, acquired a notable reputation in the field of Spanish studies and became a fellow and Tutor of St Catharine's in 1919, a Doctor of Letters of Cambridge in 1930 and finally Master of St Catharine's in 1933. One of his stories, related in a kind of grinding unpunctuated monotone, has stuck in my mind: 'I went into a restaurant in Spain and asked for the menu What's this waiter I said No meat on this menu No sir said the waiter It's Good Friday Christians don't eat meat on Good Friday Oh don't they I said I don't think much of that No sir said the waiter But there's beef-steak pudding in the kitchen for those who are weak in the faith Oh all right I said Give me some beef-steak pudding I'm weak in the faith all right.' Christopher and Chaytor used to celebrate the Holy Communion in the college chapel alternately on the Sundays in term. Christopher soon began to use wafer-bread on his Sundays, as he did at the daily celebrations which he introduced during the week; Chaytor made no protests beyond occasional low-church grunts but, when he was celebrant, stuck to his established practice of bringing with him slices of household bread which had been compressed into a pasty mass. However, there came a morning when he said to Christopher, who was standing by to assist him, 'Waddams, I've forgotten my bread. Let me have some of your wafers.' And after the service he made the memorable pronouncement: 'Good idea those wafers of yours; very convenient; I shall have them in future. Much better than that muck that I've been using: might have been baked on a witch's tombstone.' I cannot help wondering whether this extraordinary simile was derived from the Spanish folk-lore which was Chaytor's speciality.

Christopher and I had a number of holidays together, both at home and abroad. One very pleasant one was spent in Yorkshire, when we combined taking the services in a Bradford parish during the slack season with motoring about the moors. Christopher had bought a secondhand Baby Austin of the original model for ten pounds (I think I recall the exact amount, and also that he sold it later on for fifteen, in which case this must represent his only venture into the world of business). He drove in an original and unnerving way, which bore little relation to the instructions in the manuals but seemed to be somehow derived from his knowledge of applied mathematics and frequently included verbal explanations of what he was doing. It is fair to add that, neither in these early days or later when he had less venerable vehicles, did he ever meet with an accident, though twice on our first day on the moors I thought our last hour had come. For, each time on a sharp bend on Ilkley Moor of the famous song, the little Austin simply left the road and leapt through the air, coming to rest the first time just above a terrifying drop, the second under the shadow of a high stone wall, with Christopher at the wheel propounding dynamical hypotheses to explain the unanticipated phenomena. We were almost baht 'at and baht everything else, and with such a beginning it seemed to me that the chances of our survival for a fortnight were slender; but fortunately Christopher diagnosed the defect correctly as insufficiency of air in the tyres and when this was corrected we had no more trouble. Once we stayed in Paris at the Institute of St Sergius in the Rue de Crimée, for Christopher, like myself was a member of the Fellowship and we were anxious to see the life of the Russian emigration at its heart. Its main foci, apart from St Sergius', were the Student House in Montparnasse and the splendid pre-War cathedral in the Rue Daru, next door to which there lived in great simplicity the aged and much loved Archbishop Evlogi. At this time the Rector of St Sergius' was Fr Sergius Bulgakov, and we were given a great welcome on what was for me a second visit, for

I had been there with another young student several years before. One of the most attractive figures in the Institute was a very old priest of venerable appearance from the Tsarist regime of whom many stories were told. He was Otets Ioann – Father John – but was commonly known as Père Catastrophe. His nickname was derived from a legend that, when menaced by apaches or mocked by small boys – for there were two versions of the episode –, he had extended his arm while uttering the solemn formula '*Si vous – moi; vous – catastrophe*!', whereon his aggressors fled in terror. It was said that he was the model for the icon of God the Father in the chapel of the Institute; it was also said that he so strongly disapproved of the primitivism of the painter's style that he surreptitiously poured water into his paints. We were told that, after observing our deportment in chapel carefully for several days, he formulated the judgment: 'You know: those Englishmen, they are Christians.' St Sergius' was indeed a impressive institution, for it not only produced a sucession of well-trained priests to staff the churches which sprang up throughout the Russian diaspora but was also a centre of theological and cultural activity and of spirituality of the highest order. And this under circumstances of extreme economic privation and social instability which were not abolished, though they were greatly eased, by the help which came from Britain and the United States.

It was perhaps natural that, after meeting Orthodoxy in the untypical conditions of the Russian exile, we should want to see it in a country to which it was indigenous, and we decided to end a continental holiday in September 1937 with a brief spell in Rumania. Rumania had recently moved into a focal position in Anglican-Orthodox relations. In 1935 an official commission from the two churches had met in Bucharest and had produced an agreed doctrinal statement on the strength of which the Rumanian delegation recommended the acceptance of the validity of Anglican ordinations. In March 1936 the Rumanian Holy Synod concurred on condition that the Report was ratified by the Anglican Church and in June the Rumanian Patriarch Miron Cristea paid an official visit to the Archbishop of Canterbury. By January 1937 the Convocations had given the required ratification (though in the case of Canterbury in a subtly ambiguous form), so our visit, entirely unofficial as it was, came at a propitious time. And I was given one bit of very demi-semi-official business to do. I had just gone to Lincoln, and Bishop Hicks, who had led the delegation to Bucharest in 1935, was much harassed by reports that the Rumanian Church was actively supporting the Anti-Semitic policy of the

Rumanian government and he was anxious to obtain a convincing
disclaimer. Would I, he asked, impress the urgency of this upon
any ecclesiastics whom I met? I promised to do my best. (These, it
must be remembered, were in Rumania the days of King Carol II
and Madame Lupescu, Cuza and Goga, Titulescu and Tatarescu;
and the fascist Iron Guard had only just been metamorphosed into
Totul pentry Tara, 'All for the Fatherland'.)

We made our arrangements through a few students whom we had
met through the Fellowship; we anticipated no kind of formality
and were travelling light with rucksacks. Imagine our surprise
when on dismounting in Bucharest station after a long, slow
and exhausting train journey across the Transylvanian plain, we
were met not by our student friends (they came and we saw much
of them later) but by a smartly groomed young priest from the
Patriarchate in an immaculate light-grey cassock, who addressed us
in perfect American English: 'I think you are the two English priests
I am expecting; I guess you've had a lousy journey.' We were in fact
given very V.I.P. treatment and, since by a happy coincidence our
visit coincided both with a meeting of the Holy Synod and with
an official visit of a delegation from the Polish Orthodox Church
headed by Archbishop Dionisi of Warsaw, we saw the ceremonial
aspect of the Orthodox Church at its most impressive. There was a
great pontifical liturgical celebration in the cathedral on the Sunday;
a delightfully informal touch was provided by the way in which
small children would dart forward and scrape from the floor the
wax which cascaded from the triple and double candlesticks with
which the Patriarch imparted the oft-repeated blessings of the rite.
This was followed by a reception at which we were presented to the
Patriarch; fortunately we had brought cassocks in our rucksacks
and were spared the humiliation of appearing in our grubby
holiday garb at a gathering of truly Ruritanian splendour. In the
afternoon we were taken to the monastery of Cernica, which
is beautifully situated by its own lake and was a popular spot
for excursions. We were introduced there to a gentleman in a
splendid uniform with a light-blue tunic and white trousers, who
we were told was studying theology in his spare time. We were told
afterwards that his uniform was that of the high rank which he held
in the Bucharest Secret Police and when I said that it did not give an
impression of great secrecy it was explained that his was only the
official Secret Police; there were also King Carol's and Madame
Lupescu's and various others, and these were what really mattered.
(It must be remembered that in those days after the Treaty of
Trianon Rumania, however unstable politically, was psychologically

on the crest of the wave. It had received enormous accessions of territory in Transylvania, the Bukovina and Bessarabia and, as the only Orthodox country with a Latin language, believed itself to be the religious and cultural successor of the Roman Empire. Maps showing the vast square territory of *România Mare*, 'Great Rumania', were everywhere, and to this day the name of the country is officially spelt with an 'o' and not with a 'u'. It was sometimes confusing to find a town with two, or in Transylvania even three, names in different languages: Grosswardein, Nagy Varád and Oradea Mare; Hermannstadt and Sibiu. I am sure that what really makes every Rumanian tick, whatever may be the political system, is a deeply emotional and romantic patriotism and that this was as true under the socialist regime of M. Ceausescu as it was in the thirties under the ramshackle monarchy of King Carol II. But this is to anticipate.) There was a great luncheon at which all the hierarchs were present, and at which a Princess of the imperial Cantacuzeno family presided; there were many speeches, one of which Christopher was called upon to make, and we were amused to recognise that the interpreter was adroitly interpolating a passage expressing the deep concern of English people for good relations between the Poles and the Rumanians. The rest of our time in Bucharest was filled with sightseeing visits, perhaps the most memorable being to the admirably designed folk-park, in which there were typical houses brought with their inhabitants from various parts of the country. One odd feature of what, in spite of commercialisation and industrialisation, was still a definitely Balkan city was the spiked German helmets which the police had adopted as an economical use of the spoils of war.

We went on to Chisine, the former (and later) Kishinev, where the friend who met us had brought with him a journalist acquaintance, thanks to whom we became extensive and impressive front-page news in the *Gazeta Basarabiei*. Bessarabia, situated in the fertile land between the rivers Prut and Dniestr, had been seized by the Rumanians from the Russians in 1918 and was to be seized back by the Russians in 1944; it was an economic and strategic prize and Chisineu, with a population of 100,000 and the second largest city in Rumania, was its capital. It had all the features of a country town, but on our first day we were presented with a sharp contrast between the old and the new, when the peasant costumes and oxen-carts were supplemented by aeroplanes and decontamination squads in a full-dress air-raid precaution rehearsal. It was mild affair, with small aircraft zooming over and people obediently lying down to be carried off on stretchers as bangs and puffs of smoke went off at intervals, but the inhabitants seemed to be enjoying it. Perhaps that is all that could be demanded if it was true, as commonly believed, that the revenue from the stamps *Pentru Aviatiei* which were stuck on all the loaves went straight into King Carol's foreign bank-account. But Chisineu was quite delightful, and after visiting the Bishop and the great Seminary we were driven into the surrounding country to see the farms and vineyards.

The following day was memorable. After an early visit to a large girls' school we were taken to the railway station, where a big crowd had assembled to welcome a miraculous icon of the Mother of God, which was making its annual visit to the town. Chisineu was *en fête* for the occasion and most of the population was converging on the route, with church choirs taking up stragetic positions. Our driver left the congested carriage-way and took us hurtling along the tramway-tracks to get us to the station on time. When the train that was bringing the icon arrived it first decanted several quite ordinary passengers, who must have been somewhat surprised at the festal aspect of their destination, and then a tiny monk who was staggering down under the weight of his sacred burden. A choir burst into song as the vested clergy pressed forward to receive it, and at that moment a long freight train slowly and inexorably moved in between on the nearer track. This inevitably delayed the proceedings, but finally the procession got under way with a splendid mixture of dignity and informality.

The route to the cathedral was long; the day was gloriously sunny and extremely hot; the icon, which was very heavy, was carried by relays of participants, and Christopher and I were honoured by being allowed to carry it for a short distance – just about as far as we could have managed in fact, for it *was* very heavy. The route was lined by soldiers, who presented arms as the icon passed by, and at every street corner it was greeted by a church choir, who sang their sacred songs with reverence and devotion until they were obliterated by the formidable music of the brass band which led the procession and which played over and over again an air which, whatever it was, was clearly not traditional Orthodox music and which I discovered long after, to my astonishment, was that of a Welsh revivalist hymn! So the procession moved slowly along the long route under the blazing sun through crowds that struggled and fought with one another and with the police in their efforts to kiss the sacred picture. And finally, when we reached the cathedral and it had been received with prayer by the Bishop, it was laid there in the open air for the individual devotions and petitions of the people. 'How different from the home-life of our own dear Queen!' commented an English lady after seeing Sarah Bernhardt as Cleopatra; and 'How different from Lincoln Cathedral under Bishop Hicks!' I was tempted to comment after the procession in Chisineu. But this in fact was Orthodoxy, not as a theological construct in the minds of wishful-thinking Anglicans but as practised by the Orthodox. The same evening we went by train – riding in fact in the driver's cab to get the best of the view – to the frontier town of Tighina (Bender). For political reasons the frontier was virtually closed and we were told stories of people escaping from Soviet Russia over the frozen Dniestr and being conscientiously fired at by the frontier guards until they reached half way. In September the river was of course impassable; we could just see the Russian territory on the far side of its wide and sluggish stream. Nonetheless there was a wonderful atmosphere of peace in this remote and picturesque town, and my memory of Tighina is of the odour of lime trees and the clopping of our horse's hoofs as we drove round the town, and finally supper to the accompaniment of a small tzigane orchestra. Back at Chisineu, we were up early the next day to attend an ordination performed by the Bishop and were then taken in a car for a long drive through the most glorious wooded country to see the monasteries of Capriana and Condrita. Capriana was at that time a great centre of industry, with its own vineyards and cornfields, its wine-making plant, its farm and its sawmill, and I can testify that it produced from the local herbs the most pyrotechnic liqueur that I had ever tasted, with a kind of delayed explosive reaction. (This is perhaps the place to mention the popularity of a beverage called 'café Marghiloman', consisting of equal parts of Turkish coffee and brandy. The story was that excessive consumption of Turkish coffee was known to be bad for the health, but that it was also known that coffee was an antidote to alcohol. M Marghiloman brilliantly argued that, if coffee neutralised alcohol, alcohol would neutralise coffee and that therefore his particular mixture could do nobody any harm. It was certainly a very pleasant drink, and I was surprised to find on revisiting Rumania in 1971 that no one seemed to have heard of it.) The Abbot himself entertained us to an enormous lunch and weighed us on the monastery weighing-machine!

From Chisineu we went to Cernauti, the former Czernowitz, the metropolitan city of the Bukovina. Like Bessarabia, the Bukovina had been Rumanian only since 1918, but it was previously not Russian but Austrian; like Bessarabia, however, it was annexed by the Soviet Union after the Second World War. The Archbishop of Czernowitz had from 1873 been the primate of all

the Orthodox in Austria and a very splendid prelate indeed.
His palace was simply enormous, and, even now that he was
(since 1919) canonically subject to the Patriarch of Rumania in
Bucurest, there was still about the see of Cernauti a noticeable
touch of greater magnificence. When we were there the Archbishop
was Mgr Visarion Puiu, a young and vigorous man who in the two
years since his appointment had instituted a number of reforms and
was set for the highest office in the Church; his later history, like
that of his diocese, was tragic and he died years after, a broken
and pathetic figure in exile in Paris. We were met at the station
by the Archbishop's chaplain and the Prefect of Studies of the
Seminary and also by three Anglican students from Mirfield who
had been invited to spend some time studying the Orthodox Church.
One of these was Walton Hannah, who enjoyed considerable, if
passing, celebrity after his ordination for the extremely detailed
and well-informed contributions which, in his books *Darkness
Visible* and *Christian by Degrees*, he made to the debate in the
Church of England in the early nineteen-fifties about the compati-
bility (or incompatibility) of Freemasonry with membership of the
Church.[10] We stayed in the Seminary and met a good many of the
seminarians. I recall one evening when a student from Transylvania
held us enthralled with his stories; his grandfather, he said, was an
alleged vampire and had been buried at the cross-roads with a stake
through his body. When asked whether he believed in the truth of
his stories, he admitted that, sitting talking with us in Cernauti, he
was ready to doubt some of them, but added that when he was
back in his home village he accepted the lot.

By a coincidence we were at Cernauti when the Archbishop of
Warsaw broke his journey there on his way back to Poland. There
was a tremendous Liturgy and after it an equally tremendous
luncheon, at which all the local ecclesiastical and civic worthies
were present, and so were we. We were taken aback when, after
a number of speeches had been made at what we had assumed
was the end of the meal, we were presented with helpings of
roast sucking-pig and realised that it was in fact only half-time!
This was on the Sunday, and after it the Polish visitors departed;
but on the following day Archbishop Visarion (with extraordinary
thoughtfulness in view of the very humble status of Christopher
and myself) gave a luncheon for about a dozen people, with
ourselves as the principal guests. There we met the Archbishop's
nonagenarian auxiliary Bishop Ippolit, who towards the end of the
meal caused our hosts some mysterious but obvious embarrassment.
He was sitting next to the Archbishop and we could see that

he was being kept under kindly supervision, but between two of the inevitable speeches he rose to his feet and waving his wineglass in the air embarked on a vigorous speech which he demanded to have interpreted into English. One of the Rumanian priests undertook the task and, to our surprise coming as it did from an aged and presumably old-fashioned Orthodox prelate, it turned out to be a quite undiscrimating plea for Christian unity: all Christians should get together, Orthodox, Catholic, Anglicans, Lutherans, Calvinists, for all believed in Christ and their differences were apparently unimportant. But at this point the interpreter developed obvious signs of distress while Bishop Ippolit became more and more eloquent. Finally the Archbishop put his hand on his shoulder and sat him down; the rest of the speech faded away into the wineglass, while the interpreter said with obvious relief 'It is the same; I need not translate more.' We were naturally curious to know what the remarks were that had made our hosts so uncomfortable, and afterwards I enquired from one of the English students who understood Rumanian; I could hardly think that the old man had been carried away into a flood of improprieties. We then discovered why it was that all the Christians ought to get together; it was to wipe out the Jews! But I must add that this was the only expression of anti-semitism that I heard from any Rumanian ecclesiastic.

We left Cernauti the following day and travelled back to England across Poland and Germany. Sitting in the train, with a gigantic parcel of food handed in to us just before we left, we reminded each other with some amusement that in England we were of course quite unimportant people! Writing an account of our visit in *Sobornost'* I said with absolute truthfulness that from the Patriarch downwards we had received nothing but the most brotherly and Christian kindness and that we had a firm decision to revisit Rumania as soon as we could. But I was writing in December 1937, and when I went again in 1971 much had changed, though not the hospitality and the kindness. But that I must describe elsewhere, for Christopher had died in 1965.

Notes

1. Sept. and Dec. 1933.
2. *Sobornost'* is in fact simply the Russian word for 'catholicity', but because of the strong emphasis of modern Russian theology on the corporate character of the Church and its life it was felt to be specially appropriate as the name of the Fellowship's periodical.

3. *The Way of Modernism*, Cambridge U.P. (1927), 131.
4. London, Darton Longman & Todd (1963).
5. Bulgakov died in France during the War, after a long and painful illness, borne with great courage and holiness, in July 1944. Florovsky removed to the United States in 1948, achieved great distinction as a professor at Harvard and died at an advanced age in 1979.
6. Berdyaev died in 1948.
7. London, S.C.M. (1926).
8. Arseniev died in the United States in 1977.
9. If somebody says 'Ah, but perhaps there was without your knowing it', I have no answer except to suggest that perhaps the pansexualism of present-day writers leads to just as many inadequate judgments as did the prurience of their predecessors. It certainly causes misunderstanding of much of the language which male friends in the last century used in their letters to each other. But, as a colleague of mine at Oxford once observed, 'Today you can't take the dog for a walk without people suspecting the worst.'
10. It would still be instructive to study the debates in the Church Assembly on this matter in 1951 and the controversy that surrounded them. Many churchpeople, clerical and lay, were both surprised and scandalised, by the way in which highly placed prelates declared themselves to be morally exempt from any duty to justify on Christian grounds the beliefs and practices to which they had committed themselves as freemasons. On this question at least they had nothing to learn from the Vatican congregations at their most recalcitrant.

Chapter Five

Schoolmastering
and Ordination

(1928 – 1937)

'A clergyman has nothing to do but to be slovenly and selfish — read the newspaper, watch the weather, and quarrel with his wife. His curate does all the work, and the business of his own life is to dine.'

           — Jane Austen, *Mansfield Park*, ch. x.

Edmund had already gone through the service once since his ordination.

           — ibid., ch. xxxiv.

There can be no doubt about the chief reason why I was unhappy during the years which I spent from 1928 to 1931 as Senior Mathematics Master at Bablake School, Coventry; it was simply that I was incompetent and unsuccessful at my job. I had had no training in teaching, I was no good at athletics and I was a bad disciplinarian; and the then commonly held superstition that a first-class degree at an ancient university would make up for any deficiencies was certainly false in my case. From the very few senior boys who had a real interest in mathematics I got a genuine response, but how to generate that interest or provoke its simulation in younger boys when it was not there I never discovered. No doubt I had a starry-eyed expectation that a school that prided itself on antedating Eton would be a beacon of learning even in a cultural waste, but, although many of my colleagues were sensitive and thoughtful men and almost all were conscientious and unselfish, the ethos of the School, like that of the City itself, was depressingly mercantile. Although its population was approaching 200,000 and was growing with unparalleled speed, Coventry was totally devoid of cultural amenities; the propinquity of Birmingham, with its

97

great university and art gallery, only nineteen miles away may have contributed to this. It had enjoyed virtually uninterrupted prosperity, unaffected by the successive economic crises, from the Middle Ages to the twentieth century; weaving had given way to bicycles and bicycles to motor-cars. When I was there the peak of local ambition was a highly paid post in Austin Motors, and a person's social, and indeed moral, worth was estimated almost entirely in terms of the car that he possessed. The headmaster of Bablake was a priest and a doctor of science, but he showed no active concern with either science or theology; he was a prominent Freemason and was active in municipal life, he was an efficient organiser and administrator, and the school had increased in numbers under his direction. The service that it was believed (and expected) to render to the community was succinctly expressed by one of the Governors one speech-day. 'Perhaps you wonder', he said to the assembled parents, 'why we pour out our money on your children in the way that we do.' (It was of course not the Governors' money, but that may be allowed to pass.) 'We do it because we know that when they come later on to take jobs in our offices and factories we get every penny of it back.' That this avowal of misuse of public funds met with enthusiastic applause revealed much about the scale of values implicit in Coventry at this period; I should be surprised if it was very different from that of other large centres of industry or commerce.

It would be comforting if one could suppose that the Church was exercising a prophetic critique in this situation of complacent secularism, but I must admit that this was far from the case. The Cathedral had already embarked upon the career of ecumenism for which it was later to become famous, but it had also, like others in similar locations, seen one of its chief functions to lie in the canonisation of the commercial activities of the city. It is true that Coventry did not possess either the architectural or the geographical advantages that Dr Dwelly was later able to exploit so dramatically at Liverpool; one would need a very vivid imagination indeed to envisage the River Sherbourne as an adequate bride for the City of the Three Spires[1]. But the way in which the standards of the world can seduce the very elect is shown by another speech delivered at Bablake on a speech-day, this time by an archdeacon and directed explicitly to the boys. The speaker related how he had been seated at dinner opposite Sir Herbert Austin, the architect of the great motor corporation, and how he had gazed with admiration upon the great man and reflected on his unfailing devotion to an ideal. That ideal, formed in youth, was, we were told, to possess the largest automobile factory in the country; to attain it he had worked day and night, sacrificed comfort and ease, etc. etc. He had started in a small way and when his little business prospered he disposed of it and with his profits built a larger. That too succeeded and in turn gave way to an even larger one. And so the glorious saga proceeded stage by stage, until the hero, adorned with his knighthood, could sit back and look at the product of his life's devotion and say, 'I have realised my ambition. I saw the gleam and followed it.' 'Boys', exclaimed the Archdeacon, in a final burst of enthusiasm, 'Do as that great man did – follow the gleam!' The audience, of course, applauded as expected. But it seemed to me, even as the theological beginner that I then was, that one thing was lacking to the story, namely the concluding sentence: 'But God said to him, "Thou fool, this night thy soul is required of thee; and the things which thou hast prepared, whose shall they be?"' That the audience applauded did not surprise me, and I do not know whether the future Lord Austin's commercial success was the fruit of such lifelong dedication as the Archdeacon declared. That a Christian priest, however, and a dignitary of the diocese at that, should, apparently without knowing what he was doing, relate the parable of the Rich Fool and exuberantly provide it with an interpretation precisely contrary to that given by Christ, and that this should happen without his gaiters turning into red-hot asbestos, shocked me more than I can say. It did, however, help to explain the lack of prophetic fervour in the Church in Coventry: 'if gold ruste, what shall iren do?' Nevertheless, in due course, *accepit mercedem suam*, and he went to preach the gospel of unenlightened self-interest as a bishop in New Zealand.

One improbable incident is worth recording, if only because it happens to be strictly true. Bablake, in spite of its ancient origin, did not possess a school song, and the Headmaster decided to remedy this deficiency himself. The product of his labours was not perhaps much worse than most such compositions, though it was less entertaining than the parody which some of the senior boys at once devised. Instead of an original air it was set to the hymn-tune *Wir pflügen*, well-known to frequenters of harvest festivals. I need not reproduce the full text, but only the refrain, which, with a flattering estimate of the latinity of the average Bablake boy, ran as follows:

> *Floruit, floret, floreat,*
>   All Bablake's children cry.
> Through good or ill, God guard thee still,

Our boast in days gone by.

Just before speech-day copies ran short, and a reprint was hastily ordered without attention being given to careful reading of the proof. The consequence was that masters, boys and parents found their voices united in the pious prayer:

Through good or ill, God guard the still,
Our boast in days gone by.

I do not think the song was ever officially used again, after this corporate confession of illicit liquor-production throughout the centuries. It did help me later on to understand that more than triviality was involved when, in the Arian controversy of the fourth century, Christendom was divided over an iota.

I had lodgings quite close to the School and almost as near to the church of St John the Baptist, which I attended and where I became a server and a member of the Parochial Church Council. St John's was a fine medieval building, which gloried in the somewhat dubious fame of having been founded by a murderess in memory of a sodomite – by Queen Isabella in memory of her husband Edward II, to be precise. It stood for a very respectable and law-abiding form of Anglo-Catholicism, with two candles on the four-poster high altar, apparelled Gothic vestments, so-called 'English' ceremonial, strictly prayer-book services and no trace of extra-liturgical devotion to the Blessed Sacrament or of explicit devotion to the saints. The Sacrament of Penance, like the element of religion at the Victorian death-bed, 'was not absent but it was not insisted upon'. There were, of course, good Christian folk at St John's and one in particular became a close friend; and the clergy were devout and devoted priests. But, whatever had been true in earlier days, the Catholicism of St John's had become domesticated and innocuous. Militancy was left to St Peter's at the other end of the city, where Father Paul Stacy, besides being dangerously to the left in his politics, was believed to do things in church that were not strictly legal. But I have little right to criticise, as I was very much a bird of passage and during the school holidays I was usually at Hove, whither my parents had removed from London and where the exotic delights of St Bartholomew's, Brighton, were at hand. I was also able to develop my contacts with Orthodoxy, as the conferences of the Fellowship by a good chance fell in the holiday period, and this gave me my first contact not only with many more Orthodox but with a number of leading Anglican scholars as well. Having become secretary of the local branch of the English Church Union, I had opportunities of bringing some knowledge of Orthodoxy to churchpeople in the midlands; I see that in March 1931 I addressed a meeting on the subject in Nuneaton. In the following month I had been able to arrange a quite impressive gathering in Coventry itself. The chief speaker was that staunch friend of the Anglican Church, Archbishop Germanos, who held the titular see of Thyateira, but had his cathedral in London and was the official intermediary between the Ecumenical Patriarch of Constantinople and the Archbishop of Canterbury. He was accompanied by the Secretary of the Anglican and Eastern Churches Association, the Revd R. M. French, and by a distinguished lawyer Sir William Hansell, Q.C., who was to take the chair. The Bishop of Coventry, Dr Mervyn Haigh, was not normally a supporter of the E.C.U., but on this occasion he accepted our invitation and made a graceful speech of welcome to the Archbishop. (It must be remembered that at this time Anglican officialdom was ready to accept, or at any rate to overlook, almost anything in Orthodoxy on the strength of the common hostility, not always well informed, of Orthodox and Anglicans to Rome.) The meeting was held in the beautiful fourteenth-century St Mary's Hall, which was packed to the doors, and was certainly as successful as any such single meeting could be expected to be. At least it brought the existence of the Orthodox Church and a few facts about its nature to the notice to a number of churchpeople to whom it must have been previously to all intents and purposes unknown. From my own personal standpoint organising this gathering was my farewell to Coventry, for I had already resigned my appointment at Bablake and arranged for my training for the priesthood.

In retrospect I suppose that I had long had a latent vocation to the priesthood; under different circumstances it might have emerged earlier than it actually did. But I had always felt very strongly that the Church needed convinced and instructed laymen no less than it needed priests, and the priests whom I admired and respected most felt this as strongly as I did. Certainly my experience at Coventry convinced me that I was not meant to spend my life as a schoolmaster and if anyone likes to suggest that I wisely slipped into ordination because one was less likely to be sacked from the ministry than from teaching if one made a mess of it, it is not for me to reply. It did not seem quite like that to me at the time, and in coming to my decision I was helped a great deal by the advice of such wise friends as Edward Wynn and Christopher Waddams. My parents were surprised, in a way that they would not have been had my decision come some years earlier, but they very loyally gave me their encouragement in spite of the fact that my ability to support them in their old age would be much reduced and delayed. They were, I am sure, glad that our very unclerical family should produce a priest; the last one, I think, and he was only very remotely related, was James Hannington, who became the first Bishop of Eastern Equatorial Africa and was martyred by the Masai in Uganda in 1885.

With a grant from the Cleaver Trustees I went in July 1931 to Ely Theological College for the skimped year which was then considered to provide adequate training for ordination. Ely had the reputation among theological colleges for extreme Anglo-Catholicism, and Ely men were generally considered to have little hope of ecclesiastical preferment. This was puzzling, because both liturgically and doctrinally Ely differed very little from its elder sisters Cuddesdon and Lincoln; but the fact remained that no Ely man had ever become a English diocesan bishop (Edward Wynn was to be the first in 1941), while almost every one of them who had been at a theological college at all came from Cuddesdon. I do not think this reputation was based entirely on the exotic liturgical behaviour of many Ely men in the 1920s; it was far earlier than that. B. W. Randolph, who was Principal from 1891 to 1911, was virtually ostracised by his colleagues on the cathedral chapter for his views. I once discovered in the college archives a letter from Bishop Woodford, who founded the College in 1876, rebuking the Vice-Principal for having lighted candles on the altar in the college chapel, and insisting on conformity with the practice of churches throughout the diocese; if he gave way on this matter, the indignant prelate declared, 'it would paralyse my administration of the diocese'. (I was able some years later to tell Edward that I had discovered the real source of his diocesan problems; they all went back to the candles in the chapel!) The Principal in my time was a very shy, immensely tall, devout, ascetic and much respected canon named Charles John Smith; he had been Vice-Principal under Randolph and would alter nothing that Randolph had set up. The Vice-Principal, Harry Thomas, had been a missionary in Central Africa, but had been struck by lightning and was in poor health; he made a remarkable recovery and became suffragan Bishop of Taunton. The theological teaching that could be given in so short a time was, needless to say, sketchy in the extreme, but it was of course taken for granted that a great deal one's training would take place in one's early years in a parish. Two things which Ely gave me were, however, of immense and permanent value.

The first was the opportunity of life in an ordered community, temporarily cut off from disturbances and interruptions; I feel quite sure that the practice of locating theological colleges in quiet and comparatively isolated places, with opportunity for reflection and adjustment, was, on balance, very wise, and that the modern tendency to assume that what ordinands need is experience in the more difficult areas of social service is mistaken. The second benefit was the emphasis which was laid upon the formation of a regular discipline of prayer and sacramental life. It was simply taken for granted that a priest would celebrate or communicate at the Eucharist six days a week, that he would normally spend at least twenty minutes daily in mental prayer and that, either publicly or privately, he would recite the offices of Morning and Evening Prayer. Regular use of sacramental confession and the making of an annual retreat were similarly taken as a matter of course. As I look back on my subsequent life as a priest I can see that, however often I failed in keeping to it, the pattern which Ely placed before us, not as the ultimate ambition of achievement but as the normal framework within which a priest should construct his manner of life, was the great gift which we were able to take away with us. Somehow, during those ten months I was able to pass both parts of the General Ordination Examination, which must have been a fairly unexacting test. It was a time of considerable concentration, not unmixed with anxiety, with limited but much appreciated times of relaxation and a great deal of joy and fellowship. The fact that thirty of us, with little in common but our sense of priestly vocation, were able to live in rather crowded conditions with remarkably few temperamental outbursts was mainly due, under the grace of the Omnipotence, to the fact that we were all extremely busy. Now I shall indulge myself with a few reminiscences of that remarkable body the Chapter of Ely Cathedral.

The Dean, the Very Reverend Alexander Francis Kirkpatrick, was the last survivor of the band of scholars who produced the Revised Version of the Bible in 1884. He looked appropriately patriarchal and had a weak and tremulous voice; the popular imitation of his announcement of the hymn 'Hark, a thr-hilling vo-hoice is so-hounding' was *ben trovato*, but I do not think he would ever have announced a hymn. Revising the English of the Bible had strangely had the reverse effect on his own diction, which seemed to antedate even his own time. It was alleged that, when Master of his college at Cambridge, he would encourage the boat in the May Races with cries of 'Well row-ed, Sehelwyn, well ro-how-ed!', and he was alleged to have been overheard in the post-office requesting

'Pray furnish me with twelve estamp-ed envelopes.' One of our students, whose father was a friend of his, was asked to tea at the Deanery and asserted afterwards that at one stage of the meal the Dean had said 'I will remove this tea-cup from this small table unto this larger table, lest haply it fall and, falling, break.' He seemed at times to have difficulty in remembering that the War had ended, and I have a vivid impression that in a sermon, having denounced the Germans for their invasion of Belgium, his gaze fell on the boys of the King's School who were sitting beneath him and he checked himself with the proviso, 'But few of you, my dear boy-hoys, will remember those stir-hirring days when our Empire spra-hang to arms', but it is possible that my own memory may here be exercising what the biblical critics used to call 'creative imagination'. C. J. Smith told me of an occasion when, being pressed to enliven cathedral Evensong with an additional hymn, he protested 'Pray, Canon, do not fluster me; I am trying to imagine, or – pardon the neologism – to *envisage*, the precise point of the service at which the hymn should be inserted.' Many stories were told of the objects that were found in the Deanery after thirty years of his occupancy but I cannot recall them clearly.

Stories were still vivid about Robert Hatch Kennett, who had recently vacated the stall which he had held, together with the Regius Professorship of Hebrew at Cambridge, since 1903. He was a vehement Protestant and had been a sharp thorn in the side of C. J. Smith, whom he suspected of various real or imaginary subversive plots. His sermons on Old-Testament themes were famous. 'Hew down your asherim!' he would exhort the assembled farmers and shopkeepers of Ely, but most celebrated was his plea 'Put yourselves, my brethren, I beseech you, in the place of a pious Jew in the time of Antiochus Epiphanes!' But for all his prophetic vigour he was by no means a fundamentalist and was skilful in making the best of both hermeneutical worlds. 'What is the lesson that we are to learn from this story?', he is alleged to have asked rhetorically after giving a spirited account of the story of Abraham and Isaac, 'Surely, this: that, as in that ancient legend, Abraham was willing to destroy his dearest possession, his only son Isaac, in obedience to what he mistakenly believed to be the command of God, so we must be ready to sacrifice our most cherished convictions on the altar of Biblical criticism.' I am sorry not to have seen Kennett, but I should not like to have been one of his colleagues. We had to console ourselves academically with John Martin Creed, the Ely Professor, an equally liberal but less apocalyptic Biblical scholar, whom we chiefly noticed for his habit of wearing a scull-cap during the consecration at the Eucharist.

The other residentiaries were worthy men, but less sensational. There was Bishop Price, the Archdeacon, who had been Bishop of Fukien in China and who, through long contact with the Chinese, spoke in a quiet low monotone with a tonal drop at the end of the sentence ('Bishop *Price*/Was very *nice*;/There was no *finer*/Bishop in *China*', we used to say); There was Canon Vincent Watson, the Canon Missioner, an impelling preacher in his way, but with an odd habit of emphasising his points by shouting 'Listen!'; there was Canon G. W. Evans ('Uncle George'), who ran the General Ordination Examination; and there was our 'Princeps', C. J. Smith, who was the real spiritual force in the Cathedral. By and large, however, it was a depressing place, only occasionally enlivened by one of the odd characters who dwelt in the fens. Thus there was a really splendid honorary canon Edward Baldwin who claimed to have evidence that his recitation of Shakespeare was as good as that of the actor Kean and argued that this should console anyone who felt unsuccessful, as it showed that there was always something that you could do if you could discover what it was. 'You can't stop the birds from flying over your head,' this fine octogenarian thundered from the cathedral pulpit, 'but you can prevent them building their nests in your hair!'

We received instruction in ecclesiastical elocution in the Lady Chapel of the Cathedral from the cathedral choirmaster. This was extremely useful, in spite of his apparent impression that what we really needed was to be able to monotone Morning and Evening Prayer. In those days, when we could not hear our voices recorded on tape, his candid and sometimes deflating judgments were informative. 'Yes,' he said, after one of my more ambitious efforts, 'you were quite audible, you kept the right note, you went at the right speed – you know, you have a very unpleasant voice, haven't you?' We had to attend the Cathedral once on Sundays, and when the choir was on holiday we acted as a substitute; the Chapter were rather embarrassed to receive a complaint from a stranger about the deterioration of the music since his previous visit. On Sunday evenings we would cycle out in pairs to little mission churches in remote parts of the fens, where one of us would take Evening Prayer and the other would preach a sermon (previously vetted by the Principal) to a minute congregation. At one of these one of the auditors would rise and depart in the middle, not in disgust but because he was the level-crossing keeper and the train was then due. Either life was very dull or the fen-dwellers were very devout, for them to wish to receive our amateur ministrations. Ely itself was well provided with churches for a city of less than ten thousand inhabitants and, ridiculous as this will sound, on Sunday morning Morning Prayer was sung simultaneously in the choir of the Cathedral and in the Lady Chapel, as, for historical reasons, the latter was also a parish church.

It would be unjust to give the impression that the clergy of Ely and its neighbourhood were all incompetents and eccentrics. There were many good and wise priests, working under conditions of isolation and loneliness, faced sometimes with active opposition and almost always with a dead weight of indifference and worldliness; these do not provide material for entertaining anecdotes, but their names are written in the Book of Life. Few of the livings offered rich emoluments as in the days of a Victorian bishop who did so well for his kinsfolk that it was said that you could find your way across the Fens at night by the Sparkes by the wayside. I think it was a later bishop who, on enquiring from the verger about some detail of the customary behaviour of the Bishop in the Cathedral, received the reluctant and embarrassed reply, 'Well, my Lord, to tell your Lordship the honest truth, your Lordship's predecessor wasn't exactly what you might call a *churchgoing gentleman.*' In my time the Bishop was Leonard Jauncey White-Thomson, who had succeeded the scholarly Evangelical Frederic Henry Chase in 1924; he was a kindly man and caused no trouble to the College, but he avoided any close identification with its tradition.

Those were the days before bishops had largely relinquished the choice and approval of ordinands to A.C.C.M. and selection conferences, though with the already declining number of vocations it had become almost as much a matter of an ordinand choosing his bishop as of a bishop choosing his ordinands. More accurately perhaps, it was a matter of the ordinand finding a congenial parish where the incumbent had a vacancy and was prepared to invite him to fill it. Because of the shortness of the time usually spent at the theological college as well as more obvious reasons, the choice of a first curacy was of considerable importance; it was the final, and often the most important, part of a priest's training. I felt, as most of us at Ely did, the attraction of a poor, rather than an opulent parish. I had no idea of returning to the academic world, having abandoned the only subject in which I had any academic qualifications, though I had a vague hope, in which Will Spens had encouraged me, of following up my interest in the relations of religion and science, and while at Coventry I had made some tentative explorations in that direction. Although I believed I was ready to follow any clear divine guidance that I might receive,

I thought I was temperamentally more fitted to work among southerners than midlanders or northerners, and the fact that I was my parents' only child made me reluctant to be too far from them. In fact, the East or the South of London seemed to be indicated and, encouraged by Christopher Waddams who had only recently been dragged out from Christ Church, Clapham, I applied to the formidable Bishop of Southwark, Dr Cyril Forster Garbett. He received me kindly and efficiently and expressed himself ready to ordain me. He sent me to see two parishes and their incumbents. The first was Richmond-on-Thames and, in spite of its amenities and its historic associations, I decided that it was too low ecclesiastically and too high socially for me. The second was St Andrew's, Stockwell, in the triangle formed by Kennington, Clapham and Brixton, and this, I decided, was the place for which I was meant: so, fortunately for me, did the Vicar.

Stockwell was devastatingly blitzed during the Second World War, blocks of high-rise flats were built and a large number of black immigrants settled; and in all these respects it is now very different from what it was when I went there in 1932; indeed, when I returned to preach at the centenary in the 1960s I got lost on my way to the Vicarage and had to return to the Underground station to consult the map. Stockwell Green in my days had long ceased to be an open space, though some of the houses on the south side remained with their original porches and door-knockers. It was not difficult to imagine nineteenth-century business-men driving up to the City each day in their carriages. The dominant feature of the parish was Hammerton's Brewery, which emitted a variety of smells on a twenty-four-hour cycle; in the afternoon, when lorry-loads of steaming bran were discharged, a delightful warm somniferous odour spread over the neighbourhood. Between the Brewery and the Church was the very fine Hammerton Hall, presented by the firm to the Church. The Church itself was a remarkably ugly building in no particular style, but officially Romanesque, constructed in 1867 on the framework of a chapel built just a century earlier. It originally had galleries, from under which a towering pulpit was wheeled out on rails for the sermon. The galleries at the side were removed in 1924 and the pulpit derailed permanently, but the rails themselves remained as an ancient monument. It must have been about that time that Catholic teaching and cer-emonial were started. The Blessed Sacrament was reserved in an undignified and inconspicuous aumbry that conformed strictly to diocesan regulations; and it was characteristic that this was made of flimsy and inflammable wood and that the lock could easily be forced with a penknife. The parish was roughly triangular, extending from Stockwell Road, down which the L.C.C. trams thundered and screeched, to Clapham North Underground station, being bounded by Clapham Road on the north and the Southern Railway on the south. At the far end there was a neat little mission-church, dedicated to the Epiphany, which had a small and devoted congregation but was really redundant. It had an unusual history, in that it had been built in earlier and more class-conscious days by the wealthier members of the parish, not for the lower orders but for themselves, as the fashionable residential district moved from Stockwell Green towards Clapham and street after street appeared of the two-storied terrace houses so familiar in our large cities. Whether they organised mission-services for their own conversion I never found out, but it would seem to have been appropriate. We used it and the rooms beneath for scouts, guides and clubs of various kinds, as well as for one mass on Sundays. With a full range of day-schools in which to teach, confirmation classes to instruct and the South-Western Isolation Hospital to visit, we − that is, the Vicar, two curates and two Church Army sisters − had plenty to do with our time. My own particular concerns I will describe in a moment, but I must say something about the very remarkable Vicar.

Ernest Perkins St John had spent all his ministry in South London, first as a curate at St Paul's, Newington (but in fact in sole charge of a mission church) and then as Vicar of that parish until he came to Stockwell in 1930. He was very tall, had a loud voice, was the son of a colonel in the Indian Army and was probably the least intellectual priest I have ever known. He was hot-tempered, impulsive and affectionate and was proud to have learnt his religion as a layman at St Alban's, Holborn, from the Famous Father Stanton, on whose preaching he modelled his own. He sometimes appeared to have constructed a religion of his own invention and labelled it 'The Catholic Faith'; he was equally intolerant of those whom he described as either 'dirty Papists' or 'dirty Protestants', but, being a great mission-preacher himself, he was in practice extremely friendly with anyone whom he believed to preach the Gospel and he liked to have the Salvation Army band to lead outdoor processions. He was a vehement advocate of clerical celibacy and scarified any curate who showed any leaning to matrimony; and unlike many such advocates he never got married himself. He was insistent on the use of sacramental confession, except by those whom he could not persuade to use it. He had a great gift for dealing with men and boys and ran summer camps, which, like everything else of his, were conducted in an entirely original way. He liked to have at intervals what he described as 'a busting row' and was, I think, quite glad to leave St Paul's and, in due course, St Andrew's, when there were no more rows to be had because he had had and won them all. Life with him − he had his curates living with him and his bulldog in the Vicarage, all looked after by two devoted female domestics − was never dull, for it was punctuated with vigorous arguments. He had a rule that we could express as much disagreement as we wished and as forcibly as we were able, so long as we did this inside and not outside the Vicarage. This worked quite well as long as he had assistants who were young and reasonably pliable, but it is not surprising that he had never found it easy to work with people who were anywhere near his own age and degree of experience. He never bothered much about consistency, though he was difficult to defeat on this issue. Once when he had denounced a lady for spelling her name one way and pronouncing it another, I pointed out that this was precisely what he did with his own. He denied the charge vehemently: 'I spell my name Sinjun − S.T.J.O.H.N., Sinjun − and I pronounce it Sinjun', he insisted and I had to capitulate. He would not, I think, have understood Mark Twain's complaint, 'They spell it Vinci and pronounce it Vinchy; foreigners always spell better than they pronounce.' After a dispute with him one was ready to agree with Samuel Johnson's judgment on an obstinate opponent, 'Sir, I have found you an argument; but I am not obliged to find you an understanding.' His invincibility was shown by the fact that when he was at King's College, London, he had, by sheer persistence, persuaded that figure of intellectual granite Dr A. C. Headlam to allow him to proceed to ordination although he had not at the time succeeded in completing successfully the A.K.C. The perceptiveness and genuine humility which lay behind his Philistine exterior was shown by the encouragement which he gave me to develop in the parish the kind of intellectual apostolate which would have been totally beyond his own powers.

More than those of any other parish with which I have had any contact the St Andrew's people were anthusiastic for instruction, and the weekly classes which I ran had a success beyond anything to which my own theological proficiency at that time could have entitled them. I supplemented these, as time went on, by courses of lectures by distinguished outsiders in Lent and October. As we were totally unable to offer any fee to our visitors their readiness to come, and indeed in many cases to come a second and even a third time, was both unexpected and pleasing. Years later, when

I became a professional theologian myself, I appreciated how important it is, if theology is to remain healthy, for it to be in contact with the actual pastoral ministry and life of the Church. Even so, I cannot avoid some surprise at the theological galaxy which in three brief years I managed to attract to our totally obscure but nevertheless eager and appreciative parish. W. R. Matthews, Leonard Hodgson, H. L. Goudge, N. P. Williams, E. G. Selwyn, Richard Hanson (the Dean of King's College, London, not the future Bishop, who would have been then theologically in his nappy), K. D. Mackenzie, H. M. Relton,. J. A. Douglas, C. J. Smith and Christopher Waddams were indeed a formidable array, and when we ranged outside the strictly theological realm we were able to include T. S. Eliot, Sir Bernard Pares, Lord Dickinson, Leonard F. Browne and R. Ellis Roberts.

I was still able to keep up my Orthodox contacts and indeed to stimulate interest in Orthodoxy in the parish. I took parties of our people to visit the Russian church in Buckingham Palace Road (it stood where the Coach Station now is) and (although this was not orthodox in the Chalcedonian sense) the Armenian church in Kensington. I was able, by a combination of chance and skill, to present to them on the evening of November 29th 1934 the Greek Priest Father James Virvos, who had just come, bearing a large wedding-favour, from the reception after the wedding of the Duke of Kent and Princess Marina and who gave an inside account of that colourful and impressive ceremony. This was news-value indeed. The most vivid of these occasions were the four visits of orthodox bishops to take part in our Sunday evening worship: Bishop Tit Simedrea from Rumania, the Metropolitan Evlogi from the Russian emigration in Paris, Bishop Iriney Georgevic of Dalmatia, and Archbishop Germanos, whom I have also mentioned in the context of Coventry. This last function was indeed, by South London standards, spectacular. We had two English diocesans present, our own bishop Dr Richard Parsons, who had recently succeeded Dr Garbett on the latter's translation to Winchester, and Dr Frere of Truro, who was a veteran expert in Orthodox affairs and who preached the sermon. We had also Father Virvos and Archimandrite Michael Constantinides from the Greek cathedral and Father Nicholas Behr from the Russian church so it was very much a gala occasion. In marshalling the procession I almost forgot to include Father St John, who besides being the parish priest had the not unimportant function to perform of celebrating the Office! Functions such as these took a good deal of organising, but they were worth while, not only from the point of view of showmanship.

They were acts of worship and fellowship on the part of Christian communions which normally had no visible contact with each other and that, apart from anything else, gave them an intrinsic value.

My three years at Stockwell were very crowded and, in spite of the traumatic incidents inevitable to inexperience, were basically very happy. Just after my ordination to the diaconate we received our new father in God and the relaxation of tension in the diocese was palpable. For Garbett, though utterly just and straightforward, was authoritarian and inflexible, overwhelmingly conscientious and invariably punctual and efficient; an interview with him had a pre-rehearsed computerlike quality. He had a laserlike eye, and during his ordination charge, which was largely devoted to the topic of authority and obedience, each of us was convinced that it was focused directly at him. So concentrated was his control that when he was out of the diocese no confirmations were allowed, although he had two suffragans; St John once shocked him by saying, when he had unsuccessfully pleaded for an exception, 'I don't see, my Lord, why the Holy Ghost should be on holiday because you are!' Parsons, in spite of an earlier reputation for irritability, was fatherly and sympathetic, and, though he could never compete with the monumental inefficiency of dear old Winnington-Ingram across the Thames, was just sufficiently fallible to be human.[2] His chaplain told me a delightful story of his getting confused between an audience of girls at a rescue-home and one of hospital nurses and starting his address to the former by saying, 'I must just tell you what a privilege I feel it is to be speaking to so many members of what we all agree to be one of the noblest and most self-sacrificing professions in the world.' When he visited us for a confirmation, St John slipped up to me and murmured, 'Thank heaven we've got a human being for a bishop at last! He's forgotten his pastoral staff; Garbett never forgot *anything*.' He appreciated St John's evangelistic fervour and did all he could to encourage my concern with the Orthodox Church and with systematic apologetics. On Trinity Sunday 1933 he ordained me to the priesthood in Southwark Cathedral and I celebrated my first mass at St Andrew's on our Feast of Dedication two days later.

It was a High Mass and took place early in the morning, for in those days evening masses were, of course, unthinkable. There was a large congregation and it was a joyful and rumbustious occasion. Christopher Waddams acted as deacon and the senior curate, Herbert Sydenham, as subdeacon. (Herbert shortly afterwards realised a long-cherished desire to be a missionary, went out to Zanzibar diocese and became Archdeacon of Korogwe.) St John himself, as right and proper, took on the office of assistant priest, whose function at a first mass is to prevent the neophyte from making mistakes, but, as he was always intuitive rather than instructed in ceremonial matters and had merely a vague impression that his duties on this occasion consisted, in his own words, of 'standing about in an enormous cope', I found myself guiding him as much as he was guiding me. My parents, who were then living at Hove, came specially for the service, and, when I told St John that I wanted to bless a rose at the mass to give to my mother, he decided that all the congregation must be given roses – and they were! I left the sanctuary to the triumphant notes of the pseudo-Purcellian Trumpet Voluntary, and I felt that none of the young men who had been launched on the priesthood that Trinitytide had been given as encouraging a start as I had.

One of our activities which I greatly enjoyed was outdoor preaching, though St John complained, probably rightly, that Stockwell was not such a good place for it as Newington. I do not think that it visibly augmented our congregations, though it certainly helped to make the parish conscious of our existence and it broke down any tendencies in our own people to think of religion as confined to what went on within the church's four walls. I had constant struggles with St John about the Magazine, of which I was editor, as he hated writing and could never produce his monthly letter in time. He often sent it direct to the printer in his terribly illegible handwriting, with the result that it appeared one Lent as exhorting the faithful to be at the altar on Easter Day to welcome their risen Mother – a slightly advanced piece of Mariology even for St John!

The great Oxford Movement Centenary Congress came just after my priesting, and Herbert Sydenham and I did all we could to stir up our people for it. St John was initially rather tepid about it; he was suspicious of some of the people running it, who fell in the 'dirty Papist' category, and he was always reluctant to let our people realise that genuine catholicism was to be found outside his own parish. On the other hand, he was a great enthusiast and let us have our head. We took a party, singing hymns vociferously on the way, to the White City stadium for the Pontifical Mass which was celebrated by the Bishop of Colombo in the presence of the Bishop of St Albans, who acted as deputy for the sick diocesan of London. This was, I suppose, ceremonially the climax to date of all Anglo-Catholic celebrations, and it was not difficult to persuade oneself that the Movement had captured the Church of England. One need only look at the list of topics and speakers in the

Report of the Congress to see that, in whatever direction one's liturgical sympathies lie, the primary emphasis in 1933 as in 1920 was upon doctrine, scholarship, spirituality and social concern. What, if anything, went wrong with the Movement later is a quite different matter.

Though 'extreme' by Southwark-diocese standards, St Andrew's was, except for some slight transgressions in Holy Week, remarkably loyal to the 1662 Prayer Book, though St John was much upset when Garbett described him as a 'loyal Anglo-Catholic'; he felt this was an implied criticism of friends of his who weren't. (He used to say that all curates ought to be taught to repeat 'The bishops are enemies of the Catholic Faith'.) The Revised Book of 1928 was anathema, as was also any version of Scripture other than the 'original Authorised'. Most of the canon of the Roman mass was recited, but entirely silently, and the Lord's Prayer and the *Gloria in excelsis* were sung or said in the 'Prayer-Book place'. Thus the impression was given, as in many moderately high churches, that the Eucharistic Canon was simply a means of manufacturing the Blessed Sacrament, which was then used for adoration and communion. Indeed St John admitted — and I suspect this was really true of many Anglo-Catholic priests of his generation — that he found the Eucharistic Sacrifice too difficult and taught the Real Presence instead. So the eight 'O'clock mass was for 'communion' and the eleven for 'worship'. (This was, of course, before Gregory Dix had done his great work on the Eucharist.)

We never had a Corpus-Christi procession, nor did we have Benediction of the Blessed Sacrament (at least, not publicly); nor did we have a midnight mass at Christmas, though this was because St John was convinced it would attract revellers from the local pubs. Only on festivals did we normally have a full High Mass, for St John would only take part in one as celebrant. This was not due to personal conceit, but partly to his inability to learn any other function and partly to his belief that it was his place, as the parish priest, as he put it, to 'keep the service going'. He never grasped the notion of the Mass as a corporate activity in which all the various orders of the Church have their several parts to play, but thought of it rather as a kind of concert which the principal minister — himself — 'conducted'. This often had the quite unintended effect of reducing the body of the faithful to silence, for he had a stentorian voice and 'keeping the service going' usually involved allowing little time for anyone to make the responses. He said that his idea of heaven was taking part in what he described as 'Gounod's Messerlonel', and we did in fact

twice anticipate this state of beatitude with an enthusiastic and
specially gathered orchestra. Nevertheless, these were great days
and, whatever criticisms might be made of the St John régime
from the angle of strict liturgical and theological propriety, there
could be no doubt that in his five years at Stockwell, as in his
previous twenty years at Newington, he did a great work for the
glory of God and the souls of men. He was as conscious of his
limitations as of his special capacities, and he was therefore all the
more anxious to encourage his assistants to develop those areas
of work for which they had gifts different from his own. He was
not, I think, always popular with other incumbents but he was with
his own curates. Life with him was sometimes explosive but was
never dull. I was sometimes exasperated by him, but I never lost
my respect or affection for him, as was shown by my eagerness
to accompany him when he accepted the offer of St Matthew's,
Westminster. Before describing this however, I must say something
about my own personal adjustment to the pressures of the priest-
ood in those early days.

I have said already that the greatest and most lasting gift which
I took away from my brief time at Ely was the possession of a
definite framework of disciplined spirituality, of mass, offices and
mental prayer. However reluctantly I have observed it at times,
and with whatever distraction and tepidity, I am convinced that,
under the hand of God, it has done more than anything else to
preserve and stabilise my vocation as a priest. For it has been
alarmingly evident to me how many personal tragedies and collapses
of vocation in the lives of priests, to say nothing of the more
spectacular failures of highly publicised and massively equipped
ecclesiastical projects, have been traceable to the neglect or erosion
of the basic disciplines of the Christian life. It is, however, to
my mind extremely surprising that even those colleges of Catholic
tradition, such as Ely, which laid most stress upon the obligation
for the priest of systematic mental prayer gave little indication of
either the development which that prayer might undergo or the
obstacles which it might meet. It was taken for granted that to the
end of our earthly days we would perform discursive meditations
on the Ignatian model, with all the multiplicity of acts that are
peculiar to its many variants.[3] I remember C. J. Smith, in one
of his instructions, remarking rather sadly that in his experience
prayer became more and more difficult the more you practised
it, but there was no suggestion that anything could be done
about this. I read Bede Frost's *Art of Mental Prayer*, which was
published in 1931, but though he made passing reference to Dom

John Chapman's reaction against Counter-Reformation spirituality and admitted the possibility of acquired nonmystical contemplation, he devoted most of his book to such a highly systematised account of different methods of discursive prayer – Ignatian, Franciscan, Carmelite, Salesian, Liguorian, Oratorian – as to provide little help for a beginner like myself who, without having achieved any high degree of sanctity, was already finding it difficult to see the wood for the trees. I got little help in my difficulties from my confessor, who was an experienced but very austere Cowley father, and whom I could not make to understand my problem. It was not until 1935, when I had just left St Andrew's, that the recently published *Spiritual Letters* of John Chapman came into my hands and the scales fell from my eyes. I saw then for the first time clearly how theology, ascetics and spirituality are connected and that, in Chapman's words, you must pray as you can and not try to pray as you can't. But to the end of my time at Stockwell I was struggling in the morass.

One thing of which, as I look back upon my subsequent life, my three years at Stockwell has convinced me is that, whatever sphere of work he, or more importantly Almighty God, may intend him to occupy, a priest cannot do better than begin his ministry in a live but inconspicuous and preferably unfashionable parish. He will there be brought face to face with the realities of the Church's pastoral task in all its human variety as is possible in no other way. I never expected or desired, when I was ordained, anything other than a life spent in the parish ministry in South London, and, although *Deo aliter visum* and I have worked almost entirely in colleges and universities, I never cease to thank God for the day when, sent by Bishop Garbett, I knocked on the door of St Andrew's Vicarage, Stockwell.

Among the many memorable figures of my Stockwell days I will single out one for special mention. Mrs (known to all as 'Granny') Stephens was by her own reckoning our oldest inhabitant and a vigorous one at that. She looked and dressed exactly like the late Queen Victoria. She was brought to church each Sunday in a Bath chair by our Scouts and her arrival was an incident of some dignity. At parish parties she could be relied upon to oblige with a song which must have gone back to the years of her childhood; it had the rousing chorus 'And the Captain with his whiskers took a sly glance at me!' Her title as oldest inhabitant was queried by another, and less imposing, lady, concerning whose early life Granny would, I suspect for no other reasons, make veiled but sinister insinuations. 'Oh, Reverend Mascall, I couldn't soil a clergyman's ears with the things I could tell you about that woman. But if I told you how she carried on with the driver of that waggonette – '.

In 1935 St John was invited to cross the river and become Vicar of St Matthew's, Westminster. In spite of the magic of the word 'Westminster' and the fact that the church was hardly more than a stone's throw from the Abbey and the Houses of Parliament, St Matthew's was neither a fashionable nor an opulent parish, though it contained a few well-to-do people. In contrast with the lower middle-class uniformity of Stockwell, it was in fact socially extremely mixed; much of it consisted of the originally ideal but by then rather *passé* working-class flats associated with the name of Mr Peabody, but we had also a nobleman's town house, luxury flats, offices, a convent, Salvation Army and Church Army hostels and much besides. It was celebrated in church circles for its long-standing, very individual and considerably fossilised tradition of Catholic worship[4], and, like most churches in the centre of London, drew much of its congregation from outside. Its great claim to fame was its association with the great Bishop of Zanzibar, Frank Weston, who presided with such apostolic fervour over the Anglo-Catholic Congress of 1923 and had indicted the Bishops of Uganda and Mombasa for heresy and schism. It had a considerable ministry among office-workers and visitors to the metropolis, and it sometimes almost seemed as if any catholic who had an hour to wait for a train at Victoria slipped along to St Matthew's to make a quick confession! It was one of the churches that, under pressure from higher authority, dear woolly Bishop Winnington-Ingram had put under his ban for alleged liturgical (and extra-liturgical) illegalities, but he never seemed clear as to what the ban involved or indeed precisely which churches it affected; and it certainly did not prevent him from instituting Fr St John or licensing five assistants to him.

When he received the invitation St John had three curates, of whom I was now the senior, Herbert Sydenham having left for Africa in 1933. His place had been taken by a brilliant young Oxonian, Richard Ratcliff, with a double first in Greats and Theology, who devoted himself so exclusively to the pastoral ministry that he never realised the hopes that had been entertained for him in the academic world; later on he committed the unforgivable sin of matrimony, but that is another matter. The third curate, still in his diaconate, John Hankey, was a man of private means who later became a headmaster in Gloucestershire. St John never did things by halves and, having accepted St Matthew's, he sacked the curates already there and announced that he was bringing his own curates with him. In addition he somehow secured two other unappropriated deacons and the somewhat dazed people of St Matthew's found themselves invaded by an entirely new team of six, three being priests and three deacons, of whom the last three became priests in barely a year.

I cannot truthfully say that St John was really happy at St Matthew's or that St Matthew's was really happy with him. To nurse the congregation through the trauma which the violent impact of the new régime had inflicted upon them needed more patience and sensitivity than he was able to exercise. After twenty-five years in obedient South-London parishes in which tradition meant what the Vicar had just decided and the ultimate means of arbitration was the busting row, he found it very difficult to cope with people many of whom thought, and some not without justification, that their views were as good as his. It was almost inevitable that their loyalty to their settled and peculiar ways seemed to him sheer obstinacy and self-complacency, and that his impulsive innovations and improvisations seemed to them ruthless and unappreciative Philistinism. When the War came in 1939 the parish had fresh and very different problems to face, but I was no longer there to be involved in them. From a purely personal point of view I can say that my two years at St Matthew's from 1935 to 1937 were in many respects anxious and uncomfortable, but they added immensely to the range of my very limited pastoral experience. For I cannot think of any church where one would have contacts, casual or regular, with such a sheer variety of people.

Those were in fact years of considerable interest and excitement, quite apart from ecclesiastical affairs; they included the death of one sovereign, the accession and abdication of a second, and the accession of a third. I watched the funeral procession of King George V from Hyde Park and I was outside St James's Palace at the proclamation of George VI. The Abdication came as almost as great surprise to us in Westminster as to people in remoter parts of the country and, in spite of our proximity to the centres of decision, it was only very shortly before the newspapers broke their silence that we began to hear really serious rumours. This may be in part because the nearer you are to the centre, the more stories you hear and the less you tend from experience to believe any of them. I must record one comment, which I think was very typical of the general British reaction, and which I overhead from an elderly citizen whom I overtook as he shuffled along Great Peter Street. 'They say the King can do no wrong, don't they,' he soliloquised, 'Well, I say 'e's done all blurry wrong. Gawd sive the King!'

One of my functions was that of priest-sacrist and much of my time was taken up with organising services for one or other of the many church societies whose offices were in the neighbourhood. Considerable interest was provided by the fact that one never knew at any time who might walk in. When saying mass quietly one weekday morning I found that I had in my congregation literally half the episcopate of the Welsh Church; it was, one of them explained, easier in fact for them to meet in London than to converge on any spot in Wales! One afternoon the Bishop of St Albans, Michael Furse, came to fetch the Blessed Sacrament for a friend of his who was seriously ill; I do not know whether he knew that his brother of London had put St Matthew's under the Ban, but his brother of London never seemed very clear about it either. Even a diocesan bishop, if he wanted something, was likely to go where it was to be found.

I was not nearly as successful with lectures and classes at Westminster as I had been at Stockwell, chiefly, I think, because the clientele that was so avid for instruction at St Andrew's simply did not exist at St Matthew's. I did, however, get a very keen response from a study-group of well educated young women whom I was trying to introduce to the wider social implications of Christian theology. My first published book, a slight volume entitled *Death or Dogma*, the remaining copies of which were mercifully destroyed by the Luftwaffe in the Blitz, was originally delivered as talks to this group. I was acquiring a stronger conviction that I might have some kind of intellectual contribution to make to the life of the Church, though I never thought it would be in any setting other than that of the parochial ministry or that it would issue in any sizeable publications.

I had had two articles published in the journal *Theology* in 1929, when I was teaching at Coventry; they were on aspects of the relations between Christianity and science and show considerable concern with the philosophy of A. N. Whitehead, by which I was at the time a good deal influenced but not, I think, besotted. In 1935, at the end of my time at Stockwell, *Theology* published a much more substantial article, 'Three Modern Approaches to God', in which I attempted a critical assessment, not only of Whitehead but of F. R. Tennant and A. E. Taylor as well, which, as I look back on it, seems a fairly audacious thing for a neophyte like myself to undertake. In 1934 I reviewed W. C. Dampier-Whetham's *History of Science* for *Laudate*, the journal of the Anglican monks of Nashdom, and this brought me from the editor, Fr Edward Cryer, an invitation to spend Holy Week at the Abbey. Those were the

days of the amazing Abbot Denis Prideaux and I found it both
an enriching and a puzzling experience, which at that stage of my
pilgrimage it was difficult to assimilate. Neither Bernard Clements
nor Gregory Dix, who both later became close friends, was there
at the time. I should indeed have been surprised to be told that
I should one day conduct the retreat for the community. I wrote
several contributions to *Laudate* of various kinds, including a
review of the notorious Bishop Barnes's Gifford Lectures. In
1934 S.P.C.K. published under my editorship a symposium *The
Church of God* by members of the Fellowship of St Alban and St
Sergius.

It was not until my last year at St Matthew's that I became
actively concerned with the Church's mission to society. I knew
of course about the great work which the Church had done in the
slums in the last century; it was one of the glories of the Catholic
Movement. I knew vaguely about the tradition of Christian social
thinking, based on the doctrine of the Incarnation, which had been
started by F. D. Maurice and of which the later prophet Charles
Gore had died as recently as at the beginning of 1942. I knew
of the work that had been done by the privileged for their less
fortunate brethren under Christian auspices by school and college
missions and clubs and by such activities as the Cambridge fruiting
and the Oxford hop-picking campaign. I knew of the Industrial
Christian Fellowship, and I had been thrilled by the story of Fr
Basil Jellicoe's great breakthrough in the slums of Somers Town
with his foundation of the St Pancras Housing Association. St
John once asked him to talk about his work to our people at
Stockwell, and he inspired some and shocked others by the fervour
of his denunciation of our modern civilisation; he declared that
he wished not to repair it but to destroy it and to dance upon
the ruins. Its builders, he told us, with questionable exegesis but
perhaps with Somers Town in mind, had, like those of the Tower
of Babel, used slime for mortar, with similar consequences. Much
as I admired all this – and I must confess that my concern had
been one of admiration rather than of active participation – I
had, even in my then state of theological immaturity, a feeling
at the back of my mind that if social concern was to be not
either paternalistic or destructive but constructively Christian and
Catholic, it would need more systematic theological foundation
than it normally received in official Anglican circles. What was
my surprise therefore to discover that there were a number of
priests and laypeople who also felt this way and who moreover
had been doing something about if for some years, though it was

ignored in academic theological faculties. I suppose that I had
heard of the Anglo-Catholic Summer School of Sociology, which
had been founded in 1925, but it had never made any impression
on my mind, filled as that was with other things. My enlightenment
came in this way. I read in 1935 a small book called *Religion and
Social Purpose* by a layman named Maurice B. Reckitt, which,
with its combination of theological penetration, deep sense of
political and economic realities and ebulliant humour, gave me
a thrill that I had not received from any religious book since,
as a schoolboy, I had devoured G. K. Chesterton's *Orthodoxy*;
it was exciting, amusing and challenging and it made it perfectly
plain to me that to hold Catholic beliefs and yet to be conscious
of no implications in the social and political realms could only
be sign of intellectual laziness or sheer logical incapacity. Greatly
daring, I wrote to Mr Reckitt and asked him to come and talk to
some of our St Matthew's people. When he tumbled in through
the door of the clergy-house in the middle of a sentence which
he appeared to have begun somewhere near Victoria Station I not
only made the acquaintance of the wittiest speaker I have ever
known but also received my introduction to a side of the Catholic
Movement that was to mean more and more to me in the years
to come. I must, however, leave all this to a later chapter, for it
was just about this time that I was faced, quite unexpectedly, with
a radical change in my life and work, when Eric Abbott, who had
just become Warden of the Theological College at Lincoln, asked
me to join him there as Michael Ramsey's successor in the post
of Sub-Warden. Although this came as a complete surprise, I had
little hesitation in accepting. I had had five years with St John
in two very different London parishes and was feeling ready for
a change, training of ordinands was a task of vital importance in
which I felt keen to take some, if a subordinate, part, and there
would be opportunities of cultivating the areas that I now felt of
special importance in spirituality, sociology and basic dogmatic
theology. Not indeed that I felt that, with my terribly sketchy
theological training, I had nothing to learn; one of the attractions
of Lincoln was that I should have rather more time for reading,
but I hoped that, by the grace of God, I might manage to keep
about one lecture ahead of my classes. And, as I had never had
any academic training in theology at all, all my equipment as a
theologian really consists of what I was able to acquire for myself
during my eight years at Lincoln.

Notes

1. It was said that Dean Garfield Williams once refused an invitation to attend the ceremony of the espousal of Liverpool to the River Mersey on the grounds that by an unfortunate coincidence he would at that very moment be trying to make an honest woman of the Manchester Ship Canal.
2. He was known affectionately as 'Jumbo'; I do not think anyone ever dared to give a nickname to Garbett.
3. This point is well illustrated by the following story concerning Dom Gregory Dix. Some years before Vatican II he was, rather daringly, invited by Cardinal Gerlier of Lyon to give a lecture on Anglican spirituality. In the discussion he was asked by an unidentified priest whether the Anglican clergy were taught Ignatian spirituality. Dix replied that it was the only kind that most of them were taught, and that this was very unfortunate, as it was a type that was very unsuitable to English people, so that most of them, having tried it without success, abandoned prayer altogether. There was a burst of laughter and the questioner, somewhat disconcerted, sat down with the remark, 'Father, that is a truly Benedictine sentiment.' The chairman whispered to Dom Gregory, 'That was the Father Provincial of the Society of Jesus.'
4. An example of this fossilisation was provided by the strange procession that took place mass on Palm Sunday. At certain points everyone turned inwards and genuflected, while singing 'Hail, O King!', though no one appeared to know why. I discovered that this was in fact derived from the Sarum missal, which ordered that a shrine with the Blessed Sacrament and relics should be carried in the procession. Obviously this particular bit of pre-reformation devotion was more than it had been deemed safe to revive, so the ceremonies were performed in spite of the absence of the sole object that had given them any meaning. But this did not prevent their abolition being resisted as as a kind of apostasy.

Chapter Six

Lincoln and the Second World-War

(1937–1945)

Upon the north side lieth the city of the great King; God is well known in her palaces as a sure refuge.

— Psalm xlviii.2.

Lincoln Theological College — officially *Scholae Cancellarii*, the Chancellor's School — was founded in 1874, two years before Ely, and almost the first thing that struck me about it was how closely the patterns of life and worship in the two institutions resembled each other. But for some reason, whereas Ely had acquired a reputation for dangerous Catholic extremism, Lincoln was considered a model of Anglican respectability. Both had been founded by bishops — Ely by Woodford, Lincoln by Wordsworth and later fostered by the saintly Edward King — but perhaps the fact that at Lincoln the official head of the College was the Chancellor of the Cathedral and that in 1874 this was Edward White Beson, who was already well on his way to the episcopate, first of Truro and then of Canterbury, may have had something to do with it. In 1937 this office was held by James Herbert Srawley, a delightful little man, who combined a European reputation as a liturgical scholar with, apparently, an almost complete ignorance of the fact that the subject in which he was an acknowledged expert had any relevance to what went on in church. His lectures were monumental in their boredom, and even his devoted wife was on record as saying, 'Of course Herbert can make anything dull.' When Gregory Dix's book *The Shape of the Liturgy* was published, the Chancellor staggered me by making the comment, 'An excellent book. It does what I try to do in my lectures; it *makes the subject live.*' He was very deaf and, as the Vice-Chancellor was unable to speak above a whisper, it was a source of debate how

122

they managed to establish communication, but somehow they did. Gregory once remarked that conversation with him was like the versicles and responses at the end of Evensong; there was little connection between them. There could occasionally be awkward moments when he came to an office in the College chapel. When everyone else on his side was silent, a quiet but determined voice might announce from his stall, My *wounds stink* and *are corrupt, for very foolishness'* or *'I* will not *know* a wicked person.' He had, as one would have expected, a good knowledge of French and German, which he pronounced as if they were English, with sometimes unexpected results. The audience at his lectures often took some time to recognise that a character who was introduced with the name of Charlie Mayne was not a Victorian music-hall comedian but the famous emperor who was crowned in St Peter's on Christmas Day in A.D. 800. The students, who had him in great affection, for he was devoted to them, would wickedly lure him into telling anecdotes involving multiple use of the letter 'h', for his deafness together with his Lancastrian origin had rendered that consonant obscure in his speech; there was one about a horrible hullaballoo and another that involved his hollyhocks. The worst moment of all came when he had pointed out on a map the village of Shrawley, from which, he told us, his family took its name. 'You spell it differently now, Chancellor,' one of the students observed. 'Yes,' he replied, 'nowadays we drop the "h".'

The Sub-Warden was expected to be concerned specially with dogmatic theology, and a large part of the lecturing in Doctrine fell to me, as it had fallen to my predecessor, Michael Ramsey, the future Archbishop. He had written his much acclaimed book *The Gospel and the Catholic Church* in the rooms which were now allotted to me, and largely, so it was said, on the wallpaper; though as the rooms were redecorated for my occupation I could not verify this for myself. I was therefore, I felt, in a sound tradition when I wrote there my first substantial work, *He Who Is*, and my general standpoint was indicated by the sub-title which I gave it, *A Study in Traditional Theism*. I originally envisaged it as being a straightforward account of the Christian doctrine of God for beginners in theology, as I felt that such a book was badly needed. However, when I had finished it it turned out to be a re-examination of traditional natural theology, making a good deal of use of my delving into the Thomist tradition and my reading of modern philosophers, especially those who, like myself, had some acquaintance with the cosmological theories of contemporary physics and astronomy. It looked, in fact, rather suspiciously like a degree-thesis, though it had certainly not been written with that in mind or under any kind of academic supervision. Somehow or other it came to the knowledge of Roger Lloyd, who was then a canon of Winchester, and through him to that of Eric Gillett, who was one of the readers for the famous publishing firm of Longmans. It was then the end of 1942, World War II was well under way, and Longmans, who had been bombed out of their premises in the City, were wondering whether the time was propitious for serious academic theology. Very audaciously Roger Longman decided to take the risk with the very unknown author that I then was, and, having survived the hazards of wartime production, *He Who Is* saw the light of day in September 1943. It was fortunate in getting a full-page review by Ivor Thomas in the centre of the *Times Literary Supplement* and has sold steadily ever since, even achieving the respectable if gloomy status of being prescribed in university syllabuses.

While it was still in the press I had shown the manuscript to Edward Wynn, who had now become Bishop of Ely, and he had passed it on to J. S. Boys Smith, the Ely Professor of Divinity, who held a canonry in his cathedral and was moreover, though I did not know it, Chairman of the Faculty Board of Divinity. Boys Smith was, in his general theological position, a very typical Cambridge modernist and his outlook was very different from mine, but he had a genuine concern with natural theology and was anxious to encourage a neophyte, especially one with a background in the sciences. He took enormous trouble over my manuscript, made a number of valuable suggestions and, while rightly warning me that I 'would not be justified in taking any opinion of [his] as anticipating the judgment of the Committee' wrote, 'I certainly think you need feel no hesitation in submitting your book for the degree and I hope you will decide to do so.' The degree, of course, was that of Bachelor of Divinity, which Cambridge, under the influence of Bethune-Baker, had elevated almost to doctoral status (B.D.s did in fact rank above Doctors of Philosophy), and this encouragement, while it left me somewhat dazed, seemed good enough to follow. I therefore submitted the book as my thesis and was relieved, though not by now surprised, to hear soon after that my application had been approved. Of the two subsidiary requirements one caused me no trouble; the book was already on the verge of publication. The other was rather more tricky; I had to satisfy the Board that I was generally competent in theology. The standard qualification was to have received a high class in the Theological Tripos, but this hardly applied to a candidate whose sole university training had been in mathematics. There were however, alternatives, but even so elastically worded a criterion as 'the general character of the work submitted' did not seem in my case to indicate proficiency outside a very narrow specialised field. Fortunately there was an omnibus clause allowing the examiners to apply their own criterion of satisfaction, and I simply made the submission that I had been teaching theology for more than five years, while silently hoping that no details would be asked for. They were not, and in due course I was presented for the degree by another of the Cambridge modernists, the Regius Professor of Divinity, Dr Charles Raven. Cambridge was, I think, much ahead of most other universities at the time in making it as easy as possible for a man or woman to receive recognition in a faculty on the strength of his achievement without asking too many questions about his past history; nowadays transit across the frontiers is wisely easier to obtain in most universities. Now that I am a full doctor of both the ancient universties it is amusing to reflect that no academic body has ever ascertained whether I know how many Gospels there are in the New Testament and whether they were written in Greek or Sea Dyak. As far as I can judge, my entry into academic theology turned at the critical moment on the fortunate vagueness of one clause in a loosely drawn regulation. I will add to this thoroughly egotistical paragraph that Chancellor Srawley sent me a characteristically kind and enthusiastic letter of congratulation in which he wrote: 'It looks as though the dream of Lincoln becoming again a "school of theology" is coming true.'

Though I certainly did not fully recognise it at the time, it was the writing of *He Who Is* that was to bring me back into the academic world. It did me no good, however, in higher ecclesiastical circles, for it got me the reputation of being a 'Thomist'. As I was to find when it was time for me to make a move from Lincoln, although our bishops were almost completely ignorant of Thomism (one, who was reputed to be high-church, boasted in my hearing that he had never read a word of St Thomas, as if the Angelic Doctor's works were a kind of pornography), the suspicion of Thomism was as much of a disqualification in official eyes as was that of Communism or homosexuality.

The Bishop's Hostel — for this is the name of the building in which the Theological College is housed — is a large and dignified edifice to the west of the cathedral, standing on the brow of the hill and facing south over the lower and industrial part of the city; it was originally built as a hospital but had been adapted satisfactorily to its later purpose. Its position made it a very pleasant place to

live in but also, when the War came, an extremely difficult place
to render inconspicuous to raiding aircraft, as I, in my capacity
as black-out officer, was painfully aware. As it happened, only
one stick of bombs fell on Lincoln throughout the War, and that
was jettisoned by a stray plane that had lost its way; but every
night during the bombing period the sirens went at nightfall and
shortly after the German planes would be heard on their way to
the great industrial areas. Meanwhile such of our staff and students
as had no duties to perform would descend to the basement, where
our air-raid shelter was, in defiance of superstition, the converted
mortuary of the erstwhile hospital. But what were students doing
there throughout the War, it may be asked. Well, by the decision
of the Government, all candidates for ordination who had been
accepted before the beginning of the War were exempted from
conscription, and, although the supply of fresh students steadily
diminished, the vacant places were filled by students from other
theological colleges whose *almae matres* had closed in the middle of
their courses. Thus for a short time our numbers actually increased
and, although by the end of the War the supply had almost dried
up, we never in fact shut our doors. Lincoln held the honourable
position of the surviving cannibal.

In 1937 Eric Abbott had inherited as his staff Hugh Ashdown and
Bryan (G. B.) Bentley, as Chaplain and Tutor respectively. Hugh
left just after I arrived, to take over a parish in West Hartlepool;
later he became Provost of Southwark Cathedral and finally Bishop
of Newcastle. He was austere and respected, and it was said that
you could estimate the severity of his outlook in the morning by the
degree of tightening of the belt of his cassock. Bryan married and
became a priest-vicar of the cathedral in 1938, but he continued to
lecture for us in ethics and moral theology; his elder daughter, now
married to the Dean of Exeter, and with two daughters of her own,
is my god-daughter. He himself, after several years of comparative
exile in a remote Devon parish, became a canon of Windsor in
1957 and the reports of various ecclesiastical committees bear the
marks of his style to the discerning, though few carry his signature.
He was succeeded at the College as Tutor by Christopher Francis
Evans, who began his career as a Biblical scholar at Cambridge
under the dynamic and rebellious inspiration of Edwyn Hoskyns,
but in his later development in the Universities of Oxford, Durham
and London has manifested a more conventional liberalism. For
a little more than a year we enjoyed the warm and beneficient
presence as Chaplain of George Otto Simms, until his native
land charmed him back on the course which took him to the

charge, successively or simultaneously, of seven Irish dioceses and culminated in the primatial see of Armagh.

Lincoln Cathedral, like those of many other ancient dioceses, stands in a serene but formidable enclave, which is the joy of antiquarians and artists but has less to be said for it from the point of view of the Church's evangelistic and pastoral functions. Physically the Minster Yard at Lincoln is not such an impregnable fortress as, say, the Close at Salisbury, for, daunting as is the Exchequer Gate to those who approach it from the West, its Eastern approaches are entirely undefended. Nevertheless, the psychological impression of a privileged and self-conscious élite remains. Even a slight experience of a cathedral such as that of Truro, where, in contrast, the life of the city with all its variety and activity comes up to the very walls of the sacred building itself and where the homes of those responsible for its life and worship are scattered among those of the general population, helps one to understand the unwelcoming implications of the common designation of 'the Close'.

The Hostel stood well outside the Minster Yard and indeed the most commonly seen photograph of the exterior of the Exchequer Gate and the magnificent west front of the Cathedral would appear to have been taken from the window of my sitting-room. With our own chapel we stood in little need of the Cathedral's daily ministrations, though the students were supposed to attend at least one of its services every Sunday. This would have been admirable if the rites that were celebrated in the splendid edifice that announced itself to the visitor as 'the Cathedral Church of the Blessed and Glorious Virgin Mary of Lincoln' had been in any way worthy of their setting. They were in fact of a monumental dulness and dreariness and, in spite of the resources that were available, were organised – if the word can be used at all – with a kind of amateurish inefficiency of which any normal Anglo-Catholic slum parish would have been ashamed. Certainly no one would have supposed that among the residentiaries was numbered a liturgical scholar of European reputation, unless he had already discovered that, in liturgical even more than in other matters, it is rare for theoretical and practical expertise to go hand in hand. One example may be taken as typical. The Sacrist, who held his office first in conjunction with the Archdeaconry and then with the Sub-Deanery, was accustomed in virtue of his office to carry the cross at the head of processions in the Cathedral. He tended, however, to wield the cross as if it was some kind of weapon and, when it had to be lowered on passing under an arch, he would swing it suddenly and briskly under his right arm, so that its foot projected for several feet to the rear, to the alarm and confusion of those immediately behind him, as if he was about to charge with a lance against an enemy. His successor as Archdeacon once confided to me that he himself on one such occasion feared that he was about to suffer the fate of Asahel in II Samuel ii, who, it will be remembered, when following too closely upon Abner, found himself impaled on the butt end of the latter warrior's spear. Again the Sacrist held that he was also personally responsible for the smooth ordering of the procession, though the two functions might well seem to be, as they were in fact, incompossible. The consequence was that, if, as often happened, things got into a jam, the Sacrist would hand the cross to the Verger, who would then lead the procession bearing the cross in one hand and his verge in the other, while the Sacrist pulled the unruly participants into position. If, however, the cross was not being used, he would equip himself with a long wand and shift them into their rightful places with a smart tap on the posterior. He had a highly pitched and penetrating voice and on major diocesan occasions, when he was trying to reduce the prebendaries (as the honorary canons, of whom there were over fifty, were called at Lincoln) to some kind of order before the service, he would be heard plaintively appealing: 'Clergy of the diocese, line the Chapter-house; I said, *Line the Chapter-House*'. He was a high-ranking and expert figure in the model-railway world, in which it was understood the name of Archdeacon Larken gave access to lines normally closed, and would from time to time give demonstrations of his own quite extensive system to select parties from the College; I spent several fascinating hours in his attic on one such occasion, for I have had from childhood an un-realised ambition to possess a really diversified model railway of my own. Quite suddenly however, something which we never understood went wrong, though the flippant attributed it to his having been bitten by a favourite locomotive; he brought his whole concern with trains to an end, disposed of his entire equipment and, as far as I could make out, he never mentioned model railways again.

   The Bishop of Lincoln in 1937 was Nugent Hicks, generally known as 'Bumbo'. He was a massive, heavily-jowled figure who well fitted his nickname. He had a quite enormous head and it was said that when the War came it was impossible to find a steel helmet to fit him. I can quite believe this, for I remember at a garden-party shortly before, wandering round him quite fascinated to observe from different angles the gigantic silk hat which he was wearing; basically designed on the principle of two ellipses in parallel planes with their major axes at right angles, it gave the impression of having been constructed on a lathe. He had been a man of academic distinction, with a first in Greats at Balliol and then a Tutorship at Keble; later he was Principal of Cheshunt College. In 1927 he had become Bishop of Gibraltar and in that capacity had acquired a wide if somewhat short-sighted acquaintance with the Eastern Orthodox Church; like many official Anglicans of the time he tended to look on the Orthodox as a rather backward type of Anglican who were almost ready, on the basis of a common antogonism to Rome, to enter into full and visible communion with us. He had written one, and only one, book of outstanding theological importance. In *The Fullness of Sacrifice*, published in 1930, on the basis of a detailed study of Biblical sacrificial understanding, he had made a breakthrough in Anglican thought about the Eucharist which was to have considerable ecumenical significance. But I doubt whether he really saw this significance himself, and he certainly never again produced any theological work of note or cast off his Anglican romanticism. Very typical was a speech which he made at a meeting in the Cathedral to inaugurate a branch of the Fellowship of St Alban and St Sergius. He expounded, with manifest conviction, the essential identity of the belief and practice of Eastern Orthodoxy with that of central Anglicanism, as exemplified in the Sunday worship of Lincoln Cathedral, and the incompatibility of both with Roman Catholicism. He instanced in support of his thesis the use of the vernacular and the full participation of the laity in the Liturgy.[1] He also made in passing some snide remarks about young clergymen who copied modern Roman customs, having apparently forgotten that he was himself wearing a purple cassock and a pectoral cross. When time came for questions and discussion I had had about as much as I could stand, and I remarked that I had recently attended the Sunday liturgy in the cathedrals of Cologne (Roman Catholic) and Bucharest (Orthodox) as well as Lincoln. I had observed, I said, that at Bucharest, as at the High Mass at Cologne, nobody except the celebrant communicated at all, although at Cologne, unlike Bucharest, there were other masses at which there were numerous communicants. I also pointed out that, while most of those present at the Eucharist at Lincoln admittedly received communion, the great majority of the Sunday morning congregation came not to the Eucharist but to Morning Prayer and so neither communicated nor were even, like the disparaged Roman Catholics, present at the Eucharist at all. I cannot remember whether on this occasion I also instanced devotion to the Blessed Virgin as another matter on which

Orthodox practice was closer to that of Roman Catholicism than to
that of central Anglicanism, but I might well have done so; I had
recently taken part in a procession of a miraculous icon of the
Mother of God at Chisineu which came well up to the level of
Sicily or Guatemala.[2] I yield to none in my respect for Orthodoxy
and I am deeply sensible of the debt that I owe to it in my own
spiritual development; I feel therefore all the more ashamed of
the unprincipled, though usually quite sincere, way in which we
Anglicans have often used Orthodoxy as a stick to beat Rome and
as a screen to hide our own weaknesses.

Bumbo had never been famed for clarity and concision and
by the time that I came to know him, when his powers were
beginning to decline, his public utterances had reached a quite
vertiginous level of circularity and diffuseness. I do not think
I am exaggerating in saying that one of his addresses to the
College began as follows: 'All this week I have been thinking
about what I should speak to you about this evening. And as
I went on thinking all this week about what I should speak to
you about this evening, I thought I had better speak to you this
evening about something that I have been thinking about all this
week.' On another occasion, he announced his text; 'Honour all
men. Love the brotherhood. Fear God, Honour the King', and
informed us that he would show us how from any one of these
four precepts all the others could be deduced. I think that after
about twenty minutes he had managed to deduce the second and
third from the first by some rather questionable logic and I was
getting anxious as to how long the whole exercise was going to
take. Fortunately at this point he lost the thread of the argument
and concluded by saying: 'Well, now you can see how it's done,
and after all, taking one thing and another, there it is, so to speak.'
He was a committed but was not a notably active Freemason and
I imagine that, like other clerical members of the Craft, he had
managed to interpret its syncretistic religious formulas in a sense
not too violently contrary to that of the Thirty-nine Articles. His
fundamental conscientiousness was interestingly shown by the fact
that, having had to memorise the Masonic rites and repeat them
without book, he felt obliged to do the same with the Church's
Liturgy. To hear his rendering of the Ordination rite was indeed
impressive, in spite of occasional departures from the strict letter
of the printed text.

He was very much a figure of the Establishment and both he
and his wife were conscious of their place in the society of the
County; he once remarked to me that he was puzzled to hear people

speak about conflicts between the classes, in view of the excellent relations that he had observed to exist between Lord X and his butler. When the War broke out Bumbo, who had always had military sympathies, became suddenly active and issued a number of War Emergency Circulars to the clergy; one of them referred to the difficulty of obtaining what he strangely described as 'fasting food'. He was however, really a sick man and the difficulty of running his enormous diocese under the increasing strains of war-time life put a heavy burden upon him, and he died, still in office, in 1942. It would be idle to deny that, in the critical eyes of the students and even, to some degree, of the staff of the College, he had become rather a figure of fun and certainly the symbol of an age that was passing; but he was, with all his limitations and handicaps, a kindly, devout and thoughtful man. Somehow it is the ridiculous things that one remembers. When he was ill, early in the War, he committed the writing of his letter in the diocesan paper not to a suffragan but to his wife. It described the unpropitious conditions under which a social function was held − 'the Bishop was ill, war had broken out, and it was raining' − but ended on a cheerful note: 'Mr Butlin came to the rescue with his performing bears and the occasion was a great success.' More seriously we were told that the Church was in this War 'up to the hilt', for the hilt of a sword was in the form of the Cross! But I fear that this kind of superficial reflection was welcome to many of the clergy, to whom the War appeared to have made religion at last relevant to national life.[3]

The only other dignitary with whom the College had any particular concern, and that of a mainly negative kind, was the Dean, the Very Reverend Robert Andrew Mitchell. He had, I believe, had at one time something of a reputation in the Evangelical world and had for ten years been Vicar of a fashionable parish in the City of Westminster. If anything remained of his Evangelicalism at Lincoln it must have been of an extremely liberal type, for his sermons, while they were fine examples of elegant English style and were impressively delivered, were almost entirely devoid of any doctrinal content.

> Earth hath not anything to show more fair
> Than good Dean Mitchell with his snow-white hair;
> The thought how thin, the manner how intense,
> So little said, yet with what eloquence.

Thus we reflected in the Hostel, and it must be said that the Dean's attitude to the College and its works was far from helpful. I suspect that he considered any form of preparation for the ministry other than residence in an ancient university as unnecessarily wasteful of both time and money and he certainly thought that the restrained but definite churchmanship which was instilled in the College was superstitious and erroneous. Two incidents in particular in which he was involved stand out in my memory. The first is of a meeting at which he was on the platform where C. S. Lewis, who was then at the height of his fame with *The Screw-tape Letters*, was expounding in simple but uncompromising terms the basic teaching of orthodox Christianity. Now it was of course a dogma of the Dean's school of thought that intelligent modern men, and especially laymen, had no use for orthodox Christianity, which they regarded as offensive to their reason and irrelevant to their lives, but were avid for religion of an entirely undogmatic kind. Yet here was C. S. Lewis, a university don and a best-seller, defending the traditional Faith with confidence and good-humour. I can vividly remember the pathetic figure of poor Dean Mitchell, sadly shaking his head as one after another the articles of his disbelief were ruthlessly demolished. The other incident was connected with his behaviour when baptising the child of one of the residents of Minster Yard. One might have supposed that to one with his views baptism could at most be an unnecessary but tolerable ceremony, though dangerously open to superstitious interpretation. That this was his opinion can, I believe, be shown that when performing the rite he omitted every clause or epithet which affirmed or implied the doctrine of baptismal regeneration. As most of the clergy connected with the Cathedral or the College were present, this inevitably took on the character of an act of defiance, and it was certainly interpreted as such. I myself, among others, wrote to the Bishop — it was Skelton by this time — accusing the Dean of heresy. Skelton was no theologian but he had a firm grasp of the Faith and the Dean's action deeply distressed him. 'But', he said rather helplessly, 'if I say anything to him, he'll only reply that what he did was no more illegal than my use of the 1928 Prayer-Book.' Chancellor Srawley's reaction was characteristic. He was obviously disturbed by the doctrinal issue but what really upset him was the discovery that the Dean had deleted the words which offended him in certain books of common prayer, the property of the Dean and Chapter. With his strong northern sense of right and wrong and his professional concern with liturgical documents, he told me with some glee that he would make the Dean pay for the damage.

Dean Mitchell's relations with the College had never been cordial but with the coming of the War they became quite hostile, for the sight of a number of young men being trained for the ministry of the Word and Sacraments when they might have been in the armed forces of the Crown was understandably galling to an elderly cleric by whom the Gospel was understood in Erastian terms. Fortunately my personal contacts with him were very slight indeed. I only once ventured inside the sunless and dismal Victorian building on the hyperborean side of the cathedral which was the Dean's official residence, and this was to ask his permission to use one of the chapels for a service of the Fellowship of St Alban and St Sergius. I remember little of this depressing interview except his concern that the service should contain nothing of 'a Eucharistic nature'. It was characteristic of the uninviting atmosphere of the cathedral under his presidency that the chapel set apart for prayer in the cathedral was indicated simply by a dilapidated notice bearing the deterrent inscription 'Private Intercession'. Unfortunately this impression of something which had been started some time ago and then more or less forgotten was typical of the Lincoln diocese as I came to know it.

For, paradoxical as it may sound, the Lincoln diocese had never quite recovered from the effect produced by two great bishops who between them governed it from 1869 to 1910, Christopher Wordsworth, nephew of the poet, and Edward King, the hero of the famous Lincoln Judgment of 1890. Both of them had an unshakable conviction of the supernatural nature and authority of the Church (which did not prevent Wordsworth from holding that the Pope was antichrist). Both of them were outstanding for their pastoral zeal, and King, whose episcopate began in 1885, had acquired, both by his stand for the decencies of Catholic worship and by his personal holiness, an authority which lasted long after his death. It came as a great surprise to me to find in 1937 that people in Lincoln were still talking about Edward King as if he was still alive more than a quarter of a century after his death. But one of the consequences was that much that in his time had been significant and startling innovation had now come to be treasured in loyalty to him, but treasured largely as fossils with less and less relevance to the living reality of the Church. This was particularly true in the realm of worship, and the Churches which had acquired the longest reputation as strongholds of the Faith had settled into a loyal and dreary Prayer-Book catholicism, entirely untouched by the exciting developments in both thought and practice that had brought about such a transformation in the Eucharistic life of the continental churches.

The acknowledged headstone of Anglo-Catholicism in Lincoln
was the church of All Saints. I usually said mass there two or three
times a week, as I was normally able to celebrate only once a week
in the college chapel. Going to All Saints' could be a hazardous
business in the winter, as it involved descending an extremely steep
footpath which I never managed to negotiate in frosty weather
without falling once or more on my back. The Vicar was a splendid
little old Irishman from Newry, where he used to spend his holidays
with his two sisters, who made quantities of attractive tea-cosies in
the shape of Irish cottages and sold them for the benefit of the
disestablished Church. Canon Thomas Erskine Swanzy – he was
one of the half-hundred prebendaries of Lincoln and his prebend
had the intriguing title, derived from the much larger medieval
diocese, of Leighton Beau-desert – was erudite and entertaining;
he had been a gold-medallist at Trinity College, Dublin, before
reading theology at St John's College, Oxford. One could not fail
to be attracted by his eager, courteous and gentle manner, which
I always felt he must have caught from Bishop King, by whom he
had been ordained in 1894 to what was then considered the very
advanced church of St Swithin; he once told me, as of one caught in
some childhood delinquency, that as a daring young curate he had
been warned by his vicar for using the dangerous term 'Eucharist'
in a sermon. He was much respected and loved and was much in
demand as a confessor. His own preaching was of the old-fashioned
Tractarian kind, with frequent references to the Prayer Book and to
Scripture; I am almost sure that I once heard him say that one of
the things that our Lord told the Apostles during the Great Forty
Days was that people must not be admitted to communion until
they were confirmed. He referred to August 15th by the pleasant
English title of Lady Day in Harvest; he was prepared to allow
belief in the Assumption as a 'pious opinion', though I suspect
he considered its rejection as equally, if not slightly more, pious.
The Blessed Sacrament was perpetually reserved in All Saints' in a
tabernacle on the altar of a rather inconspicuous chapel, but neither
there nor, as far as I know, anywhere in the diocese, was there any
form of extra-liturgical devotion; he had had an aumbry made in
the wall of another chapel 'in case the 1928 Book was passed',
but this had of course been an unnecessary expenditure. He was
a practising member of the local lodge of Free-masons, though I
do not think this in fact weakened in any way either his belief
or his practice as a Christian priest; and I imagine that he felt
able to interpret the sagas of Hiram Abiff and King Solomon's
Temple with the same broad-minded tolerance which less orthodox

clerics have extended to the narratives of the Gospels. By the time that I came to know him he had become almost blind, though he could still read a book with the aid of a large magnifying-glass. This did not limit his mobility to any great extent but it led to a number of good-humoured anecdotes of varying plausibility. Thus it was alleged that, having bumped into the carcase of a sheep that was hanging outside a butcher's shop, he raised his hat with his customary courtesy, apologised to it and expressed the hope that he had not inconvenienced it. He had been Vicar of All Saints' since 1919 but had been curate of the same parish for the previous ten years. In 1921 he had himself acquired a curate, Norman Harding, who lived with him in the Vicarage ever since, for they were both unmarried and they became close friends. With Swanzy's increasing blindness Harding gradually took over most of the administration of the parish, and when Swanzy finally retired to his beloved Newry, he succeeded him as Vicar, having already joined him in the ranks of the prebendaries.

Harding was a thoroughly devoted, unselfish and unambitious priest, hardworking and ascetic, but almost entirely devoid of humour and imagination. He had a romantic view, not uncommon at the time, of the sober excellence of English medieval religion and, being a man of means, he had given this view generous expression by restoring a number of ancient churches in the diocese. Some of the liturgical equipment of All Saints' was also the fruit of his inspiration; I remember in particular a gigantic chasuble which completely enveloped and virtually immobilised the wearer, and a thurible which had chains of such excessive length that, when handling it, I was always afraid that I should get them round my neck and throttle myself. I imagine they had been copied from some medieval or Renaissance picture of censing angels and that it had been overlooked that human beings, unlike the holy bodiless powers, are subject to the law of gravity. Like some others of the Lincoln clergy, Harding had a positive genius for the inappropriate; it was typical that he should choose 'Gentle Jesus, meek and mild' as an introit hymn in Lent and that, having arranged a servers' festival one Easter Monday and filled All Saints' with boys and men of all ages and sizes, he inflicted upon them a repetition of the long and florid Victorian choral performance of the previous day which reduced them to impatient silence. Although he was personally unassertive his benefactions had made him the local figurehead of Catholic churchmanship, and the local direction of the Church Union, the nation-wide Anglo-Catholic organisation, had fallen into his hands. With his entirely inward-looking and pietistic mentality the only activity which he could think up for it was to go from Lincoln on bank-holiday pilgrimages to one or other of the churches which he had restored. In practice this involved a few of the city clergy, the servers from All Saints' and some middle-aged and elderly laypeople travelling by train or bus to some spot in the country, loaded with the vessels and apparatus for High Mass and Solemn Evensong. This was of course in itself a legitimate and indeed laudable activity but as the sole expression of Catholic worship and evangelism in the diocese it left much to be desired. There were, of course, a number of good Catholic priests scattered about the diocese, many of whom were struggling bravely and devoutly, frequently under conditions of loneliness and sometimes of deliberate opposition, but the lack of inspiration and leadership was lamentable. There was a society for mission and renewal founded by Chancellor Benson in 1875 under the title *Novate Novale* ('Break up your fallow-ground', Jer. iv.3, Vulg.), but it had long ceased to have any real drive. In 1943 we had a full-dress I. C. F.[4] Crusade in the industrial sector of Lincoln and got the College actively involved in it, but it was never properly followed up. The College never functioned as the intellectual and theological power-house of the diocese which I believe it was capable of becoming and which I think its percipient founders Wordsworth and Benson intended it to be. For, as much as Minster Yard though of a different kind, we too, I fear, were an enclave.

Within our walls, however, both life and work were absorbing and rewarding. The students were a remarkably mixed bag, in every respect, age, social origin, intellectual achievement, churchmanship. But all were male, and none, I think, were out-and-out Protestant fundamentalists. By no means all came from an Anglican background. At least one was a former Roman Catholic seminarian. Another, the son of an old-fashioned Baptist minister, told me that his father, on being informed that at Lincoln we had a daily Eucharist, made the puzzled comment, 'But is it not very depressing to begin each day by commemorating the Master's last sad meal with his disciples?' However, serious problems of doctrine or practice were rare, and there was a genuine sense of unity in the common life. I believe this was very largely due to the fact that there was a uniform pattern of worship which was probably nobody's ideal but to which all felt able to conform, rather than, as in some theological colleges, an alternation of 'high-church', 'low-church' and 'liberal' observances. Occasionally a student would leave, almost always by mutual consent, but, although such cases have often a sad aspect, a period in a seminary is sometimes the only way of finding whether what looks like a vocation to the priesthood is such in fact, and there need be no suggestion of either disgrace or catastrophe if the answer should turn out to be negative. Almost as important as the selection and the training of an ordinand is the choice of the parish to which he is ordained – his 'title', to use the technical term; for to a very real extent his first parish, no less than the theological college, provides an integral and special part of a priest's training. This is the more important in view of the comparative brevity of the Anglican seminary course in comparison with, say, that of the Roman Catholic Church. Many a parish offers a promising field for the labours of a mature priest, especially one with particular gifts and experiences, which could be disastrous for a young and inexperienced deacon. Nor, it must be added, has every rector or vicar, even the most devoted and capable, the special qualities needed for a good trainer of deacons.

I myself was only remotely involved in these personal issues; it was sometimes said that the Warden was concerned with the souls of the students, the Sub-Warden with their minds and the Chaplain with their bodies, and I suppose this aphorism was as true as the rather inadequate anthropological trichotomy on which it was based. Certainly I was given both time and encouragement to follow up my particular scholarly interests and I hope that something of what I acquired may have brushed off on my pupils. I have already described how my interest in the philosophy of science, itself an offshoot of my training in applied mathematics, had led to a concern with natural theology and hence to the publication of my first substantial book, *He Who Is*, in 1943. But, while I was still myself in parish work I had inevitably had to widen my thinking to embrace, however superficially, the Christian revelation. I have already mentioned two particular branches of Christian theology which, in very different ways, had forced themselves on my attention. One was Christian Spirituality – the doctrine of prayer – which had become a matter of concern to me simply because of my failure to find any help from the instruction that I had received in dealing with the obstacles (in fact quite elementary, though I did not know this) in my own attempts to pray. The other was Christian Social Doctrine or, as we insisted on calling it, Christian Sociology.[5] To many people, and indeed to many of their proponents, these appeared to stand for two conflicting and, indeed, mutually incompatible views of the nature of the Christian religion; on the one hand were the pietists, entirely absorbed in the trivialities of the sacristy and the cultivation of their own souls and indifferent to the sufferings of their fellow men and women, on the other hand were the social activists passionately concerned for the relief of human ills but indifferent to the fact that man's final destiny is not in this world but beyond the grave. While only too conscious of the fact that many professing and sincere Christians were content to identify the Christian religion with one side or the other of this dichotomy, I felt quite unable to do this myself. This was not because I felt in a state of irresoluble indecision between the two and certainly not because I felt that I had myself made a spectacular advance along either path, but because it seemed clear to me that both Spirituality and Sociology were rational consequences of the Christian revelation and that they could not therefore in fact be ultimately incompatible, even if they had often mistakenly been made to appear so. At this point I must interrupt this train of hought to describe an event which, though quite unspectacular in itself, has had, in its inner significance as well as its practical implications, the chief controlling influence in my subsequent life. On October 6th 1939 I made my first profession as a member of the Oratory of the Good Shepherd.

The Church of England Year Book lists the Oratory of the Good Shepherd under the heading of 'Religious Communities', but it simply describes it as 'a dispersed Society of unmarried priests and laymen living under a rule', and we do our best to make it plain that we are not, in the technical sense, 'religious' and that the promises under which we are professed are not, in the technical sense, 'vows'. A readable and informative account of the Oratory is given by Penelope Fitzgerald in her delightful book *The Knox Brothers* (Wilfred was one of the very early members and later became Superior), though she is, I think, inclined to exaggerate the degree of austerity which some of us practice. Fr Henry Brandreth's privately published historical sketch gives a full and accurate narrative down to the date of its writing, 1958. It is in some respects easier to depict the Oratory by saying what it is not than by saying what it is. Its unity does not depend upon its possessing a central, or indeed any, house, though experiments have been made in that direction which are unlikely to be repeated. Its members are not under any formal obligations of obedience as regards work or residence, though they have a moral obligation of consultation and of considering the general welfare of the Oratory. They have full control of their property and income, as is inevitable in a society which cannot make itself responsible for their support; but they are subject to an annual levy according to their means and have to account for the disposal of any surplus. Some corporate help is available for brethren with special needs. They are organised in local groups or 'colleges', which meet regularly in chapter, though some members have of necessity to keep in touch mainly by correspondence. They have to make a retreat each year, if possible with other members, and those who are able meet annually in General Chapter. Those in the United States and Australia have their own provincial organisation. The Manual of the Oratory describes the Aim of the Oratory as 'the adoration of God in the service of the Lord Jesus Christ and the imitation of his most holy life' and it offers for the guidance of its members the seven 'Notes' of Fellowship, Liberty, Stewardship, Labour of the Mind, the Love that makes for Peace, Discipline and Joy. But the basic obligation is that of regular prayer and, in the absence of a geographical or residential centre such as a religious order would have, this is of quite primary importance as the unifying force of the Oratory. Attendance at Mass at least five times a week, conscientious recitation of the Church's offices, a specified time for mental prayer each day (these with generous relaxation for holiday periods) and daily mention of the brethren before God, this is the structure of disciplined prayer to which the brethren commit themselves – and which, needless to say, as their formal reports manifest, they do not always manage to attain. None of us would claim to have reached a high degree of sanctity, but speaking for myself I can at least say that without the Oratory I would have spent much less time in prayer than I have spent and would have been a much less satisfactory priest than even I have been.

Stability has always been something of a problem in the Oratory, though rather less than might be expected when it is remembered that we have virtually none of the facilities for training and testing our neophytes comparable with those that a religious community is able to employ in the novitiate. There is a probationary period of at least one and at most three years, and recently we have assigned each probationer to a professed member for instruction and counsel. Profession is for one year to begin with and may be renewed for an equal or a longer period; finally, profession may be made for life, but it is a fundamental principle that all professed members enjoy equal status, irrespective of the period for which each has been professed. The form of profession makes it plain that it carries with it a firm purpose of renewal, though no formal commitment. Nobody is expected to apply for admission in the expectation that sooner or later he will find a reason for leaving; and the solemn nature of profession is underlined by the provision that any brother who develops doubts about his vocation 'shall not take any action inconsistent with his profession before the period for which he has been professed has elapsed', with a gloss to the effect that the prospect of matrimony is not an exception.

The Oratory began with a small group of chaplains in the University of Cambridge before the First World War, who felt the need of some common rule of life but it was not until 1919 that the first formal professions took place. The subsequent growth was slow and met with a number of set-backs, and when I was professed in 1939 there were only ten other members, and as five of these were closely associated with Cambridge and another, who was dean of a Cambridge college, had just resigned his membership, it is not surprising that many people had the idea that the Oratory was a kind of religious club for unmarried clergymen on the Cam. This impression was in fact false; it had had members working in Africa and Australia, as well as in parishes in England, and as it grew again, which it did remarkably in the years after the Second World War, it became much more parochial than academic. At the moment of writing, out of a membership of thirty-five (our numbers have fallen slightly during the last decade) we have not a single university don.

My own first contact (it was not more than that) with the Oratory was with Edward Wynn and Eric Milner White when I was an undergraduate at Cambridge. I occasionally went to tea at the house which the Oratory, or, rather, two or three of its members, were then running in Lady Margaret Road; it was later given to the Society of St Francis, who were far better equipped to handle it. I certainly never imagined myself becoming a member, and I had not at that time any thought of becoming a priest. (Incidentally, although the Oratory's constitution allows for laymen to be members, it has never held any for long, with the exception of an occasional ordinand on the way to the priesthood.) But my closest friend Christopher Waddams joined the Oratory soon after he returned to Cambridge in 1929 and I frequently used to stay with him at St Catherine's College, besides our having a number of holidays together both in England and on the Continent, right down to the beginning of the Second World War. It was not therefore very surprising that when I went to Lincoln and no longer had the continuous support provided by the pastoral setting of a Catholic parish, I should turn to the Oratory for the spiritual fellowship that I needed. The requirement of celibacy posed no special problem; Fr StJohn had drilled that into me in my first curacy. My decision did come as a surprise to some of my friends, who only knew of the Oratory as as the seed-bed of those notorious Catholic modernists Wilfred Knox and Alec Vidler. I would only comment on that reaction that the Oratory has never been committed to the theological outlook of even its most distinguished members and that both Wilfred and Alec were, in their pastoral ministrations, very typical and rather conservative Catholic priests. Alec's early ministry included six years in a rebel parish in the diocese of that really notorious modernist Bishop Barnes of Birmingham, and he still proudly exhibits a framed letter in which that prelate, bidding him farewell, expresses the hope that he will be more obedient to authority in the future than he has been in the past. There is no point in my relating the details of his career as Warden of St Deiniol's Library, Hawarden, Editor of the journal *Theology*, Canon of Windsor, and Dean of King's College, Cambridge, when we have his own account in his autobiography *Scenes of a Clerical Life*, but piety demands remembrance of the long service that he gave to the Oratory as Secretary-General. He now lives in retirement, as the Oratory's senior member, at Rye in Sussex, where, a patriarchcal figure with a long white beard, he inhabits the Vidler family residence, having brought his public life to its climax by filling the office of Mayor. Ironically enough, he was chosen to deliver in 1975 the official lecture for the centenary of Bishop Barnes!

Wilfred, too, has received the distinction of biography in print, not from his own pen but from that of his niece Penelope Fitzgerald in the book already mentioned. He was entirely unambitious, unselfconscious and unaesthetic; everything that he did, including his recreations of gardening and fishing, were done with a concentrated intensity which manifested his sense that time was precious. He was tone-deaf and his occasional attempts to sing mass were excruciating. He was Superior of the Oratory from 1941 until his death in 1950, and one of the great services which he did for us was to eliminate any traces of romanticism or sentimentalism; for he was quite incapable of humbug. 'That is my religion', he once remarked, pointing to a passing laundry-van which bore the name 'Loud and Western'. Not that in fact there was anything literally loud about him, for he normally spoke in a rapid and almost inaudible undertone. And his religion was Western, not in the sense that his theology was Tridentine but that its external manifestation was swift and businesslike. The Mass was essential, but, that being taken for granted, the sensible thing was to get it over as soon as possible. He would never allow the reputed liberalism of his theology to be made an excuse for the evasion of normal Catholic discipline. There was a story which came from the the final period of his life – precisely simultaneous, as it happened, with his superiorship of the Oratory – when he was Chaplain and Theology Supervisor at my own old college, Pembroke. An undergraduate came to him and told him that, having read Wilfred's writings on the New Testament, he had come to the conclusion that the sacraments had been invented by St Paul and that he therefore intended to have nothing to do with them. Wilfred, as was his custom, prodded a microscopic fire into non-existence with the poker for some time and then said in a rather depressed murmur: 'I think I ought to tell you that it is generally supposed that I know more about St Paul than anyone else in Cambridge. Do you wish to continue this discussion?' Apparently he did, for the upshot of the encounter was that the undergraduate made his first confession. The story is possibly *ben trovato* rather than *vero*, but it is typical of Wilfred's simple honesty. He would never have made such a claim about anything else – he was far too humble – but St Paul was his speciality and it was his business to know. Occassionally Wilfred would make a remark of a certain literary quality that reminded one that he was the brother of Ronnie. Thus, he remarked of a certain tedious colleague with whom he had to share fire-watching duties during the War, 'To describe the man as a B. F. would be to inflict a serious injustice upon that large body of distinguished members of the University who have hitherto been considered to have an exclusive right to that honourable title.' When, years later at Oxford, I used to meet Ronnie at intervals it struck me that, while Ronnie was indubitably more entertaining on paper (in fact I do not think Wilfred ever attempted humorous writing), Wilfred, when in the mood and if one was close enough to hear him, was the more sparkling conversationalist. I was amused on one occasion when Ronnie, having ascertained that I knew his brother, anxiously enquired whether Wilfred was becoming more inaudible or he himself was going deaf.

For some years we had in the Oratory that gifted but wayward American scholar Dr Robert Casey. When he joined us in 1940 he was a professor at Brown University, Rhode Island. He came to England, as Dean and Theological Supervisor of Sidney Sussex College, Cambridge, in 1949, but left the Oratory in 1954. He died a few years later. He was an extremely brilliant student of first-century Gnosticism and cognate matters, and combined his academic work with psychotherapeutic practice, in which he acquired professional qualifications. He was, I think, the only person I had then met who was a genuine Modernist on the Roman Catholic model. He once tried to conclude an argument with the words 'The trouble with you guys is you've never heard of Loisy', and was surprised when I suggested that the trouble with him was perhaps that he had not got beyond that point. At a meeting at which we were both speaking about the Incarnation, he propounded the thesis that Jesus was infallible in his 'Second Body' the Church but in his 'First Body' was as fallible as anyone else. When someone not unreasonably asked how the Second Body was to be identified, he replied that some people would identify it with the Church of Rome but he preferred the C. of E. Fortunately, by the time that I was asked to comment on his position he had left to catch a train. He had a refreshing way of dismissing those who did not share his attitude. Billy Graham, who was then at the climax of his success, was referred to as 'the outer darkness', and when Robert Casey was asked at a multidenominational meeting what was the difference in the United States between the Methodists and the Presbyterians he replied briefly that the Presbyterians could write their own names. Preaching a University Sermon on Ascension Day in 1951 or thereabouts, he claimed, I was told, that at last we could confidently believe in the Ascension of Jesus, because, whereas it was previously witnessed to only by New-Testament documents which were admittedly quite unhistorical, now the Pope had defined the Assumption of Mary, and if she was in heaven her Son must obviously be there too. When he was told that this sermon had caused grave offence, he simply rejoined, 'Well, they wouldn't have objected if I'd denied the Resurrection' – which was no doubt perfectly true.

The evenness of the College routine at Lincoln was frequently relieved by lectures and addresses from visitors, many of whom were distinguished and some were distinctly memorable. Dom Bernard Clements, at the height of his fame as a retreat conductor, Maurice Reckitt on Christian sociology, Robert Sencourt on St John of the Cross, George Florovsky on the Orthodox Church and George Addleshaw on the *Jeunesse Ouvrière Chrétienne* remain still vividly in my mind. Fr Florovsky's début was particularly striking. Though fluent in English he never entirely mastered English pronunciation and it was very imperfect at the time in question. Hardly any of the students had seen an Orthodox priest before and they were somewhat overawed by the mere appearance of this lanky cassocked figure with the straggly beard. But they were quite devastated by his opening sentence, which appeared to be about an Orthodox lemon being confronted with Anglican zoology. What in fact he had said was: 'The Orthodox layman, when he first meets Anglican theology, thinks it is crypto-Nestorian; the Anglican layman, when he first meets Orthodox theology, thinks it is crypto-monophysite'; and he proceeded to give a searching, but ecumenical, discourse, which included the surprising claim that St Augustine was really an Eastern father! We had frequent visits from Fr Gabriel Hebert and other members of the Society of the Sacred Mission, for their mother house at Kelham was within easy reach. Their chairmaster, a serene and quietly humorous little man called Brother Edwin, used to come over once a week to do what he could with our own students' very assorted voices. I shall say more about Fr Gabriel later on. Among my personal guests on various occasions were Christopher Waddams and Gregory Dix; both, in their different ways, were very congenial visitors but I do not remember either of them formally addressing the students. The news that Gregory Dix was around was likely to provoke mixed reactions. Chancellor Srawley was enthusiastic about *The Shape of the Liturgy* and was stimulated by it to produce a second edition of his own small but highly rated work *The Early History of the Liturgy*. The two of them would have long and profound discussions together, from which Gregory (whom the Chancellor for some obscure reason always referred to as 'Mr Dix', though he quite happily spoke of 'Dom Morin' and 'Dom Connolly') emerged hoarse and exhausted from the effort of coping with the Cancellarial deafness. Gregory's visits usually had the occult purpose of fortifying two protégés of his in parishes in the Wolds against the interferences of an ignorant and blundering archdeacon, who had spent almost all his ordained life in the Army and seemed devoid of any understanding of either theology or the Church. I could see Gregory's hand in the incumbent's explanation to the Archdeacon that he had set up a confessional in obedience to No. XXV of the XXXIX Articles, which declared that 'the Sacraments were not ordained of Christ to be gazed upon', and in the subtleties which reduced a bewildered suffragan bishop to maintaining that the incumbent's practices were 'against the law, not any particular law, but just against the law'! Much appreciated were the occasional appearances of a R.A.F. chaplain, whose uniform concealed the identity of a Roman Catholic Benedictine monk; he enjoyed sitting in the narthex of the chapel for Compline, explaining that he would not occupy a stall as she was without his habit. A very popular event was the occasional celebration of the Eastern Orthodox liturgy, when, as happened from time to time, we had an Orthodox priest staying with us. We had a musical setting of the text in English, which our own choir would carefully practise, but they were liable to be thrown into confusion by a tendency which seems endemic in the Orthodox clergy, that, however solemnly they may have committed themselves the night before, they seem unable to refrain, in the actual celebration, from rushing into any language or variant that appeals to them. As I look back on the years of the War, I find it surprising to see how many activities were possible, in spite of the obvious restrictions and the incessant exhortation to consider whether one's journey was really necessary.

The Malvern Conference of January 1941 was a formidable thing to organise and carry through even in the earlier days of a world war. To descend to a more trivial level, it was perhaps surprising that, with very little trouble, I was able to obtain permission to travel to the Irish Republic to take part in a Clergy School of the Church of Ireland. Whether or not I was able to edify the Hibernian clergy, I can have contributed little to the downfall of Hitler, and it says at least something for the concern of our Government with the preservation of culture that this kind of participation was still possible. Indeed I find myself wondering whether the Second World War may not turn out to have produced fewer obstacles to the Church's activity than may be produced by the financial inflation of the nineteen-eighties. I certainly found my brief Irish visit a welcome interlude in the drabness and dulness of war-time England. The journey itself was tedious. Because of the possible danger from submarines we were kept waiting on the boat for several hours at Holyhead for an unpublished time of departure; on landing at Dun Laoghaire I was surprised to be met by my host, who had found out the time of arrival by simply phoning the harbour – and this when there was a German embassy fully functioning in Dublin! Food was plentiful, there was no black-out and I heard only one aeroplane in a fortnight. The trains were running on peat – known locally, of course, as turf – of which there were mountains beside each station, and on the main lines there was only one train a day. The journey from Dublin to Waterford, with stops at every station for ingress and egress of living creatures of various species, was slow but full of local colour, and the Bishop's house, a beautiful classical pavilion thoughtfully separated by the wide river Suir from his cathedral, was an almost incredibly peaceful enclave for realistic theology in a world at war. Ireland was of course neutral, but it was said that so many Irishmen had illegally played truant to join the British forces that the government of Eire had informally arranged transport to save trouble. A favourite story was that of the two Irishmen in a British bombing plane on their way to an objective in Germany who were arguing furiously about their President, Eamon De Valera. 'Well, you must admit one thing:' his supporter insisted, 'At least he's kept us out of the War.' One of the less important but nevertheless interesting pieces of information with which I returned was that the enigmatic song-refrain *Caleno custure me* had been discovered to mean 'The colleen by the river Suir'. Another was that in Ireland it is socially unkind to give an informed categorical answer to an enquiry until everyone present has given a hypothetical one, based on hearsay, speculation or vague reminiscence; this is why the Irish are such splendid conversationalists.

When it became clear to everyone that at last the War was drawing to its long desired end, it became equally clear to me that my time at Lincoln should come to an end with it. In the years of reconstruction Eric Abbott would certainly be called to a new and wider sphere of work — he did in fact become Dean of King's College, London, in 1945. The new Warden, whoever he might be, would have his own ideas and would not want to inherit his predecessor's impedimenta, even if the impedimenta were happy to be inherited. It seemed to me that after some years of helping to prepare men for the ministry of the Church that I myself ought probably to be exercising that ministry in some form or another. With my complete lack of academic education in theology, I had no aspirations for a university post, unless perhaps of the chaplaincy or wardenship type; what I thought I might perhaps be offered was a parish in which there were opportunities for the sort of adult religious education that I had done at Stockwell and Westminster, with possibly some wider diocesan activities. I did not want to push myself forward, as I have always believed that a priest should be prepared to go wherever the Church needs him, and I think that other people are usually better able than oneself to judge of one's aptitude for any particular work. It did, however, come as rather a shock, though it was no doubt a salutary lesson in humility, to discover that apparently the Church did not need me anywhere at all. One bishop after another was approached in my favour; some expressed sympathy, some were evasive, some were definitely hostile, but none had anything to offer me. One indeed told me orally that he was going to recommend me for a parish that had become vacant in a well-known university town; but he wrote to me apologetically soon after to say that he had found someone else whom he thought would be more suitable —

which was very probably the case. The truth was that, apart from my personal inadequacies – and it must be admitted that dealing for some years with theological students provides a very restricted area of pastoral experience –, I had become identified with almost everything that appeared disloyal and rebellious to the ecclesiastical establishment at the time. Inter-church relationships and reunion-schemes, liturgical revision, extra-liturgical devotions, Catholic sociology, basic doctrinal orthodoxy itself – on all these matters I had become associated with persons and positions that were a nuisance to the non-party party. Worse than all these was the dreadful stigma of 'Thomism'. With Archibishop Temple I was indeed on good terms. While he never quite shook off the idealist philosophy of his early Oxonian years, he had recently shown himself increasingly ready to meet and listen to the rebellious 'younger theologians' of whom I was one. He had a deep affection for Dom Gregory Dix, the most rebellious of the lot, and he spent at least three extended periods in conference with us; for the last of these he was himself the host, at the Old Palace at Canterbury.[6] But neither he nor anybody else had any suggestions for my future, and my anxiety was increased by the fact that it was now becoming necessary for me to provide more support for my mother than I had been able to give as Sub-Warden of the Scholae Cancellarii. At this point Vigo Demant brought to my notice and advertisement in *The Times* for someone in priest's orders to teach theology and act as chaplain to the undergraduates at Christ Church, Oxford. This was a one-year appointment but it offered the prospect of election for a longer period to a status equivalent to that of a fellow at other colleges. Vigo remarked that he knew of my reluctance to apply for an appointment, but he very reasonably pointed out that if nobody ever applied for advertised vacancies one's availability was unlikely to be known. It seemed to me that, whether it was known or not, I was very unlikely, as a Cantabrigian trained only in mathematics, to be chosen to teach theology at the most prestigious college in Oxford, of which I knew virtually nothing and where I was known by virtually nobody. Wondering at my own audacity however, I sent in my application to the Dean. I received a reply that it would be seriously considered, and, after a long and agonising period of waiting, during which I was at least spared the the embarrassment of any alternative suggestions, I was asked to go for an interview on 20 January 1945.

I stayed for the week-end with Robert Mortimer, who was later to become Bishop of Exeter but at this time was a Canon of Christ Church and Professor of Moral and Pastoral Theology;

he had formerly held the position for which I was now an applicant and this was my first meeting with him. I remember little of the interview, except that Canon Jenkins, about whom I shall have more to say later, asked me whether I should be badly shocked if an undergraduate told me he did not believe in the Christian religion and I replied that I did not think that I should. I was to discover later on, as I suspected from the start, that very little is likely to emerge from such an interview that has not been discovered already from written and printed documents or will not be manifested more naturally in the more informal conditions of dinner and common-room; though I suppose that, as the candidate leaves the room, the committee are able to see whether he washes behind the ears. I do not remember feeling particularly nervous and my main impression was one of slight embarrassement and unreality, which the committee obviously felt as much as I did. (On the few occasions when I have myself been a member of such a commitee I have verified this from the other side of the table.) I felt no urge to behave like the candidate for the chaplaincy of another college who, when the Head of the College opened the proceedings with the diplomatic formula, 'I hope, Mr X, you slept well in our guest-room last night', replied, 'No, Mr Warden, I didn't sleep a wink. The bed in your guest-room is the most uncomfortable that I have ever experienced' − and acquired a majority of votes on the spot! What I believe stood me in much better stead was a conversation that I had in the common room after dinner. Everything was most tactfully and agreeably managed, but I was quietly aware that I was in fact having a few minutes' individual conversation with everyone in the room, until I found myself introduced to that formidable character Lord Cherwell, the Professor of what we would now call Experimental Physics but Oxford still designates by the antique name of Experimental Philosophy, and Winston Churchill's scientific right-hand man throughout the War. The Prof, as he was always called, became extremely interested when I told him that I had had once worked on Relativity and Quantum Theory under R. H. Fowler and we went into a huddle which must have lasted, I suppose, for nearly half an hour. I heard afterwards that the spectacle of that tough agnostic the Prof in deep and prolonged conversation with the strange Cantabrigian clergyman who had just been interviewed profoundly impressed the company, and I have always believed that I owed my election to Lord Cherwell as much as to anyone or anything else. We became in fact very good friends and I was even able on occasion to indulge in a little tactful leg-pulling. He always maintained that it was a waste of time to investigate paranormal phenomena as it was obvious that there could be nothing in them; I would point out that he was just like the scholars who refused to look through Galileo's telescope because they knew on *a priori* grounds that Jupiter could not have any satellites. His agnosticism was in fact of a very tentative kind, and readers of his biography by Lord Birkenhead will remember the document in which he described the conflict between science and religion as 'purely artificial' and anyone who maintains that such a conflict is necessary as 'an out-of-date Victorian'.[7] He was a complex character, but those who saw him only as the ruthless public figure[8] and knew nothing of the kindly aspect which appeared in private, especially towards the young, seriously misjudge him. Anyhow, whatever was the reason, on the Tuesday I received a note from the Dean at Pusey House, where I had gone on to stay for a couple of nights, telling me that the committee had decided to recommend me for election and asking me to call upon him the following day. In due course I received formal notice from the secretary of the Governing Body and I came into residence at the end of May. For the next seventeen years Christ Church was my home, as a Lecturer for the first year, and after that a Student and Tutor.

Notes

1. I was amused to find, years later, that the Rumanians pride themselves on the fact that theirs is the only Orthodox nation that has a vernacular liturgy. The Greeks, they pointed out, use patristic Greek and the Slavs use Church Slavonic, neither of which could today be possibly described as a vernacular!
2. Cf pp 92–93.
3. It was astonishing how, under the excitement of the War, many well instructed priests seemed to lose entirely their capacity of Christian judgment. I will give just four examples in my experience. (1) A most compassionate priest, who was so tender-hearted that he refused to recite the verse of the psalm about dashing the Babylonian children against the stones, vehemently maintained that the British bombing strategy should be concentrated on schools and infirmaries. 'The children of one war are the soldiers of the next;' he argued, 'The Germans have started two wars and if we don't stop them they'll start a third.' (2) Another priest wrote to me during the blitz: 'I see the Archbishop has said we ought to pray for the Germans. But I don't pray for devils.' (3) I was strongly attacked by the incumbent of a large Lincolnshire parish for saying that I was not sure that we would win the War. He maintained that we were bound to do so,

as we were defending a Christian civilisation. When I replied that the Byzantine was a Christian civilisation but fell to the Turks in 1453, he answered that, unlike ours, the Byzantine civilisation was largely corrupt and deserved to fall! (4) A preacher assured his hearers that all their moral problems about the War would vanish if they thought of it not as a war but as a crusade. No doubt the crusaders who sacked Constantinople in 1204 consoled themselves with a similar reflection!

4. Industrial Christian Fellowship.

5. It is sometimes objected that sociology is a purely empirical science, concerned simply with the way that social institutions function, and that you can no more have a Christian sociology than a Christian chemistry or a Christian mathematics. That there can be, and is, such an empirical science I agree, and its findings, when accurate, are important. Social institutions, however, are composed of human beings, and beyond the question how in fact they function there is the question how they ought to function and what ends they ought to seek, to say nothing of their prospects of achieving those ends. This is a question about which Christian theology should have something to say, because it has something to say about human beings. This is what is meant by Christian Sociology.

6. Cf F. A. Iremonger, *William Temple*, 590ff, 607ff. I can now reveal that 'X' was Michael Bruce and 'Y' was Gregory Dix.

7. *The Prof in Two Worlds*, 169f.

8. 'Lord Cherwell, that sharp-witted, sharp-tongued, pertinaceous and more than slightly conspiratorial character who had long been Churchill's closest friend and confident' (Lord (R. A.) Butler, *The Art of the Possible*, p. 109).

Chapter Seven

Four Outstanding Priests

'But I am among you as one that serves.'

– Luke xxii.27.

I intend at this point to interrupt the chronological flow of my narrative to say something about four very outstanding priests whom I was privileged to know intimately during the most productive periods of their lives. Three were members of religious communities – Dom Gregory Dix, of Nashdom Abbey, Fr Gabriel Hebert, of the Society of the Sacred Mission, and Fr Lionel Thornton, of the Community of the Resurrection; the fourth was a parish priest, Canon Charles Hutchinson. Any one of them would have merited a full-length biographical study; none has received one. My brief accounts are no substitute for that, but they have the merit of deriving from intimate personal acquaintance, and I should be sorry if my recollections of them went unrecorded.

GREGORY DIX, O.S.B.

I may have met one or two people who were more profound intellectually than Dom Gregory Dix; I have met none whose minds were more lively or more razor-like. If I had to find one adjective to describe the impact that he made on first acquaintance it would, I think, have to be 'elvish'; for, like an elf, he was small and vivacious, and, with his pointed features and tightly compressed lips, made one wonder what mischief he was going to embark upon next. For he had a tremendous sense of mischief, both in word and in action, and his comments could often have been scarifying but for the fact that, even at their most devastating, they were entirely free from malice. Although he provoked hostility in many quarters, by both his theological opinions and his ecclesiastical politics, it was rare indeed for that hostility to outlast

151

even a brief personal contact. As Fr Mark Tweedy, C.R., wrote after his death, 'one of the peculiarly noteworthy points about Gregory Dix, especially in the later period when he was known far and wide, was the genuine personal affection he inspired in those who regarded his ideas and expressed opinions as emanating from the belly of hell.'[1]

George Eglinton Alston Dix ('Gregory' in religion) came of a sober and pious family; his father was a highly respected clergyman who became Principal of the Anglican teachers' training College of St Mark and St John at Chelsea. He went up to Merton College, Oxford, to read Modern History in the extremely undisciplined days after the First World War and was as undisciplined as most of his contemporaries. His slight stature qualified him to cox the college eight, but his absence at the critical moment saved him from being sent down with the rest of the crew after they had placed an unpopular don on a bonfire. In two other noteworthy episodes he played a peripheral but not a negligible part. There was the occasion when another of the dons, while peacefully strolling in the garden was seized with a sudden violent pain which was at first believed to be lumbago but was traced to the presence in his buttock of a bullet which it was plain could only have been fired from an overlooking room whose occupant was known to possess a gun and to be somewhat irresponsible in its use. The occupant was found to be dead drunk and to be in the company of his friend Mr Dix, but the most minute search of the college revealed no trace of the weapon or of any means by which it could have been removed undetected, though circumstantial evidence pointed clearly to Dix as the agent. Only later and under a promise of immunity did he explain that, realising that any attempt by him to conceal it would certainly be detected, he had made it up into a parcel, addressed it to himself and, when the porter's back was turned, deposited it with tradesmen's deliveries in the lodge. The other episode was that of the famous lecture by Dr Emil Busch.

During and after the War news had been filtering through of the sensational developments in therapeutic method of the great Viennese psycho-analysts Freud and Jung but there had been virtually no personal interchange as yet. Intense interest was therefore aroused by the announcement of a lecture on the subject to be delivered in Oxford by the distinguished authority Dr Emil Busch under the auspices of a society called the Oxford and Home Counties Psychological Association. A number of senior members of the University were impressed by the importance of the occasion and promised to attend. What neither they nor anybody outside a strictly guarded circle knew was that the whole thing was a carefully organised undergraduate hoax, with George Dix in a key position. He had in fact two functions to perform, theoretical and practical respectively. The former was to write Dr Busch's lecture for him, which Dix did by selecting and editing passages from a psychological journal; the second was to stand by the switchboard and plunge the hall into darkness when, as it was felt was bound to happen, the audience began to see through the deception. I do not know whether the text has been anywhere preserved, but if so I have never seen it; but two memorable fragments of whose authenticity I have been assured are 'In psychology causes always come after their effects' and 'Consciousness is not so much as fluid as a background'. As it happened, Dix had to delegate the second function to a fellow-conspirator, because on the great night he was himself in bed with influenza. He described the astonishment which he experienced when later in the evening a kindly don, who had heard of his interest in the lecture and of his disappointment at being prevented from attending, came to tell him that it had been an outstanding success and that various distinguished senior members present had paid glowing tributes to the erudition of Dr Busch and the importance of his discoveries. At the totally unexpected news that the hoax had gone right through the evening entirely undetected, Dix, who was curing his influenza by the time-honoured remedy of whisky, became so hilarious that his visitor, misinterpreting the reason, remarked that because one had flu there was no reason to drink oneself silly and departed in a huff. It was, I believe, only when an undergraduate journal published two photographs of Dr Busch, one with his beard and the other without, that the dreadful truth began to be known, and by then too many senior people had compromised themselves for much to be done about it. But there had been, Dix told me, two very anxious moments. The first was before the lecture, when Dr Busch was seized with a fit of nervousness and took so much alcohol to restore his courage that he was almost unable to appear at all; the second was when a questioner asked how his views related to those of Dr Jung. Dr Busch had in fact never heard of Jung, as his lecture had been based entirely on Freud, but his presence of mind did not desert him. 'Jung? Jung?!' he exploded, 'His apple-cart upsetten ist!' And no one dared to mention Jung again.

In spite of the turbulence of his academic career (it culminated in 1923 with a second class which did no justice to his ability), Dix was clear that he had a vocation to the priesthood. After a minimal period at Wells Theological College, where he established a great veneration for the erudite and eccentric Dean Armitage Robinson, he was ordained to a lecture ship at Keble College.[2] Very soon he felt the attraction of the religious life and began the association with Nashdom Abbey which culminated in his taking solemn monastic vows in 1940. I shall not attempt to describe the subsequent period, which included some years in West Africa in the diocese of Accra, for my own acquaintance with him began only shortly before the Second World War. From then until his death in 1952 our friendship steadily deepened.

We met a number of times before and in the early days of the War, frequently in London. I often stayed during my vacations at the famous church of All Saints, Margaret Street, where his Benedictine confrere Dom Bernard Clements was doing a great work in the pulpit, in the confessional and on the radio, and Gregory was a frequent and often unexpected visitor. Also we were both quite deeply associated with the apostolate which that very impressive woman Berta Travers was exercising at the Pax House and the Dacre Press. She was the widow of Canon Duncan Travers of the Universities Mission to Central Africa and had also formed a close link with the Benedictine nuns of West Malling in Kent. Soon after I left St Matthew's, Westminster, she opened in Victoria Street the Pax House for the sale of religious books and works of art, especially those from abroad. This, however, was merely the base for a more ambitious project, in the form of a new Anglican publishing firm with an unimpeachably Catholic orientation; thus the Dacre Press came into being. My own contribution to its lists was a small work on St John of the Cross entitled *A Guide to Mount Carmel*[3] and the paper-back series *Signposts*, which I edited in conjunction with Julian Casserley. Gregory, however, having largely taken over informally the editorial direction of the Press, made it the vehicle not only for several minor but quite important writings of his own, but also for one of the major theological works of this century, his massive *Shape of the Liturgy*; but more of that later. With the War, both Gregory's community and the Dacre Press went into traumatic up-heavals. Gregory himself went to look after his brother Ronald's church of St Michael, Beaconsfield, in the absence of the latter as an army chaplain. Mrs Travers, anticipating the need of a bolt-hole for staff and stock in the imminent holocaust, rented a little house in the same outer suburb and, as my father had quite recently died, she asked my mother to look after it for her. She invited me to stay there whenever I wished and it was on these visits that I got to know Gregory really well, to profit from his amazing scholarship and to appreciate the intense spirituality and pastoral zeal that lay behind the scintillating and resilient exterior that those in authority often found so disconcerting. Many was the time when we sat into the small hours while he instructed me in topics ranging from the liturgical practices of Carthusian nuns to the contemporary iniquities of the Anglican episcopate.

His time as a parish-priest was highly successful and his charm and zeal amply compensated for a certain lack of system. He and his brother Ronnie had an intense admiration for each other and confusingly referred to each other as 'Brother Bill'. St Michael's was not an independent parish and Gregory was skilful in handling the Rector. He was determined to introduce the Mass of the Presanctified on Good Friday, and the letter in which he solicited Bishop Kirk's approval for this ancient and scriptural rite and assured his Lordship that he had no intention of importing the Peruvian Jesuit devotion of the Three Hours was a superb example of Gregorian guile. St Michael's was very close to the Roman Catholic church and presbytery, and Gregory's courteous attentions both puzzled and embarrassed the resident monsignor. When the encyclical *Summi Pontificatus* was published, Gregory preached an enthusiastic sermon about it and urged the congregation to buy it; when his own supply of copies ran short, he sent down to St Teresa's for some of theirs only to find that they had never heard of it. He vigorously supported Cardinal Hinsley's early venture into ecumenism, the Sword of the Spirit, and prodded a somewhat reluctant monsignor into doing something about it. On one occasion he turned up on the presbytery doorstep with the complaint 'I'm sorry, Father, but this lady is a member of my congregation whom your curate is preparing to be received into the Roman Catholic Church and I find that what he's teaching her is all wrong.' Gregory's sermons were first-class and they were prepared with as much care for the little flock of St Michael's as for a university. They were written on oddly folded sheets of paper which were turned and manipulated as the discourse proceeded and were delivered with wit and bite and a gripping spiritual intensity.

Gregory was accompanied to Beaconsfield by Dom Maurus Benson, a delightful Scotsman with a pawky sense of humour and a capacity for looking on the gloomy side of things which was somehow never depressing. Once in a letter, after listing a formidable catalogue of calamities, he concluded, 'The cat at least is looking cheerful, but I suspect it is nursing some secret sorrow.' It was difficult to realise that he had been an officer in the Indian Army, for he had a quite unmilitary bearing. I gathered however that that there was a mess-room where his initials were traced in bullet-holes on the wall and that he had taken part in the last charge with lances in actual war in which the Army was ever engaged. One day, walking with a companion at Beaconsfield, he passed two soldiers in greasy overalls carrying spanners. Maurus fell into silence and gloom. Then: 'Isn't this a *ghastly* war?', he muttered. More than any one I have known he had the supreme Benedictine virtue of humility; he had literally no opinion of himself at all. Though professed as a choir-monk he had originally no thought of ordination, and when it was decided that he ought to become a priest the notion filled him with horror. He told me in consternation that his essay for the diaconate had been given first place, and he could only take this as a sign of the appallingly low standard of the other candidates. 'What was the subject of the essay?' I enquired, and was told that it was some topic connected with the Rule of St Benedict. 'Well,' I replied, 'you might after all have been expected to know something about *that*', and he seemed somewhat comforted. Later on, his place at Beaconsfield was taken by Dom Augustine Morris, the future abbot. My mother became devoted to 'the Doms' and on occasions of domestic crisis would go in and cook for them.

Gregory exercised a wide but largely unseen ministry as a confessor and as director or advisor to several religious communities; in the latter office he was frequently in conflict with episcopal policy, especially on liturgical questions. There is a characteristic story of an interview which he had with that hot-tempered authoritarian Bishop Garbett about the goings-on of some nuns in the diocese of Winchester. The Bishop became progressively more irritated as Gregory took books off the shelves of the Bishop's library and cut the leaves in order to read passages justifying the legality of the nuns' practices. In fact tempers rose more and more on both sides – or so it seemed – until both Garbett and Gregory were gesticulating and shouting furiously. However, while the episcopal anger was genuine, the monastic was only simulated, and Gregory suddenly became perfectly calm. 'Don't you think, my Lord,' he enquired, 'that we are both becoming rather undignified?' and left the outraged pontiff reduced to speechlessness. A minor but amusing incident at this epoch occurred when a verger at Norwich Cathedral tried to charge him for admission to the chapels. 'Out of my sight, man!' cried Gregory, as he swept him aside, 'We *built* this place!'

He was always indignant at the way in which he felt the pastoral work of the Church was being swamped by its growing administrative machinery; the Church of England, he pointed out, supported one lay official for every twenty working clergymen. He was particularly outspoken when, in order to finance the building of the new Church House at Westminster, an operation which was under the guidance of Bishop Partridge of Portsmouth, it was suggested that a levy of a penny in the pound should be placed upon the missionary societies. In a scathing speech he recalled the administrative hypertrophy of the Avignon papacy. They taxed the bishops, they taxed the parishes, they taxed the sacraments, they even taxed sin, he fulminated, and in the end men rose and tore the Church asunder. You, he said, would tax sin if you believed in it, but in default of that you want to tax the missions. Do that if you will, but call things by their proper names; let this exaction be known for ever as 'Partridge's Pence'. No more was heard of it.

Again, there was an occasion when Greogory himself had been expounding the nature of Christian unity, as a theological and spiritual reality rooted in the death and resurrection of Christ. In his audience was Bishop Headlam of Gloucester, whose capacity for casting forth his ice-like morsels was proverbial, and who cuttingly observed that, having listened to a young man's dream, we should now get down to hard facts. Gregory simply boiled over. 'I have always understood', he said, 'that it was old men who dream dreams and that young men see visions. I would rather that what I have spoken about was described as a vision than as a dream. But if the Bishop of Gloucester prefers to call it a young man's dream I will not object and I will tell him who first dreamed it. It was dreamed by a young man the night before he died and you will find it described in the seventeenth chapter of the Gospel according to St John.'

His frequent and undisguised lack of respect for those in authority was due to a conviction that, in order to turn the Church into something simple to understand and easy to administer, well-meaning but short-sighted and intellectually lazy bureaucrats were trying to impose upon its life and its worship a structure that was really incompatible with its true nature as the Body of Christ. If he got a little quiet fun out of making them look foolish, well, so much the better, but that was not the primary object of the exercise. It is noteworthy that those in office who had a note of real greatness in them — men such as Walter Frere, Kenneth Kirk and William Temple —, though they might at times disagree with him and even be exasperated by him, never lost their respect and affection for him. As a scholar Gregory was erudite, brilliant and provocative — and, to those who did not appreciate his inveterate ebullience, perennially precocious.[4] In 1933, Gregory, then just in his thirties, seriously offended and alienated one of the leading Anglo-Catholic theologians by two articles in the Nashdom periodical *Laudate*. Norman Powell Williams, universally but rather unsuitably known as 'Nippy', had been Lady Margaret Professor and Canon of Christ Church, Oxford, since 1927. In his earlier days he had been one of the group of young priests who founded the Society of St Peter and St Paul and who, with their defiant introduction of counter-reformation devotion and Baroque art, had been quite as irritating to the Anglican establishment as Gregory was ever to become. He had a highly ingenious mind and a splendid, if overwhelming, literary style.

He maintained his basic catholicism until his early death in 1942 and as Sub-Dean had initiated badly needed liturgical reforms which took half a century to mature. But, having now become part of the establishment, he directed his talents to justifying the Anglican Church, not merely as, under the providence of God, a product of history, but as the manifestation of a specially pure and authentic type of Catholicism. His opportunity came in 1933, the centenary year of the Oxford Movement, when, together with Charles Harris of Hereford, he edited a symposium with the significant title *Northern Catholicism*. In his Foreword and in his own essay on the Theology of the Movement, Williams adumbrated the thesis that throughout history Northern Europe had manifested a more rational and less superstitious presentation of the Catholic Faith than was characteristic of the mediterranean zone; and he appealed to Tacitus to prove the special qualifications of the Nordic peoples for this task. It is notable that the other essays in the book show practically no tendency to support or assume, or even to be conscious of the thesis which, in its editor's view, the book was intended to advance, and it must, I think, be judged as a rare but serious lapse of a very distinguished scholar into fantasy and wishful thinking. To Gregory this essay in racialism seemed to be theologically outrageous and historically false. Even at that early date he was impressed by the conservatism of Rome and by the religious ebullience of Scandinavia. In two articles entitled 'Nordic Spirituality' and 'Northern Catholicism'[5] he tore Williams's thesis to shreds with an irony and humour that are so entertaining that the reader can easily overlook the devastating argument that they embody. His reproduction of Williams's impression of Nordic worship, with our fair-haired ancestors sitting round on damp logs under grey and weeping skies, breathing into their brazen casques their unsuperstitious devotions, with a lack of emphasis on their tendency to slip into human sacrifice, is as funny as anything that I have read. Williams was not, of course, alone among Anglicans in holding the Nordic myth, but when, nearly half a century later, we think of the lines upon which dialogue between Rome and ourselves is now conducted it is possible to admire the longsightedness of the young man Dix in 1933.

Gregory had already begun work on the critical edition of the *Apostolic Tradition* of Hippolytus which was published in 1937 and which was described by no less an authority than Dr Henry Chadwick as 'still very necessary' thirty years later. In 1938 he published in *Laudate* a series of articles on Jurisdiction in the Early Church in which he argued that it was 'the sacramental and prophetic function of the bishop which mattered in the early Church and not what the Middle Ages were to call his *potestas jurisdictionis*'; Dr T. M. Parker, in introducing their republication in 1974, made the significant comment: 'To my knowledge, nobody before Dom Gregory saw this point so trenchantly and so clearly.' His famous lecture on the Theology of Confirmation in Relation to Baptism, which I heard him deliver under Dr Cross's aegis in the chapter-house at Christ Church in 1946, aroused the indignation of those who, for reasons of Protestant ecumenism, wished to downgrade the sacrament of Confirmation. His collaboration with Kenneth Kirk in the same year in organising the symposium entitled *The Apostolic Ministry* produced a similar reaction from those who for similar reasons wished to minimise the significance of episcopacy. Way back in 1937 he had contributed to Gabriel Hebert's symposium *The Parish Communion*, but the work by which he will be chiefly remembered is the massive volume entitled *The Shape of the Liturgy* which, as he said, took him fourteen years to prepare and fourteen months to write and which appeared in 1945. It contained a great deal of minute technical analysis and argument about the detailed development of the various liturgical rites of Christendom. Its central and dominating theme, however, is the existence of the Christian as crucified with Christ and risen with him into his Body the Church, as that existence is embodied in the Sacrament in which the Church's nature is proclaimed and its life maintained throughout the centuries. In the preface to the book Gregory bewailed the common assumption that liturgiologists were experts in a remote and mysterious realm of research which could have no practical bearing on what went on in the ordinary parish church. 'Liturgists', he maintained, 'have no particular reason to be pleased with the mandarin-like position thus accorded them. They are in reality only students of what actually goes on in every parish or other church in christendom and went on before there were special buildings called churches, ever since thirteen men met for supper in an upper room at Jerusalem — the "common prayer" of christians.'[6] The almost uproarious reception which the book received was undoubtedly due to the fact that it gave many of the clergy and laity for the first time a clear understanding of the nature of the rite for which they were assembled round the altar and of the tremendous wonder of the part which it played in the life of the redeemed human race. It had indeed other attractions: it contained a splendid refutation of the views of the liberal scholars who traced the origin of the Eucharist to something other than the institution of Christ; it exposed the well-intentioned but disastrous historical ignorance which produced the novel rites of sixteenth-century Protestantism; it brought into full view the largely overlaid and forgotten significance of the traditional rites of Catholic Christendom; and — this, it must be confessed, was not the least of its attractions for many Anglo-Catholics — it showed up as bumbling amateurs the modern Anglican bishops, with their continual restraints upon Catholic devotion and their opportunistically conceived books of 1927 and 1928. Perhaps more than anything else however, at a time when theological books had achieved a quite abysmal nadir of dulness, Gregory Dix was writing about theology in a style that was lucid, sparkling, at times amusing and indeed ironical, and which in the appropriate contexts could rise to great heights of eloquence. I would indeed be prepared to maintain that Gregory was, though unrecognised at large, one of the greatest prose stylists of this century, and I would instance two particular passages in *The Shape* in support of my claim. The first consists of the final pages of the chapter on the Sanctification of Time, in which he speaks of the consequences for good and evil of the acceptance of the Faith by Rome:

> For three and a half centuries — for ten times as long as Augustine saw it, ever since the Tower of Babel — 'Two loves had built two cities', — and now at last came the final creative synthesis of the whole of antiquity. In one swift generation *c.* A.D. 375–410 the *Civitas Romana* bowed itself at last to enter the City of God, and was baptised upon its deathbed like so many of its sons. But it died christian in the end, which was all that mattered after it was dead ...
>
> So the last christian generation of the old Roman world looked wistfully into the future knowing the end had come, and turned to God. In all its unhappiness and carnality that world had always loved beauty; and now there was given it a glimpse of the eternal

Beauty. And it cried out in breathless wonder with Augustine, 'Too late have I loved Thee, Beauty so ancient and so new!' ...

The whole hard structure of the *civitas terrena*, the earthly city that had thought itself eternal, was now ready to dissolve into a different future. Gibbon was right. The foundation of the empire was loosened by the waters of baptism, for the empire's real foundation was the terrible pagan dream of human power. Its brief christian dream of the City of God which alone is eternal was broken by the roaring crash of the sack of Rome by the Goths in A.D. 410. The world went hurrying into the darkness of seven long barbarian centuries, but pregnant now with all the mediaeval and modern future. It was the achievement of the church in the single century that had passed since Diocletian that, though all else changed in human life, it was certain to be a christian world, that centred all its life upon the eucharist.[7]

The second passage, beginning with the question 'Was ever another command so obeyed?', covers two pages right at the end of the book,[8] too long to be quoted in full and too much of a unity to bear abbreviation, in which Gregory uses all the evocative power of his wonderful style to describe what the Eucharist has meant in the lives of individual men and women and in the history of the nations down the Christian centuries. 'One could fill many pages', he writes, 'with the reasons why men have done this, and not tell a hundredth part of them. And best of all, week by week and month by month, on a hundred thousand successive Sundays, faithfully, unfailingly, across all the parishes of Christendom, the pastors have done this just to *make* the *plebs sancta Dei* − the holy common people of God.' How this passage affects other people I do not know, but for myself I can only say that it is one of the very few passages in literature which, because of its sheer intense concern with living humanity, invariably brings me close to tears.

Because of his skill as a controversialist in the most keenly fought battles of the church politics of his time, Gregory was frequently suspected and sometimes accused of distorting his facts to buttress his desired conclusions, especially by those who had no hesitation in distorting their facts to buttress theirs. That he never did this consciously or deliberately I am convinced, and in fact many of his views were as novel and startling to text-book Anglo-Catholics as they were to the official Anglican establishment. He could sometimes weaken a good case by over-statement, as I think he did in the controversy about Confirmation. What he said about Frere was also true about himself, that 'he never forgot or wasted an acquired fact, but he could not always let facts master him.'[9] After his early death in his fifty-first year a quite unfair attempt was made to represent him as a second-rate scholar whose following had been built up by demagogy and charlatanism. To discover how unfounded such a calumny is one need only mention his name to any competent continental scholar in liturgiology and patrology; of course he had his blind spots and made his mistakes, but what scholar does not? In his later years he became more and more respected as a leader of Anglo-Catholic opinion and policy; from 1946 until his death in 1952 he was a Proctor in Convocation and did much to avert the serious threat of schism caused by the formation of the Church of South India in 1947. While he was convinced of the fundamental wrong-headedness of most of the approaches to Christian unity favoured by Anglican officialdom (for he considered them as designed to perpetuate the very distortions of Christianity by which the situation of *disunity* had been produced), he was passionately concerned to disinter and exorcise the real causes of our divisions. It will, I think, be instructive to recall a little bit of theological history in which he was involved in the mid-1940s.

The report which was published in 1947 under the title *Catholicity: a Study in the Conflict of Christian Traditions in the West* says in its Preface that in November 1945 the Archbishop of Canterbury 'invited Dom Gregory Dix to convene a group of Anglicans of the "Catholic" school of thought to examine the causes of the deadlock which occurs in discussion between Catholics and Protestants and to consider whether any synthesis between Catholicism and Protestantism is possible.' The knowledgeable will no doubt suspect that the initial stimulus may have come from Dom Gregory rather than from Dr Fisher, and so in fact it was. The idea was, in fact, that three groups should simultaneously work on the problem, the other two consisting of Anglican Evangelicals and Free-Churchmen respectively. However, for what Dr Fisher described as 'various reasons', the other two groups did not get to work until the 'Catholic' group, which, under Gregory's encouragement acted with amazing rapidity, had actually completed its assignment, presented it to Dr Fisher and put it on sale. The other two reports, when they appeared, thus largely took the form of replies to the first one; this was not the original idea, though whether it was what Gregory expected to happen I just do not know. Dr Fisher, to judge by the Foreword which he contributed, was not too satisfied; but, in the headmasterly manner which was not unnatural to him, he gave it a patronising beta-minus as an 'honest attempt' which 'should serve a useful purpose'. 'Readers may wish to alter some of its proportions and to dissent from some of its judgments; but they will profit by the survey ... It shows perhaps more of anxiety to avoid wrong methods than of ability to elaborate a right method.' With the advantage of hindsight I find it interesting to list the names of the recipients of this lukewarm commendation, with their future appointments: A.M. Ramsey (Archbishop of Canterbury); H.J. Carpenter (Bishop of Oxford); R.C. Mortimer (Bishop of Exeter); E.R. Morgan (Bishop of Truro); A.R. Reeves (Bishop of Johannesburg); E.S. Abbott (Dean of Westminster); V.A. Demant (Regius Professor, Oxford); F.W. Green; C.H. Smyth; A.M. Farrer; A.G. Hebert, S.S.M.; L.S. Thornton, C.R.; T.S. Eliot; and, of course, Gregory Dix, O.S.B. Phew! What was the Report's conclusion, anyhow? Well, not so much a conclusion as a policy and an orientation:

> not to take our contemporary systems or 'isms' or Church traditions and try to piece them together, either as a whole or in selected items, but rather *to go behind our contemporary systems* and strive for the recovery of the fulness of Tradition within the thought and worship and order and life of each of the sundered portions of Christendom.

This is not the place for an assessment of this whole operation; I attempted that in a book entitled *The Recovery of Unity* in 1958, but it is well to remind ourselves that it was in 1945 that Gregory Dix assembled this team under the instruction, or at least with the connivance, of the Primate of All England. We should also, as we look back thirty-five years later with Vatican II in between, appreciate the faith and vision of the monk to whose initiative it was due.

I was not a member of the *Catholicity* group, but I was involved in a smaller and quieter but, in those days, even more audacious enterprise, when Gregory arranged a conference at Nashdom between four Jesuit fathers, led by that inflexible old moral theologian Fr Joyce, and four Anglicans, of whom I was one and Vigo Demant, Gabriel Hebert and Gregory himself the others. It was all extremely secret, though it took place with official approval, and no results were either formulated or published. In these days such a meeting would of course hardly invite comment, but at the time its mere occurrence was astonishing and was likely to lead to the gravest apprehensions among the authorities of both churches. But Gregory was deeply convinced that the recovery of the authentic Christian tradition was to be sought in Western Catholicism rather than in Protestantism or in the Anglicised version of Eastern Orthodoxy which was cherished by many of our bishops. It was not, however, to the post-Tridentine or even the medieval West that he looked for guidance, but rather to the pre-Constantinian liturgy, with its profound sense of the Church as the Body of Christ and the *plebs sancta Dei*, 'the holy common people of God'. Yet neither, again, was he a 'catacomb romantic'. While he had a horror of Erastianism which gave him a sympathy with sixteenth-century Puritanism that some found surprising, he held that the Church's 'entrance into the world' in the fourth century was a vocation from God in the actual circumstances of history and therefore morally inevitable. He saw this 'sanctification of time' as carrying within it grave spiritual dangers, and it was in this that he saw the life of the consecrated religious, whether in the archetypal form of the desert fathers or in its various adaptations and manifestations in the subsequent life of the Church, as concerned not just with the salvation of the individual monk or nun but with the welfare of the family of God as a whole. He had little use, theologically, for the Byzantine elements in the later liturgical development of the Orthodox East and was sometimes unfair to them, though he admitted once to me that the modern Eastern liturgy appealed to him in his occasional Dionysian moments. In a mischievous mood he described the function of the clergy in that rite as that of a spiritual bomb-disposal squad, provided with the necessary protective equipment, immunising a dangerous object which had come down from the sky. In fact however, for all his lack of sympathetic rapport with their way of worship, he had a great admiration for their persistent loyalty to Christian truth and their faithfulness under centuries of persecution. 'Orthodoxy', he wrote,

> is a far greater and more Christian thing than Byzantinism – rich in faith and holiness and above all in martyrs . . . It will be fascinating to see what it makes of its magnificent patristic heritage in the modern world when it has been everywhere set free from its old entanglement with autocracy. One thing it will assuredly keep is the Byzantine rite by which all orthodoxy worships, and has saved itself from extinction by worshipping. This is the joint creation of Greek christian theology and the old Hellenic poetic spirit, working together on a Syrian rite. Along with the *Digest* of Justinian it is the greatest legacy of Byzantine thought to the world.[10]

This is not the language of either ridicule or contempt, and I think Gregory's greatest quality was his readiness to appreciate Christian reality even under forms that he found unattractive or even misguided. I was enormously impressed when, years after his death, a prominent Baptist minister told me of his personal admiration and affection for Gregory and of the help and inspiration which he had derived from his meetings with him.

The intense activity of his later years led many to wonder whether it was really compatible with the life of a Benedictine monk. Not only did his membership of Convocation give him, in the words of the Jubilee Book of the Nashdom Community, 'ample scope for what his opponents would have called intrigue and his friends diplomacy', so that he was once described in a newspaper as 'the man who runs the Church of England',[11] but he was heavily involved in the foundation of the American house which has since become an independent abbey and in an exhausting programme of lecturing and preaching. No one was more conscious of this danger than Gregory himself, but it was evident to those who knew him that beneath the waspishness and the talent for conspiracy there was an infectious love for human beings and an increasing holiness. It was the same Gregory who was anathema to much of the Anglican establishment to whom a small girl ran up in excitement at Beaconsfield with the news 'I've got Mickey Mouse on my new knickers; what have you got on yours?' and who on his death-bed was counselling those who had come to rely on his wisdom. I last saw him when he was staying in Oxford with the Farrers not long before his death, when he was, as it was hoped, convalescing after a horrid and painful operation; he was as lively and entertaining as ever and I had no idea how desperately ill he really was. I can only endorse the words which Fr Tweedy wrote about him:

> The real man of God could be discerned by anyone who cared to look; but not all did. The exterior was so attractive. His 'wicked' rapier-thrusts and gay stories were repeated up and down the land, not least by himself ... No man ever more enjoyed being himself ... Yet the depths of those eyes held kindness and sympathy, the smile often brought encouragement to the young student or ordinand, and the monkish look proved in the end to be no counterfeit.
>
> Of his heroic last days, let it suffice to record that all the mischief had gone, and nothing but holiness remained. God had had his way with him.[12]

One is tempted to speculate how he might have continued to influence both the liturgy and the politics of the Church of England if he had lived, as might well have been expected, for another twenty years or more. We can at least be sure that if we could now have his comments on some of the changes that have occurred since his death, they would be devastating; but also it is clear that many of the more satisfactory developments, especially in the realm of liturgy, have been largely due to his influence. It is instructive to read the last chapter of *The Shape*, remembering the impact which it had upon many of the bishops, by whom the chief reason for Prayer-Book revision was conceived as being to prevent the lower clergy from breaking the law. Against a wider backcloth, remembering that *The Shape* was published in 1945, it comes nowadays as something of a shock to recall that Rome did not allow the most obviously rational fragment of liturgical reform — the restoration of the Paschal Vigil to the night-time — until 1951; Gregory once told me that the Benedictines had repeatedly petitioned to be allowed to make this change in the privacy of their monasteries and had as repeatedly been refused. Gregory was, of course, not the only Anglican writer on either the principles or the practice of liturgy; E. C. Ratcliff was working away at the top level of scholarship, and Gabriel Hebert had written his fascinating *Liturgy and Society* as long ago as 1935; Gregory himself had contributed to the symposium *The Parish Communion* in 1937. But it was *The Shape* which is his memorial, as it deserves to be. On some controversial points he laid himself open to criticism, which he both welcomed and received; he was about to produce a revised edition at the time of his death. The vision remains, by which he lived and which he communicated to others, as vivid and relevant as it was more than forty-five years ago:

> Over against the dissatisfied 'acquisitive Man' and his no less avid successor the dehumanised 'Mass-Man' of our economically focussed societies insecurely organised for time, christianity sets the type of 'Eucharistic Man' — man giving thanks with the product of his labours upon the gifts of God, and daily rejoicing with his fellows in the worshipping society which is grounded in eternity. This is man to whom it was promised on the night before Calvary that he should henceforth eat and drink at the table of God and be a king. This is not only a more joyful and more humane ideal. It is the divine and only authentic conception of the meaning of all human life, and its realisation is in the eucharist.[13]

My own copy of The *Shape* is inscribed in Gregory's handwriting: E.M. *sylleitourgo* Gr.D. O.S.B.

GABRIEL HEBERT, S.S.M.

One of our advantages at Lincoln was that of being within easy reach of Kelham, where the Society of the Sacred Mission had its central house, its theological seminary and the great square chapel, dominated by Jagger's realistic rood, which was looked on by many Anglicans as embodying the ideal setting for the liturgy. A trip to Kelham made a pleasant outing from Lincoln for any of us on a Saturday. Thus began my friendship with Fr Gabriel Hebert, who had just turned fifty and was already in the public eye as that desirable but none too common character, the theologian whose work is at once readable, relevant and reliable. With his tall, slightly bending figure, his beaked profile, his eager gait and his high-pitched faintly slobbering cackle, he always reminded me of a large and purposeful, but wholly benevolent, vulture. The Kelham students used to reproduce, with kindly exaggeration, his rendering of the apostolic protestation: 'Are they Hebrews? So am I ... I speak as a fool; I am more.' His concern with ordinands had given his theology a markedly pastoral orientation, which did not commend it in English academic circles, though it earned him an honorary doctorate in Scotland, where the concept of theology as the science of God and of other beings in relation to God has suffered less erosion. When we met, he had already made a great impression in 1935 with his book *Liturgy and Society*, in which he had tried to acclimatise the principles of the continental Liturgical Movement in the setting of Anglicanism. It was an enlightening and inspiring work, in spite of some idiosyncrasies, and, together with the symposium *The Parish Communion*, with which, as editor, he followed it in 1937, it did something to lessen the danger with which the Movement in the Church of England is always threatened, of treating the Sunday Eucharist as simply a less boring form of service, especially for the young, than choral mattins or as the expression of a purely human kind of togetherness. Gabriel was now engaged on a new work, *The Throne of David*, which, as he said, was to explain 'why the Christian Faith, which is catholic and for all mankind, is nevertheless still so Hebraic that we continue to use liturgical forms which speak of "Jerusalem" and "the Throne of David"; why, in short, our Bible consists of two Testaments.'[14] Thus, though the word was hardly used, this was an essay in the 'typology' of which later on we were to hear a great deal. It is fair to notice that Gabriel was very clear, unlike many practitioners of the art, of the distinction between harmless but fanciful applications of the Old-Testament words and stories for devotional edification – what has been described as 'good clean fun for the long winter evenings' – and the recognition that the great prophetic types recorded in the writings of the Ancient Dispensation are fulfilled in Christ and his Church and mediated in the Sacraments – *et antiquum documentum novo cedat ritui*.

Gabriel read to me various fragments of the work in progress, and I can hear now his excited cackle: 'Ow, I say, I must read this bit to you; it's awfully good.' He brought the completed manuscript to Lincoln to show to me, and when we went in to lunch, he took it with him and placed it on his chair and sat on it. 'Gabriel,' I said reprovingly, 'You can't do that.' 'Why can't I?' he enquired. 'Why,' I replied, 'You can't sit on the Throne of David.' He was delighted. After it was published I picked up from a basket outside a second-hand shop a copy of a nineteenth-century novel called *The Throne of David*, by the Reverend J. H. Ingraham, LL. D. I bought it and sent it to Gabriel, and had this delightful reply:

My dear Eric,
Thank you very much. I feel quite put to shame by my predecessor's inventive genius and his descriptive talent. Witness the unforgettable description of the morning ritual of the priests at sunrise by the banks of the Euphrates − copied no doubt from the morning devotions of the author with his curates & churchwardens by the banks of the Mississippi − or again the parade of the Israelite Home Guard near Jericho, all trained soldiers, but armed with billhooks and scythes only, because the Philistines had disarmed them. There is a touch of genius about the gifted author.

With immeasurable gratitude,

Yrs, Gabriel Hebert S. S. M.

Gabriel must have been one of the first English scholars to make a thorough study of the work of contemporary Swedish theologians; he not only learnt their language but produced at the beginning of the 1930s translations of no less than three of their major works: Brilioth's *Eucharistic Faith and Practice* in 1930, Aulén's *Christus Victor* in 1931 and the first part of Nygren's *Agape and Eros* in 1932. He always had a sympathy for Lutherans, whom he felt were often judged unjustly and not least by his friend Gregory Dix. At the conference at Nashdom with the four Jesuits, one of the few difficult moments was a confrontation, in which Gabriel repeatedly insisted that Luther was *terribly sincere* and Fr Joyce as often reiterated that Luther was *a bad man* − two assertions which were not logically incompatible but difficult to synthetise. I believe, however, that he later became more critical, and that his failure to complete the translation of Nygren's book was connected with this. He was gentler than Gregory towards Cranmer, but I suspect this was due more to pity for his predicament and admiration for his prose than to agreement with his theology; he quoted Fr Kelly as saying that 'the age of the Renaissance was a paradise of bullies, and Cranmer was a commonplace citizen made to be bullied.'[15] He certainly did not accept the myth of a peculiarly pure 'Northern Catholicism'; he once pointed out that in fact Northern Catholicism had existed for centuries and remarked that 'one of the results of the developments of "northern catholicism" was that there had to be a Reformation.'[16] But he did, I think, believe that not just the Anglican Church, but Anglicanism as a specific form of Christian thinking and living, had a unique and peculiar excellence, and I do not think Gregory believed this. If I was to speculate why two men remained in the Church of England, I should say, with some hesitation, that Gregory was convinced that it offered the only feasible means of bringing the Gospel to the great mass of English people, while Gabriel really believed in something called Anglicanism. But what either of them would say if we could question him now I have really no idea.

Gabriel was not, in my opinion, an eccentric but he was certainly a character, if the distinction can be accepted. Two incidents recur to my mind, trivial in themselves but recognisable to those who knew him as typical of this intelligent but fundamentally simple Christian man. We were crossing Nottingham together one late afternoon. 'Let's have some tea,' he said, 'I know an awfully jolly place; it's called the Moo-Cow.' In we went and he asked for two cups of tea 'and some of those awfully jolly cookies.' And it seemed impossible that it could have been called anything else. The other incident was at Birmingham in 1940, at a conference under William Temple's leadership between what were known as the older and younger theologians. Gabriel was perched on a coal-box at one end of the fireplace, with his knees up to his chin, looking more like a kindly vulture than ever, while somebody was laboriously propounding the thesis that the language of devotion ought not always to be interpreted literally. Suddenly Gabriel came to life. 'I'm going to give some flowers to our Lady!' he crowed. We all gazed at him in astonishment. 'Some people would say that means I think she's inside the statue,' he continued, 'Isn't that silly of them?' and lapsed into chuckles. He had made his point.

After I left Lincoln in 1945 we had few opportunities of meeting. He continued to be active theologically to his death in 1963 but these later years are outside the range of this book.

LIONEL THORNTON, C.R.

I think I must have first met Lionel Thornton in April 1936 at Mirfield, at the conference between Anglican and Russian Orthodox theologians which Bishop Walter Frere organised two years before his death. I got to know Lionel really well though through the summer-schools which the Fellowship of St Alban and St Sergius ran from 1946 onwards, first at St Helen's School, Abingdon, and then from 1956 at St Stephen's College, Broadstairs, and which we both attended with hardly a break until his own death in 1960. He was naturally shy and abstracted, and the students who sat under him at Mirfield regarded him as an Olympian figure, dwelling in a realm of typological contemplation which it would be dreadful to invade. Fr Tweedy, who like him belonged to the Community of the Resurrection, has written of his own delighted astonishment, at the way in which Lionel, having been inveigled by him with some trepidation to Abingdon as a guestspeaker, took to the family-party setting like a duck to water and promptly decided to come every year. I cannot do better than reproduce Fr Tweedy's own words:

> To members of his Community it appeared that something hitherto latent in their brother Lionel had been brought out entirely by the Fellowship. More and more, in the intervals between scholarly discussions with his intellectual equals, he throve on the companionship of the young. And the young soon realised the kind of person they were dealing with, piercing without difficulty beneath that roughish husk which his shyness had built round him. So it would happen that after a theological paper by L. T., first through one of us, later direct to him, young people – 'simple souls', they would call themselves – came to ask for elementary exposition in the afternoon of what he had said in the morning. And he would give it delightedly. He used to say that he could deal with highbrows or lowbrows but not middlebrows. So some of those with no theological background really had him at his best. He felt particularly at home in young feminine society – one would guess this was a quite new feature in his life. His liking for them was only matched by their devotion to him. Once, after I had staged a rencontre with him for some who were too shy to ask for themselves, he referred to them afterwards as 'those young women you got me into the summer house with'. Enjoyment had been mutual and conversation, I bargain, entirely theological and by no means shallow.[17]

I have quoted this passage at length, because I think it contains the key to much about him that people found puzzling. He had a fine and penetrating intelligence, but with it a kind of wondering seriousness, not unlike that of a child. As Fr Tweedy says, 'a good deal of private explanation to Lionel was always necessary of any but the most unsubtle jokes', and, although this was in many ways undoubtedly a handicap, it had the compensating advantage that he found it natural and easy to take everybody equally seriously.

He was a large and rather lumbering person and always walked with a stick, though he had no obvious infirmity. I was told that he had started the stick under medical advice when he had some temporary lameness and that, never having had any definite instructions to discontinue it, had, as a good and obedient religious, simply gone on using it. He lived strictly according to rule and, unlike some of his brethren, said a private mass daily if it was at all possible. He had little aesthetic sense, or perhaps it would be truer to say that his aesthetic sense found its satisfaction almost wholly in the intellectual and spiritual realm.

He was as clearly a Cambridge man as Gregory Dix and Gabriel Hebert were Oxonians. He got a first class at Emmanuel College in Theology and the Carus Greek Testament prize in 1907 and he acquired there the photographic memory of the Biblical text that was the essential foundation of his very much later work. But his early published work was apologetic and historical rather than exegetical. He joined the Mirfield community in 1915, when its dominant intellectual was John Neville Figgis, and, with his books *Conduct and the Supernatural* (1916) and *Richard Hooker: A Study in his Theology* (1924), followed by his contribution on The Christian Conception of God to *Essays Catholic and Critical* in 1926, he might have seemed to have become simply a very able but quite conformist member of the liberal Catholic school. However, in 1928 – year of the ill-dated Revised Prayer-Book, though this, I think, was purely coincidental – he published a book which, to those who managed to read and appreciate it, suggested something very different. Lionel's literary style was always stodgy and elephantine, but in *The Incarnate Lord* it earns the adjective 'unreadable' as justly as any book that anybody has in fact managed to read. It is extremely long, often obscure, turgid in style and irritatingly repetitive – in fact it often quotes at length from itself; I read it when I was a schoolmaster at Coventry because it was the only book that I had in my bedroom when I was quarantined with chicken-pox. It is couched in a philosophical idiom which was novel, debatable and highly complicated, though it had the advantage of coming out of a scientific rather than a classical setting. Nevertheless, I believe it was potentially an important work and one ahead of its time; and it was certainly significant of its author's basic attitude and presuppositions. For, when liberal Anglo-Catholics in general were making subtle adjustments to bring the Christian revelation into line with modern thought, Lionel Thornton, in *The Incarnate Lord*, was making drastic modifications in a contemporary philosophical system in order to bring it into line with the Christian revelation. In fact, he was doing with the philosophy of A. N. Whitehead what St Thomas Aquinas had done with the philosophy of Aristotle; the only trouble is that the leucocephalite philosophy has proved to be less enduring than the peripatetic, though my own opinion is that, apart from his doctrine of the relation of God to the world (a very large exception, admittedly!), Whitehead's general metaphysic has a lot of truth in it. I am, however, concerned at the moment simply to show where it was that, as early as the late 1920s, Lionel knew his primary loyalty to lie and where he had taken his stand. And it is interesting to notice that, as late as 1959, an out-and-out process-theologian like Dr W. N. Pittenger[18], no less than Boys-Smith and Bezzant in 1928, would recognise this and reproach him for it. A decade later, in Lionel's own mind, the situation had become perfectly clear; and, in the Preface to *The Common Life in the Body of Christ*, which was completed in 1939 though the War delayed its publication until 1942, he wrote:

In *The Incarnate Lord* (1928) an attempt was made to relate the revelation of God in Christ to current philosophy. But now another problem presented itself. What if the Gospel becomes obscured by our presuppositions and preoccupations, so that we neither see the scope of its application nor suffer it to speak for itself? The conviction grew that this danger was present in the theological situation of today. In particular it became clear that certain aspects of the New Testament were not receiving the attention which was due to them.

Thus, as Lionel said, he 'found himself launched upon a fresh inquiry into biblical theology' and in particular into 'three aspects of Scripture, namely (1) its function as the medium of revelation, (2) the unity which it manifests and (3) the nature of the authority which it possesses.'[19]

Lionel was now openly committed as a Biblical theologian and all his future writings conformed to this profession; forgotten were Whitehead and the philosophy of organism. It must be stressed that he saw himself as a Biblical *theologian* and not as a textual or historical scholar whose special sphere of interest happened to be the Bible. In 1946 he contributed an essay on The Body of Christ in the New Testament to Kenneth Kirk's (or should we rather say Gregory Dix's?) symposium *The Apostolic Ministry* and this was followed up by the loosely knit trilogy to which he gave the overall title *The Form of the Servant*: *Revelation and the*

Modern World (1950), *The Dominion of Christ* (1952) and *Christ and the Church* (1956). Interpolated into the series was the volume *Confirmation: its Place in the Baptismal Mystery* (1954), in which Lionel defended Gregory's thesis that Confirmation is an integral part of Christian Initiation against Dr G. W. H. Lampe's book *The Seal of the Spirit*. Lionel's fundamental thesis, which was strangely given little attention by his opponents and his defenders alike, is set out in the opening pages of the first volume of the trilogy in which he explains the overall title. Under the heading 'Revelation in its Human Setting' he put the question 'What is the relation between revealed religion and its cultural environment?' and rejected both of two answers commonly given, namely (1) that it simply transcends the environment and (2) that it is the product of the environment. Rather, he maintained, revelation *masters* its environment and it does this because God identifies himself with human history and enters into it in order to transform it. This '"mastery" in God's mode of action towards the order within which he manifests himself ... is all of one piece with the action of Jesus Christ when he took a towel and girded himself to wash the disciples' feet.'[20] 'God's self-identification with the minutiae of contemporary life and thought is all of one piece with the doctrine of the incarnation.'

Yet, Lionel insisted, this must not be taken in a merely immanentist way:

> This total adjustment to environment was a supreme work of condescension which left nothing as it was before. It was an agonising conflict in which the Creater wrestled with his fallen world in order to redeem it; a conflict like that of Peniel [Genesis xxxii.24f] in which the divine wrestler emptied his own strength into the human wrestler, in which, as on Calvary, God suffered defeat in order that Man might be victorious, God came down to the level of our trivialities in order that those same trivialities might be taken up into a context of surpassing significance. Such is the general character of revelation; and it carries this corollary, that nothing in scripture is too trivial to be relevant.[21]

Lionel's principle that God and divine revelation enter into his creation not to be submerged by it but to master it seems to me to be of central importance; it holds the answer to much unsound Christology, especially of the kenotic type. It would be interesting to correlate it with the Constitution of Vatican II on Divine Revelation. I would direct attention specially to his assertion that 'nothing in scripture is too trivial to be relevant', for it may explain much in his later writing that many readers found fantastic and undisciplined. For, even less than that of Gabriel Hebert a decade earlier, did Lionel Thornton's appearance in the guise of a Biblical scholar commend him to the established practitioners of the art. To them what mattered above all else was that Biblical study should be a coldly analytical study, conducted in accordance with canons as authoritative for the secularist as for the Christian believer. For Lionel, Holy Scripture was a gift from God to his Church, given 'at divers times and in divers manners', here a little and there a little, and garnered into the Body of Christ, in whom alone it becomes really and fully intelligible. This, I believe, explains his joy in a typological method and technique which to many appeared outrageously arbitrary and indefensible, and also the disarming way, used especially in oral discussion, in which, when one had confessed one's inability to see the typological coherence of two particular Biblical texts, he would try to resolve the problem, not by more careful study and analysis of those but by introducing several new ones, which might well be even more obscure to the baffled disciple. In fact, as regards method, Lionel might seem to be an outstanding example of the type of teacher whose idea of simplifying a problem is to make it more complicated. This was emphatically not due to any love of obscurity for its own sake and equally surely not due to any desire to pose as a pundit – for he was modest to the point of naivety – but to the conviction that Scripture was an immense and wonderful vehicle of the divine revelation, built around and focused upon the figure of the Incarnate Lord, and it was a matter of comparative indifference if some of the arguments were speculative and others implausible as long as one was clear about the structure as a whole. For Lionel's typology was meant to dazzle with a vision rather than to silence with an argument, though his vision had the detail of a mosaic rather than the atmospheric haze of a painting by Turner; and it was the failure to understand this that often misled other people and, I fear, sometimes even misled him.

I think in fact that his individual types had a tendency to get loose on their own, in a way that Austin Farrer's, for example, did only very rarely, and this could be disastrous when, as in the Confirmation controversy, he launched into unrestrained typologising when careful critical judgment was called for. Those of us who found typology difficult to practice in any case looked on with combined admiration and amusement at the obvious disfavour with which the two typological gold-medallists Thornton and Farrer regarded each other's typological techniques. I could never quite appreciate the tremendous significance for the Sacrament of Confirmation which Lionel saw in the fact that the Israelites, after crossing Jordan, were circumcised with stone – that is, *Petrine* – knives. But I believe that the real key to Lionel's later writing was that he had, in these days when almost all biblical scholars, whether 'conservative' or 'liberal in their sympathies and their conclusions, are irrestibly pressurised into approaching Scripture from an external standpoint, it had somehow become second nature with Lionel to study it from within, as a grateful and humble son of Christ's Church, to which it belonged and through which he had received it. It was not that he condemned the critical method as intrinsically evil, but he thought the Scripture did not yield up its authentic fruits that way. If we want to discover why the Fathers of the early Church interpreted Scripture in the way that they did, we should not, I suggest, approach them as so many modern patristic scholars do, as if they were cultural aborigines, with an arrested spiritual development and grievously handicapped by the lack of our academic techniques, but simply try to catch some fragment of the insight of our contemporary Lionel Thornton. However he might seem to be cruising in the solitariness of his own intellectual stratosphere, he was happiest and at his most natural expounding the Word of God to a little group of young people in the garden at Abingdon. But I cannot do better than conclude my memories of Lionel with a description by Fr Mark Tweedy of a series of talks given by him on the theme of *Apokatastasis*, the summing up of all things in Christ:

> The whole thing was a mosaic of Scripture, and the serious listener needed to keep fingers in several pages at once of a Greek Testament (not to mention a Septuagint, if he had one). As Fr Lionel proceeded, always slowly, sometimes almost ponderously, one knew that this was Biblical theology at the very source. No matter if one missed a thread or two in his tangled skein: it was a *religious* experience. Sooner or later there would come the passage – as so often at Mirfield when delineating to his brethren ideas which were fermenting for one of his books – when his eyes would close as he looked upward and his voice would take on a curious semi-chanting tone, as he seemed to lose consciousness for a few moments of everything but the word of God which he was expounding. Almost he was enraptured. For most of us there has been no closer experience of an intellectual

contemplative communing to himself as it were, of the things of God.[22]

CANON CHARLES HUTCHINSON

One of the most versatile and devoted priests I have been fortunate enough to know well was Charles Walsham Hutchinson, 'Father Hutch' to his very diversified and widely scattered flock. I first heard of him in Edward Wynn's rooms when I was an undergraduate, and I listened entranced to Edward's story of how he went to help Hutch in his South-London parish over Christmas and was sent off without warning late at night on a rickety bicycle to an imperfectly defined destination to entertain a large mob of boys from the training-ship *Britannia* who were being looked after over the festive season. But I first got to know him when I went to stay with him in his vicarage at St John's, Waterloo Road, during one of my early vacations from Lincoln. He was short, thick-set and bald and had a remarkable resemblance to Benito Mussolini; and, as he spent a great many of his holidays in Italy, I could never understand how he avoided assassination, as, unlike his visual prototype, he was not of course provided with an armed bodyguard. He was of middle-class and by no means opulent origin and had worked in a London office; he was however convinced that he had a vocation to the priesthood and, like many other men for whom King's College, London, provided facilities in a similar situation, he acquired an A. K. C. and was ordained to a parish in Woolwich just before the First World War. He had already developed a remarkable gift for work among boys, and in those days work among boys in South London could be a tough proposition indeed. In spite of his limited formal education he had a great aesthetic sensitivity and developed a vast range of contacts with the literary and the dramatic world. He read voraciously and visited the theatre whenever he could; he became one of the leading officials of the Actors' Church Union. To stay with him was to meet a succession of unexpected celebrities. At Waterloo Road he had to lunch one day that splendid and formidable personality Lilian Baylis, the transforming genius of the Old Vic and the Sadlers Wells; they were old friends and had been involved together in many projects for the material and spiritual welfare of the theatrical profession. This must have been shortly before her death, but she was full of vigour and volubility; she reminded me in appearance of a garrulous seaside landlady and gave an impression of being festooned with amber necklaces. In her faintly cockney accent she described how she had been trying to restrain a young actress from an indiscretion – 'So I said, "Don't, my dear, it'd be so bloody silly"; well I mean it would have, wouldn't it?' – and how she had been trying to improve the elocution of the curate – 'Oh, my Gawd, it was *awful*!' The parish included Waterloo Station, which was not only, like most large termini, surrounded by a run-down area containing more than the normal proportion of slums and brothels, but also, in the days before transatlantic aviation, provided one of the main passenger inlets to the metropolis from the United States. Hutch had some fascinating stories about some of the new residents which his parish acquired when the New York police, having had a clean-up of the criminal elements in their city, put all those who turned out to be of British nationality on the boat to Southampton, whence they took the train to Waterloo to continue their activities in London. Hutch had on his mantelpiece a beautiful but horrifying flick-knife, which one of them had presented to him as a token of respect for religion. One story which I recall was of a character named Moggy Morgan, whose forehead was tattooed with the legend 'Hail, Columbia'; by his own account he had had the inscription made after one of his numerous conversions to a life of virtue, but according to one of his friends it had been made forcibly by his business partners, who had become doubtful of his *bona fides* and wished him to have a permanent mark of identity. Somehow it seemed wholly appropriate, if not indeed inevitable, that it was Hutch who found himself at the centre of this influx, for he had a delight and an aptitude for unusual situations; and one of the things that I admired most about him was the way in which he would make straight for any person who, either by misfortune or by fault of his own, had fallen outside the orbit of conventional society. The unfamiliar always appealed to him, especially if it made demands on his compassion.

Great as the contrast was, it was therefore not unsuitable that in 1943 Hutch was asked to go to Istanbul as chaplain to the Anglican Church and the British Embassy. His natural sociability and adaptability made him popular in diplomatic society and his deep pastoral sense made him ideal for ministering to the small and scattered Anglican flock, who were an easy prey to loneliness. Although he had had previously no experience of the Orthodox Church, his natural perceptiveness and curiosity, together with his sensitivity to the inner reality of Orthodox liturgy and spirituality, made him rapidly welcome in the Patriarchate. It was during his time that the future Pope John XXIII was Apostolic Delegate at

Istanbul, and Hutch had on the mantelpiece, near to the flick-knife, a photograph of himself with Mgr Roncalli, both in black suits with trousers. Some years later, pointing to this photo and two more formal autographed portraits which stood beside it, he remarked to me, 'I think I am probably the only Anglican clergyman who has been kissed by the Pope, the Ecumenical Patriarch and the Patriarch of Moscow; and, you know, they all smelt of garlic.'

In 1947 he came back to England as Vicar of St Bartholomew's, Brighton, the great brick edifice with, it is said, the second highest nave in Europe, which is visible, towering out of the valley on the left-hand side, just before the train enters Brighton Station. It was after this that I really got to know Father Hutch, for on a number of occasions until he retired in 1962 he invited me to stay with him. This was always delightful, for I am devoted to Brighton itself, which is one of the few English seaside resorts that has maintained its distinctive character; readers of Osbert Sitwell and Margaret Barton's *Brighton*, D. L. Murray's *Regency* and Professor E. W. Gilbert's *Brighton: Old Ocean's Bauble* will know what I mean.

> Long shalt thou laugh thine enemies to scorn,
> Proud as Phoenicia, queen of watering places!
> Boys yet unbreech'd, and virgins yet unborn,
> On thy bleak downs shall tan their blooming faces,[23]

though it is on the beaches rather than the downs that the tanning process of 'old Ocean's bauble, glittering Brighton' is now conducted. It was an unfailing joy to celebrate the High Mass beneath the great red and green baldachino of the splendid church where as a boy I had first seen what Catholic worship could be. The sheer scale of St Bart's was borne in on one when, having sung the *Dominus vobiscum* from the altar, one waited for several seconds for the response to come from what seemed to be the far side of the horizon but was in fact the choir high in the great gallery. And, of course, there was Hutch himself, of whom it was truer than of most, that he counted nothing human alien to him.

Hutch was an entrancing raconteur, who never seemed to be able to go anywhere without interesting and amusing things happening to him. Yet, strangely, I can at this length of time remember hardly any of his stories; and I think the reason must be that what made his experiences interesting was simply the fact that it was he to whom they happened; without his spontaneity to give them life there was often very little in them. It was certainly not that he played fast and loose with the facts in order to provide them with embellishment. I heard most of his stories many times and, while I always enjoyed them, they never showed signs of development or improvement. They always began with an almost rubrical uniformity. Hutch would wipe his hand down his face in a characteristic gesture and say, 'You know, it's a very remarkable thing . . .' And as he told it it certainly was.

One of his stories at least I must preserve from oblivion. Hutch had a friend, a wealthy and somewhat eccentric priest, who designed his own vestments and who took him one day into the sacristy to see his latest acquisition, which lay under a dust-cover. He whipped the cover off and revealed to Hutch's astonished view the dazzling figure of a gigantic queen bee, surrounded by smaller bees, embroidered on the back of a chasuble. To Hutch's startled enquiry of its significance the reply was casually given, 'Oh, my dear Father, don't you realise? Our Lady surrounded by the saints.' 'Oh, of course,' Hutch answered, recovering his equilibrium, 'how stupid of me.' 'Wait a moment', said the proud owner, and whipped the vestment over, to reveal the front view of a vigorously depicted elephant. Again Hutch was shocked into displaying his ignorance of ecclesiastical symbolism, and again enlightenment came. 'Oh, my dear Father, surely you know this: the emblem of sacerdotal chastity.' What was the effect on the devotion of the faithful of the alternation of these zoological representations during the celebration of the Mass I find it difficult to imagine, but I doubt whether that would have occurred to the celebrant. If, however, one is tempted to suppose that the south-coast resorts attract rather more than their share of idiosyncratic clergy, one might recall the words of Dr A. L. Wigan, in his book on the climate of Brighton, that 'nowhere can be found a set of men, whose blameless lives, whose zeal and talents mingled with the highest discretion, and whose active and disinterested exertions in the cause of humanity, do greater honour to their noble profession.'[24]

Hutch was an active open-air kind of man, in spite of his involvement in literature and the theatre, and in his earlier years, like many of the urban clergy, he had run very successful camps for boys; he remarked as a sign of the radical change that had come over the outlook and interests of the young that he was no longer – this was in the 1950s – able to make contact with them on this level as before. He was a keen swimmer and, at Brighton, would often dash down to the sea for a plunge before Mass. He would tell in his inimitable way of an occasion in his Istanbul days when he was invited to a great festival at the seminary which in those times existed on the Island of Halki in the Sea of Marmora.

After the great patriarchal Liturgy and the vast banquet which
followed it, Hutch lured one of the students away to find a quiet
beach for a bathe. In this they were successful, but as they lay
dozing on the sand afterwards in apparently complete isolation
Hutch was astonished to see the surface of the sea heaving as an
obviously living object approached the shore. As it came near it
raised above the water a black and shiny head as of some legendary
seamonster. 'Whatever is this?', Hutch anxiously enquired of his
companion. 'Do not take notice', came the reply, 'It is the Great
Archimandrite'; and that highly-placed cleric emerged in a state
of nudity from the sea with his long black hair hanging over
his face.

Hutch was a well-informed amateur of food and drink, though
he was moderate and abstemious and was far from making a god
of his belly. He knew which Brighton restaurants were good and
cheap, and if one took him out to dinner the sensible thing was to
let him choose both the place and the menu. Indeed, as he was sure
to take over the proceedings in any case, it was as well to invite
him to do this at the start. His sheer unselfconscious enjoyment
enabled him to do this without offence either to his host or to
the staff, though it could cause some surprised amusement, and I
envied him the ease with which he would slip into the kitchen to
establish good relations with the chef. An evening out with Hutch
was always a joy, whether as host or guest.

He was not without literary gifts, though he published little or
nothing. He once read me a delightful ballade with the refrain
'What did you do about it all?', supposedly addressed to a
medieval abbot on the approach of spring, and there must have
been other poems and essays. I suggested to him that he should
write his memoirs and I hoped that after he retired in 1962 he
would concentrate on doing this, for they would have been both
instructive and entertaining; nothing, however, came of this. He
settled down in a small house in Hove very happily for the last few
years of his life and was mourned when he died by men and women
in every station of life from bishops to criminals. It was appropriate
that he had been photographed with Angelo Roncalli, for in the
totally different conditions of their ministries, they shared the same
spontaneous priestly concern for men and women as such.

Notes

1. *Sobornost'*, winter 1952, p. 538.

2. I cannot recall the details of the saga about the documents for his ordination, at a time when the diocese of Oxford was vacant; but they included his successful refusal to pay fees to a lay official for writing letters from himself to himself in several different legal capacities.
3. I heard that this caused some irritation among tourists when it was inadvertently stocked by a bookshop in Jerusalem near the bus-stop for the earthly and not the spiritual mount!
4. Once, when I had mildly crossed swords with Bishop Hunkin, Gregory, who had had just concluded a much more serious controversy with that prelate, sent me a card accusing me of having potted his pigeon. He himself had just been referred to Genesis xxxvii.33: 'Joseph is without doubt torn in pieces'!
5. *Laudate*, XI (1933), pp. 152ff, 208ff.
6. *The Shape* ..., p. xiii.
7. *The Shape* ..., pp. 387, 395, 396.
8. ibid., pp. 744f.
9. *Walter Howard Frere*, ed. C. S. Phillips, p. 125.
10. *The Shape* ..., p. 548. This is, of course, the precise problem with which really sensitive and perceptive Orthodox thinkers in the United States, such as Dr John Meyendorff and Dr Alexander Schmemann, are grappling today.
11. The following verses, circulated (privately) at the time, may give some impression of the effect that Gregory's activity had produced:

Night upon Lambeth Palace,
  Storm over Breadsall Mount!
Who are the men that matter?
  Who are the chaps that count?
Is it the boys in gaiters,
  Rushing about all day,
Springing from lunch at Amsterdam
  To dine in the U.S.A.?
Is it the brave archdeacons,
  Slaving from nine till six?
Oh no, no, says Fleet Street,
  It's Dr Gregory Dix.

Gloom in the Athenaeum,
  Darkness and dirty looks!
Bishops huddled in corners,
  Reading their Contact Books.
Flickers the flame of Fisher,
  Waver the words of Woods,
Faint and vague is the voice of Haigh,
  Garbett's *not* the goods.
The glory that was Pollock,
  The grandeur that was Hicks,

Gone to a monk at Nashdom,
  Gone to Gregory Dix.

Twilight over Geneva,
  Ecumenical haze!
No new deal for Stephen Neill,
  No more *Songs of Praise*.
Faint through the mists of Merseyside
  Booms the ghostly knell,
No more croaks from Raven,
  No more chimes from Bell.
No more Derby sweepstakes,
  No more crashing bricks,
No more Cambridge Sermons,
  But heaps of Gregory Dix.

Rainclouds over the Abbey,
  Sturm and also *drang*!
Shivers the shade of Randall,
  Weeps the wraith of Lang.
No more doles for Dashwood,
  No more Church House games.
Deep distress for Good Queen Bess
  And also Bad King James.
No more oil and water
  Striving in vain to mix:
Ichabod for the Big Black Rod,
  And all through Gregory Dix.

Notes: Breadsall Mount: the residence of the Bishop of Derby, Dr A. E. J. Rawlinson. Cambridge Sermon: the famous university sermon of Dr G. F. Fisher on November 3rd 1946, pleading for the non-episcopal churches to 'take episcopacy into their systems'.

12. art. cit., p. 540.
13. *The Shape* ..., Introduction, p. xviii.
14. *The Throne of David*, p. 7.
15. *Liturgy and Society*, p. 171.
16. *Christendom*, XII (1942), p. 257.
17. *Sobornost'*, winter-spring 1961, pp. 202f.
18. *The Word Incarnate*, pp. 107ff.
19. op. cit., p. vii.
20. *Revelation and the Modern World*, p. 5.
21. ibid., p. 6.
22. art. cit., p. 203.
23. Horace and James Smith, *Horace in London* (1813).
24. Quoted by E. W. Gilbert, *Brighton* ..., p. 201.

Chapter Eight

Extra-Curricular Activities

(1937–1962)

Heureux qui comme Ulysse a fait un beau voyage.
— Joachim du Bellay

Eight years as Sub-Warden at Lincoln, seventeen years as a don at Oxford and finally eleven years as a Professor in London provided me with ample vacations in which to indulge my extra-curricular interests and activities, though I can truthfully say that most of these had some relation to my commitment as a theologian. I shall describe some of these before continuing my central narrative from the point which it has now reached, namely my election as a lecturer at Christ Church in 1945. Eight plus seventeen plus eleven adds up to thirty-six, and in the course of those thirty-six years I suppose that I preached in most of the historic churches of the Catholic Movement, frequently conducting the Good-Friday devotion of the Three Hours, which was in those days an almost compulsory feature of any well-run parish. All Saints', Margaret Street, and St Mary's, Graham Street, in London; St Bartholomew's and St Paul's, Brighton; St Benedict's, Ardwick, Manchester; Little St Mary's and St Giles's, Cambridge; St Paul's and SS Mary and John, Oxford; St Stephen's, Bournemouth; St Barnabas', Tunbridge Wells; All Saints', Hereford – these are some that come to mind. At Margaret Street I spent some quite long spells, first with Dom Bernard Clements, then with Cyril Tomkinson and lastly with Kenneth Ross, three outstanding priests of very different types and all very hospitable to a struggling theologian; I typed the final text of my first serious theological work, *He Who Is*, at Margaret Street on a typewriter borrowed from the Pax House. After the War, for some years running I spent part of the summer at St

Bartholomew's, Brighton, with Charles Hutchinson, about whom I have written elsewhere in this book, and several times with Billy Favell at St Paul's in that same resort. Brighton, with its location in my own family's Sussex background, its Regency rakishness and its wealth of Victorian churches, has always fascinated me; and D. L. Murray's novel *Regency*, while perhaps not quite in the front rank of English fiction, catches its atmosphere quite remarkably. To find two friends of long standing established as vicars of famous churches in the town gave me plenty of stimulus for exercising my well-known capacity for being a guest.

One very odd experience was that of preaching at Eton College when the bombing was at its height. How such an unlikely thing took place when I was a completely obscure member of the staff at Lincoln with no public-school connections I cannot imagine; and in fact when my mother told an acquaintance of hers who occupied grace-and-favour apartments at Windsor Castle, the latter lady simply said, 'Oh no, I don't think that can be so.' The invitation came, of course, from the Provost, Lord Quickswood (better known perhaps as Lord Hugh Cecil), with whom I stayed over the week-end. There was a peculiar Alice-in-Wonderland air of unreality about the whole proceedings; as soon as one had crossed the threshold and been received by the butler, one appeared to have left not only the War but the last century and a half behind. Quickswood used words like 'ain't' and dropped his aitches in a way which in a lesser mortal would have been uneducated but in a Cecil was no doubt a mark of ancient lineage. To my enquiry whether the War had made things difficult he replied vaguely that he thought they had lost one of the servants; he had not only a butler but a valet as well. He was an excellent host and an entertaining conversationalist. My apology for not having brought evening clothes was of course accepted, but I sensed a faint note of surprise; he not only dressed for dinner, but wore knee-breeches and silk stockings. Just after we started dinner on the Saturday the air-raid sirens sounded; no comment was made, but the butler murmured an apology and withdrew for a moment before reappearaing in A.R.P. overalls over his suit to continue serving the meal. A first-class raid rapidly developed and it was plain that the Luftwaffe was bombing the railway at Slough; but we treated it with aristocratic disdain. However one terrific crash shook the house when the Provost had his glass half-way to his mouth, and he shot its contents over the table. 'Oh dem!', he exclaimed loftily, as the butler rushed forward with a napkin. One felt that the Cecils were ready to be blown to death if need be but they were not going to interrupt their meal for an Austrian house-painter. At breakfast on Sunday he told me that we should be lunching in college and asked me what I would like to drink at that meal. Surprised at this enquiry so early, I said the first thing I could think of, which was beer. 'Very well,' he replied, 'I'll have some sent across. I don't think much of what they give you there.' Everything seemed to have been arranged in order to demoralise the preacher. The Provost kindly explained that if the head of the school disapproved of the sermon he would turn his back to the preacher and the rest of the school would follow suit. The preacher was 'pokered' to the pulpit to soft music between the serried ranks of the congregation, who had nothing to do but stare at him as he proceeded. A 'purple' air-raid warning was in force, which meant that if it was changed to 'red' the service would step abruptly and the chapel would be evacuated; I was hoping this would happen before the sermon began, but in fact it never happened at all. Nor did the head of the school turn his back, and to my great surprise I was asked to preach again; which I did, though this time I declined the Provost's invitation and stayed with a friend near by. I have never really enjoyed preaching to a school, or to any institution with its own private corporate mythology; however careful one is, one can always drop the most ghastly brick; like the visiting preacher who, expounding the parable of the rich fool, exhorted his hearers to pull down their barns. How could the poor man know that at that school 'barns' was the official slang for trousers?

I have already described how I made my first acquaintance with Russian Orthodoxy while I was still at Cambridge, in the winter of 1927, and maintained it as a schoolmaster and as a young parish-priest.[1] Indeed for most of that time I was chairman of the Executive Committee of the Fellowship of St Alban and St Sergius, but I gave up that office when I went to Lincoln and took on the editorship of the journal *Sobornost'* instead.[2] The bulk of the Fellowship's membership in those days was domiciled in Britain and France and the annual conference was almost always at High Leigh in Hertfordshire, though many local gatherings took place of various types and sizes. When the War came, the Fellowship fell apart into two mutually isolated sections; the old type of conference ceased, but other types of gathering, such as camps, were sometimes possible, and the upheavals of population which the War produced on the continent of Europe brought about fresh contacts between Orthodoxy and the Churches of the West. Somehow I managed to maintain an exigueus *Sobornost'*, on a paper-ration reduced to one-fifth, until the return of peace, when I gladly handed it over to new management. The reintegration of the Fellowship took place remarkably smoothly. Several of the foundation-members, notably Father Sergius Bulgakov, had died; others, such as Father George Florovsky, migrated to the United States, and in recent years St Vladimir's Seminary in the State of New York has eclipsed the Institute of St Sergius in Paris as the leading centre of Russian Orthodoxy in the West; the most distinguished Russian Orthodox theologian now alive, Dr John Meyendorff, is firmly rooted in the New World. The Fellowship is now an international and indeed an intercontinental association, with two established houses in Britain alone: St Basil's in London and SS Gregory and Macrina in Oxford. When the annual conferences were resumed after the War in the extended and more relaxed form of summer-schools – until 1955 usually at St Helen's School, Abingdon, and after that date at St Stephen's School, Broadstairs – some impressive new figures emerged on both sides. Fr Lionel Thornton, C. R., about whom I have written elsewhere in this book, became an invariable participant until his death in 1960. H. A. ('Bert') Hodges, Professor of Philosophy at Reading University, came every year with his family until a breakdown in health forced his early retirement. A Methodist who had become an Anglican – and remained one, although he seemed to find in Orthodoxy the expression of Christianity that best met both his religious and his intellectual demands –, he devoted his last years to preparing for publication his mature thought as a Christian philosopher. He died in 1976.

An equally familiar family (if the verbal solecism may be allowed) was that of Vladimir Lossky from Paris. When he died suddenly in his early fifties in 1958 he had already become known to some English readers by his recently published book *The Mystical Theology of the Eastern Church*,[3] which, unlike many books by Orthodox writers, is clear and systematic. He was a quietly vivacious, stocky little man, always ready for a theological discussion, and anyone who may remember 'Ecumenism Exemplified' in my little book of verses *Pi in the High* may be interested to learn that the original Palamite and Thomist who inspired it were not the Orthodox monk and the Dominican friar of Barbara Jones's admirable illustration but Vladimir Lossky and myself; indeed the original version of the poem was recited by us together at an informal concert at Abingdon. His wife Maddalena was a woman of deep devotion and amazing vitality, who not only coped with conspicuous success with the care of a lay-theologian husband and four gifted children in the difficult conditions of emigration and war, but was a talented and indefatigable choirmistress. She once told me, in reply to an enquiry, that the longer she sang the liturgical music the less tired she became!

When one recognised how uncompromising was Vladimir's adherence to the tradition of Eastern orthodoxy it came as a surprise to discover that his major academic achievement was a study of the person and thought of the Dominican mystic Master Eckhart. This extended over a period of twenty-five years and culminated in the preparation for the doctorate of the Sorbonne of the massive volume *Théologie négative et Connaissance de Dieu chez Maître Eckhart*, which appeared posthumously in 1960; I was deeply touched to receive a copy from Maddalena. Vladimir himself had become convinced that the negative strain in Eckhart counterbalanced what he felt to be the exaggerated rationalism of the dominant theology of the medieval West and approximated to the 'apophaticism' which he held to be fundamental to the Eastern tradition; whether he was right or wrong in this estimate, it is significant that his book appeared with an admiring preface by such an impenitent and indeed Thomistic an occidental as Etienne Gilson. It is because I believe that in Vladimir Lossky we lost a really great theologian that, more than twenty years after his death, I wish to re-emphasise the three characteristics of his theological method to which I pointed in writing his obituary[4], for I believe they have much to teach all who are involved in ecumenism on the theological level, and especially in the reconciliation of East and West.

First, then, there was a deliberate effort of clarity and discrimination, a feature which is none too common among theologians of either the Orthodox or the Anglican Church. I do not think that I ever came away from a conversation with Vladimir without feeling that some issue had been made clear to me which was formerly obscure. Indeed, although there was nothing Latin about his theology, it always seemed to me that his mind showed some of the more admirable Latin, and indeed French, features in its determination to avoid any kind of ambiguity or obscurity. I have not always found it easy to discover what an Orthodox thinker really held about a difficult theological question; but there was never any doubt in the case of Vladimir Lossky.

Secondly, there was his courteous but persistent adherence to the traditional positions of the Orthodox Church. Many Orthodox thinkers who have come into contact with the West have been ready and anxious to soft-pedal the classical formulations in the interest of ecumenical understanding; not so Lossky. He would never admit that the *Filioque*[5] was a matter of indifference. On the contrary, he was inclined to trace from it all that he considered to be distorted or displaced in Western theology, and not least the authoritarian Papacy; indeed I sometimes flippantly suggested that he attributed to it everything bad in Western Europe, including Napoleon and Hitler! As I understood him, the Palamite doctrine of the divine essence and the divine energies was no mere *theologoumenon* but a direct consequence, if not indeed a constituent, of the deposit of faith; though this was a point on which I was hoping to question him if he had not been so suddenly taken from us. There was, however, nothing obstinate or truculent about his loyalty to Orthodox tradition; no one could have been more modest and humble and more willing to learn from others. But I do not think he would have been happy with the more recent readiness of many Anglicans to abandon the *Filioque* as a concession to the obstinacy of the Orthodox, when it is accompanied by indifference to their theological objections and even by disbelief in the Trinity.

For – and this is my third point – one always knew with Lossky that for him it was the truth that mattered and not its verbal formulation; no one was less a slave to words than he. I can remember vividly a long conversation in the garden at Abingdon about the doctrine of sanctifying grace, at the end of which Vladimir remained as convinced of the incoherence and inadequacy of the Western concept of the created supernatural as I was of the unintelligibility of the Eastern distinction between the divine essence and energies. (It is reproduced in stylised form as the discussion between the Thomist and the Palamite in my books *Existence and Analogy*, pp. 151ff, and *Via Media*, pp. 162ff.) And yet he was ready and anxious to assert that he and I were both trying to express in the limited and halting terms of human speech the same mysterious and inexhaustible reality, namely the participation by a creature in the life of the Holy Trinity without destruction of its creaturely status. One was always sure with Vladimir that there would be no scoring of debating points and no merely verbal victories. For beneath all his incisive intellectual brilliance there was the religion of a profoundly humble and devout son of the Orthodox Church.

When I wrote Vladimir's obituary I suggested that relations between Anglicanism and Orthodoxy had got into a condition approaching stalemate and that this was largely due to a failure in theological method. 'I wonder', I wrote,

> whether the trouble is that we have never got very much beneath
> the surface. Perhaps if we had started by discussing the great basic

truths which we professedly hold in common we might have found that beneath the common inheritance there were hitherto unsuspected differences of interpretation and understanding which were the real, though unrecognised, obstacles to unity. And then we might have done something towards resolving them. There are very few books that can help us if we ever take up this task, but Vladimir Lossky's *Mystical Theology of the Eastern Church* is one of them.

In my book *The Recovery of Unity*, which was published in this same year 1958 (and in which, incidentally, I gave a fairly searching critique of Bert Hodges's particular interpretation of the significance of Orthodoxy for Anglicanism), I tried to apply this method to some of the major theological confrontations in the history of Christendon – Grace, Eucharist, Ministry and Papacy – and to carry the discussion a stage further than the above quotation suggests. For it had become plain to me, not only that our really genuine differences might be other than we had originally supposed them to be, but that, paradoxical as this may seem, the difficulty in resolving them arose very largely from certain assumptions which we held in common, which were in fact highly debatable but which, just because they were held in common, were never disputed and were frequently unrecognised. Now to attain, even imperfectly, to this type of theological insight clearly needs careful and sympathetic theological co-operation in a setting of Christian life and worship, conducted not with the aim of victory over an antagonist or even for the satisfaction of achieving a tolerable compromise, but as a humble and grateful service to the truth revealed in Christ. For myself I can say quite sincerely that a great part of such understanding as I have managed to acquire goes back to those often impromptu talks at Abingdon in the nineteen-forties and -fifties, unassisted by any of the conventional academic paraphernalia, with Vladimir Lossky, Bert Hodges, Lionel Thornton[6] and Derwas Chitty (Derwas, who appeared to have been at the university with St Gregory Nazianzen and who knew all about the sanitary arrangements of a stylite's column). These were often enlivened by the briefer visits of such meteoric figures as Fr Lev Gillet (who was more fluent in English than most Englishmen but pronounced it exactly as if it was French), Gregory Dix, Antony Blum (whom we first knew as a young doctor working in the slums of Paris and saw pass successively through the stages of monastic profession, ordination to the priesthood and consecration to the episcopate), Gabriel Hebert, and many others not less distinguished whom to name

> ... would need a thousand tongues,
> A brazen throat and adamantine lungs.

After I left Oxford in 1962 my active participation in the Fellowship gradually decreased, for a number of reasons. Other activities became increasingly pressing, the Fellowship was flourishing and had plenty of younger members ready and able to take over from their elders; and I have seen too many cases of vigorous organisations gradually turning into gerontocracies and finally into necrocracies to wish ever to hold on to power myself. I am still a member, and a complete run of *Sobornost'* adorns the shelves of my study. I shall never cease to be grateful for those few days over fifty years ago in snow-bound St Albans when I had my first concrete experience of a Catholicism wider than Anglicanism.

My concern with Christian sociology, which had been kindled by Maurice Reckitt when I was still a curate in Westminster, now found expression in attending the annual Christendom Conferences and Anglo-Catholic Summer-Schools of Sociology and in reading (and sometimes writing for) the journal *Christendom*, of which Maurice was Editor. The creative event from which all these derived was the transformation of the Church Socialist League into the new League of the Kingdom of God in 1923 under the impact of an amazingly dynamic Anglican priest named Percy Widdrington. This was carried out on the grounds that Christian sociology ought not take its principles from secular sources but from Catholic dogma and experience, and that, necessary as it is for the Church and its members to be involved in the hard realities of contemporary living and dying – and Widdrington himself dwelt in no academic ivory castle-, the battle for a Christian social order must begin in the realm of faith and thought. Reckitt was already in the movement, and the best account of it is in his biography of Widdrington, published after the latter's death in 1959. It was enthusiastically taken up by Anglo-Catholics in the days of the great Congresses with such notable figures as Fr Reginald Tribe, S.S.M., Fr Lionel Thornton, C. R., and G. D. Rosanthal, and the much-quoted words of Bishop Frank Weston's address to the 1923 Congress – 'You cannot claim to worship Jesus in the Tabernacle, if you do not pity Jesus in the slum' – almost became a slogan of the movement. Two very weighty recruits on the intellectual side – both ex-nonconformists – were V. A. Demant, who from 1929 to 1933 had been Director of Research for the Christian Social Council and had produced important material on unemployment, and W. G. Peck, who later, from 1936 to

1951, was to organise clergy schools for the Industrial Christian Fellowship.

I am not sure whether T. S. Eliot and Charles Williams were strictly to be described as members of the L.K.G. — membership was in any case a rather indefinite and fluid concept, but they were frequently at meetings and Williams in particular could on occasion make striking interventions. I came in with a wave of younger people, more or less independently of one another: Julian Langmead Casserley, Bryan Bentley, Patrick McLaughlin, David Peck (son of W. G.), Herbert Rees and, less committedly, Donald MacKinnon. In retrospect, one of the most remarkable features of the Christendom Group and its gatherings was the extraordinary note of excitement and indeed of jubilation which characterised them. This no doubt owed something to the sheer entertainment value of such brilliant talkers as Reckitt and Williams, but it rested on something far deeper than that, namely the conviction that Christian social ethics did not consist simply in persuading people to pursue more diligently and conscientiously the tasks on which they were already engaged but in critically examining, from the standpoint of Christian belief about the nature, destiny and predicament of man, the validity of those tasks and of the whole mass of human activity of which they were part. For it seemed obvious to us that, if a social and economic structure is constructed to achieve other than genuinely human values, its efficient and conscientious operation will result not in human happiness but in misery and frustration.[7] This is why we were so critical of capitalist economics and interested in proposals for financial reform. Mr John Oliver[8] is quite mistaken in suggesting that the Christendom Group committed itself to Major Douglas's scheme of Social Credit, though certainly some of our leading members were sympathetic — probably too sympathetic — to it. What we were convinced of was the necessity of subordinating financial values to real ones; to be hungry because there was no food was tragic but made sense, but to be hungry because, although there was plenty of food, there was no money to buy it, simply proved either the incompetence or the rapacity of the financial experts. I tried to express the theology involved in simple language in a small book in the 'Signposts' series called *Man: His Origin and Destiny*. In this I argued that there are four orders of being: God, Man, Things and Money; and that each exists for the one before: Man for the glory of God, Things for the good of Man, Money for the production and distribution of Things. However, the argument went, with man's modern repudiation of the supremacy of God, the whole scheme has not just lost its first member but has gone entirely into reverse: Things are for the production of Money; Man is for the production and consumption of Things; and a very hypothetical God is for the convenience of Man. I gave several specific examples to justify this analysis, and it still seems to me to be sound. Indeed I believe that, with the necessary adjustments to a different historical situation, it is as true of 1980 as of 1940. There is, however, one difference and it is all to our credit, for it shows that some of the assertions which when we made them were ridiculed as fantasies and indeed heresies have now become orthodox and commonplace; and the chief of these is that of the essentially abstract and conventional character of Money in relation to Things and Man. Nevertheless, illusions die hard, and recent events have shown trade-unionists and top executives alike clinging to the belief that higher wages are the key to personal prosperity. But it would in any case be quite wrong to suppose that Social Credit was the main concern of the Christendom Group. Hitler became Chancellor in 1933, Mussolini invaded Ethiopia in 1935, and the Spanish Civil War lasted from 1936 to 1939; I do not think this last conflict caused quite as sharp a division among us as it did among many Roman Catholics, but if tempers rose no higher than they did it was because we were trying to see the issues in the light of Catholic theology and not simply of emotional reactions and sympathies.

The title of one conference, 'Right or Left or – ?', at least showed an attempt at a distinctive Christian stance. As the World War became imminent and when it finally broke out, we became much concerned both with its theological interpretation as a judgment of God on our civilisation and also with detailed practical questions of the ethics of war under modern conditions. This incidentally attracted one of the rudest letters I have ever received. The Dean of Wells, the Very Reverend R. H. Malden, who was later revealed as the anonymous author for many years of the generously barbed prefaces to *Crockford's Clerical Directory*, made a speech in Convocation in which he seemed to me to have quite clearly misstated St Thomas Aquinas's teaching as to what constituted a just war. I wrote to him very politely questioning his interpretation. His reply was superb; it began 'Dear Sir, If you will take a word of advice from one who is presumably older than yourself ...' and ended 'I have neither time nor inclination for any further correspondence with you,' but entirely evaded the point. This left me with no alternative but to continue the argument in the *Church Times*; I was apparently not the only person who had demurred, as a letter was printed shortly after in that paper beginning 'Letters from unknown persons in various parts of the country . . .' and bearing the signature of the Dean of Wells. Malden was in fact typical of a number of ecclesiastical dignitaries of his time, who were so convinced of their status in the universe that to be dictatorial and insulting was second nature to them and it never occurred to them that anyone could doubt its propriety; some of them were in fact quite nice in private to those who had been privileged with the entrée. But they really belonged to another century.

Like any other group of people who were gripped by a strong conviction the Christendom Group was accused of being introverted and inbred; but I do not think this was true, and it was certainly not exclusive. I have never known any circle in which such violent arguments took place. It was indeed sometimes accused of claiming to be the only authentic Anglican voice on social questions. John Oliver is probably correct in writing that 'in 1933 the Christendom Group was at the height of its popularity and influence, and its outlook was to dominate the Malvern Conference of 1941, but it never succeeded in permeating the Church of England as a whole.'[9]

The Malvern Conference, held at a time when many thought that the end of the War was much closer than in fact it proved to be, was a characteristic brain-child of its chairman William Temple, embodying both his strengths and his weaknesses. It was far too large in its membership, and lasted far too short a time, to provide an adequate discussion of its enormous subject, The Life of the Church and the Order of Society; the official element was massive but largely uninstructed, constructive argument was impossible and was not really attempted, and, when finally the Conference was asked to accept without amendment a number of resolutions which the chairman frankly declared represented his impression of what the Conference believed, Alec Vidler rose and protested that it was improper for people to assent to propositions which they had not thoroughly considered. His point was ignored, as also was one which I had made earlier and which I think is worth recording as showing the way in which theology can become relevant. Temple had a firm conviction of the social implications of the Eucharist and in particular of the fact that the Church brings the bread and wine to God as the products of man's labour upon the fruits of the earth and that God accepts them, transforms them and gives them back in their transformed state. But how, in such a very mixed gathering of Anglicans, was that state to be described? Clearly, Temple was timid of saying in so many words that the elements were now Christ's body and blood; so he hit on the ingenious device of asserting that they were returned to us 'charged with spiritual power'. It was here that I put in my protest. If we said they were Christ's body and blood, we were, I held, being scriptural and Christian and loyal to the evangelical truth of our personal relation to Jesus; but 'charged with spiritual power' seemed to me to be not even personal, let alone Christian; it was at best a metaphor from electrostatics and at worst could be sheer gnosticism; and it encouraged the notion, which I knew that Temple in fact repudiated, that Christianity was a purely spiritual religion. I cannot remember how much of this I was in fact allowed to expound, but I know that my protest was brushed aside. Temple was a great man and he took an interest, if a detached one, in our work; his suggestion, which raised such a furore in the business world in 1942, that the creation of credit by private persons and corporations should be prohibited, was fully in line with our stress on the basically functional and ancillary character of finance. But even he, when it came to the point, was inclined to rely for the Church's social witness on the general ethical conscience of Christians rather than on systematic theological thought, or at most to look on the latter as a useful boost for the former. After the War, although individual members of the Christendom Group were still articulate, it gradually ceased to function as an identifiable entity, largely owing to the dispersal, for a variety of reasons, among which change of religious allegiance, personal problems, pressure of other concerns and sheer geographical separation all played a part, of the young recruits of the nineteen-thirties. Since then there has been no lack of vociferous Anglican utterance on fashionable social matters; there has not been very much systematic theological thought by Anglicans in the social field. Then again there has not been very much systematic theological thought by Anglicans in any field at all. I am, however, encouraged by the recent emergence of the Jubilee Group, which is, as I see it, trying under much more difficult circumstances to do essentially the same task that we were attacking half a century ago. No doubt they will make their mistakes as we made ours, but it is significant that they have come, as we came, not out of the theological faculties of the universities or the central organisations of the ecclesiastical establishment, but out of the front line of the Church's pastoral ministry.

It would be pointless and futile for me to write at length about all or most of the memorable people with whom I had contact through the Christendom Group. Some, such as T. S. Eliot and

Dorothy L. Sayers, have been the subject of detailed studies which render anything that I could say about them superfluous. There are, however, two about whom I feel it may be worth while to record my memories, Maurice Reckitt himself, who died in his ninety-fourth year in 1980, and Charles Williams, who died suddenly in early middle age in 1945. Maurice had been an outstandingly good-looking young man, with a remarkable likeness to the future Earl of Avon. He was devoted to his wife, to ballroom dancing and to croquet, in the last of which he acquired international status; he once said that there were no men who could beat him at the game but quite a few women. Unlike some lay apologists for religion he was a loyal and steady practising, though sometimes exasperated, churchman and was a member of the Church Assembly for some years. His literary output, both of books and of articles, was continuous and extensive; it was almost entirely in the field of Christian sociology. His style was lucid and entertaining, and is in the most striking contrast imaginable to the turgid dullness of most theological writing at the present day. It was in the spoken word, however, that he excelled for pungency and wit, and the effect was enhanced by the peculiar high-pitched emphasis which exploded in the last accented syllable of his sentences and which was so infectious that his hearers tended to adopt it unconsciously themselves, temporarily and in some cases even permanently. He had a story about a M.P. who, whenever he could think of a joke, made it and, whenever he could not, assumed a severe expression and declared 'This is no time for frivolity'. The first part of this story might well have applied to Maurice himself; and what good jokes they were! That they were always relevant and never malicious I must add. Take, for example, this extract from the small book which first emboldened me to write to him:

I remember hearing a tale of a man who went to call upon a neighbour and was greeted at the door by the growls of an apparently ferocious dog. His friend expostulated with his pusillanimity. 'The dog's perfectly harmless,' he said, 'you know it and I know it.' 'Possibly,' his friend replied, 'but does the dog know it?' The Church is a Divine Society essentially at issue with the cupidity, the cruelty, the cynicism and the insensibility of the plutocratic world order by which it is everywhere surrounded. You know it and I know it. But does the dog know it? Does the Church, in its external character as a human association of churchgoers, claiming with very varying degrees of knowledge and enthusiasm the Christian name, in any true sense know these things? Would not it – and the world upon which it reacted – look very different if it did?[10]

Or this, from the same work:

> If you had told any typical Christian thinker in any century from
> the twelfth to the sixteenth century that religion had nothing to do
> with economics, and that bishops must not intrude in these matters
> upon the deliberations of laymen – propositions which to many
> of the correspondents to our newspapers appear to be axiomatic –
> he would either have trembled for your faith or feared for your
> reason. He would have regarded you, in short, as either a heretic
> or a lunatic.[11]

One of the most useful functions of Maurice's interventions was to
bring life to a discussion that had run into a rut of boredom. There
was a meeting at which someone was elaborating at unnecessary
length the relevant but uncontroverted thesis that the effects of the
fall had extended beyond man into the material world as a whole.
Suddenly from the depths of a basketwork chair came the clarion
voice of Maurice: 'I know – "Groaning and travailing, groaning
and travailing"!' And that summed the argument up. But the best
example of this enviable gift that I can remember comes from an
annual public meeting of the Cowley, Wantage and All Saints
Missionary Association. It was a hot summer afternoon and the
audience had been reduced to a state of somnolence by a series
of utterances from worthy but boring clerics, when Maurice was
called upon to speak. 'I find it difficult', he began, 'to understand
why I should be here as the only layman on a platform otherwise
entirely occupied by the clergy. I can only suppose that I am here
for the same reason for which the cannibal attended the missionary
meeting. *I represent the point of view of the consumer!*' The note
of triumph on which the last sentence culminated evoked a burst
of laughter after which his hearers hung on every word.

Though his style was admirable for its lucidity, his handwriting
manifested a standard of illegibility which it is granted to few to
attain, an illegibility which derived not, as with most bad writers,
from omitting vital graphic elements but from over-writing several
times, so that the finished product resembled weeds rather than
words. Maurice's own recipe for interpreting it was: 'Throw it
on the floor and walk round it; then some of it'll leap out at
you.' This frequently worked; but most of his friends would try
to arrange that their letters reach him on a Monday, when his
secretary would produce a neatly typewritten reply.

Maurice was a wealthy man, as the trade name 'Reckitt and
Coleman' would suggest; he was also a generous one, and before
his death he had set up the Christendom Trust to set forward the

Christian social thinking to which his own life had been dedicated. He described his own vocation as 'being available', and Vigo Demant described him on his ninetieth birthday as 'one of the few fairly rich men who will get through the needle's eye'. His tombstone bears a sentence of G. K. Chesterton's which he was fond of quoting: 'One must somehow find a way of loving the world without trusting it.'

Charles Williams — novelist, poet, dramatist and brilliant lay theologian — was certainly one of the most invigorating and stimulating men that it has been my good fortune to encounter. A conversation between him and Maurice Reckitt was as entertaining a display of spontaneous wit and wisdom as I can remember to have experienced. Yet in other respects than the intensity of their Christian conviction and the speed of their mental reactions they might seem to have had little in common. Physically, Williams was not particularly impressive until one noticed the vivacity of his facial expressions. He was rather below middle height and peered through rather thick glasses. It was in the excitability and volubility of his speech that his enormous interior energy and enthusiasm were manifested and became infectious. Though largely self-educated, he was a man of profound intellectual depth and, with this, of great spiritual integrity. With the emotional temperament of a Welshman and the accent and sense of humour of a cockney, the impression which an audience received from him on their first meeting could begin with a kind of stunned incredulity, which rapidly passed into wild enthusiasm. I vividly remember the effect which he produced on the students of Lincoln Theological College by reciting the opening lines of Milton's *Paradise Lost*:

> Of man's first disobedience an' the fruit
> Of that ferbidden tree, 'oose mortal tiste
> Brort death into the world and all our wow . . .
> Sing, 'eavenly muse, that on the sicred top . . . ,

which was probably more like Milton's own pronunciation than the etiolated accents of our modern academics!

Most readers of Williams easily recognise how deeply concerned he was to emphasise the goodness and authenticity of the physical, including the sexual, aspect of human existence and human nature, 'the holy and glorious flesh' as he sometimes described it. What they do not always understand is that, with all the exuberance with which he would extol the glories of romantic love, he was firmly and no less exuberantly committed to the great traditional

Christian values of chastity, fidelity and monogamy. C. S. Lewis describes in one of his letters the impact made by a lecture given by Williams on Milton's *Comus*:

> We actually heard a lecture on *Comus* which put the importance where Milton put it. In fact the lecture was a panegyric of chastity. Just imagine the incredulity with which (at first) an audience of undergraduates listened to something so unheard of. But he beat them in the end.
>
>   He is an ugly man with rather a cockney voice. But no one ever thinks of this for five minutes after he has begun speaking. His face becomes almost angelic. Both in public and in private he is of nearly all the men I have met the one whose address most overflows with *love*. It is simply irresistible. These young men and women were lapping up what he said about Chastity before the end of the hour. It's a big thing to have done.[12]

Nevertheless, with all his enthusiasm for the romantic nature of married love, Williams made no pretence of glossing over the more banal aspects of domesticity. I remember him describing how he used to make early-morning tea for his wife. 'I usually enjoy doing it. But there are times when there's nothing that I want to do less. And then I say to myself, "Well, dash it all, I am married to the woman!" And then I get up and make it.'

It would be quite wrong to suppose that with his intense aesthetic sensibility Williams was inclined to underrate the importance of the rational and intellectual aspect of human experience. He once arrived rather late at a meeting at which I was speaking, I forget about what topic. In the discussion after my speech he mentioned that he had just come from Fleet Street, where everyone seemed to be living in a world of false values. 'I've just seen a poster saying "Tragic Death of a Peer". Just fancy that – what is there tragic about the death of a peer? And then, when I came into this room I heard Father Mascall saying, "What is really important is to be careful how we define our terms." And my heart leapt up when I beheld a rinebow in the sky!'

At the risk of being outrageously egoistic I will dare to illustrate this same point from a review which Williams wrote in 1943 of my first serious theological work *He Who Is* in the now defunct journal *Time and Tide*. He began by saying that in writing on philosophical theology I had confirmed the line in *Comus* where the Elder Brother says that philosophy is

> a perpetual feast of nectar's sweets
> Where no crude surfeit reigns ...

and then continued:

> This is supposed to be a simile of intellectual satisfaction. So it
> is, but it is also a perfectly correct literal statement. There was a
> moment in *He Who Is* when I found myself savouring a particular
> doctrine with an almost physical delight; and, except from false
> fear, I do not know why I say almost. It was in my mouth 'sweet
> as honey'; it melted exquisitely into my corporeal organism and
> bestowed a richness. Perhaps the Apocalyptic John also was talking
> more sense than we know when he spoke of 'eating a book'. It
> would be humbling if we discovered that the saints and prophets
> were physiologically as well as psychologically accurate. The physical
> effect of intellectual ideas has still to be examined by psycho-analysts
> and doctors. We shall yet perhaps see graphs showing the relative
> effects on a fifty-years-old one-legged west-country industrialist of
> the Platonic ideas, the Cartesian dualism and the geo-politics of
> Houshofer.[13]

No doubt it will come as a surprise to some that 'the particular
doctrine in question was that of the self-sufficiency of God', even
when he added that 'one's physical reactions have nothing to
do – at least, calculably – with the truth of the doctrine, nor
was the doctrine new, but I have quoted this passage simply in
order to show how very organically in Williams's view of reality
the intellectual and the aesthetic were mutually integrated. Indeed
I think that one of the reasons for his concern with the language of
poetry was that it seemed to him that aesthetic images were often
more successful than conceptual forms in expressing the depth and
the multiplicity of the real world. I once very daringly asked him
whether the line, in one of the Taliessin poems, 'The feet of creation
walk backward through the waters' was meant as a description of
the effects of sin and the Fall. With characteristic humility he
replied after a moment's thought, 'I have never thought of that
before, but it is certainly one of the things that it means.' Paradoxical and even frivolous as this answer might seem, there could
hardly be a clearer spontaneous avowal that the poet's function
is not to give expression to the dredged-up precipitates of his
own subconscious but to witness to his imperfect but nevertheless
authentic perceptions of the manifold aspects of objective reality.
This, however, is not the place for a discussion of William's theology,
fascinating as that topic would be.

One last recollection; I cannot recall the context of this incident,
but it is entirely characteristic and I tell it as I rememeber it.
Williams told us that he had been having his hair cut, and the

barber had told him that he (the barber) had just got engaged to be married. 'He said to me, "Yer know, sir, it makes yer feel just fine. I felt that if a bloke 'ad dotted me in the eye I'd 'ave stood 'im a pint." I leapt out of the chair and seized him by the hand and said, "My friend, do you know that's just what Dante said in the *Vita Nuova*: 'Such warmth of charity came upon me that most certainly in that moment if anyone had done me an injury I would have forgiven him.'?".' What effect this had on the other occupants of the barber's saloon Williams did not tell us; I imagine that to him his reaction was the most natural thing in the world. For if ever there was a Christian to whom it was obvious that grace does not destroy nature but perfects it, that Christian was Charles Williams, for whom 'there [was] only one reason why anything should be loved on this earth – because God loves it.'[14]

In these days, when for so many professional theologians the fundamental theological categories seem to be drabness and obscurity, it is comforting to remember the life and work of this inspired and inspiring layman. But indeed Williams and Reckitt were only two of a number of highly intelligent lay men and women – T. S. Eliot, Dorothy L. Sayers and C. S. Lewis spring at once to mind – whom the Anglican Church possessed in those days, who wrote grippingly, lucidly and enlighteningly because they were convinced of the truth of orthodox Christianity and of its relevance to the problems of mankind. The strength of their conviction gave their writings more, not less, apologetic force.

I have mentioned my conviction that Sociology and Spirituality, so far from being either alternative or conflicting interpretations of the Catholic religion, were integral aspects of it. In this I was clearly in accord with the basic principles of the Christendom Group, though in its earlier years its members had given little attention to the relation between the two. It was to give this a concrete expression that some of us younger people pressed for the holding of a retreat in which, while the traditional pattern of silence and sacramental worship would be retained, the addresses would have a social as well as an individual orientation. As conductor we invited William George Peck, whose books, especially *The Salvation of Modern Man*, showed him to have just that grasp of Christian dogma combined with sensitivity to its practical implications that was needed; his addresses made the substance of another volume, *Return to Holiness*, which I would still recommend to aspiring retreat-conductors. In some ways the experiment was hardly a success; the participants were few in number and showed a regrettable tendency for coming and going. In retrospect it was clear that our attempt to wed Sociology and Spirituality had too much of the brashness of a shotgun-marriage; nevertheless we had made our point. This was in the early nineteen-forties, and it is good to find, nearly forty years later, Kenneth Leech's 'Study of Spirituality' entitled *Soul Friend* coming out of the heart of so very socially conscious a body as the Jubilee Group. My initial concern with the theology of spirituality had arisen from those personal problems in prayer to which I have already referred and in coping with which I had been much helped by the *Spiritual Letters* of Dom John Chapman. From this I had been led on to Chapman's magisterial article 'Mysticism, Christian, Roman Catholic' in the *Encyclopaedia of Religion and Ethics*, with its vindication of contemplation as a normal element of Christian prayer. Taking many of the 'correct' authors on the way with variable profit, I became quite fascinated by the great Spanish mystics St Teresa of Avila and St John of the Cross. St John in particular appealed to me, not only because of the intrinsic importance of his subject, but also because of the extraordinary technique which he adopted to deal with it. He first of all wrote three poems, which are considered as among the finest lyrics in the Spanish tongue; then he wrote allegorical commentaries on them which are neither complete in themselves nor consistent with one another. This would seem an unpromising way of writing a scientific account of any subject whatever; nevertheless it is remarkably successful, and one can only suppose that St John knew his own business best. He had in fact that rare combination the mind of both a poet and a philosopher, and this produced a highly specific technique of communication; he was also a saint, and had something important to communicate. As a result of my study I produced for my fellow-neophytes a brief summary and analysis of St John's most elaborate commentary, *The Ascent of Mount Carmel*; it was the publication of this by the Dacre Press that led to a long and fruitful association with the Benedictine nuns of West Malling. It came about like this.

I have already mentioned the link between the nuns and Mrs Berta Travers, the founder and owner of the Dacre Press. With the approach of war the nuns found their life becoming progressively more difficult, surrounded as they were in Kent by Air Force stations and under the threat of invasion. Mrs Travers, who was a lady of formidable efficiency and forcefulness, took the matter into her own hands and evacuated the whole community by motor coach to a large house which she had secured at Fownhope in Herefordshire on the banks of the River Wye, where they remained until the return of peace. It was through her that I received an invitation from the Abbess to conduct the community retreat in the summer of 1940. My first impulse was to refuse on grounds of sheer inexperience, but, encouraged and advised by Gregory Dix, I decided that, provided I gave the sisters straightforward dogma in an assimilable form, I was at least unlikely to do them any harm. In subsequent experience with religious communities, especially contemplatives, I found that this was in fact the most useful service that a theologian could perform for them.

Religious have of course their own problems, whose solution can need sensitive and expert handling, but by and large they are the easiest people to have in retreat because they have achieved at least some degree of maturity in the spiritual life; I always felt with the Malling nuns that if I had merely recited the Greek alphabet it would have provided them with material for prayer for an hour! It is much more difficult to give a retreat to a miscellaneous collection of lay people who have never been in retreat before. However, as things worked out, my visits to the nuns, though they became numerous, were usually for a different reason. During the war they had a succession of chaplains who, while admirable at their work, were either physically infirm or musically limited and for whom therefore the long and elaborate ceremonies of Holy Week presented special problems. As there was no teaching at Lincoln during Holy Week and the College was in semi-retreat, I was able to go to Fownhope for that period, or at any rate for the last three days, and take over the chaplain's duties. To spend the sacred season for five successive years with a contemplative Benedictine community was for me a deep spiritual experience which I count myself fortunate to have enjoyed. It was, I must admit, physically exacting, especially for a single-handed priest on Holy Saturday morning. For these were the days of the unreformed liturgy, and when one had blessed the new fire, sung the *Exultet*, chanted the twelve prophecies (and by the time one had got to number twelve one was likely to stumble at the third listing of *sonitum tubae, fistulae, et citharae, sambucae, et psalterii, et symphoniae, et omnis generis musicorum!*) and sung the first Mass of Easter, all on an empty stomach, one seemed to have been up for quite a long time. Everything of course, was in Latin, the choir parts exquisitely sung with a beauty and devotion that put to shame the croaking of the celebrant, for the community had for many years defied the thunders of bishops and primates in order to worship by the same rite as their fellow Benedictines throughout the world. (Recently they have entirely reversed their policy and now, with episcopal approval, worship with an English rite of their own devising which is used by no other congregation in Christendom.) After they returned to Malling I frequently visited them there, for the Oratory of the Good Shepherd met there for a number of years for annual retreat and General Chapter, and twice – in 1950 and 1951 – I celebrated the Holy Week ceremonies for them again. One unusual service which I was able to perform was to assist a young Swiss Orthodox woman who was living there to tidy up the English of a degree thesis on Ralph Cudworth which she was writing for the University of Basel; her further history as an Orthodox nun living in an Anglican Benedictine convent and later as the foundress of her own community can be read in the volume *Mother Maria: her life in letters*, published after her death in 1977. It is an inspiring account of very unusual but genuine ecumenism, resulting not from planning as such but as the by-product of a heroic life dedicated simply to the will of God. The history of Malling Abbey as a whole is in fact a history of hiddenness and the last thing that the nuns would desire is any kind of sensational publicity. I will therefore mention only their great abbess Mother Magdalen Mary, who not only guided them through long years of episcopal harrassment and the upheaval of World War II but also exercised a remarkable influence upon many priests and layfolk who came to her from outside. She finally made the renunciation of which not all superiors are capable and relinquished her office to a younger successor some time before she died. I met her many times and I always felt that entering her presence was like going into a room where a lamp was burning.

There is of course a grape-vine among religious communities, and having made contact with one I found invitations coming from others. The leading men's communities – Cowley, Nashdom, Mirfield and Kelham – were already familiar to me; Kelham I have already mentioned as close neighbours to us at Lincoln; with the others I had stayed on various occasions, often formally or informally in retreat. But – and here as so often I am running ahead of my narrative – I was both surprised and terrified to be asked by all three at different times to conduct their community retreat. I will only say that they were all both indulgent and appreciative and that I certainly derived from them far more than they could have derived from me. Of the women's communities, Burnham Abbey and Fairacres among the contemplative, Wantage, East Grinstead, Malvern and Westcote among the active, asked me either to conduct their retreats or to give them lectures, and I often felt that, especially for the contemplatives, it was for the second of these functions that, as a theologian, I could be of most use. For unless prayer has the great Christian truths to feed upon it is bound to become weak and straggly, and in the end to feed simply on itself and starve to death. This is all the more necessary at a time when few people have received in their childhood the basic Christian formation that once could be taken for granted. There seem indeed to be cases in which a sense of vocation to the religious life seems almost to have preceded conversion to Christianity, and this is not altogether surprising when it is remembered that religious communities have flourished outside as well as inside the Christian Church. One of the most interesting discoveries that one makes in interviewing members of an enclosed community is that of the extraordinary variety of the backgrounds, social, intellectual, temperamental and physiological, from which God has called them to contribute to what might appear from its visible aspects to be a very uniform type of life. Now however, I must return to May 1945 and Christ Church, Oxford.

Notes

1. Cf p. 80 supra.
2. The journal was first printed in 1932 and took the title *Sobornost'* ('Catholicity') in 1935. Under that title it was renumbered in seven successive series and in 1979 incorporated the (Roman Catholic) *Eastern Churches Review*.
3. English translation 1957. The original was published in French in 1944.
4. *Sobornost'*, summer 1958, 568f.
5. I.e., the Western insertion of the words 'and from the Son' after 'who proceeds from the Father' in the section of the Creed concerning the Holy Spirit.
6. Cf pp 169–176.
7. In Demant's phrase, 'you cannot rationalise a contradiction in terms.'
8. *The Church and Social Order*, (1968), ch. vi.
9. op. cit., p. 185.
10. *Religion and Social Purpose* (1935), p. 53.
11. ibid., pp. 12f.
12. *Letters of C. S. Lewis*, p. 196.
13. *Time and Tide*, 9 Oct. 1943.
14. *He came down from Heaven*, p. 141.

Chapter Nine

Oxford:
Place and Personalities

(1945 – 1962)

'Can this be Oxford? This the place?'
(He cries) 'of which my father said
The tutoring was a damned disgrace,
The creed a mummery, stuffed and dead?'
        – Hilaire Belloc, *Dedicatory Ode*

'He was brought up in the – ' with a shiver
of repugnance ' – the House.'
        – Charles Dickens, *Our Mutual Friend*, I, xvi.

'Sir, it is a great thing to dine with the Canons
of Christ-Church.'
        – Samuel Johnson, Boswell's *Life*, 20/3/1776.

For the sake of readers to whom it is unfamiliar a brief note on the constitution of that peculiar institution Christ Church, Oxford, may be here in place.

When in 1532 King Henry VIII refounded Thomas Wolsey's Cardinal's College as his own King Henry VIII's College he may already have had a more grandiose plan in mind. Be that as it may, in 1545 he refounded it in a new form as both a college of Oxford University and also the cathedral establishment of the newly founded diocese of Oxford. Thus the Dean and Canons – the Chapter – of the Cathedral were also the Governing Body of the College. and therefore, in contrast to every other college in the two ancient universities, it possessed no Fellows. Both those who taught and researched and those who studied were, if they were members of the Foundation, called indifferently 'Students.' In 1867 university reform came in; the senior Students were admitted to the Governing Body, in which they soon outnumbered the Chapter, but they still kept their title of Students, no longer as a token of inferiority but of distinction, though the junior Students became Scholars as everywhere else. Thus there has come about the strange situation of a college in which there are no Fellows and in which nobody can be a Student unless he is a member of the Governing Body. Add to this that there are Lecturers who do, and Lecturers who do not, lecture, and the possibilities of misunderstanding are obvious. Strangers are sometimes surprised when a mature gentleman in his sixties is pointed out as 'just one of our Students'. Officially Christ Church is 'the House of the Cathedral Church of Christ in Oxford'; it is often referred to simply as 'the House', though to overdo the term is a preciosity and the notion that it must never be called a college is simply false. Furthermore, although the biverbal from 'Christ Church' is now invariable, there is plenty of precedent for the univerbal from 'Christchurch'. 'Christchurch College' would have upset nobody in the eighteenth century.

In my time there were six Canons, of whom five held theological professorships and the sixth was the Archdeacon of Oxford, and something under forty Students, of whom I was one. I was commonly, though not officially, known as 'the Clerical Student', which always suggested to me that I was learning shorthand and typewriting. In fact, I was entirely responsible, under the Dean, for the pastoral care of the undergraduates. The cathedral, as such, was the entire responsibility of the Dean and Canons, though, as it was also the college chapel, the College had certain rights in it, which were virtually limited to the holding of an extremely dull service called College Prayers, which took the place of cathedral mattins at 10 o'clock on Sunday mornings in term; the Dean, the Canons and myself each preached at this service once each term. The relations between the two sides of the House – the College and the Cathedral – were to some extent governed by statute but were largely a matter of agreement, much of which was tacit and informal. Potentially it contained the seeds of conflict and from time to time some student, with a real or imaginary grievance or just an anti-clerical sense of mischief, would try to cause trouble. But this never got very far, for feelings in general were friendly and most people were too busy with their jobs to want to waste time and energy in squabbling. I must confess however that I felt sympathy, though not agreement, with the honest disbelievers in our midst, for they saw the most imposing, if not the most comfortable, accomodation in the College occupied by the Dean and Canons, who were, from the unbeliever's standpoint, wholly devoted to the propagation of error and the performance of mumbo-jumbo. I sometimes tried to imagine how I would feel if I saw their residences inhabited by professors of astrology, necromancy, phrenology, haruspication and gyromancy. I sometimes wondered whether the Chapter had ever seriously considered whether, as a body of Christian priests and not just a group of privileged academics, they were exercising their intellectual apostolate in the most efficient manner; but personally I found them kind and encouraging and ready to let me do my own job in my own way. How well I did it is not for me to judge.

The Chapter of Christ Church when I first came to know it contained a rich variety of personalities, though they perhaps hardly justified the description which was once applied to them by that expert in the succinct Arthur Couratin. Arthur, who was the Principal of St Stephen's House and Bishop Kirk's unpaid master of ceremonies, always came to the cathedral with a posse of servers from his seminary whenever some pontifical function, such as an ordination, was to take place. The Dean, John Lowe, who I think mildly resented these invasions while secretly admiring the efficiency with which they were conducted, remarked shortly before one of them, 'I suppose we shall have Arthur Couratin here next Sunday with his travelling circus.' This was repeated to Arthur, and it drew from him the devastating comment, made in the mincing manner which he kept for such occasions, 'Well, old man, I'd rather belong to a travelling circus than a permanent freak-show.'[1] The implied reference was no doubt exaggerated, but the Chapter of Christ Church when I came to know it was certainly a remarkable assortment of clergyman.

Dean Lowe was gremial to the House as a Rhodes Scholar from Canada. He was intensely conscientious, very unimaginative, temperamentally shy. He was devoid of small talk but could on occasion make a brilliant and amusing speech. There appeared to be no upper threshold to the amount of work that he could do, but, as with all such people, the truth was simply that his threshold was vastly higher than is normal and the tragedy was that he reached it. For, having become Vice-Chancellor of the University without the usual preliminary grooming, as the result of an emergency in 1948, and having filled that office for the usual three years with great distinction (they included, for example, the delicate business of M. Antonin Besse's foundation of St Antony's College), he was almost immediately struck down with a cerebral thrombosis from which he never fully recovered. He resigned from the Deanery in September 1959 and died less than a year later.

Whether, if he had been spared the burden of University and College administration and given the leisure to devote himself primarily to scholarship, he would have become the great New-Testament scholar that some have suggested it is difficult to say. Certainly, with his great power of application and of attention to detail, he could have produced an outstanding example of the type of commentary of which we have seen many — perhaps too many — examples in recent years. That he had the kind of sensitivity and intuitiveness which is needed if Biblical scholarship is to receive its badly needed regeneration and if the uniqueness of the scriptural wood is not to be overlooked in the conscientious enumeration of its individual trees is however doubtful. Nevertheless there were occasional signs that, behind a façade that was almost entirely moralistic and even positivistic, John Lowe had an inarticulate sense of the supernatural realm. I will simply illustrate this by an incident which I think will surprise any of my readers who knew him as much as it surprised me at the time.

There had been incidents connected with an undergraduate's set of rooms which, after eliminating all the obvious explanations, I had come, in my pastoral capacity and after taking advice from other priests of experience, to diagnose with reluctance as a case for exorcism. I will not describe the phenomena which had disturbed the undergraduate in question, who was a devout and emotionally stable ordinand, but it seemed clear to me that he was not a victim of the pranks of other undergraduates and that I myself was not on this occasion the object of the honourable sport of pulling the chaplain's leg. Two other relevant points were, first, that I am very far from seeing evil spirits at every street corner and, second, that I was proposing to exorcise not a person but a place, a much less hazardous proceeding. It was no concern of the Canons, as they had no spiritual jurisdiction over the undergraduates, but I felt that I ought to consult the Dean, who had (Christ Church is extra-diocesan and the Dean is therefore its spiritual head, as a kind of abbot *nullius*); and I wondered how ever, with his down-to-earth mind, he would take this. Would he think that I was even more of a medieval than he had imagined and that I was about to start exorcising everyone? I need not have worried. Before I had done more than outline the data of the problem and was wondering how to introduce my proposed solution, he interrupted slightly impatiently, 'Don't you think this is probably a case for exorcism? I think Arthur Couratin does it for the diocese and can let you have the form that is used. You had better just let me see it and then carry on.' I did as he suggested and the manifestations ceased forthwith. I swore the few undergraduates who knew about it to secrecy and that was the end of the matter. But it showed me a new side of John Lowe.

The only Canon who did not hold a professorial chair was Gerald Allen, the Archdeacon of Oxford, the one member of the Chapter who was appointed by the Bishop of Oxford and not by the Crown. He was also Bishop Suffragan of Dorchester and I do not think anyone can ever have enjoyed being a bishop more. He was really kindly and humble but he had little sense of humour, and his conviction of the importance of the episcopal office led his utterances to resemble the Catholic Truth Society's translations of papal encyclicals. 'This august sacramental rite which we have this day administered in this glorious basilica of Saint Barnabas ...' were the opening words of his sermon after confirming a few children in the suburb of Jericho. 'Consecrated hands, however unworthy, should at least be clean', he once remarked to me as he removed a particle of dirt from one of his finger-nails. Because St Birinus had been Bishop of Dorchester in the seventh century, long before the diocese of Oxford had been heard of, he was allowed to celebrate Mass from the throne in Dorchester Abbey on the feast of the saint; and servers from St Stephen's House (directed of course by Father Couratin) and the choir from the cathedral would accompany him on that occasion. Unhappily the feast falls in December and the large and beautiful church was unheated; it was alleged that every body taking part was almost frozen to death with the exception of the pontiff, who was maintained in a pyrotechnic state by his own interior enthusiasm. It was said that on one occasion he imparted blessings with such vigour during the procession of entry that his episcopal ring flew off his finger and that the proceedings were held up until it was found – on the stone that had originally covered the grave of St Birinus! But this no doubt is one of the legends which the faithful are free to doubt without mortal sin. Somehow or other I was never there for these festivals.

Gerald Allen always reminded me of a pouter pigeon ruffling itself, and his nickname 'Puffles' seemed highly appropriate. He lived with his stepmother ('My steppers', as he described her) in the Archdeacon's Lodgings on the north side of Tom Quad, the Great Quadrangle. They were devoted to each other, and she was devoted to the choirboys, to whom she showed many kindnesses. She would stand at her window as they crossed the Quad on

their way to the cathedral each day, and they greeted each other
with mutual wavings. Puffles was well in with the landed gentry
and nobility of Oxfordshire and he always managed to give the
impression that, although the Church was rightly impartial in
matters of party politics, it was obvious that Conservative was the
only possible thing for a thoughtful churchman to be. He would
clearly have loved to be a diocesan and not a mere suffragan;
it is, however, perhaps as well that he was not, as he always
gave a faint impression of being a figure of fun. Unless my ears
deceived me, I once overheard him saying to the Archbishop of
Westminster at a party at Campion Hall, 'I believe your Eminence
was the youngest cardinal in the Roman Catholic Church; I was
once the youngest bishop in the Church of England.' He had a
delightful complacency about the condition of the Church and
would maintain with enthusiasm that the C. of E. was doing
much better than Rome, especially (so he claimed) in the matter
of converts.

The impressive position of Regius Professor of Divinity was held
by Leonard Hodgson, a kindly and conscientious man of definite
but moderate opinions, much trusted and respected. He had held
the chair of Christian Apologetics at General Theological Seminary
in New York City from 1925 to 1931 and, while inclined to attribute
over-much importance to the concept of evolution in theology,
stood theologically well to the right of the self-styled 'modern
churchmen'. When Kenneth Kirk became Bishop of Oxford in
1937 and vacated the chair of Moral and Pastoral Theology in
which he had done so much to raise Anglican moral theology
to a genuinely professional status, Hodgson, to the surprise of
many, was chosen to succeed him. Hodgson had far too strong
a moral sense to neglect any task with which he was entrusted, but
I think it is true to say that, whereas for Kirk moral theology was
a systematic and scientific discipline with its own special norms and
principles, for Hodgson, as for most Anglicans, it was something
much less elaborate and almost instinctive, at any rate for well
brought-up people. To say that all it demanded was that one
should say one's prayers and wash behind the ears is no doubt
unfair but is not a complete travesty. At any rate, moral theology
made no marked advances in Oxford under Hodgson and, when
the Crown enabled him in 1944 to exchange his chair and stall for
the adjacent *sediae* of Divinity unparticularised, he was obviously
glad to be freed of the trammels. Both in the theological faculty
and in the College he was a benevolent and beneficent influence; he
was invariably kind and thoughtful and I shall always feel grateful

for the encouragement that he gave me at a turning point in my theological career, especially as he cannot have entirely approved of the direction my theology was taking.

His successor in the Moral Theology chair was Robert Cecil Mortimer. 'Bob', as he was always called, was no newcomer to Christ Church; he was in fact my immediate predecessor as Clerical Student, in a period that included virtually the whole of the Second World War. He had acquired a reputation for lassitude that was not entirely deserved, for he was one of those people who do a great deal more than they appear to be doing. He was himself a disciple of Kenneth Kirk and understood better than most people the sometimes perplexingly elaborate tactics of that very outstanding prelate. 'If you want to understand Kenneth', he once said to me, 'you must remember that if he wants to pick that glass off the table he will go into the corner of the room and take it by a flanking movement.' Bob reinstated the traditional shape of moral theology which it had had under Kirk, while adding the expertise in canon law which he had himself acquired. When he became Bishop of Exeter in 1949 he applied his knowledge in a wider context in Convocation and later in the House of Lords. He told me with some amusement of an occasion when, after he had been addressing a meeting in a provincial diocese on the moral theology of gambling, an elderly cleric rose and said, 'I should just like to say two things. The first is that I am sorry that the speaker has just become a bishop. And the second is that I am sorry that the speaker is an Oxford man, because I am an Oxford man myself.' Of all the members of the Chapter Bob was the most approachable and convivial and I found his counsel most helpful when I was still finding my feet as a don, though he never tried to pressurise me into following his methods.

The least visible member of the Chapter was the Regius Professor of Hebrew, Herbert Danby, who occupied the house at the south-west corner of the Quad once inhabited by the great Dr Pusey. In the long years that he had spent as a canon in Jerusalem he had acquired a great reputation for both scholarship and accessibility, but back in Oxford he had become, through bad health and failing eyesight, almost a recluse in the bosom of his family, though it was said that he was still in frequent demand as a source of up-to-date information on events in Palestine. He hardly ever dined in hall and all that most people saw of him was his slightly bent figure scurrying between his house and the cathedral. It was said that when somebody remarked to him upon the severity of a quite desperately cold winter, he replied that he had not noticed it as he had not been out — which could not have been quite true, as he never missed the minimum of his duties in the Cathedral. His churchmanship was low-church rather than evangelical, and he could celebrate the Lord's Supper at a speed which would have made an old-fashioned Jesuit green with envy. His sermons were invariably on Old-Testament themes of the less blood-thirsty type and, although their content was inoffensive, they were delivered with a kind of concentrated expectoration which reminded me of a passionate but self-restrained viper. At a time when many Christian theologians were turning to Hebrew documents for light upon the period of primitive Christianity, Danby maintained that these were really entirely useless for the purpose, on the grounds that as we have them they are post-Christian in date. As far as I know, no other Hebrew expert went to quite this extreme, but who was I in any case to judge? I heard him expound this self-denying theme with vigour on one of his rare extra-curricular appearances, in a paper which he read to the Oxford Society of Historical Theology under the appropriate title 'The Irrelevant Rabbi'. He died of cancer in 1953 and was succeeded by Cuthbert Simpson, of whom I shall have much to say later.

If Herbert Danby was the least visible member of the Chapter, Leslie Cross (his first name, Frank, was never used) was certainly the least audible. Leslie was immensely learned, intensely devout, kind and generous to a degree — and agonisingly shy. He had originally studied Chemistry, in which he had a science degree from London University, but changed over to Theology while at Balliol and won all the honours and prizes in his newly adopted subject. His transition in churchmanship from modernism to Anglo-catholicism was marked by his successive holding of appointments at Ripon Hall and at Pusey House; and when in 1930 he wrote his first book, *Religion and the Reign of Science*, he dedicated it to the three institutions from which he had, as he said, learnt respectively his science, his theology and his religion. From his earlier interest in philosophical theology he gradually moved into historical theology and in particular into patristics, in which he acquired an international reputation. In 1944 he became Lady Margaret Professor and Canon of Christ Church and moved, with his father and his sister, into the uncomfortable and rambling building on the south side of the Cathedral called Priory House. Its discomfort did not deter him, for he was a man of austere and spartan personal habits; and its extensiveness enabled him to manifest his generosity in providing accomodation for a succession of needy undergraduates and researchers. In one respect he was as a scholar a disappointment. Chiefly, I believe, through his shyness and his terror of being drawn into controversy, he never produced the great constructive works of theology or moved into the position of leadership in the Catholic movement to which his intellectual equipment would have entitled him. Instead, he devoted himself to the organisation of a series of mammoth international patristic and Biblical conferences and grand editorial projects.

When he planned the first patristic conference in 1951 he expected an attendance of about fifty, to be compactly accommodated in Christ Church; in fact two hundred applied to come and further accomodation had to be sought in other colleges. Subsequent conferences, held at four-year intervals, rose steadily to double this size by 1967. The explanation for this remarkable success lies mainly in Leslie's capacity for what I can only describe as academic commercial travelling. For, in spite of his normal silence and withdrawal, he would go on long journeys to universities and religious houses on the continent, travelling always in the most economical way, maintaining and extending contacts with other patristic scholars. Furthermore, in order to give the participants full value for their money, he would arrange programmes of quite inhuman concentration and intensity and, in the cynical but probably accurate conviction that people come to conferences much more to talk than to listen, he would arrange that, in addition to the plenary sessions, there were four or five parallel sequences of twenty-minute papers. In these periods anyone who wished had an opportunity to deliver himself on his pet topic, whether there was anyone to listen to him or not and regardless of the fact that three or four other specialists were simultaneously indulging themselves in the same way. I always wondered whether any obscure hoaxer ever got away with a paper on a recently discovered but fictitious writing by a non-existent desert father; it would not have been difficult to do this. As resident in Christ Church I was always made a member of the Conferences, and my protests that I was not a patristic scholar were met by Leslie with his usual weapon of silence. My actual participation was largely limited to the unofficial but acceptable function of rescuing exhausted conferenciers whom I found wandering in a dazed condition in the Quad and taking them up to my rooms to be restored not inappropriately with Cyprus sherry.

The Biblical Conferences, which took place in the interstices of the patristic conferences, took very much the same form, but they were addressed primarily to the parish clergy; for, in the Biblical field, there were already regular international gatherings of professional scholars. Leslie's intention was that they should bring the best and newest fruits of academic scholarship to those who were engaged in the Church's pastoral and evangelistic ministry. Whether or not they were as successful in this as he hoped, they testify to his real concern and sense of responsibility for the Church's basic and essential function. For, much as his shyness concealed them, he had that concern and that sense, far more indeed than the majority of academic theologians; and, in anything that did not involve him in public appearance and social intercourse, he gave himself to it unsparingly. He took tremendous interest in his students and in the incumbents of the Christ-Church parishes, of which there were a very large number. He spent large parts of the vacations acting as chaplain to several enclosed communities of nuns, where he found not only more opportunity for uninterrupted study than even in the labyrinth of Priory House but also the atmosphere of contemplative prayer. For at the heart of his scholarship was a very profound spirituality.

His two chief editorial activities were with the *Patristic Greek Lexicon* and the *Oxford Dictionary of the Christian Church*. The former of these had been initiated in 1906 and, like many such projects, had acquired such a perennial character that no one appeared to expect, and hardly even to desire, that it would ever be completed. Leslie took it over in 1941 but, sharing as he did a sense of timelessness that would have done credit to any of the Fathers, he was the last person to be influenced by any note of urgency. In 1948 it was more or less forcibly extracted from him and transferred to Dr Geoffrey Lampe, under whose editorship, to the openmouthed astonishment of the learned world, it saw the light of day in five sections between 1961 and 1968. This precedent augured badly for the other work, which in an embryonic form had been in Leslie's care since 1939, but when he came to Christ Church it imperceptibly began to develop. Year after year if one went into his study one saw galley-proofs hanging from clothes-pegs round the walls like washing on the line. He amassed a very large body of contributors, who were duly acknowledged *en bloc*, but their material was editorially processed and not separately attributed; to demur was futile in face of the silent weapon. There was, I believe, a long hold-up through differences with the University Press. The Press envisaged a compact work, without bibliographies and a limited sale; Leslie was planning a comprehensive one-volume encyclopaedia, with full bibliographies to every article, which any self-respecting clergyman would be ashamed to be without. The cold war of silence ensued and finally the Press capitulated to Leslie's

E.L. Mascall at his desk.

Anglo-Russian Committee, Mirfield, Bishop of Bradford and
Rev. E.L.Mascall.

A group of Brethren at West Malling Abbey (Fr. Mascall on the
left).

Lincoln Theological Studies.

Lincoln, summer 1942.
E.L. Mascall, E.S. Abbot, Dr J.H. Srawley, C.F. Evans.

With the Bishop of Johannesburg, Rosettenville, August 1969.

General Chapter, Elfinsward 1969.

Zagreb, August 1971.
VIth International Mariological Congress.

Visit of H.M. the Queen and H.R.H. Prince Philip to King's
College, London, 27th June 1972.

An audience with the Pope in 1974.

complete indifference to time. He was triumphantly proved to be right, when the *O.D.C.C.* suddenly appeared in 1958 and successive reprints followed. By this time I had entirely forgotten what I had contributed, and so I imagine had most of the other contributors; my own share cannot have been large, judging by the size of my cheque, but my free copy of the work was more valuable. I always kept it within reach when I was teaching and the comprehensive bibliographies were always my first refuge for further information on any topic. The second edition, which, after his death in 1968, was brought to publication in 1974 by his wonderfully competent secretary and literary executor Miss E. A. Livingstone I have found quite indispensable. His sermons were excellent in substance but were delivered in an intolerable and expressionless grinding monotone.

I have left to the end the one member of the Chapter to whom Arthur Couratin's label might have applied with little exaggeration – the Regius Professor of Ecclesiastical History, Dr Claude Jenkins, a man of whom our organist and choirmaster Sydney Watson used to remark 'All stories are true'. He died at Tunbridge Wells in the Christmas vacation of 1958/9, advanced in years but still in Office; for canon-professors did not have to retire unless they wished to, and he had made it quite clear that he did not wish. He had in fact been given a dinner by his friends and admirers in celebration of his longevity some time previously, and, although he had accepted the invitation, it was plain that he suspected it concealed a hint of an unwelcome nature. He began his reply to the toast with the words 'Being as I am of a modest but not of a retiring disposition,' which was clearly a polite way of saying 'You needn't think that you'll get rid of me by giving me a meal.' When the news of his death arrived in common-room Sydney remarked to me, 'Well, the last of the real Oxford eccentrics has gone'; and all that I could think of replying was, 'Be careful, Sydney; in how many common-rooms this evening are they saying, "Now that Jenkins has gone, only Watson and Mascall are left."?'

Jenkins's character was an amazing mixture of sweetness and obstinacy. He had a large number of grievances against Christ Church and various of its members, almost all of which were, as far I could find out, entirely without foundation, but, as he bore them in an entirely forgiving and unvindictive spirit, they never spoilt his personal relations though they made him absolutely inflexible about his official rights and privileges or what he believed to be such. He lived in Tom Quad in an enormous house which he simultaneously alleged to be unfit for human habitation and to have been adroitly foisted on him by its rightful occupant. He had originally had his aged mother living with him, but, after first his mother and then his housekeeper died, he lived entirely alone and uncared-for. He resisted any attempt to improve his living conditions as a highly nefarious scheme on the part of the College to invade his rights, if not indeed to infringe the royal prerogative, since he held his chair and his stall by appointment from the Crown. The sole heating equipment of his house that he used was a small electric fire with one bar. He came into common-room before dinner on a bitterly frigid evening, when there was snow on the ground and sleet was falling and he himself looked absolutely perishing, and remarked, rather uncharacteristically yet with a note of pride, 'My house must be the coldest house in Oxford.' 'Yes, Jenkins,' I replied somewhat impatiently, 'I expect it is, but isn't that because you have no heating in it?' 'That,' he answered after a moment's pause, as of one upon whom a previously unrecognised truth had now dawned, 'may very well be the case'; 'but,' he added, recovering himself and refusing to be defrauded out of a valued distinction, 'the fact remains, *it is the coldest house in Oxford.*' The mental process behind this interchange was typical of Jenkins in his later years, when his sense of cause and effect appeared to go progressively into reverse. His assertion 'Lecturers are better-off than professors in these days; they aren't charged so much income-tax' was typical; and when he was unwillingly forced by the College to allow workmen to deal with the dry-rot which was visibly eroding his house, he appeared to be convinced that it was the invasion by the workmen that had produced the dry-rot and not *vice versa.* He allowed the weeds in his garden to grow to a height of something like eight feet and explained that he was setting up a bird-sanctuary. I do not know what avine creatures it harboured, but it was believed to be the immediate source of a stoat which appeared in the adjacent garden of the Deanery and was hunted down by a co-operative enterprise conducted by the Dean's cat and dog. Once when I regretted that Jenkins grew no flowers in his garden he astonished me by asserting that nothing would grow in it because the soil was suffering from natural decay. This seemed unlikely, in view of the flourishing condition of the bird-sanctuary, but I suggested that perhaps the natural decay might be corrected by horticultural therapeutics. 'No', Jenkins replied, sadly shaking his head, 'It's well known that when soil is suffering from natural decay nothing can be done about it.'

He dined in hall every night in term, except on Thursday, when as

Senior Librarian of the Union Society he dined with the Committee before the weekly debate. His appetite was enormous, and he would annex any loose food within reach, presumably for consumption at home the following day. His first action after the saying of grace was a prestidigitous wave of the hand over the toast-rack, after which that receptacle was magically almost empty. If the menu included either beef-olives or cherries, he would pick up those convenient fruits from his plate, suck them free of the adherent liquid and place them in his waistcoat-pocket. On one occasion Sydney, having been over-plentifully served with olives, said to me 'I am going to send some of these to Claude.' Ignoring my horrified protests he placed them on a plate and sent them round by the butler, who murmered a complimentary message in the Canon's ear. Instead of manifesting offence, as I had feared, Claude signalled his gratitude, and the olives went to join the other spoils in his pocket. When we had a buffet lunch, as we did before meetings of Governing Body, he would bring in a large woollen muffler, in which he would secrete a succession of foodstuffs, but gorgonzola cheese would be wrapped in a filthy and never renewed bandana handkerchief, liberally stained with the snuff to which he was addicted. He rarely or never drank alcohol, but after dinner he would let his coffee get cold and then pour it into a tumbler, which he filled up with soda-water. On one of the rare occasions when he dined in another college – I think he had preached first in their chapel – one of the fellows came to see me beforehand to get briefed about the appropriate entertainment. I suggested that the provision of a number of conveniently placed receptacles containing nuts, fruit, biscuits etc. would be appreciated but I added that I could not guarantee that Jenkins would be as uninhibited when playing away as on his home ground. I need not have worried. His hosts behaved most lavishly – I was told incidentally that so many wished to dine that they had to ballot for places – and he was at the top of his form. I was told that after his departure a pile of food was found under his chair, having slipped from his pocket, but that this was considerately sent round to his house afterwards. *Se non e vero* ... And I have a vivid memory of him at the Vice-Chancellor's garden-party in his full doctoral scarlet, secreting cream buns in the pocket of his cassock.

His smoking mixture was revolting; it was a mixture of leaves picked up in Christ Church Meadow and cigar- and cigarette-ends abstracted from the common-room ash-trays. His great time for these spoils was the summer gaudy, when large numbers of cigars were smoked at the College's expense. Jenkins explained to me that he considered it was necessary as a matter of etiquette for at least one of the hosts to outstay the last of the guests and he always fulfilled this hospitable function; but scavenging was certainly as impelling a motive as etiquette. When his normal sources ran short, he could be seen picking up fag-ends in the street. He had a number of pre-war Woolworth sixpenny pipes, their bowls choked with deposit, in which he incinerated this dreadful composition.

The stories about him were legion. Typical was that told me by a colleague who was working in Lambeth Palace Library, where Jenkins was still honorary Librarian and paid regular visits. Having difficulty in finding a volume, my colleague enlisted the help of Jenkins, whom he spotted immersed in a book. Jenkins interrupted his reading, extracted from an inner pocket a piece of recognisable Christ Church high-table toast, placed this in his own volume as a bookmark and, having courteously rendered the assistance requested, replaced the toast in his pocket and went on reading; presumably the toast was part of his lunch.

He was asked one year to propose the toast of Pusey House at the annual luncheon of that institution. 'I find it difficult', he began, 'to understand why I should have been chosen to fulfil this function, as I never even saw Dr Pusey' – which was hardly surprising as Pusey died in 1882. 'But', he continued, 'I can say that three times I saw Cardinal Newman', and he went on to describe how, when he was a small boy at Birmingham, people had pointed out to him a bent and fragile old clergyman as being the famous cardinal. It happened that the following year I was myself asked to propose this toast in Jenkins's presence, and I felt that the opportunity was too good to miss. So I first of all recalled his words on the previous occasion and then continued: 'Now I can in fact go one better than Dr Jenkins. For though like him I never saw Dr Pusey, unlike him I never saw Cardinal Newman either.' Jenkins was delighted.

His sermons nearly always followed a regular pattern. They would open in some such was as this: 'Three hundred and seven years ago next Tuesday a young man was walking down the street of a city in the north of Italy.' The story would be developed but the name of its hero would be carefully concealed until the *dénouement* was reached, when it would be revealed in an almost casual way: 'Thus it was that Polycarp of Smyrna ...' or ' ... Benjamin Franklin ...' or whoever it might be. A Jenkins sermon thus had for its hearers something of the exciting character of a guessing game, with the added possibility – which I think was once realised – that this time he would forget to reveal the hero's identity altogether. An exception to the pattern was the sermon which he preached for the quatercentenary of the House's foundation; in it he took us on a kind of Cook's tour of the College, ending with the splendid pronouncement: ' ... and even the Meadow Buildings, under the mellowing hand of time, are slightly less repulsive than when they were first erected.' He always arranged to preach on the Sunday when, for some obscure reason, the small boys of the Dragon School were brought to matins in the Cathedral. On this occasion he would describe with great enthusiasm and a wealth of lurid detail some specially unpleasant experience, such as that of being eaten piecemeal by a tiger; the adults in the congregation might be turning green with nausea, but the small boys would have their tongues hanging out with eager anticipation. He was a slight, though unintentional, embarrassment to visiting preachers. Owing to the extraordinary furnishing arrangements of the Cathedral, the field of vision of the preacher was almost entirely occupied by the Sub-Dean's stall, and Jenkins was Sub-Dean. As towards the end of his time he invariably slept throughout the sermon and occasionally slid off his seat in the process, he could have a somewhat damping effect; though from comments which he made afterwards there was reason to believe that he sometimes dreamt a sermon to take the place of the one through which he had slept.

His sole extravagance was the purchase of books, of which at his death he had, I believe, thirty thousand. He spent his vacations at either Malvern or Tunbridge Wells, in both of which towns there were secondhand bookshops of which he must have been one of the principal customers. Shortly after his return at the beginning of each term several crates full of spoils would be delivered at his lodging; many of these remained unpacked to the time of his death, for they had simply overwhelmed him. Many of them were the kind of books – Victorian parish histories and the like – which one can hardly imagine anyone wanting but which, if anyone did want them, it might be impossible to find. In spite of its size the house was inadequate to accomodate them; in the corners of each room piles of books were thrown down anyhow like sand in the corner of a builder's yard, and the bath, which was not used for its normal purpose, was a kind of dump for odd printed scraps. It was only just possible to push one's way up the staircase, for on every step there were piles of books extending high out of reach; in fact the view of the staircase-wall reminded me of a sectional diagram of geological strata in an atlas, and one could see how the conformation had readjusted itself after a cataclysm had occurred through the removal of a book from one of the lower levels. He was very indignant at the suggestion that books were ever stolen from libraries and insisted that apparent thefts were in fact cases of absent-mindedness; this may indeed be true to some extent, for it would be absurd to give any other explanation for the books which were found in his house after his death. He once showed me a book which contained the plate of a well-known library and in which he had inserted a signed declaration that he had bought it in a shop and not stolen it from the library; otherwise, he said, someone doing research would defame him posthumously. I remarked that I thought this was a very poor safeguard, since anyone suspecting him of theft would be equally ready to accuse him of perjury. Jenkins was scandalised. 'That,' he said, 'is the remark I would expect from a moral theologian.' This was the worst thing he could say of anyone, for he was persuaded that Kenneth Kirk and N. P. Williams between them had been responsible for most of his grievances.

He delivered innumerable lectures, more probably than anyone else in Oxford, for, although he would put on a new course at intervals, he could never bring himself to take one off. He told me once that he was going to lecture on George II. 'I did not know that he was one of your specialities,' I said. 'Well, I had lectured on all the other Georges, so I thought I ought to add this,' he replied, in a splendid repudiation of the alleged excessive specialisation of Oxford. 'Which aspect of his reign are you going to deal with?' I enquired. 'All aspects,' he firmly asserted. Whether all his lectures had even a minimal audience was doubtful; an inquisitive investigator alleged that careful peeping revealed him lecturing eloquently to an entirely empty room. An American research student told how he presented himself at the appointed time for a course of lectures scheduled to be given at 'the Professor's lodging' and how, when repeated ringing of the door-bell at last produced the Professor in cassock and gown and with his bands under one ear, Jenkins looked straight at him, bent down and took in the milk, and shut the door in his face. Renewed tintinnabulations were more successful and the two got on very good terms. Americans were always fascinated by Jenkins, who represented everything that they had come to Oxford hoping to see; when I was in New York in 1958 I was delighted to see in the *New York Times* a photograph of Jenkins walking down Oriel Street in full academic dress, which must have been supplied by one of our transatlantic visitors. One of the subjects on which he voluntarily offered instruction, on the ground that it was culpably neglected by the University, was Greek palaeography, and he continued in this conviction even after the University had appointed a lecturer in the subject, who was moreover a member of our common-room.

His scholarship was immense but unsystematic and unco-ordinated. His mind, like his house, resembled a vast waste-paper basket, in which anything that was needed was bound to turn up if you went on turning it over long enough. He edited a number of historical documents, but was the author of no major historical work. He had grave distaste for the application of scientific technology to historical research and even for the methods of archaeology. History was for him something to be done by the study of documents and inscriptions; to excavate a site or, still more, to open a tomb, was vaguely felt to be indecent and ungentlemanly. Like shooting a sitting pheasant, it killed the bird, but it was the wrong way to do it. And because it might settle a seemingly permanent controversy by taking a short cut, it was also, I think, felt to spoil the fun. Jenkins amassed an immense number of research students − more in fact than he could properly cope with − but he was kind and encouraging and they loved him for his oddities. He had acquired the one position which he really wanted and for which he believed he was fitted, and the chief ground on which he justified his refusal to contemplate resignation was that, if he went, certain sinister persons in positions of influence would scheme to get various undesirable and unsuitable candidates considered for his place.

Although his obstinacy exasperated anyone who had official dealings with him to the verge of insanity, he was a genial and fascinating conversationalist, and until his final decrepitude I would always try to put a guest next to him in common-room. He would pull up his sleeve and lay a thick train of snuff several inches long along his wrist; by the end of the evening this would run across his upper lip from ear to ear. His death reduced our bill for snuff by one half, and in his will he left an endowment for its supply. Though he became shabbier and shabbier and his clothes lost their buttons to the point that his trousers were secured strategically by an enormous safety-pin, he always put on an old-fashioned dress-coat for dinner. The one exception was when we were graciously honoured by the presence of the King and Queen and were regally instructed not to dress for dinner; Jenkins interpreted the command whole-heartedly and appeared in a very light grey flannel suit which was never seen before or after. Even at this distance memories of him keep crowding back; how he kept accounts in a number of banks, in case the manager should be dishonest; how he fed the goldfish daily because he feared they were undernourished. His antipathy for cats was even greater than that for moral theologians: 'If they were larger,' he would say with a shudder, 'they'd *eat us*.' Even when seriously ill, he refused to see a doctor, because, as he insisted with a somewhat imperfect application of inductive logic, all the people he had known who died had seen doctors first. He was miserly towards himself and rapacious towards Christ Church; but this was because he conceived it his duty to obtain retribution to the last farthing, and to the last beef-olive, for the amenities of which he believed he had been defrauded; he was extremely generous in secret to individuals and institutions whom he knew to be really needy. He once made an eloquent plea that nursemaids with perambulators should be admitted to Christ Church Meadow, and was undeterred by the information that there were no nursemaids now and that perambulators had been admitted to the Meadow for years. He would reduce the said services in the Cathedral to confusion by reciting the psalms on a different system to that used by everyone else, not, he explained to me, because he liked upsetting his colleagues but because the method they used had been introduced by the late Canon N. P. Williams and he felt conscientiously obliged to manifest his disapproval of everything done by that sinister cleric. Through sheer conservatism he had refused to take the D.D. on his academic attainments, but insisted on taking it by the earlier method, which, as Melbourne said of the Garter, 'had no damned merit in it'. However, for all his conservatism he was a firm supporter of the women's colleges, both morally and materially, and at his death he left them the first choice from his books. Each morning for some days I saw, from my rooms across the quad two fellows of St Anne's going into his house on their work of selection, and emerging several hours later in a somewhat dishevelled condition, like archaeologists from a newly reopened pyramid. I understood that about half of his collection of 30,000 went to St Anne's and half were disposed of to a bookseller, who kept half of these on his shelves and sold the remainder for pulping. I was allowed to take a couple. My first choice was a copy of Archbishop Davidson's second charge to the Canterbury diocese, autographed by the author to Jenkins in gratitude for his help with it; the second − highly appropriate! − was a Victorian book on Cats, ranging from the jungle to the domestic variety and illustrated with delightful oleographs.

I have devoted more space to Jenkins than to all the rest of the Canons, but that is because there was so much more to say about him, and even so, much has begun to fade and more must have been forgotten. Was it, for example, once or more than once that, when he went to the lectern in the Cathedral, common-room sugar cascaded from his cassock to the delight of the choirboys? The alarm clock that he took in to his lectures may not, as some said, have been set so as to wake up either himself or his audience at the end of the lecture, but I know that he carefully set it when conducting the *viva* for a D. Phil. degree, to the amusement of his fellow-examiner, the Dean of Wells. Many who never knew him personally liked to see his stocky figure as, in a filthy cassock and gown, he proceeded to lecture in the chapter-house with the alarm clock dangling from his finger, or, in his flat clerical hat and dilapidated brown raincoat, he stood feeding high-table toast to the goldfish. Readers of the novels of Michael Innes (our colleague J. I. M. Stewart) may like to know that Dr Stringfellow was closely modelled on Canon Jenkins. I suppose I knew him about as well as anybody, having lived on the other side of Tom Quad for the last twelve years of his life, but I could never solve the basic Jenkinsian enigma: Was he a perfectly unselfconscious eccentric, just doing what came naturally to him, however different it might be from what came naturally to everyone else? Or did he spend long hours in profound cogitation, devising and elaborating new forms of eccentricity, outlandish enough to ensure that he would be remembered by them and credited with them, and yet not quite so outrageous as to exclude him from decent society, put him in the hands of the police or relegate him to a mental hospital? Or was there something of each? I have never been quite sure, but he was certainly, as Robin Dundas wrote, Senior Common Room's 'oldest, most lovable, and most idiosyncratic member'.

Most colleges, if they are lucky (and some if they are unlucky) have resident in them some elderly bachelor don who, to under-graduates and visitors, if not always to his colleagues, has become a kind of visible image or symbol of the place. Such when I went to Christ Church, was Robert Hamilton Dundas ('Robin' to a few close friends, 'D' to almost everyone else). Surprising as it was to most people if they discovered it, he was, in the terminology of an earlier day, not gremial but a squill[2]; for, although, with the exception of a year's teaching at Liverpool and military services in the First World War, the whole of his life after graduation had been that of a Christ Church don, he had won a first class in Mods and another in Greats at New College. He was an Etonian and had a deep loyalty and affection for the foundation of King Henry VI, but his down-to-earth Scottish realism preserved him from any foolish snobbishness. He had a typically Caledonian combination of personal austerity and economy with generosity and – when it seemed called for – lavishness. His gruff manner could be initially off-putting until one recognised that it concealed an intense, and even embarrassing, personal interest and concern. He tried to know every undergraduate in the House and to help with their personal problems; this interest in their pupils was not welcome to all his colleagues and could even lead to mild, but unjustified, suspicion of his motives. He had piles of books filled with their details, recorded in minute and abbreviated symbols which sometimes even he misinterpreted. He told against himself the story of his enquiry 'Your father was a missionary, wasn't he?' which produced the surprised reply 'No, sir; he was in the army and was reported missing in the War' and D's own comment 'Oh, so that's what "miss" meant in my notes.' Another undergraduate told me that, entering D's room when D was studying his records, he introduced himself with his name, 'Maddox, sir'. 'Oh yes,' said D, not looking up but turning over his pages, 'let me see, you've got red hair, haven't you?' D was convinced that many undergraduates, coming from sheltered surroundings, were caused acute perplexity and misery through ignorance of the facts of life and he resolved to remedy this defect in their education. 'You parsons', he told me good-humouredly, 'don't know how to help these young men'; and he had drawn up five questions by asking which he claimed he could immediately find out how much they needed to know. What apparently never occurred to him, but what I soon found out, was that boys, from some schools at least, arrived already briefed by their seniors with two sets of answers to make according as they did or did not wish to lure D into giving the proffered course of instruction. Or did this possibility occur to him after all, and was he prepared to expose himself to quiet ridicule as the cost of being able to help the occasional undergraduate who was genuinely in need of instruction? He was quite capable of taking the risk. Of one thing I am quite sure, that he was a man of rigid personal morality, though he had an almost obsessional interest in certain matters, which was easily misinterpreted and made him less welcome in certain schools than he would have liked to be; for he had made himself a kind of unofficial commercial traveller or liaison officer between the House and many public schools.

His moral standards were clearly if brutally expressed by the rebuke which I heard him make more than once in common-room when a guest, on being offered snuff, made the common but foolish remark that he was prepared to try anything once: '"Provided it's morally right" – mind you add that. Otherwise you'll start off with women, go on with boys and end up with dogs.' He was either an atheist or an agnostic; I was never quite sure which, but it was plain that, with the deep human compassion that lay behind his gruff exterior, it was the fact of suffering that hindered him from belief. Even the spoiling of a children's party by rain was to him scandalous callousness on the part of any allegedly existent God of goodness. He was, however, in no way militant in his unbelief and kept on the best terms with the clergy; and once he was convinced that I had the welfare of the young men at heart he became one of my strongest supporters. He occupied a large, untidy and musty set of rooms in the north-west corner of Tom Quad which had once belonged to Charles Dogson, the shy mathematician who achieved fame as Lewis Carroll, the author of *Alice in Wonderland*. To protect him from the inroads of tourists the college porters were strictly forbidden to reveal to enquirers the whereabouts of Lewis Carroll's rooms, but D was always delighted to show them to friends of his colleagues. For he was a devoted Carroll fan, and was visibly disappointed when Princess Margaret, who lunched in Hall one day, admitted that neither she nor her sister had much enjoyed *Alice* as children. D was an enthusiast for bathing, but it had to be done unmixed and in the nude, and therefore in the enclave called Parsons Pleasure. In my early days he took me for a walk in the Parks and as we drifted towards the north-east I guessed that the object of the operation was to make a new convert. Sure enough we found ourselves there and he clearly hoped for an enthusiastic reaction. However, the sight of several naked middle-aged gentlemen lying about on the grass in a steamy and stuffy enclosure produced no effect on me except a very mild sensation of nausea, and the matter was never raised again. *A propos* D and Parsons Pleasure I was told a characteristic story of an occasion when the bathers in that sanctuary were surprised by the appearance of a boat which, by some inadvertence, contained female occupants. The sun-bathers hastily wrapped their towels round their loins, with the exception of D, who wrapped his towel round his head. When they all unwound themselves, D remarked, 'I don't know how people recognise you, but they recognise me by my face.'

D's Scottish sense of economy extended to the literary realm and he was famous for his laconic postcards and notes. When an undergraduate whom he had rebuked for musical activity during prohibited hours replied cheekily that his friends considered that he was an accomplished musician and therefore ought to be allowed to indulge his art whenever the mood seized him, D simply rejoined

'You aren't and they don't and you mustn't.' When he was in New Zealand he sent a picture-postcard of the Blue Lake and the Green Lake, with his own brief comment 'Neither is either D.' When the wife of a former pupil gave birth to twins, D simply sent a telegram saying 'Six cheers. D.' Every spring the same grubby scrap of paper was pinned up at the foot of his staircase with the information:

> The Dwarf Iris (*iris reticulata*) in the College Garden is now in flower and is worth a visit from almost anyone.

(The delicate hint that there were some whose lack of aesthetic appreciation would make a visit pointless was thoroughly in character.) But for generations of Christ Church men his outstanding literary work was the annual report in which his genius for astringent but never malicious depiction of his colleagues had just the field of exercise that he enjoyed.

More often than not it fell to him to preside in common-room over the circulation of port and snuff. He was a great inhaler of snuff, though he never had any during the vacation, which he spent in Scotland with his sister; I always felt that the paroxyam which followed his first pinch after long abstinence was the real official opening of term. He had been very much shaken towards the end of the War by the theft in a train of his luggage, which contained the material for a life's work of classical scholarship; but he recovered very rapidly from the blow and, intense as was his interest in the world of antiquity, he was much more concerned with persons than with academic research. In 1954 he ceased to be a Tutor and in 1957 to be a Student and member of Governing Body, but in view of his long service he was still allowed to keep his rooms in college. His health was then just beginning to fail, as I could perceive since my rooms were at that time on the same staircase and floor as his. He was taken seriously ill at the end of the Long Vacation of 1960 and died swiftly and peacefully. His biography, *'D': Portrait of a Don*, was written by a former pupil, Roger Venables.

When I came to the House in May 1945, between V-E and V-J Days, its conditions were, of course, very abnormal, though not so much as those of some other colleges. We had no governmental or military institutions parked upon us, and the fact that the remaining undergraduates of Brasenose had moved into Meadow Buildings meant that together with our own small group we had at least the minimal appearance of a college as popularly conceived. As I recall it, the only Student, apart from D, who was actually living in College (of course the Chapter were in their self-contained residences) was Edward Farquhar Buzzard, the Regius Professor of Medicine, a tough old atheist with a not very impressive academic beginning but distinguished in the world of amateur Soccer and formerly neurologist to King George V. He died in December 1945 and the discussions in common-room about his memorial service left me, as a timid and uninfluential newcomer, puzzled, to say the last, at the revelation which they gave me of the academic attitude to the Christian religion.

It was the custom at Christ Church, on the death of a Canon or Student, to have in the Cathedral a service, based on the Burial Service of the Prayer Book and therefore opening with the three sentences of which the first is a very explicit expression of Christian belief. Surprisingly perhaps, nobody seemed ever to have raised objections on the ground of the convictions or lack of convictions of the departed until Buzzard's relations pointed out that it would be more honest to omit the first two sentences and simply begin with the indisputable assertion that he brought nothing into the world and could certainly carry nothing out. Once attention had been called to the point there was general agreement that the objection was very reasonable, until the organist made the counter-objection that the three sentences were set as one continuous musical composition and it was difficult to begin in the middle of a bar. The point was referred back to the family, who capitulated immediately and intimated that they would never have raised the matter if they had suspected that it would upset the music. So Buzzard vicariously professed belief in the Redeemer and the Resurrection at his memorial service in spite of his unbelief during his lifetime; but I was left with a very mystified impression of the mental condition of my new colleagues, especially as no one had expressed any qualms about the rest of the service, which was even more explicitly Christian. But this was quite typical of college chapels, and the chaplain of another college told me of a similar service at which a don who did not believe in God delivered an impressive panegyric upon another who had not believed in survival. More recently, I notice, the custom has arisen, in such cases, of having a memorial concert with appropriate speeches in a secular building; macabre and possibly unconvincing as such a function must be, at least it testifies to a vestigial desire for the consolations of religious emotion even when religious conviction has departed. I am far from despising the tenderness of the bereaved for their loved ones or even the respect of academics for their deceased colleagues, but there is something pathetic about the artificiality and the sense of helplessness of these contrived functions in contrast with the unselfconscious practicality with which Catholic Christianity goes about its ministry to the departed.

Of the other older Students of the House who had carried on during the War, two died not very long after my arrival: John Barrington-Ward, the acting Steward, a notable classical scholar, who did a great deal to make my living conditions reasonably tolerable in the immediate post-war austerity, and Captain Hutchinson, the Treasurer, whose comment on being confronted with the common-room lunch was 'Wouldn't feed it to me hounds' and who appropriately fell dead from his horse in the hunting field. When he was told that his financial theories had been falsified by the events of the preceding three centuries, he was alleged to have replied, 'You must remember that the last three hundred years have been a very abnormal period.' Keith Feiling, the historian of Conservatism, was with us and the scientists of course were around. Alex Russell, the chemistry tutor, who kept the record of past members of the House, had the most capacious memory for biographical detail of anyone I have ever known; he must have remembered more facts about many of them than they could remember about themselves. But the Common Room really came to life with the return from the War of such notable figures as J. C. (later to be Sir John) Masterman and with the influx of newly elected Students and lecturers who were needed to cope with the flood of post-War undergraduates. 'J. C.' was a man of extreme versatility, distinguished as a historian but also a top-level athlete in several sports, a more than competent novelist and dramatist — I still have the copy of his play *Marshal Ney* which he gave me —, and, during the War, centrally involved in organising the British counter-espionage service. (Incidentally, although his fascinating book *The Double-Cross System* was published in 1972, I never heard him refer to this particular activity.) His 'Oxford Guide-Book' entitled *To Teach the Senators Wisdom* contains quite the best collection of university anecdotes that I know, and I have, I hope and believe, refrained, though with difficulty, from plagiarising it. He and D were close friends of long standing; both were bachelors and their rooms were adjacent in Tom Quad. However while D, as I have said, was a regretful unbeliever, J. C. had the conscientious unexciting established religion of the English country, gentleman. He was always courteous to the clergy and we were on the friendliest terms, but he liked to include in his books a college chaplain of the most footling type. When he left Christ Church and became Provost of Worcester College in 1947 he insisted, so I heard, that any undergraduate of the latter institution who wished to avoid chapel should give his reasons to the Provost; I wonder whether any undergraduate ever asked the Provost to give *his* reasons for *attending* it! They would have been interesting.

Even to mention the names of all the colleagues whom I had during my seventeen years at Christ Church would of course be impossible. I cannot, however, omit the Heatons, for during much of my time the social life of the House centred round them. Trevor Heaton was tutor in physiology and also for many years presided as curator in Senior Common Room. His charming and gracious wife Irene was the sister of George VI's biographer John Wheeler Bennett. They lived in a most attractive house, No. 40 St Giles; it had been originally a coaching inn and had absorbed the gardens on either side. From this strategic spot they dispensed a lavish but unostentatious hospitality. Shortly after my arrival I was invited to lunch and was given before the meal a glass of a reddish-brown liquid which seemed to be devoid of alcoholic content and tasted very much like beef-tea; this, it was afterwards divulged, was sherry bottled in the accession-year of Queen Victoria, several bottles of which had been discovered concealed in a gift of wine made to Trevor and Irene on the occasion of their marriage. Irene was specially good in befriending the wives of young researchers, who were often overlooked and lonely in Oxford, and I always took care to let her know of any such. I met her one day taking hot food in a container to a young don and his wife who were both in bed with flu. I told her once that she should be known as 'Jerusalem on high', because she was the mother of us all! Trevor retired from his tutorial studentship in 1954 but continued as curator until 1962, when they left Oxford and went to live in Chichester, where Irene continued her care for others in a new setting. Trevor's health rapidly deteriorated, his sight failed, but he lived on till 1972. Irene lived on into her eighties, as active as ever, and finally died peacefully in her sleep. In her later years she acquired a remarkable resemblance to the Queen Mother. It seemed highly appropriate that, when their son visited in his home village a Nigerian student whom they had befriended in Oxford, he found that the grateful African had given his humble dwelling the name '40 St Giles'!

A real tregedy in my time was the suicide in 1959 of Michael Beresford Foster. Michael, who taught philosophy and whose interest was in ethics and culture rather than in metaphysics, was away in the Army when I came to the House; it was typical of him that he had enlisted as a private without a word to anyone, for he was entirely unambitious and unselfish. He had come, via a brief involvement with Dr Buchman, to an intense evangelical Christianity. Though rarely critical and never denunciatory of others, he set himself a standard of moral commitment that was virtually impossible of attainment this side of the Parousia. It was, I believe, this paradoxical sense of living under a moral demand which it was impossible to satisfy that, acting upon a temperament naturally subject to fits of deep depression, led to the crisis in which he took his life. As Vigo Demant said, in a magnificent sermon in the Cathedral on the Sunday after Michael's death, he came by a hair's breadth only short of complete sanctity; he had all the marks of holiness, but just missed the joy of the saints. This was all the more surprising because he had formed a close association with the Franciscans at Cerne Abbas and seemed happier with them than anywhere else; but although he had been won by their simplicity, somehow he never caught their joy.

The antediluvian type of don, the type who could boast of having once been an anachronism, then become an abuse and finally ended up a crying scandal, had of course become extinct before my time, but there were still in Oxford a few who might be described as survivals. Christ Church still remembered, though I had never met them, the gourmet who, having been entertained to dinner by a wealthy married couple with every thinkable profusion of food and drink, turned to his hostess with the remark, 'I suppose, Mrs X, that you have your main meal in the middle of the day?', and the hedonist who claimed to direct his life by the four maxims 'Live and let die', 'Self not service', 'Anything to give pain' and 'The best is good enough for me'. The doyen of these coelocanths was undoubtedly William Nelson Stocker, of Brasenose College. He had taken his M.A. degree in 1877 (the Next senior fellow took his in 1919!) and had retired from teaching for over thirty years. He still lived in college and took his daily exercise, measured it was said by a pedometer. I met him only once, when I was dining as the guest of one of his colleagues, and witnessed a somewhat embarrassing episode when another fellow was trying to introduce to him a guest of his own. 'What's his name? Speak up. Can't hear you. What's he called?' grumbled Stocker in reply to the other's repeated attempts to establish communication. Another colleague came to the rescue. 'I think I can help', he said and placing his lips close to the nonagenarian's ear said in a penetrating undertone 'It's Mr Z, and old member of the College.' The message got through, and Stocker turned and blinked at the young man, who was standing in awkward silence. 'Not the Mr Z I knew', he said and turned his back, leaving us wondering whether the Mr Z whom he *had* known was the father, grandfather or possibly even great-grandfather of the one who had just been introduced to him. He was found by his servant early one morning lying on his bedroom floor, having fallen the previous night and been unable to get up. 'Can't get any attention in this damned college', he remarked as he was picked up. He was taken to hospital, as it was thought that the experience might have been unnerving for a man of his age, but he was found to be quite unharmed and came back into college for a further spell of picturesque antiquity.

Much younger and more active but still in his way a survival was the Master of Pembroke College, Dr Frederick Homes Dudden. During the First World War he had been the incumbent in succession of two fashionable west-end parishes, St John's, Notting Hill, and Holy Trinity, Sloane Street. I think it was of the former of these that he remarked in my hearing that it was an ideal parish as it contained no poor people, though according to Osbert Lancaster he used to refer bitterly to 'years of penance in the draughty parish-halls of North Kensington'. Anyhow, in 1918 he became Master of Pembroke, an office which until 1937 was held with a canonry of Gloucester Cathedral; as under the statutes which governed his election the Master was compelled with advancing age neither to continue to perform his duties nor to retire from office, he appointed a deputy in due course but went on living in the Master's lodgings until his death. I met him on a number of occasions, as Christ Church and Pembroke used to share alternately senior-common-room facilities during the Long Vacation. He was a tall and handsome man of distinguished and aristocratic bearing and always made me think of the first Duke of Wellington; if one met him in the street he would touch his hat with two fingers unless he was with his wife, in which case he lifted his hat with a courtly gesture. Though comfortably circumstanced he was alleged to have preached a moving sermon about toiling up the steep and stony path with bruised and bleeding feet and to have remarked that, while as an ordained clergyman of the Church of England he was constrained to believe in a future life, he would personally have much preferred extinction. He commented disapprovingly on the fact that the Vicar of St Aldate's was holding open-air services outside the college, but added more cheerfully that they were badly attended. During the Lambeth Conference he observed that there seemed to be a lot of bishops about but that he gathered there was some kind of meeting taking place in London. He made an impressive public appearance in 1948, when, as the senior surviving ex-Vice-Chancellor (he had been Vice-Chancellor from 1929 to

1932), it fell to him to preside at the meeting of Convocation which received the Chancellor's nomination of a successor to Dr Stallybrass, the only Vice-Chancellor on record to have died in office. He wrote three authoritative full-length biographical works, on St Gregory the Great, St Ambrose and — improbably enough, after the other two — the English novelist Joseph Fielding; I cannot help feeling that he would have been most at home with the last.

One of the leading figures in the theological field was Robert Henry Lightfoot, Fellow of New College and Dean Ireland's Professor of Exegesis. His reputation as a New-Testament scholar was based on his Bampton Lectures of 1934 on History and Interpretation in the Gospels, and, largely on the strength of a much-quoted sentence about 'the whisper of [Jesus'] voice and the outskirts of his ways', he acquired the reputation of an extreme liberal, which in fact his later writings hardly justified. In 1956 when his long-awaited commentary on St John's Gospel was published posthumously, he was revealed as what his manner and attitude had always suggested, at bottom a simple and devout Evangelical. His two great interests were The *Journal of Theological Studies*, of which he was Editor, and the Oxford Society of Historical Theology, of which he was Secretary. On the former he imposed a uniformity of style, in accordance with his own standards of linguistic correctness, which reduced variety and enhanced dulness; he wrote to me explaining that he could not possibly allow the pages of the *J.T.S.* to be sullied by the neologism of 'to get' used intransitively. You could get *something* but were not allowed to get *anywhere.* He would sometimes send me a book to review, usually with the instruction not to write too much about it, which suited me quite well, as it provided me with volumes that I wanted in return for very little work. It reflected, however, the assumption which the contents and the arrangements of his hopefully named journal indicated, that for it and its editor 'theology' did not mean, as it had throughout the history of Christendom, the study of God and of his creatures in relation to him, but such aspects of archaeology, textual and literary criticism and history, especially those involving non-Latin alphabets, as had some connection with religious institutions and movements. Some years later, after Lightfoot's retirement, I actually had a theological study published in the Journal of Theological Studies; it was about St Anselm's ontological argument, and I had a modest sense of triumph.

The Oxford Society of Historical Theology was a useful institution, but I doubt whether it had quite the importance which

Lightfoot attributed to it. That importance was illustrated by his shocked reaction when John Lowe, during his year of office as President, informed him that he proposed to miss a meeting on the grounds (*a*) that he was not interested in the subject and (*b*) that there was a film which he wanted to see at the time. 'One would have supposed', Lightfoot commented, 'that the Dean of Christ Church, having been elected as President of one of the most distinguished societies in the world, would not have treated it in so cavalier a manner'. The first meeting which I attended was on October 23rd 1945, when the veteran Nonconformist scholar Dr W. F. Lofthouse delivered a rather dull presidential address on Jeremiah and Paul. Some solemnity was added to the occasion by the fact that it took place immediately after a ceremony in which the University had conferred honorary degrees on several of the War leaders, for a number of the doctors came straight on still wearing their scarlet robes. However my gravity was somewhat jeopardised during the discussion, in which both the President and the Secretary had taken part, when someone conflated the two as Dr Lighthouse! Lightfoot retired from the Secretaryship in 1948 but remained on the Committee until he ceased to be Professor two years later. The occasion of his retirement was lugubrious and embarrassing. It was a dull October afternoon in the library of the distinguished Unitarian institution Manchester College, a dignified building with stained-glass windows representing such themes as the triumph of enlightenment over superstition. Lightfoot laid down office in an emotional and indeed tearful speech, whereupon Leslie Cross, who had just succeeded to the Presidency, rose to his feet and proceeded to read, in his appallingly sepulchral voice, an appreciation which sounded almost exactly like an obituary from *The Times*. He then delivered his Presidential Address, on the History of Athanasian Studies in Oxford; it was of enormous length and before it had finished night was falling and his hearers were creeping out unobtrusively one by one in order to get to dinner in hall. The Society survived Lightfoot's departure and continued in a rather half-hearted and dwindling condition, in spite of – or was it because of? – the erudition and specialisation of most of the papers that were read to it. Paradoxically, as time went on fewer of the theological professionals were coming to the meetings and my own Presidential Address in 1961, which I devoted to the subject of Sonship and Sacrifice with particular relation to the Eucharist, received a very minimal and lukewarm response.

Lightfoot's reputed scepticism was largely due to a conscientious reluctance to accept conclusions on insufficient evidence; 'If only they would say, "We don't know."', he sometimes lamented. On the other hand, once he was convinced it was impossible to shake him, and difficult even to persuade him that those who differed from him could possibly be sincere. Of these convictions none was held with more pasionate fervour than the view that St Mark's Gospel had originally ended with verse eight of chapter sixteen. He would tremble from head to foot with emotion when defending this thesis and I was told by an eye-witness that considerable embarrassment was produced when he read a paper at Cambridge on the subject. For in his audience there were the two distinguished New-Testament scholars C. H. Dodd and Wilfred Knox, neither of whom held his view. Lightfoot, in a state of extreme agitation and distress, prefaced the reading of his paper by saying that he found himself in one of the most painful situations of his life, since he was obliged to declare in their presence that two friends for whose scholarly competence and intellectual integrity he had always had the highest respect had committed themselves to expressing a view about the ending of St Mark that could not possibly be held by any honest man. He then burst into tears, and so did the two delinquents whom he had denounced. It would be easy to write off as a pedant and a fusspot a man who could rebuke a colleague for arriving three minutes early for an appointment and who could send a note to the college chaplain asking him to articulate more carefully the 'o' in 'creator', but Lightfoot's pupils were devoted to him and were much – perhaps too much – influenced by him, as was shown by the fact that, while several of them could entertain their friends by deliberate imitations of him, there were more who imitated him without intending to do so. The introduction which Dr D. E. Nineham contributed to the memorial volume *Studies in the Gospels* is a moving tribute to the fundamental goodness and kindness of this shy and meticulous scholar.

One of my closest friends at Oxford was Austin Farrer, who was I suppose one of the most original and versatile theologians of this century. He had an attractive elusiveness and would appear in a room without having very obviously entered it; I always felt that both he and his wife Katharine might sprout small gossamer wings at any moment and fly out through the window. His writings fell into two very sharply contrasted types; there were works on philosophical theology, which were closely reasoned with numerous and minute distinctions, and there were works on Biblical exegesis and typology, which were imaginative and suggestive, sometimes to the point of fantasy. People who did not know him found this baffling, but the answer was that his mind was, in a very rare combination, both that of a philosopher and of a poet. (Another example is that of the Swiss theologian Hans Urs von Balthasar.) Nor was his typology based upon chance and isolated similarities; he was critical of his fellow-typologist Lionel Thornton on just this score. The principle that governed his exegesis was that the thought and writing of the New-Testament writers was dominated by the conscious, or more frequently unconscious, assumption that the words and deeds of Christ were the fulfilment of the great Old-Testament themes. This did not mean that, like the contemporary scholars of the 'demythologising' school, he thought the Gospels were imaginative writings with little historical basis; on the contrary, for him God was himself the supreme typologist, who had arranged both the prophetic character of the events and the interpretative skill of the evangelists. Admittedly, at times his suggestions strained the credulity of his hearers; is Aenon near Salim, where John baptised (John iii. 23) really an echo of Elim, where there were twelve springs of water (Exodus xv. 27)? I remember vividly an occasion when a passage which, by an oversight, had been applied to one pair of Jewish patriarchs was, in the next lecture, shown to apply even more accurately to another. But then, as Austin himself remarked, with the modest humour which was one of his most attractive traits, if it would have been very clever for a German scholar to have discovered this mistake, it must have been even more clever for Austin to have discovered it himself! His friend C. S. C. Williams, in his commentary on The Acts of the Apostles, produced a brilliant piece of Farrerian typologising on Acts x – xii which no one has ever been quite sure whether to take altogether seriously or not. But two things need to be remembered before one dismisses Austin's typology as the undisciplined exuberance of an over-fertile imagination. The first is that he himself drew a sharp distinction between the central typological themes, which he held to be firmly based, and what he would describe as 'luxury points' of detail, which could be accepted or rejected without harm to the structure as a whole. The second point is that, while rejoicing in imaginative detail, Austin always saw this detail as lying within the great pattern of type and antitype, of prophecy and fulfilment, which related God's redemptive acts in Jewish history to his supreme redemptive act in Christ. Furthermore, while being ready to subject his own work to a *retractatio* that would not have been unworthy of his great namesake of Hippo (thus his books on both St Mark and the Apocalypse were followed by subsequent works that amounted almost to recantations), he always held that an author was not usually the best critic of his own work. He once remarked that he appeared to have a flair for producing his kind of stuff but it was for others to decide whether it was worth anything. There was something much more magisterial and synthetic about his handling of typology than was characteristic of the even more elaborate but less co-ordinated typologising of Lionel Thornton; it was indeed amusing to lesser mortals to note the mingled appreciation and reserve with which these two able practitioners of the same art regarded each other's work. The method was less happy in the hands of some of Austin's disciples who were infected by his enthusiasm but lacked both his ability and his sense of humour. In addition, while he was highly critical of the work of many New-Testament scholars and rejected many of their conclusions, he was perfectly well equipped to engage in the more humdrum type of Biblical scholarship, as in his article 'On Dispensing with Q', in the Lightfoot memorial volume, in which he launched a full-scale attack on one of the most tenaciously held hypotheses about the composition of the Gospels; it may not have routed the ranks of Tuscany but it drew their reluctant cheers.

Fundamental to Austin Farrer's Biblical exegesis was the conviction, deeply congenial to the poetic side of his nature, that religious truth is far more adequately expressed through images than through concepts. Indeed it was apparent to him that it was precisely this method that had been chosen by God himself in inspiring the scriptural writers. He never worked out in detail an epistemology of the image, parallel to the many epistemologies of the concept which philosophers have devised; the nearest that he came to this was in his Bampton Lectures, *The Glass of Vision.* He described these as an attempt to bring together his thoughts on three things – the sense of metaphysical philosophy, the sense of scriptural revelation and the sense of poetry. He was clearly more interested in showing how images worked – especially the great scriptural images – than in constructing a formal theory about them. There is a glowing passage in which he displays the monumental way in which the New Testament amasses and interlocks the great images which it employs to declare the mystery of the Holy Trinity. To understand them, he held, it is not necessary or indeed possible to find purely conceptual equivalents for them or to get behind them to a non-metaphorical understanding of fact; the images themselves illuminate us. Furthermore, the images through which the Christian revelation is mediated to us do not function simply in virtue of their iconic character, by being the sort of images they are. Their efficacy does not depend merely on the

natural power of the human mind to recognise likenesses, to
abstract universals from particulars and so on; they were provided
by God to his ancient people the Jews, they were taken by Christ
and refashioned and synthetised, and this work continues in the
Apostles and the Church. Here Austin's epistemology of the image
coalesces with his doctrine about revelation and about the way in
which that revelation is communicated and developed. He was, I
believe, on the way to formulating and commending a theology
of Biblical inspiration which would have made possible the use
of a sound critical method without abandoning the accumulated
fruits of scriptural devotion throughout the Christian ages. It was
however very difficult to get his writing taken seriously, and it
must be confessed that he was at least partly to blame for this
in the light of some of his more audacious speculations.

It was a source of joy to Austin's many friends when he was
lured back to philosophical theology proper by his election as
Gifford Lecturer at Edinburgh for 1956. He chose for his topic
the well-worn subject of the Freedom of the Will, but he treated
it with remarkable freshness. Like almost everything he wrote, his
Giffords appeal as much to the ear as to the eye, in spite (or
because) of their highly polished literary form. He was in fact
one of the few recent writers in the fields of philosophy and
theology who seem to have paid much attention to style as
such, though he never allowed his power of writing to cover
up gaps in the argument. *The Freedom of the Will* was written
in a soliloquising idiom that was rarely absent from his books but
was more prominent here than in most; it provided him with a
medium in which objections could be stated amply and could be
refuted, though his critics complained not altogether justly that
he was rather unfairly conducting both sides of the argument.
Certainly the book runs on rapidly and happily, and the reader is
sometimes surprised to find how far he has been taken; the method
is nevertheless well adapted to the subject under treatment, in which
introspection and the registration of its results play an inevitable
and constructive part. As he himself said, 'to keep myself and
my readers awake, I have used the device of a running debate
between the doctrines of freedom and of necessity', and indeed
one of the most attractive features of his style in general was his
obvious consciousness of the existence and the circumstances of his
audience, a consciousness of which so many modern theologians
seem to be almost totally devoid. It may be worth recording here
that he had, in his oral utterances, two quite distinct styles.
His formal exposition of a well worked-out theme was polished,

elegant and quietly humorous, whether in the pulpit or in the lecture-room; but in wrestling with a topic that he was still in the process of mastering he could be inarticulate, incoherent and floundering, and apparently on the point of crawling on the floor or climbing up the curtains. It was nevertheless from such manifestations of the work in progress that one gathered something of the working of his very unusual type of mind.

In the opinion of many, Austin Farrer was the finest preacher of his generation, as much at home in a college chapel as in the university pulpit. As he seems never to have preached except from a fully written manuscript, many of his sermons were collected and published after his death. As chaplain of Trinity College from 1935 to 1960 it fell to him to deliver a homily every Sunday at the college Eucharist, and he put himself under the admirable, but unusual, discipline of writing a sermon that should be no longer than the portion of the Gospel that it was ideally concerned to expound. Some of the results are to be found in a small volume entitled *The Crown of the Year*, which has been of great utility to many less spontaneous, but more voluble, clerics.

Austin's influence in the intellectual life of Oxford was immense, but he made an impact far beyond the bounds of college and university. To me his most impressive intellectual characteristics was his ability to take full account of contemporary fashions in thought and action, both sacred and secular, without ever being carried away by them. Both the excessively linguistic bias of English philosophy and the excessively sceptical outlook of German New-Testament criticism failed to throw him off his balance. He was, in the Anglican setting, an almost perfect example of what Cardinal Suenens has happily called the 'extreme centre'. It would, however, be quite false to suppose that his impact was solely, or even chiefly, in the intellectual realm.

For all his brilliance, and his deceptively distracted appearance, Austin Farrer was the antithesis of the detached and desiccated Oxford don of popular fiction. For some years at Trinity he played a highly important part in the life of the college behind a beautifully written notice which read:

> The Junior Dean
> may best be seen
> from 10 a.m.
> to 10.15.

though his constant accessibility to both young and old far

outstripped the exiguous limits thus indicated. Modest and shy as he was by temperament, he had a remarkable capacity for winning the confidence of seniors and juniors alike and he was untiring in helping them to solve their problems, both wordly and spiritual. When Keble College elected him as its Warden in 1960 it wisely protected him from having his scholarship submerged under the mass of administration that usually quenches the intellectual activity of the modern head of a house, but he was in fact a very capable administrator. He was a charming companion on any social occasion and an accomplished writer of humorous verse in English, Greek and Latin. We frequently exchanged verses, though mine were perforce always in the vernacular. When he was elected to the Wardenship, which took place on St Matthias's Day after a long interregnum, I sent him the following:

> When Judas left, in ultimate disgrace,
> Explosively, and went to his own place,
> The Eleven solved their problem in a trice
> And filled the vacancy by casting dice.
> They hailed Matthias' apostolic reign,
> And no one ever heard of him again.
> When Keble's Warden, with his record clean,
> Reluctantly became Westminster's Dean,
> The Fellows, huddled in their winter coats,
> Spent weeks and weeks before they cast their votes.
> But, patience justified, at last they found
> One with whose praise all Christendom shall sound.

It produced this from Austin in reply:

> Quoth Peter, 'Our Economist
> Has burst asunder in the midst.
> Now who can tell if we should trust us
> To good Matthias or to Justus?
> Between the even and the odd
> Seek we the arbitrament of God.'
> They cast the die, heaven ruled the bias,
> Up came the odd, and marked Matthias.
> Though no one could have meant it, he
> Turned out a pure nonentity;
> He simply vanished in the blue
> Like Thaddee, or Bartholomew.

The following will appeal to those who have even a slight knowledge of the classical tongues:

The Scrolls and Tablets now their truths disclose,
Ventris digesting these and *Gaster* those.

And this I received from Edinburgh, written on the back of a post-card of Raeburn's well-known painting of a solitary cleric skating on a frozen loch:

While the fierce hounds of *Calvin*'s savage pack
Skate on thin ice, half hoping it will crack,
The Gifford Lecturer from Oxford's strand
Makes circles round them and returns to land.

No one who knew Austin would suspect any malice in either of these!

I saw little of the Farrers after I left Oxford in 1962, but the news of his sudden death in December 1968 came as a shock, as did that of his widow Katharine not long after. Those who lamented that he was not appointed to any of the chairs which his intellectual gifts would have so fittingly adorned could take comfort from the reflection that it was his vocation to write not only on paper but also on human souls. Katharine was herself an accomplished writer, who had several novels to her credit and also performed with accuracy and grace the not very easy task of translating writings by the French Catholic existentialist Gabriel Marcel. After I congratulated her on her first novel *The Missing Link* I received from her the following verse:

What, did you buy for ten and six
The book I should have given you gratis?
My pride is puffed; my conscience pricks.
What *did* you buy for ten and six?
A work the just have labelled *vix*,
And milder critics, *query*, *satis*.
What? Did you *buy*, for ten and six,
The book I should have sent you gratis?

To which I replied:

Of course I paid my ten and six,
And would have spent my utmost penny.
You say the critics marked it *vix*?
It never cost them *one* and six.
I scorn that greedy race of ticks;
The mark that I assign is *bene*.
Of course I paid my ten and six;
I *would* have spent my utmost penny.

After the publication of *The Cretan Counterfeit* I sent her some verses, too long alas to reproduce here, inspired by the variety of the social backgrounds with which that sensational crime-story suggested its author must have been acquainted. They began 'Where did you spend your early life – / In Lewisham, Soho, or Crete?', and received a reply beginning 'We used to live at Rickmansworth / When all the locals called it Ricky.' I also sent her the following, which was based on the fact that one of her characters was a restaurateur who kept rabbits in his back yard to supply his famous chicken dish:

> I used to dine at restaurants in Soho,
> But now I shall not pass that way again.
> You've shattered my illusions at one blow.
> I used to dine at restaurants in Soho.
> Creamed chicken was my weakness, you must know;
> The very *thought* of rabbit gives me pain.
> I *used* to dine at restaurants in Soho,
> But *now* – I shall not pass that way again.

Oxford must have lost a great deal with the passing of the Farrers.

To return to Christ Church. In the last half of my time I received much help from the friendship and counsel of Cuthbert Aikman Simpson, who came to us from General Theological Seminary in New York City as Canon and Regius Professor of Hebrew in 1954 after Danby's death and was appointed Dean in 1959. Like his predecessor John Lowe, he was a Canadian by birth and had been a Rhodes Scholar of the House – he came of farming stock in Prince Edward Island, the smallest province of the Dominion – but was temperamentally extremely different. He was expansive and forthcoming, and he and his wife Jessie made the South-West Lodging and later the Deanery an open house of welcome to old and young alike. He was warm-hearted, generous, impulsive and hot-tempered and General 'Cuthbert's outbursts' were legendary. They were sudden and violent and often their only signal was an ominous twitching of his upper lip, but they were quickly over and left no ill feeling behind; they always reminded me of milk boiling over from a saucepan. He had deep loyalties, and even the mildest criticism of his friend Stephen Bayne, who held the oddly-named post of Executive Officer of the Anglican Communion, or of the theologian Paul Tillich was sure to produce an outburst. A distinguished Canadian who was staying with him told me that he was very nearly thrown out of the Deanery for expressing disagreement with Tillich's views. Cuthbert's doglike devotion to Tillich was always a puzzle to me, for his own Churchmanship was a very definite and rather old-fashioned Anglo-Catholicism quite unlike Tillich's idiosyncratic and undogmatic Protestantism; I never dared to question him about this, but I suspect it was based upon admiration for Tillich's sermons and ignorance of his theology. I have since wondered how Cuthbert would have reacted to the posthumous revelations of Tillich's sexual behaviour, for he himself had retained from his own social origin an almost puritanital respect for traditional moral values. As a scholar he was, I think, thorough and responsible rather than original. His interest in people made him a very good teacher and he was always generously willing to give off the record some Old-Testament tuition to such of my pupils as needed it. But his concern as a priest and pastor was primary to everything else and I found myself frequently consulting him when I had a difficult pastoral problem. His bucolic background would sometimes express itself in (for a cleric) an unusual and unconventional diction. 'God damn it man,' he would ejaculate, 'What's the bloody fool up to now?', when told of some irritating piece of stupidity. He would privately refer to his colleague Claude Jenkins in exasperated but affectionate terms as 'the old bastard'. There was a widely told story of his returning late one night in a taxi and telling the driver to drive into Tom Quad. 'I don't think the Dean likes us to drive in,' oblected the driver, who had not recognised the identity of his passenger. 'I am the bloody Dean,' Cuthbert replied, 'Drive in.' Characteristic, though involving no expletives, was a remark made by him in the Church of St Mary Magdalen, Oxford, when acting as assistant priest at Pontifical High Mass on Palm Sunday on the first occasion after the introduction of the revised rite. Not surprisingly a moment occurred when the ceremony came to a halt with everyone wondering what to do next. In the silence Cuthbert's mildly but definitely transatlantic accents were heard: 'O.K., Father; it's all under control. We're doing fine.' He was certainly a refreshing influence in an academic institution; I forget who it was who said that he fell back on reason when all else failed.

His appointment by the Crown as the second Canadian-born Dean in succession gave rise to all kinds of speculation about occult political influence – was it part of a desperate attempt to keep Canada in the Commonwealth? – but it had a very simple explanation. The members of the Governing Body were asked who they would like and they unitedly asked for Dr Simpson. But his appointment raised an unforeseen matter of international protocol.

For Cuthbert when he went to New York had become a naturalised citizen of the United States, and the Dean of Christ Church has to take at his installation an oath of allegiance to the British sovereign. The U.S. State Department alleged that if he did this he would be committing a disloyal and illegal act and incurring goodness knows what penalties under U.S. law; the English lawyers alleged that unless he did it he could not become Dean. Cuthbert himself proposed to solve the problem by re-assuming his original Canadian nationality. But then the authorities changed their minds. The State Department decided that, as the matter was purely ecclesiastical, they could turn a blind eye, and the English lawyers decided that, as he was a foreigner, he need not take the oath. So everything ended happily, with Cuthbert in the Dean's stall and, together with his dearly loved Jessie, in the Deanery.

From the point of view of the College his Deanship was highly satisfactory. Administration was not his chief interest, but he had plenty of help in that activity and his unfailing enthusiasm for the House led to some impressive expansions under his rule, notably the building of a new quadrangle and the equipment of a new picture-gallery, to the material basis of which his transatlantic contacts were of no little help. Without doubt however, the chief contribution made by Cuthbert and Jessie was that of sheer Christian friendship, which was manifested in many personal and private ways, and, although her death in 1961, was, in Vigo Demant's words, 'a dreadful personal calamity for him' from which he never fully recovered, his friendliness and generosity and his pastoral concern were unabated. After I came to London in 1962 I almost always stayed with him in the Deanery whenever I visited Oxford.

No account of Cuthbert Simpson could be adequate without some mention of the transformation which he brought about in the cathedral. It is not, I think, unfair to say that, while most of them performed their duties conscientiously, the great majority of members of the chapter of Christ Church in the past had looked upon the upkeep of the cathedral and its services as a tiresome burden upon their academic interests and activities. A notable exception was N. P. Williams, who held the Lady Margaret Professorship throughout the nineteen-thirties; maintaining that Christ Church was a cathedral with its teaching side abnormally developed and not a cathedral and a college existing side by side, he had taken in hand the furnishing of the cathedral and the ordering of its services and had introduced many of the accompaniments of Catholic worship. But he died in 1943 with the work uncompleted and nobody was enthusiastic enough to carry it through. When I came in 1945, the Holy Communion was still celebrated by three clerics in surplices and hoods at eight o'clock on Sundays and by one in a cope on weekdays; and there was a Sung Eucharist (with the ministers in copes) only on alternate Sundays. The bishop's Eucharists were an exception; full eucharistic vestments were worn and Arthur Couratin came with a full complement of servers. The general impression though was of something going on from habit in which most of those taking part had little real conviction, and I always felt that the Sung Eucharist seemed mainly to be regarded as an excuse for a sacred concert performed by the choir; any real sense or understanding of the Liturgy was totally lacking and at the end those who had in fact been celebrating the tremendous mystery of redemption would be played out by soft devotional strains. Cuthbert, on the other hand, finding himself in charge of an ancient and historic cathedral, was seized with the vision of making it a great and noble centre of Christian liturgy, and he very largely succeeded. Under his direction much was done to the fabric of the building itself; the spire was restored, the interior was cleaned, the many heraldic devices were coloured and gilded and improvements made in the chapels and in the chapter-house. But more important were the changes in the services. The Eucharist was sung with solemnity every, and not merely every other, Sunday, the proper Eucharistic vestments were gradually introduced, and, although nothing could control the vagaries of individual canons, an impressive measure of Catholic behaviour became the norm. Much of this happened after I left Oxford and one of the most important, though least spectacular, innovations, the perpetual reservation of the Blessed Sacrament, did not take place until after his death. He was anxious to make the cathedral the effective centre of the Diocese of Oxford and to break down the remains of the absurd traditional hostility between the Bishop of Oxford and the Dean of Christ Church, between the Diocese and the College. He encouraged individual parishes to come and celebrate their Sunday Eucharist in the cathedral, bringing their own apparatus of worship with them; this sometimes resulted in the cathedral being permeated by a hitherto unfamiliar scent! His desire to make visitors feel at home scandalised the vergers, who looked upon their job as the marshalling of the worshippers in disciplined ranks and the exclusion of late comers, and, when Cuthbert instructed them to fasten on the door as soon as the service began a notice saying 'Worship is now in progress. Please come in and take a seat.' or words to that effect, they were quite scandalised. But I think that later on they got the message.

Cuthbert died peacefully in his sleep at the end of June 1969 and it came as a surprise to realise that he was in his seventy-eighth year, for he had been vigorous and full of initiative to the last. He was a great Dean, a great character and above all a great priest.

Now however, having written at some length about the society in which I found myself in post-World-War-Two Oxford, I must say something about the part − the very minor part − which I played in its life.

Notes

1. I must preserve from oblivion Arthur's equally characteristic remark when someone bewailed the way in which Archbishop Fisher had ruined the dignity of a great episcopal procession by his slovenly lounging demeanour as its climactic figure: 'Well, old man, you can't have *Aladdin* without the Widow Twankey.' Many people compared Dr Fisher with a headmaster; no one but Arthur would have thought of him as a pantomime dame!
2. *Esquilinus*.

Chapter Ten

Oxford:
Sixteen Years a Student

(1945 – 1962)

Let not Ambition mock their useful toil,
Their homely joys, and destiny obscure;
– Thomas Gray, *Elegy written in a Country Churchyard*

The immediate post-war period at Oxford was abnormal and interesting. There were boys coming up straight from school again as well as the swarm of demobilised warriors anxious to prepare themselves for jobs in civilian life, and the two groups mixed on the whole much better than might have been expected. Many of the warriors had achieved high commissioned rank, which they tactfully concealed from view; many had acquired wives and even children, who were not so easily concealed. In fact the married couples were a very pleasant feature of the period; they lived in considerable discomfort, often in bed-sitters with the baby behind a screen. The wives were with hardly an exception capable and level-headed young women, and I often thought that only a capable and level-headed young woman would have allowed her husband to bring her to share the austerities of two years in post-war Oxford. One temporary but refreshing element was provided by a small number of demobilised United-States servicemen who were awaiting transport across the Atlantic and were allowed by arrangement to count a term or two at Oxford towards the academic course which they were going to take up at home. They were practically the first Americans I had met and I found them almost all charming and considerate. When one had them to tea – and even the simplest entertaining in those days of rationing had its difficulties, which I only partly circumvented by exchanging soap-coupons for bread-coupons with married colleagues – they would frequently present one with confectionery which they had received from home, explaining charmingly that

246

to bring some food with one was an old American custom. There was a marked air of seriousness, in marked contrast to that which enlivened the universities after the First World War; the conflict had been longer and the age of the ex-warriors was correspondingly higher, and it was less easy the second time to feel sure that one had just taken part in the war which would end all wars. One unexpected feature was the popularity of societies of all kinds; meetings were invariably crowded in a way that was not, I think, wholly explained by the inflated number of undergraduates.

Among the sets of rooms that were vacant I chose one on the ground-floor of Canterbury Quad. This had the advantage, from the pastoral point of view, of being readily accessible to undergraduates and, from that of worldly comfort, of being one of the few with an electric fire. Christ Church had never emerged psychologically from the era when coal and servants were equally plentiful, though by the end of the war they had become equally exiguous. When Farquhar Buzzard died at the end of 1945, I moved into the rooms which he had occupied on the first floor in Tom Quad and, when J. C. Masterman went to be Provost of Worcester in 1947, into the similar but larger set now vacant on the adjacent staircase, and this remained my college home for the rest of my Oxford days. It was indeed a large set, even by Christ Church standards; I had, in addition to my bedroom, which looked into the quadrangle, a large and a small sitting room, which were separated by a pantry, and a study; these formed a circular sequence, beginning and ending in an ample lobby. From this last, a staircase led to the bathroom and a roomy spare bedroom. To prevent callers giving up in despair, I put notices on the doors to encourage them in penetrating this labyrinth. J.C. had used most of the space simply to house his bookcases, and was himself to be found in the tiny study, like a queen-bee in the central cell of her hive; but I decided to make full use of this eccentric but impressive suite of rooms and, when I had a large party, as I occasionally did when I got firmly established, I would throw the doors open and make use of the whole sequence. The set − or, it would be more accurate to say, its external walls − overlapped Wolsey's unfinished sixteenth-century work with that of the following century, and their junction was marked by a transverse wall three feet thick, through which my study and my bedroom were connected by an archway. The internal partitions and floors were of much flimsier structure, and my smaller sitting room had been given a low ceiling above which an undergraduate's set had been skilfully inserted. I came in one evening to find the ceiling visibly rising and falling in a most alarming way under thunderous bumps from above, while quantities of dust descended all over the room. I went up to investigate and discovered a mixed party in progress; a game was being played which involved all the participants leaping in the air simultaneously as high as they could. I pointed out to their host that, whatever the rules of the College said on the matter, the laws of nature would ensure that unless the game ceased forthwith the party would continue in my sitting room! My big problem was that of heating my large room, which I tried to cope with first by oil- and then by gas-heaters; but the really insuperable enemy, as with most ancient buildings, was draughts, for as soon as one had been tracked down and its way of entry blocked, it would infuriatingly discover another, hitherto unknown, and proceed to make use of that. Nevertheless, I became very fond of my rooms and counted myself very lucky to have secured them; they were excellently situated for pastoral purposes, being immediately over the Junior Common Room, and also for modest entertaining of friends and colleagues. On a Sunday morning, after College Prayers, I would gather up such of my colleagues and their families as were there and any old members of the House who were week-ending in Oxford, and offer them refreshment in my rooms. The refreshment, about which I made no concealment, was Cyprus sherry, and I was interested that on two occasions high-court judges, having enquired the identity of this unfamiliar beverage, made a note of the address of the supplier, in order to get some for themselves. I also used it for undergraduate parties and it amused me when they expressed appreciation of what they took to be some rare and expensive vintage.

I had, of course, to provide my own furniture, but, apart from carpets and curtains, this was less of a problem than I anticipated. For large rooms both need and invite large things to fill them, and I was fortunate in being able to buy a number of extremely good pieces of furniture second-hand at very low prices for the simple reason that they were far too large for most modern dwellings to accomodate them. There were two oil-paintings belonging to the College already on the walls, one a fine pseudo-Vandyke of King Charles I and the other a sombre but impressive portrait by Herkomer of the nineteenth-century theologian H. P. Liddon. (The House's enormous collection of portraits of distinguished members is exhibited rather according to the eminence of the artist than of the subject.) When after the War our artistic treasures were brought out from the places where they had been hidden from the possible depredations of Field-Marshal Goering, it was discovered that a number of paintings had been stowed away in one of the attics in Tom Quad under the extraordinary impression that they would be safe there during air-raids, and it was decided that any senior member who wished could hang some in his rooms. So I spent an afternoon there with a young colleague and we emerged with what appeared to be a Vandyke and several Raphaels, heavily adorned with dust and damp and mouse-tracks. The Raphaels have been given the non-commital addition 'School of' but the Vandyke is accepted as the work of the Master; it hung in my rooms for several years until, somewhat to my relief, the Curator of Pictures decided it ought to be in a more secure place. It is a sepia drawing in which the most prominent feature is the end-elevation of a horse; and it represents either Venus arming Mars before the Battle or Venus disarming Mars after the Battle, no one seems quite certain which.

Christ Church in 1945 still bore a faint aroma of the past, when it had been largely a playground for the aristocracy, none of whom would have condescended to take a degree. The University Calendar still printed every year the list of its undergraduate members, headed by the Earl of Home, who had matriculated in 1892, and containing a large number of members of the peerage and such other distinguished persons as the Maharajah of Indore. But this was really a matter of the past and, although Christ Church still got perhaps more than its share of the upper class, it was difficult now for anyone to acquire, and still more to retain, a place in the College without maintaining some standard of academic respectability. One problem facing the Colleges just after the War was that of the shortage of teaching staff, and for several years I found myself not only teaching the small number of men whom we had for the Theology School but also helping out with philosophy for P.P.E. (Philosophy, Politics and Economics, or 'Modern Greats'), and also with elementary Mathematics and Latin for the Pass Degree.

English became an unwontedly popular subject at this time, possibly because of an impression, certainly not justified in practice, that it was a soft option which one could get through by reading a few novels. I was given the job of unearthing from the various recesses of Oxford people who were able and willing to teach those of our men who wished to study it. This particular chore ceased when we elected an English tutor of our own, but throughout my time I performed this task with regard to Chinese and Geography; in this last capacity I used regularly to receive unsolicited and splendidly produced literature from the Dominican Republic extolling the beneficent activities of the President, General Truhillo, and his kinsfolk. I still occasionally meet some middle-aged civil servant or lawyer who reminds me that I gave him his first acquaintance with the writings of Descartes, Berkeley, Locke and Hume. I did not find it easy to teach the very varied syllabus of the Theology School, never having read a first degree in Theology myself, but by a fair amount of informal interchange with tutors in other Colleges – a common Oxford practice, which had in any case the advantage of providing one's pupils with some variety – I got through without too many disasters. (Incidentally, I think that undergraduates have become much more demanding for perfect teaching than they used to be. I do not think this is altogether unreasonable, but in my days one was quite prepared to have, and could even take a certain pride in having, a teacher whose mind operated at such an impenetrable depth of academic profundity as to be incommunicable to others and possibly even unintelligible to himself; this could provide the better pupil with valuable mental exertion, but was hard upon the dimmer types. Nowadays many pupils, going to the other extreme, seem to expect to have all their thinking done for them.) My pastoral responsibilities extended to the whole College, or at least to the junior part of it. At any rate this was the interpretation placed upon the dignified and flattering, but conveniently vague, language of the Statute which empowered the Governing Body to 'appoint ... a person in Holy Orders of the Church of England who may be deemed eminently qualified to give religious and theological instruction to the undergraduate members of the House, and to be a Student of the House as a place of religion, learning and education' and laid upon me 'the condition of taking such part in the religious and theological teaching, and performing such duties with respect to the Chapel Services and the discipline and educational work of the House as may from time to time be assigned to him by the Governing Body.' In fact no such duties were ever formally assigned to me and I was given complete freedom in doing my job. I can remember only one occasion, in my seventeen years, when a tutor protested that I had come between him and one of his pupils and only one occasion when I protested to the Dean that one of the Canons had interfered with my pastoral policy behind my back.

The Dean and the Canons were almost invariably anxious to encourage me in my pastoral task and to make it easy for me, but it was, I think, already becoming an anachronism for the cathedral of the diocese to be also a college chapel. There was also the added complication that all the Canons were members of the Governing Body and all but one held university professorships in the Faculty of Theology. In spite of the general goodwill, pastorally the association of cathedral and college was on the whole a handicap. In contrast with other colleges (New College and Magdalen, with their choir schools were a partial exception), where the functioning of the chapels depended entirely on the voluntary support of their members, Christ Church, with its imposing cathedral establishment, encouraged the common British assumption that religion is some-thing laid on by the establishment which needs for its survival nothing more than an attitude of benevolent non-opposition, while it did little to satisfy those who felt the demand for a more personal expression of their faith. In fact, the real centres of Church life in Oxford were only to a very small degree to be found in the college chapels; Pusey House for the 'High' and St Aldate's for the 'Low', with St Ebbe's for the downright fundamentalist, offered much more outlet for enthusiasm and commitment. From time to time groups of various colour would spring up among undergraduates in the House, and they could try the patience of someone like myself who was trying with mixed results to make some impact on the nominal Anglicans who formed the bulk of our undergraduates. The Protestants, who at one time included a group with the pretentious title 'The Christians of Christ Church', for the most part left me severely alone, except when they came with unsuccessful requests for interdenominational communion services. The Anglo-Catholics, who gravitated towards Pusey House or towards St Mary Magdalen's Church (to which Christ Church appointed in 1946 that very remarkable priest Colin Stephenson[1]), would sometimes scandalise the vergers by reciting the Rosary in the cathedral before Evensong on a weekday, but were not very often seen there, except to serve at an early celebration or for some pontifical function. I took every opportunity that I could of making contacts with undergraduates, I gave innumerable tea- and sherry-parties and invited them to hear gramophone records; though profoundly unathletic myself I spent much time, especially in my earlier years, on the river bank and the sports field, and every now and again these contacts proved fruitful. I had a fairly steady succession of candidates for confirmation, many of whom (such has been the decay of religion in the home) were candidates for baptism also; but I was always conscious, in spite of my attempts to link them up with their home parishes, of our weakness in not having a normal and active Eucharistic community in which to give them not merely instruction but also practical training in the life of the Church. There were always some, though never many, candidates for ordination, some of whom wisely decided that they had not a vocation to the priesthood after all, and others who discovered their vocation during their undergraduate years. A few – and these some of the best – came up as ordinands, then became doubtful and went in for a secular career, and then some years later, with greater experience and maturity, resolved their doubt and offered themselves for ordination again. Whether it is ideal that an ordinand should read a degree in Theology at the university, having regard to the fact that he will have in any case to go on to a theological college, is itself a matter of opinion; a lot will depend on the ordinand himself and a lot will – or at any rate should – depend on what the university in question understands by theology. Only once was I approached by an undergraduate whose ideas of the priesthood appeared to have been derived entirely from the novels of Jane Austen and Trollope, if indeed he had ever exerted himself sufficiently to read them. He was a younger son of a county family which had the patronage of the parish in which the family mansion stood; the incumbent was an elderly man who had developed regrettable high-church tendencies, including what was described as 'ringing an electric bell during the service', and the idea was that this young hopeful should be ordained to succeed him in a few years' time. Although the family had the reputation of being keen supporters of the Established Church, there was apparently no conception of the priesthood as involving anything in the way of personal conviction, vocation or training or of the parish as anything but a pleasant niche for a country gentleman. It was not difficult to disillusion him, but I suppose that a century earlier there were a number of young men like him at the House.

Every three years the life of the University was considerably disrupted for a week by a mission to the undergraduates, of which the high lights were the addresses given each evening in the Sheldonian Theatre by the principal missioner. Originally the missions had been run in three simultaneous but independent sections, Anglican, Free-church and fundamentalist respectively, but more recently the Anglicans and Free-churchmen had combined their efforts, on the theory that they had no disagreements on the fundamental Christian doctrines and that if, in the course of the mission-week, you could convert someone to belief in God and Christ you could leave it to whatever church he joined to add the rest later. I was never quite convinced by this argument, for I think what usually converts people is the life of an actual worshipping community, and that even one's presentation of the basic Christian doctrines will depend on one's beliefs about the Church and its life. This was rather painfully illustrated at the end of one of the missions when it was arranged that the final address should be given not, as was usual, by the principal missioner but by the Archbishop of Canterbury, Dr Geoffrey Fisher. Conscious of the mixed nature of his audience, the Primate embarked on an unconvincing attempt to minimise the significance of the divisions between Christians. Some people, he said, asserted that we differed about the Ministry, but that was absurd; we all had a ministry. And some asserted that we differed about the Sacraments, but that too was absurd; for we all had sacraments. And some asserted that we differed about the Church, but we were all agreed about that: if you were baptised you were a member of the Church, and if you were not baptised you were not. I think his Grace would have been shocked to know that his well-intentioned glossing over of serious problems caused grave, though presumably unanticipated, offence; for among the supporters of the Mission were Congregationalists and Baptists, who rejected any strict relation between baptism and membership of the Church! It is of course impossibly difficult to assess the spiritual effects of such an endeavour, but I must admit that, in view of the enormous work of preparation involved and the call that this made on the time and effort of dons and undergraduates alike, I faced the prospect of a mission with less than unmixed enthusiasm. Missions were certainly no substitute for the quiet work of the college chaplains, difficult as it was at Oxford to get that informal relation between chaplain and undergraduates which had long been taken for granted at Cambridge and which seemed to prevent any Cambridge chaplain from ever getting to bed before one in the morning.

One of the most useful organisations throughout my time in Oxford was the Socratic Club, which existed as a forum for the discussion of basic religious questions and had C. S. Lewis for its presiding genius. It included both senior and junior members of the University and, at time when Oxford philosophy was heavily dominated by the prestigious figures of Gilbert Ryle and A. J. Ayer and had only just emerged from the spectral phase of logical positivism, it provided a valuable battle-ground for religious apologetics. There were some hard-hitting debates, especially when Lewis himself was involved, and the Socratic did as much as anything to make religion in general and Christianity in particular intellectually respectable in those post-war years. Lewis and I met frequently but we never became really intimate, and I have nothing to add to the many studies of his life and work which have appeared since his death. He was in his time certainly the leading Christian apologist and it was interesting to note the embarrassment that mention of him often caused to atheists and agnostics, who could not bring themselves to believe that so obviously intelligent a man could really hold the views that he professed; such a work as his famous *Screwtape Letters* was frequently dismissed as a brilliant *tour de force*.

More private and inconspicuous but in its way perhaps of not less value was the small group of philosophers and theologians which Michael Foster and I got together just after his return from the Army and of which I was secretary until I left Oxford. In Basil Mitchell's words:

> The nearest thing to a manifesto was the choice of a name, 'The Metaphysicals'. This title voiced a common dissatisfaction with the restrictions which tacitly governed philosophical discussion at a time when 'metaphysical' was the rudest word in the philosopher's vocabulary. In an atmosphere thick with inhibitions, we wanted to be free to ask what questions we liked, even of some of them turned out to be 'ultimate questions' of an allegedly unanswerable and, indeed, unaskable sort.[2]

We met in one another's rooms, with a minimum of programme and organisation, and in our early days we certainly had no thought of publication. Nevertheless, after ten years of discussions such of us as survived came to the conclusion that we had sufficient in common to justify our speaking to such of the outside world as was prepared to listen to us. The upshot was the set of essays published in 1957 under the title *Faith and Logic: Oxford Essays in Philosophical Theology*, and the authors, apart from Mitchell and Foster, were Austin Farrer, Ian Crombie, G. C. Stead, J. R. Lucas and R. M. Hare; I was exempted from contributing as I was at the time engaged in writing my Bampton Lectures. The book had a modest, though not a spectacular success; at least it served as a sign that even in Oxford, the home of linguistic positivism, there were some who had not bowed down to Baal.

The even tenor of life at Christ Church was punctuated by a number of interruptions, the first of which fell quite early in my time. In 1545 King Henry VIII had refounded the College on the basis of Cardinal Wolsey's earlier foundation of 1525 and his own transitional 'King Henry VIII's College' of 1532. Oddly enough, in spite of the House today having direct continuity with the royal polygamist and enjoying the status of a royal foundation, it has always felt itself as being Wolsey's offspring rather than Henry's. There are two statues of the disgraced Cardinal and none of the monarch who disgraced him; his tasselled hat appears everywhere, in stone, in painting and on writing-paper, and the arms of the House are based on his. Nevertheless the quatercentenary (or, as *The Times* persistently described it, the quadringenary) of the existing foundation fell in 1945 and, allowing for the fact that the War was then virtually unfinished, it was decided to postpone any celebrations to the following year. So, on October 24th 1946, King George VI and his consort, who earlier in the day had been opening the new building of the Bodleian Library, came to Founder's Prayers in the Cathedral and then to dinner in Hall, after which they came down into the Senior Common Room, where a representative selection of members of the House were presented. I was not one of these and I have no illustrations dicta to record; my main memory of the evening is drinking the loyal toast while singing 'Here's a health unto his Majesty' in a crouching position, owing to my neighbour having firmly planted his foot on the sleeve of my gown as we rose and ignoring in his patriotic enthusiasm my frantic pleas to remove it. This was the occasion, which I have mentioned elsewhere, on which Canon Jenkins made his one and only appearance in a light grey flannel suit. A more ambitious, though less august, celebration was the performance the following month in the College Hall of Shakespeare's *Henry VIII*; with the exception of the female characters, those involved, whether as cast, producers or scene-shifters, were all undergraduates. *Henry VIII* is not generally considered to be one of Shakespeare's greatest plays, but, dealing as it does largely with the relations between the House's two founders, its presentation in the magnificent hall built by the former of them was highly appropriate to the occasion and its pageant character lent itself to an effective accompaniment of splendour. As with undergraduate productions in general it all but got out of hand; as rehearsals proceded the stage was gradually extended until it occupied a quarter of the Hall and one began to wonder whether any room would be left for an audience. Batteries of flood-lamps were introduced, and quantities of electrical apparatus which one suspected had earlier served a more military purpose. The stage was delineated by great flats rising almost to the roof; this I could not help feeling was a mistake, as the intention had been to reproduce this slice of Tudor history in its splendid original Tudor setting, whereas the actual scenic setting that emerged might have come from any modern experimental theatre group. However, a good time was certainly had by all, though I am not sure of the effect on some people's examination results. The general opinion in senior circles was that a disturbance of this kind could be tolerated once in four hundred years but that if it had gone on for another week Christ Church would have come to an end. As it was, normality was rapidly restored and High Table restored to Hall from its exile in S.C.R. The following term we faced a severer ordeal.

Just before the Hilary Term began I walked along the Isis to Iffley and felt unpleasantly hot wearing an overcoat. The following night it began to snow and we did not see the ground again for something like seven weeks. That in itself might have been endurable and even pleasant, other things being equal; but other things were certainly not. I have already described the primitive nature of our heating arrangements in College; but, as those who go back to that time will remember, there was a nation-wide fuel crisis and most of us were undernourished after six years of war. It was not surprising that an unpleasant and obstinate gastric infection ran round the college; I was one of its victims. I had by this time moved into Tom Quad, into Buzzard's former rooms, which at least had two rather ancient gas-fires. These suddenly ceased to function and investigation revealed a blockage in the main pipe which served my rooms. When dismantled, this was discovered to be completely blocked with ice, which had condensed from the water-vapour in the gas; the main pipe ran up the wall of my open staircase, which faced east and had been exposed day and night to freezing winds for several weeks. The gas company put in a new pipe but left it equally exposed as the old one, so I lagged it myself with newspapers. In retrospect this was a very minor incident, but it amuses me to observe my hearers' incredulity when I tell them that in Christ Church it was so cold that even the gas pipes froze; it is, however, the sober truth. One of the more amusing aspects of the great freeze was the costumes which people adopted in their attempt to keep warm. Some of these, belonging to ex-warriors who had served in arctic or mountainous regions were remarkable indeed; there was one man who walked about in what looked like the complete skin of a yak. Canon Jenkins appeared more and more nearly globular as he presumably added more and more items of clothing under his cassock, until finally he put his raincoat over it and so, when seen from behind, had two light brown tails hanging down under his surplice. When the longed-for thaw came damage was visible everywhere in the shape of cracked and chipped stonework, but the most immediate result of the melting of country-wide accumulations of snow was of course widespread flooding. My own private flood came through the ceiling of my large sitting room, which was immediately under the outside roof; its source was the snow which had drifted under the eaves and built up between the roof and the plaster ceiling. When the deluge descended I rushed down to get help and the first person I met was the Head Porter who was standing in the Quad. 'There's nothing that can be done, sir,' he replied helplessly when I explained my problem, 'It's coming through every roof in the College.' So it was, but unlike the burst pipes which also made their presence known in many places, this particular inundation, though ample, soon stopped of its own accord. Christ Church Meadow was deeply flooded, and not only the Meadow itself but the raised paths round it. I put on gum-boots and attempted to walk round in order to enjoy the view of Meadow Buildings and Merton College across the water, but I had to give up the attempt as the current was so strong that I should have been swept off my feet. When the flood partially subsided and the path re-emerged, I obtained the desired view and I realised to my astonishment that, when seen reflected in water, the universally execrated Meadow Buildings (I have recorded Canon Jenkins's abusive description of them in his quatercentenary sermon) looked elegant and well-proportioned. And then the explanation dawned upon me. They had been built in 1862—5 from the design of a discipline of Ruskin named Thomas Newenham Deane in highly imitative Venetian style and, whether the architect realised this or not, needed to be seen with a reflected counterpart. Indeed, so slavishly imitative are they that they lack any kind of plinth and rise straight out of the grass as if out of the water of a Venetian canal. Meadow Buildings are in fact a fine example of the triumph of the doctrinaire over the appropriate.

Some of the saddest victims of combined frost and flood were the magnificent trees in the Meadow. Their roots had become loosened and many of them were elms infected by the disease to which that species is particularly vulnerable. When one night a great storm of wind arose they came down like ninepins. From my rooms in Tom Quad I could hear the distant crashes with which they fell, and when the wind fell in the morning and I went out into the Meadow I met a scene of devastation. Something like a score of giants had fallen; a few snapped in twain but most simply torn up by the roots. (And in fact the replanting of the Meadow was one of our steady problems during my time at the House.) But the woes of our frozen winter received ample, and indeed extreme, compensation in one of the longest, hottest and driest summers on record, by the end of which not a blade of green grass was visible on the brown earth. 1947 was indeed a year of extremes. One casualty, as we believed, was the fig-vine, whose limbs were spread out to catch the sun on the north wall of the college garden and which provided fruit for the dons if the undergraduates did not get to it first. According to tradition it had, in its embrionic condition, been brought from the Holy Land in the seventeenth century by Edward Pococke, the then Regius Professor of Hebrew and Canon of Christ Church. There was therefore lamentation, though not surprise, when this aged vegetable appeared to have succumbed to the great frost. Its withered branches were cut off to the ground and nothing was left but a stump, and this only because it was considered to be too much trouble to dig it up. What was our astonishment when the following year there appeared from this apparently lifeless stump at ground-level tiny green filaments, from which in a couple of years the whole vine was reconstituted and ready to bear fruit once more! Mention of the Hebrew Professorship brings to my mind the great controversy which convulsed the University at the end of the nineteen-fifties about what was inaccurately called its secularisation or its laicisation.

The story was as follows. Since 1630 the Regius Professorship of Hebrew had been attached to a canonry of Christ Church, which provided its incumbent with both a stipend and a residence, though in recent years the stipend had become inadequate and had had to be supplemented by the University to bring it up to the level of that of other chairs. This of course meant that it could only be held by an Anglican priest and, with the decline of Hebrew studies among the clergy, the field of candidates when it fell vacant was likely to be limited; some people thought it significant that after Danby's death his successor had to be found in America. The matter was complicated by the fact that one of the leading Hebrew scholars in Oxford, though himself holding a position which removed him from the field of possible candidates, was a violent anti-clerical and was habitually more offensive both to and about other people than anyone else in Oxford. Once, at a meeting of the Society of Historical Theology in Campion Hall, the Jesuit College, in the course of a paper about the Hebrew Scrolls, he managed to introduce two quite gratuitous insults to his hosts. He had convinced himself of two propositions, that the churches were empty because the clergy knew no Hebrew and that there was no Anglican priest who was competent to hold a Hebrew chair. When Cuthbert Simpson resigned the chair to become Dean of Christ Church the balloon went up, and a proposal was brought before the University to separate the Hebrew chair from the canonry. A really farcical situation resulted. The impression was widely produced, largely by the anti-clerical whom I have mentioned, that to carry the proposal would be to deal a deadly blow, certainly against the Anglican Church and probably against organised religion; and it was amusing, when the crucial decision was taken, to see people turning up in the Sheldonian Theatre to cast their vote who had no interest whatever in Hebrew but thought that they were driving nail in the coffin of Christianity. The proposal was of course carried, but I do not think either the Church or religion suffered at all as a result. It did however carry the consequences that the whole of the Professor's stipend now became a charge on the University and that the former contribution from the canonry was set free for specifically church purposes, neither of which results can have been very welcome to some of those who had been most enthusiastic for the separation. As a final touch, when a Professor was appointed under the new regulation, he turned out to be a Scottish Presbyterian minister, a member of a species not noticeably more acceptable to anticlericals than that of the Anglican clergy.

A more wide reaching and more protracted controversy was that concerning the proposed road through Christ Church Meadow; it went on with undulations in intensity during practically the whole of my time. The problem from which it arose was simple in its essence but extremely complicated in its details. Oxford, like many other ancient cities, was suffering from a steadily growing congestion of traffic, and the intense concentration of buildings of unique beauty and historic interest in the central area made the simple and obvious solution of ruthless demolition and straightforward road-widening entirely unacceptable. The area most obviously affected was the High Street, fringed as it was with colleges and also in effect a main arterial highway. Solving Oxford's traffic problem thus appeared to many as primarily 'getting the traffic out of the High', and when in May 1945 the Oxford City Council engaged Mr Thomas Sharp as its consultant to prepare a report on the planning and development of the city it was widely anticipated that his proposals would include provision of a new road running east and west across Christ Church Meadow. And so, when his report appeared two years later, they did.

At first sight nothing could appear more reasonable. On the one hand was the High, getting more and more congested, noisy, polluted with petrol-fumes and generally spoilt; on the other, less than a quarter of a mile to the south, the Meadow empty and unutilised. Furthermore, unscrupulous critics could – and did – plausibly make it appear that Christ Church was keeping a monopolistic grasp on the Meadow for its own mysterious but presumably selfish ends, whereas, in the words of the College Report for 1955, 'for 400 years the House has spent large sums on maintaining and beautifying the Meadow, with the sole object of preserving its amenities, for ourselves, naturally, but also for the whole of Oxford, which enjoys them and pays no single penny towards their upkeep.' I shall not attempt to narrate the complicated subsequent story. No less than thirteen different schemes were proposed at one time or another. If there was to be a road through the Meadow how far to the south could it be? Could it be in a trench or even in a tunnel? Could it even be on the far side of the river? And need there be a road to the south of the High at all? The University affirmed its opposition to any inner relief roads, but some influential members dissented, especially some whose colleges were on or near the High, and among these was the Warden of New College, A. H. Smith, a kindly but romantic and unpractical man who when he became Vice-Chancellor tried to feel a personal concern with all the undergraduates in the University. I was provoked to send to the *Oxford Magazine* the following verse, inspired by a famous poem of G. K. Chesterton on an even more distinguished Smith:

> Oxford's Preservation Trust,
>   A.H. Smith,
> You are on it; is that just,
>   Smith, Oh Smith?
> As the Warden of your College
>   You are good as good could be,
> And your services to knowledge
>   Cannot be assessed by me.
> So discuss Kant's sense of duty
>   And interpret Plato's myth;
> But preserving Oxford's beauty –
>   Chuck it, Smith!

So the arguments dragged on. The Minister, Mr Duncan Sands, ordered an Enquiry. Christ Church issued a writ against the Minister, challenging his action as *ultra vires*. But when I left Oxford in 1962 the then Minister had accepted the proposal of a road across the Meadow 300 yards from the nearest point of Christ Church. I have been totally outside the subsequent discussions and all I know is that when I am writing in 1980 the Meadow is still inviolate. One thing always seemed clear to me, that it was ridiculous to devise plans for roads *through* Oxford while the relief road *round* Oxford was unfinished and therefore virtually unused; for obviously the much needed completion of the latter, whenever it took place, would radically alter the flow of traffic and therefore the needed solution. This proved to be the case when the Donnington Bridge above Iffley Lock was opened and made the ring-road complete. But it is horrifying to contemplate the amount of time and effort that were wasted over a scheme that was both unattractive and unnecessary.

Various functions in the Latin language survive at Oxford from its more literate past. One of these is the Latin Communion conducted in the church of St Mary the Virgin by the Vice-Chancellor and Proctors or, if, as is now almost always the case, they are not in Holy Orders, by deputies appointed by them. In 1949 Denis Page, who was Senior Proctor, asked me to assist John Lowe by reading the Epistle and Gospel at this service and presented me with a suitably inscribed volume in recognition of this task. I was certainly less distinguished than the celebrant as a classical scholar but more familiar with the celebration of the Holy Mysteries in the Latin tongue. I was puzzled to find inserted into the book given me to use on this occasion a typewritten vestry prayer in Latin which struck me as being vaguely familiar but somehow not quite right. I suddenly realised that it was a Latin translation of a collect from the 1928 Prayer Book which the translator did not know was itself a rather free translation of the Latin collect for the Feast of Corpus Christi. I now confess to the world for the first time that, of my own mere motion and without any authorisation whatever, I removed this spurious hack translation from the volume belonging to the University of Oxford and substituted the authentic original *Deus, qui nobis sub sacramento mirabili* ... On another occasion I was asked to sing the Latin Litany.

Another Latin function which fell to me was the Bodleian Oration in 1956. According to ancient statute or custom — I am not sure which — at the annual visitation of the Bodleian Library by the Curators an oration has to be delivered in Latin by a Master of Arts of Christ Church, who receives a suitable emolument for his pains. The duty of the Orator is, in alternate years, to voice the praise of Sir Thomas Bodley and of Hebrew studies. I believe that at one time the Bodlein Oration had fallen into neglect and contempt; there was one fixed text on each topic, which was handed on from one Orator to the next and was gabbled through in a perfunctory and inaudible way. More recently, however, some dignity had been restored to the function; an original, though fairly brief, discourse was expected and the Orator was invited to lunch with the Curators after. Even so, it was somewhat difficult to find continually new aspects of Thomas Bodley to praise, if not of Hebrew studies, and

I decided to be entertaining rather than learned and to argue a mock scholastic thesis in the style of St Thomas Aquinas. The Vice-Chancellor at the time was the formidable Maurice Bowra and I was relieved to see his expression of puzzlement give way to a broad smile as he realised what I was doing. The Latin text can be found in the *Oxford University Gazette* for November 15th 1956; the following is a literal translation:

Most Distinguished Vice-Chancellor, Eminent Proctors, Most Worthy Curators, Most Learned Deputy-Head-Librarian, Lord-Doctors, Masters:

The Question is proposed today WHETHER THOMAS BODLEY WAS A GOOD MAN.

We proceed thus to the Question:

First Objection. It appears that Thomas Bodley was not a good man. For it is said (Eccles. xii. 12) *Of the making of many books there is no end*; which is manifestly confirmed by this Library. But that which has no end tends to infinity. But every infinite is imperfect, as the Philosopher says, And he who builds a Library causes many books to be, because nobody wants to print books unless there is a possibility of selling them. But it is impossible for him who causes the imperfect to be good. Therefore, neither was Thomas Bodley good.

Second Objection. Furthermore, it is certain and is confirmed by the senses that the books which are buried in the Bodleian Library have for the greatest part never been opened or their pages cut, although for their housing and feeding much money and much labour are necessary. Moreover, if there were no Library, there could be constructed in its place a building dedicated to the reception of mechanical vehicles, which is manifestly desirable. Nevertheless, while the Library remains, to build such a receptacle appears in no degree possible. Therefore, all his benefactions whatsoever notwithstanding, Thomas Bodley ought not to be judged as simply good.

But on the other hand there is what the Swan of Avon says (*The Tempest*, I. ii. 109), *My Library was dukedom large enough*.

I reply that it must be said that it has been shown by the Philosopher, that the first mover in any order of motions is the cause of all that are of that order, in which opinion the Angelic Doctor agrees. And he shows that the good of man is the good of the intellect. It follows therefore that founders and benefactors of colleges, libraries and other such are worthy of all praise. Such was Thomas Bodley. Furthermore, it is manifest that the greatest praise belongs to those who provoke others to follow and imitate their good example. And this also is true of Thomas Bodley. For he not only fostered its construction and adorned that most beautiful building for the use of the University and its teaching, but also initiated that succession, uninterrupted until now, of most generous benefactors, such as in this present year are Mr Osborn of Yale in the United States of America, certain learned professors of the University of Moscow, the most illustrious Head Librarian of Pekin and many others. Therefore is the most talented knight Thomas Bodley to be praised as the First Mover, in whom, as effects in their cause, all his successors are in some way included.

To the First Objection it must be said that it does not follow that everyone who does something imperfect is altogether bad. Granted therefore that it is bad to make many books, it would not follow that Thomas Bodley was devoid of all good. However, the aforesaid supposition is not certain. For a certain wise man has said *The more the merrier*, and all men agree that someone who increases the joy of nations does a good work. Furthermore it must be said that 'infinite' has two meanings: one of that which stretches itself for its own sake, and this is manifestly bad, as is shown in the fable of the toad; the other of that which tends to the perfection of some end, such as good morals, the natural sciences and other such things, and this can be good. And this is true of the Bodleian Library, whose earlier part has just been happily renewed and redecorated.

To the Second Objection it must be said that other ways of solving the traffic problem can be thought out than the destruction of the ancient amenities of our University. Furthermore, if certain books are not read, the remedy is not to destroy them but to increase the number of readers. The University ought therefore to become much larger or (what would be much better) at any rate more studious, which is a consummation devoutly to be wished.

The Objections are thus resolved and the conclusion is confirmed that THOMAS BODLEY WAS A GOOD MAN.

I wondered whether I should receive a rebuke for my frivolous behaviour on a solemn occasion, but in fact the audience seemed to be grateful for a little light relief. However, when, in the hope that I might have initiated a new tradition, I suggested to my successor the following year that he might deliver his oration in goliardic verse, my example was ignored. I did wonder however what some foreign readers thought when the international *Journal of Documentation* printed my oration as a matter of routine.

The great Christ Church function each year was the Summer

Gaudy, which I have already mentioned as Canon Jenkins's chief source of cigar-butts. All colleges have their annual festivities ('Gaudies', from *Gaude* = rejoice, at Oxford, simply 'Feasts' at Cambridge), to which they invite their old members in batches according to seniority and which provide pleasant opportunities of reunion with one's contemporaries. (I must, however, admit that, on recently attending a Feast at my own Pembroke, Cambridge, it was forcefully borne in on me that, while an individual man in his seventies or eighties may appear impressive and dignified and even on occasion handsome, a hundred or more septuagenarians and octogenarians together can give rather too much an impression of the Pool of Bethesda having a day out.) When it was the year of one of the older batches, it was interesting to spot various eminent persons colourfully adorned with stars and ribbands, but I enjoyed more the younger years when there would be men whom I had known as undergraduates and some as my own pupils. The Christ Church Gaudy, however, had never quite the unalloyed domestic character which was found at other colleges; for by long tradition it was always held on the evening of the Encaenia, that is the ceremony at which the University confers honorary degrees on distinguished outsiders. It was the invariable custom to invite these honorands as guests to the Gaudy and even to ask one or two of them to reply to the toast. This gave our Gaudy a peculiar double character as both domestic and imposing, and the latter characteristic was emphasised by the splendid setting of Wolsey's hall. It also tended to make the proceedings inordinately long, until drastic measures were taken to shorten them. The Dean had been expected to make two speeches, one being a kind of headmaster's report on the year's progress; this was eventually dropped on the quite sufficient ground that everyone received it all in print anyhow. The other reform was a drastic reduction in the number of speeches, especially those made by our distinguished visitors. Having listened to an enormous number of after-dinner speeches in my life (though fortunately I have very rarely had to make one), I have been struck by one uniform characteristic which they have almost without exception possessed, namely that, while some have been good and some have been bad, they have invariably been too long. It seems to be a law of nature that anybody, even if he has complained most bitterly about the volubility of other speakers, has only to get on his feet with food and drink inside him to release a verbal flood which it is impossible for him to control. I can recall one nightmare occasion at a Gaudy when the toast of the Guests was to be replied to first by a Conservative minister and then by a

Labour ex-minister. The Conservative's speech was quite unsuitable to the occasion and was quite clearly really an election-address; it was also very long. The Labourite, no doubt feeling the challenge, retaliated with an election address on the other side; it was not quite so long and he seemed to realise this, for on coming to the end he launched out on a second address which, added to the first, gave him the better aggregate. This was a specially bad example, and neither speech was much good anyhow, but even among those rare after-dinner speakers whose material and presentation were first-class I find it difficult to think of any whose effect would not have been improved by pruning.

Like other colleges, Christ Church was much in demand as a locale for conferences during the vacations, and these fell roughly into the two categories of the commercial and the cultural. The former were highly favoured by the Steward on account of their lavish expenditure and their high consumption of alcohol; of these the international bankers were most notable, and I can think of one occasion when, their entertainment having been subsidised on successive days by a number of the British banks, the College enjoyed for a week something of the atmosphere of a protracted bump supper. The cultural conferences, on the other hand, in spite of their tendency to request cut-prices and to keep low on the drinks, were felt by most of us to be more in accordance with the nature of the House as a place of religion and sound learning. To a resident observer like myself it was delightful to observe the particular characteristics of the various groups that we briefly housed within our walls. One of the earliest consisted of about a hundred leading surgeons, one of whom went down with appendicitis on arrival and was operated on by one of his colleagues; they provided an impressive note of opulence by the luxurious cars which they parked in the Meadow. My chief re-collection, however, is of the fascination with which I watched them methodically dissecting their breakfast herrings with anatomical precision. Another early conference was that of the International Red Cross; they had a service in the Cathedral and a great party in the Hall. The organiser, a high army officer, anxiously asked me whether I thought the service could be devised to be acceptable to atheists, as representatives of Soviet Russia would be present; I assured him that I was confident that the Dean would have thought of this point! At the party I received a vivid reminder of the disparity of our cultures. A nice young Canadian nurse who had been gazing open-mouthed at the roof of the Hall caught my eye as she lowered her gaze. 'My!' she said in awe-struck tones, 'It's old.' 'No so old,' I replied, 'only about four hundred years; there are older things in Oxford.' 'Four hundred years?', she gasped, 'I guess we'd call that old in my country.' A few minutes later I found myself talking to a Chinaman, who himself looked well on to his century. 'Have you found the old buildings in Oxford interesting?' I enquired, to be met with a look of blank incomprehension. Clearly, to him nothing more recent than the Great Wall of China could be accounted old. The Headmasters' Conference were another welcome group; from my window overlooking Tom Quad I derived some amusement from seeing them scurrying into the Hall after break, for all the world like reluctant schoolboys. I have never really lost the conception, derived from my own schooldays, of a Headmaster as an impeccable and Olympian figure and indeed of 'headmaster' as a word which hardly admitted of a plural. Very agreeable in a different way were the members of the International Methodist Conference, who came to us one year; while they were with us the Buttery closed down, though I never discovered whether this was due simply to lack of custom or whether it was due to a ban imposed by the management to keep temptation out of the way of weaker brethren. And of course at regular intervals there were the great Patristic and Biblical Conferences organised by Leslie Cross; I have said something about them already.[3]

Ecclesiastically the great annual occasion at Christ Church was St Frideswide's Day, October 19th. Frideswide was an eighth-century princess who founded a nunnery on the present site of Christ Church. Although her foundation was short-lived and was succeeded by a house of Augustinian canons, she was canonised shortly before 1500 and her body was given an imposing shrine. Needless to say, this was destroyed at the Dissolution, but the bones of the saint were preserved in secret and finally, in 1561, the extraordinary decision was taken to mingle them with the remains of Catherine, the widow of the reformer Peter Martyr. The mixed relics were then reintered in the Cathedral, presumably as a protection against future violation, whatever party might be in power. *Nunc coeunt pietas atque superstitio* wrote a contemporary epitaphist, leaving the reader to decide which lady represented piety and which superstition. Anyhow, there St Frideswide is, beneath a brass plate in the floor of the Lady Chapel which makes no mention of poor Catherine Martyr, surrounded by four gilded candlesticks and inviting the veneration of the faithful. On the Feast of the Saint the Bishop always celebrated the Eucharist with considerable solemnity in the morning – this was one of the occasions when Arthur Couratin attended with his 'travelling circus' – and, after

Evensong, a procession would be made to the shrine singing the not obviously very appropriate hymn 'Jerusalem, my happy home'. This service, simple in itself, could involve complications in practice, for not only was St Frideswide patron of the Cathedral and the Diocese but also of the University and the City, so that delicate questions of precedence and seating could arise. Even ecclesiastically there were unsettled .questions, so that the Dean walked in with the Bishop on his left and out with the Bishop on his right. When in addition the Vice-Chancellor and Proctors had to be accomodated and also the Lord Mayor and Corporation that there could be problems is obvious. They were in fact solved, I believe, by careful timing, so that the different groups never clashed and so never had to give way to each other, but some consternation was caused when last-minute arrangements had to be made to receive Princess Margaret, who was coming with a party from Blenheim Palace! Like most of the cathedral ceremonial these functions had been planned by N. P. Williams, who was one of the canons from 1927 to 1943, and this was, I believe, the explanation of a sermon preached by Claude Jenkins on St Frideswide's Day 1952, which fell on a Sunday, in which that venerable eccentric passionately repudiated the authenticity of the saint whose festival was being celebrated. Jenkins, it will be remembered, felt obliged to register his opposition to everything that Williams had done or said; and Williams, when the Festival had fallen on a Sunday, had preached a sermon defending the substantial accuracy of the Frideswidean tradition. Jenkins had thus simply been hurling the last word in his argument across the Stygian flood.

Christ Church possessed the patronage of more than eighty parishes, chiefly in rather remote country districts, more than any other college in either Oxford or Cambridge. These had been acquired in the days when fellows of colleges (and this included most of the students of Christ Church) had to be ordained but were not allowed to be married. Thus there was a constant movement of dons into parishes and a number of patient young women scattered over the country whose fiancés were waiting for vacancies. (Incidentally, the commonly held view that Victorian common-rooms were stocked entirely by elderly eccentrics is quite false; most colleges had one or two stranded coelocanths who could become very eccentric indeed, but the majority of fellows were young men on their way to marriage and college livings or, less often, to some other niche of public life.) This situation had of course become completely obsolete. None of our livings were held by former Students and few even by Christ Church men;

and the Benefices Committee, which consisted of the Dean and
Canons and three Students, of whom I was one, often found it
difficult to fill the vacancies. We did, however, resist the obvious
temptation to dispose of our parishes to the local bishops or local
patronage boards, for we administered various trusts, in particular
one derived from the seventeenth-century divine Robert South,
for the assistance of our incumbents. Not only could we help in
such matters as expenses of illnesses and purchase of motor cars
but – which was especially appreciated by their wives – in making
their houses more practicable under modern conditions. We also
presented them each year with some recently published theological
work, in the hope that some of them might read it. Difficult as
it is to justify private patronage on theoretical grounds, I think
we made it work fairly well in practice and that we maintained
friendly relations with our incumbents and – what was less easily
established – with their people. For, when a vacancy occurred, the
Parochial Church Council would almost always ask us to appoint a
man in his forties, married, musical, good with young people, not
'extreme', driving a car and, if possible, possessing private means,
and it was often difficult to persuade them that there was not an
unending supply of clerics meeting this specification.

Mention of the South Trust reminds me that some trusts were
very odd indeed. I recall one, founded by a clergyman, which was
to pay for a sermon to be preached at twenty-year intervals on
the subject of the moral progress of the human race during the
previous twenty years. Fortunately, when the time came for the
first appointment of a preacher to be made, it was discovered
that the income of the trust was insufficient to satisfy one of the
conditions, which was that a printed copy of the sermon was to be
sent to every theological college in the Anglican Communion, of
which in fact there were more than two hundred. Faced with this
impasse we were relieved to discover a further provision, which was
that if the primary intention proved impossible to fulfil the whole of
the endowment was to be given to the funds of a specified Canadian
diocese. So we were able to shed a tiresome and useless chore to
the benefit of a needy and deserving church.

Life in college was extremely pleasant and became progressively
more so, as I advanced imperceptibly from being the unfledged
newcomer of 1945 to being the senior Student resident in college
eighteen years later. I rented from the College a small house
in North Oxford for my mother, and until her death from a
heart-attack in 1953 I spent a great deal of the vacations there
with her, though I normally slept in college during full term. (My

father had died in 1940 at Parkstone in Dorset, where he and my mother went to live in retirement shortly before the War.) Later on I took lessons in driving and bought a car. To my own surprise, not less than my instructor's, I got through my test at the first attempt, and I got a great of pleasure exploring the countryside. I was, however, a thoroughly bad driver, having learnt too late in life, and had a number of accidents, though luckily no serious ones. When I left Oxford in 1962 I got rid of my car with a sense of relief. I still hold a driving license, but wild horses (if that is the appropriate metaphor) would not persuade me to drive in London.

As far I could, I avoided getting involved in administrative and organisational activities, both academic and ecclesiastic, being neither attracted by them nor competent in them. Fortunately there are plenty of people well qualified in both respects. I was thus able to concentrate on teaching, pastoral work and scholarship, and, having ample vacations, spent a lot of time addressing conferences and conducting retreats, the latter mainly for religious communities. I have always believed that one of the most important functions, and alas one of the most neglected duties, of the professional theologian is that of interpreting the historic and traditional faith of the Church to the contemporary world and I have tried to make this work of *haute vulgarisation* one of my primary concerns. Inevitably I was drawn into current controversies. I contributed my share, and perhaps more than my share, to pamphlet- and article-warfare, on South-Indian Reunion, Anglican-Presbyterian relations, the validity of Anglican orders and similar topics. But I also wrote eight serious volumes on philosophical and dogmatic theology. *Existence and Analogy* (1949) was a sequel to *He Who Is*, which I had published while at Lincoln; it and *Words and Images* (1957) were written as replies to the linguistic positivism which dominated Oxford philosophy. *Christ, the Christian and the Church* (1946) and *Corpus Christi* (1953) were contributions to dogmatic theology on the mutually related topics of the Incarnation, the Church and the Eucharist. *Via Media* (1956) argued that on the cardinal points of Christian doctrine, orthodoxy consists in holding together two notions which appear to be, but are not, incompatible; *The Recovery of Unity* (1958) argued that doctrinal deadlocks between the different Christian denominations were due much more to uncriticised assumptions held in common than to consciously recognised disagreements. In their different ways both these last two books were works of reconciliation, but their reception showed that antagonists are not always grateful to be deprived of the grounds of their quarrel! In a separate category were the Bampton Lectures which I delivered in 1956 on *Christian Theology and Natural Science*. Ever since my undergraduate days at Cambridge I had toyed with the idea of one day writing a book on the relation between modern science and the Christian Faith and and here, I felt, was my opportunity. The electors to the Bampton Lectureship are, in theory, all the heads of the Oxford Colleges, the range of treatment is virtually unlimited and the candidates submit their own syllabuses, and the lectures – or a condensed version of each – are delivered on eight Sunday mornings in the University church. The Lecturer cannot draw his stipend until he has delivered a printed copy of the text to each of the electors. Some Lecturers have exhibited a remarkable unworldliness in not publishing their texts for months or even years. I resolved to set an example of efficiency in this if in no other respect. With the co-operation of my publishers, Longmans, I arranged for copies to be on sale in the bookshops the day after the last lecture was given, and immediately after delivering the last lecture I personally toured the colleges in the spring sunshine and served a copy on each of the electors before lunch. While preparing the lectures I had had many opportunities of sucking the brains of scientific colleagues for information, which was patiently and generously given, and the two real howlers in the published text – 'geocentrism' for 'heliocentrism', and temporal for causal antecedence in a statement of general relativity – were due to my own mind having jumped a cog in a moment of abstraction. *The Importance of Being Human* consisted of the Bampton Lectures delivered in Columbia University, New York City, on my first visit to the United States in 1958. Apart from the name there is little in common between the the foundation established by the learned prebendary of Salisbury at Oxford in 1751 and that made centuries later by his remote kinswoman Mrs Ada Byron Bampton Tremaine in the New World. Now John Bampton prudently stipulated that no person should ever be Bampton Lecturer more than once and this provision has been scrupulously observed. It therefore gave me both satisfaction and mild amusement to reflect that, without any violation of law or morality, I had been enabled to appear in the hitherto unknown role of the man who had been Bampton Lecturer twice.

As time had gone on, not only had my theological writing and research, and the other calls upon me that those brought with them, steadily increased, but also I began to feel that pastoral charge was beginning to suffer. Being a chaplain with the young calls for something more than athletic good-fellowship; it needs maturity and sensitivity at the least. But, at least as far as I was concerned, I was conscious that I was doing it with less patience and resilience, and with less understanding, after ten years than after five, and with less after fifteen than after ten. It was not, I must stress, that I wanted to be free from pastoral concern; I have always held that for the Church's theological and pastoral functions to become isolated from each other is disastrous for both, but I realised that in this particular specialised pastoral field I was rapidly becoming stale and it was alarmingly clear to me that if I remained in it until I reached the age of retirement I should by then be in a complete rut. Furthermore, quite apart from the normal generation gap arising from the sheer passage of time, there had come about in the nineteen-fifties a change of psychological climate among the young which can best be described by saying that, whereas their traditional grievance had consisted of a complaint against their exclusion from the privileges of adult society and a demand to be let in, now they were insisting on building up a culture of their own and fleeing from that of their elders as from the plague. I do not think this was simply a sign of increased wickedness in the young, many of whom seemed to be more serious and compassionate than had been those of my own generation, but it strengthened my suspicion that I had probably been the Clerical Student of Christ Church for as long as was good either for the job or for my own soul. I had seen enough examples of the way in which, under the comforts of life in Senior Common Room, an unmarried clerical don could gradually succomb to a kind of fatty degeneration of the spirit to be aware of the danger-signals in my own case.

> Not for ever by still waters
>   Would we idly rest and stay;
> But would smite the living fountains
>   From the rocks along our way.

What, however, was the way where the rocks would offer living fountains to my smiting? For one who was becoming increasingly active in theological research a professorial chair was of course the ideal, but professorial chairs were hard to come by, and, although my own work had ranged over a good many − perhaps too many − topics which I believed to be of considerable theological importance, they were not those to which most theological chairs were in fact assigned. I had, in fact, been offered the Ely

Professorship at Cambridge, but it was attached to a canonry in Ely Cathedral and would have involved dividing my time between the University and the lonely cathedral-city sixteen miles to the north, with a canonical residence of combined medieval picturesqueness and inconvenience. Difficult as it was to refuse such an invitation from my own *Alma Mater Cantabrigia*, I came reluctantly to the conclusion that, while there might be some who could cope with it, such amphibious existence was not for me. That I was right has been confirmed by a noticeable tendency of Ely Professors to glide into other chairs when the opportunity has arisen. What was at least workable at Christ Church, where the cathedral and the university were in the same city, was far less so where the stall and the chair were separated by a tract of the most desolate land in the country. I was much less perplexed, though not less surprised, when in the summer of 1961 the Dean of King's College, London, Sydney Evans, came to ask me whether I would accept the newly established chair of Historical Theology at that College. I duly consulted my brethren in the Oratory of the Good Shepherd and with their unanimous encouragement I agreed. That this would involve a definite break both in my manner of living and in the pattern of my work was obvious, and I found the prospect both slightly intimidating and refreshingly challenging. But once I had made the move I never felt the slightest regret or doubt as to its rightness, though I must confess to an occasional twinge of nostalgia in the summer for the lawns and gardens of Oxford. The reason was, I believe, almost entirely due to the extreme diversity of the two jobs and their settings. Had they been fairly similar, as for example if I had moved from Oxford to Cambridge, there would have been constant opportunities of comparison and evaluation, but between Oxford and London there was virtually nothing to compare. What I can truthfully say is that I was extremely happy in both places and I count myself extremely fortunate to have had this variety of experience.

Looking back on my seventeen years at Oxford I find it very difficult to see them falling into any kind of continuous history and even to assign any particular remembered incident to one year rather than another. I never made any attempt to write up a systematic diary and my record of engagements is incomplete and in places illegible. Also, I have an almost totally unhistorical memory; I can remember innumerable anecdotes but am hopeless at reproducing a detailed narrative, and with any event of history I consider myself lucky to locate it in the correct century. Even when I had only just left it, Oxford in my memory was a fabric studded with jewels of varied value rather than the growing and developing plant that in fact it was. Many of those jewels were of course personal encounters, some transitory, others repeated and developing into lasting friendships. The Christ Church Common Room was a place where one met a number of distinguished people and a larger number of undistinguished ones, and frequently the undistinguished were the more attractive and interesting. A frequent guest was the Warden of Wadham, the inexhaustable conversationalist Sir Maurice Bowra, to whom a particular type of epigram was always, and usually accurately, attributed: 'This is one of those books which it is very difficult to pick up once you have laid it down'; 'By migrating from X College to Y College, Mr A has raised the academic standard of both institutions'; 'Mr B has now entered upon a wider realm of uselessness'. There was at one time a steady stream of High-Court judges whom our then Law Tutor, a figure straight out of Dickens, had an apparently hypnotic power of luring to preside at undergraduate moots. There were royal visits, in which I was never more than a very peripheral participant. There were various undergraduate extravagances, mostly harmless and amusing without being particularly noteworthy, but one of a degree of lunacy which entitles it to be remembered. The central figure in it was a wealthy, brainless and idle young man, of a type common in Christ Church before the First World War but mercifully almost extinct after the Second; he was already in trouble with the Proctors and his academic life was hanging by a thread. Late one night he heard on the radio the news that Princess Elizabeth, our Visitor's daughter, had given birth to a son, the present Prince of Wales. He was nothing if not patriotic and, in the slightly alcoholic condition in which he was, it seemed obvious to him that the Dean, if given the good news, would give immediate instructions for the cathedral bells to be rung, an operation which, in his complete ignorance of campanology, he assumed to be much more easily initiated that in fact it was. Repeated ringing of the Deanery doorbell produced the Dean in his dressing-gown, but John Lowe, loyal to the Royal Family like most Canadians though he was, took the request as both ill-timed and impracticable and brusquely shut the door. The young man, scandalised but undeterred, decided that if no one else would ring the bells he would do it himself and made his way to the cathedral. Unfortunately, his knowledge of the history of Christ Church did not include the fact that in the eighteen-seventies the bells had been removed from the cathedral tower to a new location over the hall-staircase and he spent some time trying to get into the locked cathedral. Finally he found an open door, but it led only into the coal-store and, after fruitlessly crawling over the coals in the darkness to the detriment of his evening clothes, he disconsolately abandoned the enterprise. A more entertaining episode, and one which had a larger audience, was that of the swan which was discovered one morning swimming in Mercury (the pond in the centre of Tom Quad) with a black bow tie round its neck. It was not surprisingly in a furious temper and violently resisted all attempts to lure it out. Finally an official of the Port of London Authority arrived with an instrument like a very large butterfly-net. 'How did it get in I'd like to know?', he enquired. 'Flew in', replied the Porter. 'What, with that tie round its neck?' objected the official. 'You don't think it'd be admitted if it wasn't properly dressed, do you?' came the answer. Then, in a remarkable exhibition of legerdemain, the official slipped the net over the bird, removed it from the water by a rapid twisting movement and carted it off over his shoulder squarking its protests. And this is perhaps as good a note as any on which to conclude my memories of Oxford.

Notes

1. Fr Stephenson, who succeeded an equally (but very differently) remarkable priest, Bartle Hack, had been a naval chaplain in the War. He left Oxford in 1957 to become Custodian of the Shrine of our Lady at Walsingham. His own highly entertaining autobiography *Merrily on High* makes any further account of him superfluous.
2. *Faith and Logic*, p. 1.
3. See pp. 213

Chapter Eleven

Back in London

(1962 –)

There is one matter which I beg you to bring to the King's
notice yet again before your departure; this is the proposed
foundation of a university of London. You have my authority
to tell His Majesty of my absolute conviction that the imple-
mentation of this plan would bring about England's ruin.
– Metternich to the Austrian Ambassador in London, 1825.

The whole of my career as a university don was spent in two
institutions having a dual academic and ecclesiastical character,
though in almost every other respect King's College, London,
and Christ Church, Oxford, were vastly different from each other.
Both, however, had as their official founders monarchs whose
flamboyant profession of the Christian religion went with certain
ethical weaknesses, especially in the matrimonial field. King's came
into being early in the nineteenth century as the Church's reply
to the godless foundation which under the portentous title of
'The University of London' had been set up in Bloomsbury in
1826 through the efforts of Jeremy Bentham, Henry Brougham,
James Mill and Joseph Hume. The scheme for King's College was
launched with the active support of Archibishop Manners-Sutton
and the Duke of Wellington, though, as the grant of the site was
not signed by King George IV until June 1829, a bare year before
his death, it is clear that if any monarch was practically concerned
with the College's early years it must rather have been William
IV. In the course of time King's, together with the Bloomsbury
foundation (now more modestly renamed University College) and
a host of other more or less self-governing institutions, became
part of that amorphous but distinguished sprawl now called the
University of London.

One condition of the granting of the site between the Strand and
the Thames was that the new building should complete the east end
of the river frontage of Somerset House. This equipped the College

with a beautiful, expensive and inconvenient edifice, in which as time went on every device of basements, mezzanines and the like was improvised to obtain extra floor-space. Visitors, especially those from America, who know of the distinguished reputation of King's for learning and research are frequently baffled by the exiguous nature of the buildings in which the results have been achieved. 'But where is your campus?' they ask, not realising that they are standing on it. Two advantages have accrued from this, in spite of the obvious drawbacks. One is that, when all that was possible had been done to acquire and build on neighbouring sites, King's was physically unable to succumb to temptations to excessive expansion; the other is that working under difficult conditions keeps you mentally on your feet and prevents that intellectual flabbiness to which more opulent academic institutions in another hemisphere are sometimes subject.

I will not attempt to narrate the story of the vicissitudes and transformations through which King's has passed in the century and a half of its existence; that has been done admirably by Dr Gordon Huelin in the history which he wrote for the sesquicentenary.[1] Largely but not wholly through the steadily increasing financial stress, the exclusively Anglican control of the College had been gradually modified, though it was still a very recognisably Anglican institution. What will happen under the new Charter which has just come into force remains to be seen. I shall describe the set-up as it was when I came in 1962 and still remained when I retired in 1973. Like that of Christ Church it was intensely complicated, depended largely on informal convention and, because people were on the whole friendly and co-operative, worked quite well in practice. I can only record my own experience of both places as being quite unlike that of that respected but glacial personality Dr A. C. Headlam,[2] who had been successively Principal of King's and Canon of Christ Church and who was alleged at King's College/Christ Church to have said that the Governing Body of Christ Church/Council of King's College was the most unpleasant body to which he had ever belonged with the possible exception of the Council of King's College/the Governing Body of Christ Church.

Under the new constitution, which dated from 1908, King's College consisted of two distinct but inter-related institutions, both of which were fully recognised Schools of the University. One was the Theological Department, which continued to be governed by the Council. The other bore the cumbersome name of 'The University of London King's College'; it consisted of the remaining faculties and was administered by a body called the Delegacy, which was legally a committee of the Senate of the University but was in practice an independent governing body. The original site and buildings were the property of the Council and only the Department was entitled to teach theology, but U.L.K.C. was much larger than the Department and much wealthier, as it was in receipt of government subsidies, which the Department as a denominational concern was unable to claim. In this last respect the Department was in the same situation as the two other denominational colleges, Richmond College (Methodist) and New College (Congregational), which were also Schools of the University and had comparable financial difficulties. Considerable mitigation of the problem of providing an adequate theological staff was provided by the setting up in 1956 of a number of theological teaching posts with no denominational orientation within U.L.G.C. as constituents of the Faculty of Arts. The holders of these, together with those in the Department, formed an overlapping informal Faculty of Theology for the dual College; and all of them were members of the Faculty of Theology of the University. Seen in cold print such an arrangement may well appear as too phantasmagorean to be viable in actual practice, but it did in fact work successfully for seventy years. It was indeed a good example of the proverbial English genius for compromise, with all its strengths and weaknesses, and it is perhaps significant that the only member of the Faculty during my eleven years who seemed totally unable to come to terms with its working was not in fact English. The centre of King's, geographically and psychologically, was the chapel, a remarkable edifice in cast-iron Byzantine style by Gilbert Scott of 1864; and the religious tradition, which had become established as what might be described as ecumenically orientated centre-to-high Anglicanism, was under the control of the Dean and the Chaplain, both of whom were appointed by the Council.

King's was not only a bicorporate but also a bicephalic body, but any suggestion that this gave it a purely Siamese character may be corrected by the reminder that the two bodies at least shared a common circulation. Its two heads were the Dean on the Council side and the Principal on that of the Delegacy, but when either of those offices fell vacant there was always mutual consultation and both of them were always members of the two governing bodies. More than anything else, the smooth working of the College depended on their co-operation, and if ever the Dean and the Principal had ceased to be on speaking terms or had even been seriously at variance the College would have come to a standstill. An almost equal responsibility rested on the

Secretary, upon whom the two sides chiefly converged. One thing that struck me at King's, even more than at Christ Church, was that with the occasional exceptions inevitable in so large a body, even those who had no personal conviction of the truth of Christianity or commitment to Christian practice, had a very sympathetic attitude to the place occupied by the Chapel and the Theological Department in the life of the place. Without wishing to sentimentalise or romanticise the situation, I believe this was because it gave to King's a structure and a form without which it is only too easy for a large college to lose any real sense of corporate identity and to degenerate into a jungle of warring faculties, each jockeying for its own position and trying to seize the largest possible share of the available spoils. King's was certainly not a place of refreshment, light and peace in which the writ of original sin did not run, but it was the only multi-faculty school of the University in which a chapel and Christian thinking had a recognised place. This gave it a character of which even its unbelieving members were conscious; and I think the word 'structure' describes this character.

The two sides of the theological faculty were so closely integrated in practice that the average student for the B.D. degree, and even the ordinand who was adding to that the qualification of A.K.C.[3] was usually quite unconscious as to the side to which any particular one of his teachers belonged. In fact I was the only Professor on the Council side, until an endowment was raised to found a chair of Social and Moral Theology in memory of F. D. Maurice, and Gordon Dunstan was appointed as its first holder. There were five theological professors on the Delegacy side and a number of readers and lecturers on each. The title of my chair – Historical Theology – perhaps needs explanation, as I have no pretensions to be a historian. In the past, theology at King's had been classified as either 'Biblical' or 'historical'; the word 'dogmatic', though acceptable enough in Scotland, was considered to have dangerous suggestions in an English setting and everything that was not Biblical was called historical. But it was quite clear that what what I was needed to teach was dogmatic theology and that was what I did, though I kept the boundaries flexible and in fact worked in very close contact with the specialists in philosophy of religion. In status (and also in salary!) there was full identity.

One important responsibility of the Theological Department had been the preparation of candidates for ordination and it was for this purpose that the Council had set up a hostel in Mecklenburgh Square; in 1914 this was replaced by the large but inconvenient building in Vincent Square which was completed in 1929. By my time a scheme of training, unique to King's, had been evolved which had acquired a very high reputation. This covered four years in all; the first three, of which the third was normally spent at the Hostel in Vincent Square, were devoted to work for the A.K.C. and, in most cases, for the B.D. as well; a combined course had been devised, in which the specifically Anglican element was of course the sole responsibility of the Theological Department. Then for his fourth year the ordinand went to Warminster, where the former missionary college of St Boniface had been leased to the Council as a place where his final preparation for ordination could take place and where, free from the inevitable distractions of three years in the metropolis, he could spend a period of quiet study and thought and deepen his spiritual life. This highly desirable fourth year was the creation of Eric Abbott, who, on leaving Lincoln to become Dean of King's, made its institution a condition of his acceptance. When in 1969 it was decided to transfer the fourth year to St Augustine's College, Canterbury, chiefly on the ground that this would offer more opportunities for experience of useful activities, I was in a minority of one in voting against the move. For I was convinced that, after three years in London, even if the third was kept in the Vincent Square Hostel, activities, useful or otherwise, were the last things that an ordinand needed. But all this is now a matter of the past, since, with the new Charter of 1980, the Theological Department and the A.K.C. have ceased to exist and the ordinand at King's must read a straightforward degree and go on to a theological college elsewhere.

One unique institution at King's was the oddly named 'Non-theological A.K.C.'. It was in fact an optional theological course for students in faculties other than theology. It involved attending a weekly theological lecture for two terms in each of three years and also taking an examination. It was noticeably popular among the scientists, and round about three hundred students would receive the diploma each year, which for a college of under three thousand in all was striking.

I have already remarked on the enormous difference beteen the conditions of life and work in Christ Church and at King's. In place of an eight-week term and, for a college chaplain, a seven day week, I now had an eleven-week term with Saturdays and Sundays free, the undergraduates dispersing to play games on Wednesday afternoons and hardly anything taking place in the evenings. From the point of view of fatigue the greater length of term was amply made up for by the more leisurely tempo of the

week, and this was, I am sure, to the benefit of the College as well
as the individual. For at Oxford one's time-table was so crowded
that discussions of important matters were often ill-prepared and
hurried through by distracted and exhausted people, while finding
time for some urgent and unforeseen business could be virtually
impossible. Surprisingly, I found more academic repose at King's
than at Christ Church, at any rate during term. King's was, and
had been for years, a mixed and non-residential college, though
we had hostels for men and, later on, for women as well. The
provision of living accomodation within reasable distance and at
reasonable cost for students in the metropolis presents a major
problem, which the time and expense of transport accentuates; I
was always impressed by the effort and ingenuity which our young
men and women showed in organising and maintaining a quite
vigorous athletic and social life centred in the very inadequate
accomodation which was all that could be offered them. In one
respect our students were, I think, quite unique: through the period
when the academic community throughout the First World was
disorganised by student revolts and violence, King's remained free
from any serious disturbance. Various explanations were offered for
this phenomenon, such as a tradition of good relations, fortified by
tact and understanding. Cynics attributed much to the fact that the
London School of Economics, which was one of the storm-centres
of unrest, was less than half a mile away and there was a deeply
held conviction at King's that whatever the L.S.E. did King's must
do the opposite; it was even suggested, not quite seriously, that
unrest at L.S.E. had been secretly fomented by sinister *agents
provocateurs* from south of the Strand. Rather more seriously, it
was sometimes remarked that, while King's was the only School
of the University that included all the other seven faculties (it had
set up a faculty of Music in 1964 and was the only School to
do so), it had firmly resisted any pressure to welcome the faculty
of Economics and Political Science within its doors. Our students
were certainly not unconcerned with human welfare, but their social
conscience tended to express itself in less disruptive ways.

In a different manner, residence was a problem for professors
and lecturers as well as for students. At Oxford and Cambridge a
don, if unmarried, normally lives in college and, if married, usually
rents one of the houses within easy reach which his (or in these days
her) college has bought or built for such as he. But in London no
such provision exists and he is at the mercy of the property market
and public or private transport. I had colleagues who lived as far
away as Brighton, Eastbourne or even Avebury, though the more

distant had usually some overnight accomodation closer at hand. I was determined to live in a London clergy-house if it was at all possible, for several reasons. Partly because I am a Londonder and therefore like living in London (though I cannot understand anyone who was not one wanting to do so), partly because the idea of a long journey as a commuter appalled me, while living on my own in the centre of London would have been beyond my means, but chiefly because of my conviction of the importance for academic theologians of keeping in close relation with the pastoral and evangelistic ministry of the Church and of the serious harm that has been done both to theology and to the Church when they have failed to do this. Parishes with clergy-houses are, however, much scarcer than once they were, and I was therefore extremely fortunate when Fr Stephen (F. E. P. S.) Langton, the Vicar of the well-known Anglo-Catholic parish of St Mary's, Graham Street, near Sloane Square, asked me if I would like to occupy the vacant flat in his Presbytery; and I have lived there ever since, taking a modest, but for me a deeply enriching part under him and his two successors in the sacramental and liturgical life of that quite unique parish. It was with real pleasure that in 1980 I dedicated my book *Whatever Happened to the Human Mind?* to 'the Priests and People of Saint Mary's in Pimlico, who for many years have provided this grateful author with an altar and a home'.

One consequence of the peculiar history of King's College was that the rooms of the theological faculty, instead of being concentrated in one place, were widely distributed throughout the buildings; this played an unobtrusive part in preserving the unifying function on which I have already remarked. My own room had a superb prospect overlooking the river; it was on the ground floor as approached from the main entrance in the Strand but was two floors up when one looked out of the large windows. Originally the waters of the Thames had lapped against the college buildings, and the now functionless water-gate of Somerset House remains as a memorial of this; but the construction of the Victoria Embankment in the 1860s, with the roadway on top and the District Railway underneath, barred King's from any direct contact with the river. By a margin of an inch or two I was able to fit into my room the fine mahogany and oak bookcases I brought with me from Oxford and which I had bought very cheaply simply because of their size; when I retired from King's in 1973 there was nothing to be done except give them to the college, for no ordinary modern dwelling could contain them. As long as I was alone I could work undisturbed even with the windows open in summer, for the noise of the traffic was so uniform that I was unconscious of its existence, but unless the windows were closed conversation was impossible for its sheer level in decibels. Around, above and below me were the rooms of the Department of Chemistry; they were friendly neighbours, and the smells which they produced were pleasant as often as disgusting. There was one unfortunate incident, when they left a plastic bag containing corrosive waste in the room over mine for the week-end and the contents dissolved their integuments and came through my ceiling some time on the Sunday. But, fortunately, none of my books were damaged, and the chemists were very apologetic and not a little ashamed, since they might have been expected more than most people to know about the properties of dangerous substances.

The view from my room was a constant distraction. It was fascinating to watch the traffic on the river, with barges taking fuel up to the power-stations and pleasure-boats taking parties down to Greenwich; and at the turn of the tide all the lightly moored boats would unanimously swing round. Almost opposite my windows was Captain R. F. Scott's famous ship *The Discovery*; it was visited by a constant stream of sightseers, of whom I frequently resolved to be one, though at the end of my eleven years this resolution, like some others, remained alas unfulfilled. At intervals *Discovery* would rather surprisingly fly the flag of an admiral, and I gathered that, by one of those delightful fictions of which the Royal Navy is full, this meant that it had been borrowed for the day by some recently appointed but shipless admiral, who had to fly his flag on a ship before he could draw his pay. Across the water I watched the Queen Elizabeth Hall gradually rear its massive structure; further to the East was the ugly cuboid of London Weekend Television, so familiar on their screens to TV addicts, and after dark there shone out against the evening sky the vertical and electric slogan OXO. I have never been what used to be described as a 'South-bank theologian', but at least I can claim that for over a decade I was a theologian who had a superb view of the South Bank.[4] For, as reference to a street-map makes plain, King's is just about half way along that superb curve of the Thames which extends from Westminister to St Paul's (Strangers are surprised to discover that the shortest way from the Abbey to St Paul's is not along Whitehall and the Strand, but across Westminister Bridge and along the South Bank.) From the raised promenade over the Temple Underground station (fare from Sloane Square in 1962 8d, now 80p!), both the tower of Big Ben and the dome of St Paul's stand out above the intervening buildings. One of my most moving experiences at

King's came on the day in June 1963 when I looked out of my window and saw in both directions that, quite spontaneously, all the buildings had their flags at half-mast for the death of Pope John XXIII.

I have always been conscious of the danger of asserting universal negatives, but I felt confident in asserting that no other academic institution than King's College enclosed in its area both an Underground station and a Roman bath. The station is Aldwich, on the quaint but useful shuttle service that runs during rush-hours to Holborn on the Piccadilly line; the 'Roman bath' has been alleged by sceptics to be only an eighteenth-century folly, but has established itself as an ancient monument. I find myself wondering, however, whether, with the extension of the Metro in the city of Rome, King's may one day have even this title to uniqueness challenged. In any case the need to preserve these two antiquities was one of the many obstacles that the College encountered when it decided to replace by systematically designed modern buildings in the 1960s the collection of largely ramshackle and miscellaneous property which it had gradually acquired along the Strand and in Surrey Street. I shall not attempt to narrate the story of the discussions and negotiations, and finally the constructional activities of Messrs Higgs and Hill, which culminated in the opening of the New Strand Building by Her Majesty the Queen in June 1972. For many months nothing seemed to be happening except the excavation of a deeper and deeper hole, at the bottom of which men could be dimly seen crawling in the mud, but as soon as something appeared above ground-level visible growth became astonishingly rapid. To the relief of everyone except the archaeologists nothing of interest was discovered on the site − not even the tiniest Mithraic temple, although three basement floors were excavated. But in one minor respect I myself had reason to be grateful for these operations, for they provided me for several years with the subject-matter for the frivolous verses, usually in the style of some more distinguished poet than myself, which I was in the habit of circulating to my friends at Christmas time. I will quote just two of them here, the first in the style of the great Augustans, the second provoked by that inspired doggerelist William McGonagall.

1967

ACHILLES' Wrath, to *Greece* the direful Spring
Of Wos unnumber'd − this let HOMER sing;
With haughty JUNO's unrelenting Hate,

Arms and the Man may VIRGIL celebrate;
While *Albion*'s Prophets amplifie their Scope
(DRYDEN turns VIRGIL, HOMER'S turn'd by POPE),
That each aspiring Artisan may know
Proud AGAMEMNON's Might and DIDO's Wo,
And *Rome*'s grand Origin and *Ilium*'s Fall
May edify the most mechanicall ...

Relinquishing this too presumptuous Dream,
A lowlier, though not a lowly, Theme,
Shall occupy my less ambitious Lyre,
Be less exacting towards the NINEFOLD QUIRE,
Temper to Possibility Endeavour,
Leave *Helicon* for *London*'s murkier River,
Quit HOMER's, VIRGIL's, DANTE's, MILTON's Crew,
And seek *Parnassus* in *West Central Two*.

Therefore descend, LONDINIENSIAN MUSE,
Whether thou broodest o'er the *Evening News*
Or perchest on those newly cleansed Walls
Where impious Pigeons desecrate *Saint Paul's*.
In pensive contemplation dost thou range
The silent Cloisters of the *Stock Exchange*,
Or thine aethereal Lungs dost thou inflate
With fishy Incense steamed from *Billingsgate*? ...
Where e'er thou art, I beg thee now to land
Just opposite *Saint Marie's* in the *Strand*,
That me with epic Fire thou may'st infuse.
Descend, descend, LONDINIENSIAN MUSE! ...

Awake, my muse, and leave all lower Things
For high Ambition and the Pride of KING'S!
Bend all thy Powers, concèntrating thy Knowledge,
To praise KING GEORGE THE FOURTH and this his *Colledge*.
Praise all its members, in their severall Ways,
But chiefly THE PROFESSORS thou shalt praise,
A Group so learned that they seem to be,
In each, all Faculties' Epitome.
If to their Share some donnish Errors fall,
Look on their Faces; that explains 'em all.

But where, thou askest, may this Colledge be
Which I must celebrate in Poesy?
MUSE, when thou first descended'st to the Ground,
Thou then didst see a Cavity profound,
With sweating Multitudes, that crawl like Lice,
And many a grim mechanicall Device,
And horrid Darkness and impervious Mire

Such as could *Troglodytes* alone desire.
There mirky Burrows stretch in Stygian Gloom,
An endless, still-encreasing *Catacomb*;
And, of that wallowing, despairing Rout,
Many go in, but never one comes out.
All Hope abandon, ye who enter here!
A sanguine Lion[5] guards its Portals drear,
With hideous Mien and Ululations gruff.

This the Colledge, MUSE. Now, do thy Stuff!

(*But the Muse fainted and is now King's College Hospital*)

1972

McGONAGALL IN THE STRAND

O beautiful building in the Strand!
I hope all my readers will understand
That I am not referring to the Church of St Mary,
About which opinions may legitimately vary,
Nor am I referring to the Church of St Clement's,
Where the bells play at frequent intervals 'Oranges and Lemons'.
I am prasing the beautiful new building of King's College,
Which all men agree is a very important centre of knowledge.

O beautiful building in the Strand!
I do not know by whom it was planned,
But the money came from the University Grants Committee,
Who considered it was a crying shame and a pity
That King's College had not got a better frontage
To show itself off to greater advantage.
In fact a great many respectable persons say
That they had sometimes been looking for the College the livelong
      day

And finally found themselves in the Roman Bath,
Which made the passers-by unfeelingly laugh,
Although it was a crying shame and a pity
And a real disgrace to our famous city,
To say nothing of the inconvenience to King's College,
Which all men agree is a very important centre of knowledge.

The building was erected by Messrs Higgs & Hill,
Who threw themselves into the business with a will.
First of all they had to demolish the existing edifices
By swinging a large ball which scored both hits and misses
And brought huge lumps of masonry down with a noise of thunder,

Which caused all the passers-by to stop and wonder
And say 'Good heavens, King's College is falling to bits!
There has been nothing like this since the days of the blitz!
I hope they are not going to destroy King's College,
Which all men agree is a very important centre of knowledge.'

When the existing edifices had been cleared away,
Messrs Higgs & Hill proceeded without any delay
To dig in the ground a very deep hole,
At the bottom of which men were crawling about like mole
s And pouring in the very large quantities of concrete
Without which the foundations would not have been complete,
Until finally after many weeks' delay
The building rose above ground-level into the light of day,
At which the Principal and the Dean both cried 'Hooray!
We shall soon be occupying the new buildings of King's College,
Which all men agree is a very important centre of knowledge.'

Our gracious QUEEN was sitting at breakfast in Buckingham Palace
(She is beloved by all her subjects and none ever bear her malice),
When she heard an exclamation from the Duke of Edinburgh,
Which made her wonder whether he had been seized with sudden
      sorrow,
But soon she saw he was expressing delight
At something in *The Times* which had burst upon his sight
And caused him very extreme gratification
As of very great advantage to the whole nation.
'My dear,' he said, 'I am very glad to see,
Among other news about London University,
That a new building has been erected at King's College,
Which all men agree is a very important centre of knowledge.'

Then our gracious QUEEN, who has always her subjects' welfare
      at heart,
Made a magnanimous decision, which she did then impart,
To visit the building for its official inauguration,
And thus give very great joy to the whole nation,
On the twenty-seventh day of June nineteen seventy-two,
Which will long be remembered for years not a few.

Oh it was a beautiful summer day,
And all the people who worked in the Strand did say
'Why are these crowds assembling from far and near?
Something very important must be happening here!',
And others, who were better informed, did say
'Yes indeed, Her Majesty the QUEEN is coming this way,
Accompanied by His Royal Highness Prince Philip, the Duke of
      Edinburgh,

Which will cause very much satisfaction and drive away all sorrow,
To inaugurate the new building of King's College,
Which all men agree is a very important centre of knowledge.'

Oh it was indeed a glorious sight,
With very important people to left and right!
The Principal, Sir John Hackett, G.C.B., D.S.O., M.A., LL.D., was
 there seen,
Together with the Reverend Canon Sydney Hall Evans, M.A., B.D.,
 the Dean,
And there was seen the Right Worshipful the Lord Mayor of
 Westminster,
Whose presence was very propitious and not at all sinister,
And other distinguished persons in Church and State,
Whose accumulated intellectual power was very great
In science and arts of very considerable diversity,
Such as are studied in London University,
And specially in such an institution as King's College,
Which all men agree is a very important centre of knowledge.

When the sun set upon this happy scene
Everyone sang with vigour 'God save our gracious QUEEN',
After which they expressed great satisfaction
At the successful conclusion of the whole transaction,
On the twenty-seventh day of June nineteen seventy-two,
Which will long be remembered for years not a few,
As a notable day in the history of King's College,
Which all men agree is a very important centre of knowledge.

This is the end of this truthful chronicle,
Posthumously communicated by Mr William McGonagall.

Social life in a London college was inevitably small when compared with that of Oxford. With residence widely dispersed and
the general tendency to get away home as soon as possible after
tea, opportunities of meeting one's colleagues with their spouses
were limited to the reception at the beginning of the academic year
and occasional common-room dinners and buffet-suppers, none of
which were very well attended. This merely reflected one of the
problems of modern metropolitan life; at Oxford one could ask
people to drinks before dinner without being expected to invite
them to a meal, but it is hardly hospitable to do this in London,
where they may have a journey of an hour or more before getting
anything to eat. The chief, if not the only, opportunity of getting
to know one's Colleagues at King's was at lunch-time, and I cannot
help thinking that the College must have suffered from the recent

abolition of a separate luncheon-room for the academic staff. I made many friendly contacts over the luncheon-table with people in other faculties than my own, and not least with a variety of scientists. I was also agreeably surprised to find that I had more frequent opportunities of meeting my fellow-theologians at King's than I had had at Oxford. For, apart from the two small groups at Richmond and New Colleges, the whole of the theological faculty of London University was concentrated in King's and was working under the same roof, whereas at Oxford, with the exception of Christ Church, the theological don in any college was usually a solitary figure. I cannot, however, say that this concentration of theologians, numerically impressive as it was with seven professors and a dozen or more other teachers, was the source of creative Christian thought and judgment that might have been expected. For, whether through excessive modesty or some other cause, they seemed to show little concern or interest in one another's subjects, and while they were accepted by the College as a whole as a congenial element with a civilising and cohensive influence, neither they nor anyone else showed much consciousness of Christianity as a comprehensive belief about man's origin, destiny, predicament and resources, with consequences for his welfare here and hereafter. But this is largely, I think, because theology, as understood in modern universities, is not really one discipline at all, but a collection of fragments of various disciplines, each having some, though not all having the same, relation to Christianity.

The teaching method which I came into at King's might be roughly described as a combination of Oxbridge and Redbrick. We had not sufficient teachers to give each student a weekly tutorial, but we tried to give sufficient individual attention to supplement a comprehensive scheme of lectures. This gave professors rather more individual and class work than they would have at the ancient universities, but I found this enjoyable and refreshing, in spite of an inability, which has increased as I have got older, to remember any student if I have seen him at intervals of more than a fortnight. I have always sympathised with the remark attributed to Dean Strong of Christ Church: 'I remember your name, but I forget your face'; I usually find I have forgotten both. One of the most agreeable jobs I had to do at King's was supervising advanced students for higher degrees. I only had one while I was at Oxford, for this work usually falls to professors; that pupil is now a professor himself, at Windsor, Ontario, and I have twice stayed with him there. At King's I had a constant sequence; many of them came from the United States, and, although one is inevitably taking a chance with someone whom one cannot interview, I was never once let down. One of them is now a Jesuit provincial; his thesis was on the spirituality of von Hugel. One was a Presbyterian from New Zealand; his concern, which was very topical in his home-church at the time, was with miracles. There was an American Episcopalian priest, who worked on the eschatology of St Augustine and Teilhard de Chardin; he went to a country parish forty miles to the south of Los Angeles, where I visited him later and was given (of all things!) a ride in a buggy. There was another American, a Lutheran this time, who was also concerned with Teilhard, but in connection with Karl Marx; he made so many contacts with Marxists in search of information that I began to fear that he might raise the suspicions of the State Department!; he now has a chair in North Carolina. There was a Capuchin Franciscan from the States; he did a brilliant thesis on divine impassibility and went back to teach at Georgetown University in Washington, D.C. And there were others besides.

One unexpected fact emerged from the remodelled degree of Master of Theology. It was primarily intended in order that the brighter man or woman, having taken the first degree in Theology (i.e., at London, the B.D.), should spend a further year in study of a slightly more specialised kind. What had not been envisaged was that it was an admirable refresher course for a more mature person, such as a teacher, who could get a year's leave of absence. It seemed to be specially attractive to Roman Catholic sisters in teaching orders, if they could persuade their superiors to spare them for the necessary time. I had several; they were splendid pupils, worked like beavers, and the extra experience and maturity which they brought to their studies was a tremendous help. Cardinal Heenan told me how gladly he gave permission to them to come to King's. One of them could cover a page in an hour with more words in neat and legible handwriting than anyone I have ever known; she is now a headmistress and I hope her pupils write as plainly. One amusing difficulty arose over the tendency of religious after Vatican II to revert to their baptismal names and surnames, so that, for example, Sister Monica Seraphina of Aaron's-Rod-that-Budded would stand revealed as plain Bridget Murphy. The University Senate House was rightly lynx-eyed in its examination of the credentials of candidates, in view of its many experiences of deception in the past. Now it happened that I had one candidate who, for reasons which I cannot now remember, had had no less than three different names in the past and had certificates bearing each of them. I forwarded these with what seemed to me to be satisfactory material in support. I was therefore taken aback to receive a message from the Senate House saying that, although the documents I had submitted were adequate to prove that two of the ladies mentioned were identical with each other, nothing in fact showed that either of them was identical with the third!

One of the functions expected of a don is the marking of examination papers. At Oxford I had always managed to avoid examining for the Final Honours School; I justified this to myself for three reasons: first that I find the task almost intolerably tedious and therefore think that I am not a good examiner, secondly that there were plenty of young married dons anxious to earn the fee and quite capable of doing the job, and thirdly because I had never taken a first degree in Theology and thought the job had better be left to those who had. At London however it was difficult to avoid, though the problem was lessened by the fact that, instead of the tiny group of examiners who were expected to cover the whole School at Oxford, London appointed a body of about twenty, so there was less need to feign omniscience. I still think examining is the one really repulsive element in academic life. In my experience, the nadir was reached in the overseas scripts of the paper in Christian Ethics in the now extinct External Pass B.D. Degree. Most of the scripts fell into three classes, mainly according to their place of origin: (1) those whose writers considered all that you needed to do Christian ethics was to say your prayers and wash behind the ears; (2) those intended to convert the examiners to either (*a*) nuclear disarmament or (*b*) contraception; (3) those which, regardless of the questions asked, consisted of a set of essays on (*a*) verbal inspiration of the Bible, (*b*) total corruption and (*c*) justification by faith alone. On the other hand, I have always enjoyed examining for higher degrees, and especially for the Ph.D., whether at London or elsewhere, though I have sometimes disagreed with my colleagues as to what one should look for in a thesis. I agree about the importance of care, accuracy, clarity, consistency and the other academic virtues. But what I hope to see is not just the minute application of a technique but the understanding and the operation of theological principles. I want to see the functioning of a mind that has learnt to think theologically, that, for example, in studying a Biblical or patristic text, can enter into and interpret the mind of the writer. I fear that a great deal of training in our theological faculties tends to inhibit rather than to stimulate this ability. It is for this reason that I rejoice to find 'loose ends' in a thesis, for they may, one hopes, be the sign that the candidate does not intend to cease thinking about theology as soon as the scarlet hood had descended

on his shoulders. But how many Ph.D. theses have been deposited
in the archives of university libraries as signs that their writers have
now finished with theology!

From 1968 to 1971 I held the appointment of Dean of the Faculty
of Theology in the University. This was less impressive than it sounds
and the sole duty which it involved was attending the ceremonies of
presentation of graduates and standing in silence while they were
presented. (This was not a ceremony of conferring the degrees,
though even the Chancellor herself appeared not to realise this, as the
degrees had already been acquired without any ceremony at all.) It
was a duty of extreme boredom, espe- cially on the occasions in
March and May when several hundred newly-fledged bachelors and
masters appeared in the Albert Hall, which was the only building
large enough for the ceremony. The Chancellor — for many years
that office had been held by Her Majesty the Queen Mother — almost
always presided in person, and I was always astonished at the way in
which, for two hours with only the briefest interval, her attention
never wandered as she greeted with a smile and a nod each of the
apparently never ending sequence of young men and women who
wound round the Hall and passed before her. Only once do I recall
any unexpected diversion and this happened at a Higher-Degree
ceremony in the Senate House when fortunately the Vice-Chancellor
and not the Chancellor was presiding. I had observed in the front row
a middle-aged doctor whose restless behaviour suggested that he had
been indulging in premature alcoholic celebration of his academic
advancement, and this was confirmed by the fact that, after being
'hooded' and given the customary handshake by the Vice-Chancellor,
he stepped back and uttered a loud and original formula of
appreciation, only just failing to somersault to his destruction
through the geraniums which lined the edge of the platform. The one
really enjoyable occasion was the Foundation Day ceremony in
November, when the Chancellor herself conferred the honorary
degrees after presiding at the Foundation Dinner. She would greet the
guests individually at the head of the great staircase in the Senate
House, would make a speech which showed much more personal
expression of opinion than is frequent in royal utterances, and after
the ceremony would mingle informally with the company until some
who lived at a distance were discreetly slipping away in defiance of
protocol while her energy and animation were unexhausted.

By the sheer accident of being Dean of the Faculty in 1969 I
found myself involved as a representative of the University in
the discussions which resulted in Heythrop College becoming a
School of the University in 1971. Originally founded at Louvain

in 1614 for the education of English Jesuit students, it had after a number of vicissitudes settled in 1926 near Chipping Norton in an imposing mansion, originally built by a Victorian tycoon, to which it had made very large additions. (I had once slept there in the splendid guest-room and was impressed by the way in which, when I sneezed on waking, the noise of my sternutation echoed round the ceiling in the darkness.) But, pleasant as was its situation and ample and well-equipped as were its facilities, its isolation was more and more felt to be a drawback and, in line with a widespread trend in the Jesuit order, the possibilities were explored of moving into a university town. Oxford already had Campion Hall, and London was an obvious possibility with its existing provision for the incorporation of self-governing and self-supporting denominational institutions. A scheme was drawn up remarkably quickly in view of the fact that not only the University and the Society of Jesus but also the Roman Catholic hierarchy had to be persuaded of its acceptability, to say nothing of the material problems involved in disposing of a mansion in the country and acquiring adequate premises in the metropolis. However, all the obstacles were overcome, Heythrop College was granted a royal charter, and in 1974, while retaining the name of its former rural location, it opened in the West End of London in Cavendish Square, in a fine Palladian building previously occupied by a teaching order of sisters and fittingly adorned with a striking statue of the Madonna and Child by Sir Jacob Epstein. I was elected to the Governing Body and remained a member for some years, until, after retiring from my chair, I found myself becoming progressively less and less in touch with the affairs of the University and I asked not to be re-elected. I valued my involvement with Heythrop very highly indeed; its staff, which was not entirely Jesuit or even entirely Roman Catholic, was both distinguished and extremely friendly, and I feel it as a privilege to have played even a small part in an enterprise which almost doubled the academic strength of the Faculty. It is pleasant to have as a souvenir a copy of the Humble Petition in which Her Majesty the Queen Mother informed her august Daughter of the fact *inter alia* that in 1626 King Maximilian of Bavaria set the example of granting the College a Charter in the city of Liége.

One of the most interesting and productive of the various groups into which I was drawn in London was one which met at the Institute of Advanced Legal Studies under the benevolent control of the Director of the Institute, Professor (now Sir) Norman Anderson, best known to the outside world as Chairman of the

House of Laity of the General Synod of the Church of England. Its precise composition varied from time to time according to the topics which were under discussion, but it drew people from a large variety of academic and professional disciplines, lawyers, medical men, scientists, sociologists, theologians, politicians, to name the chief. The subjects discussed were usually such as overlapped into several fields and the group was of real value in bringing together people who had a common interest in a particular problem but approached it from often quite different angles and normally had little opportunity to pool their thought and experience. It was fascinating, and also extremely instructive, to observe the different ways in which a question such as drug-addiction would be approached by, say, a moral theologican, a lawyer, a doctor, a social worker and a politician or to contrast the attitudes to press-freedom and the law of libel of an English and an American expert in jurisprudence. One of the topics we discussed that specially interested me was that of the moral aspects of molecular biology and genetic engineering.

Of the various religious societies with which I was connected at this time one in particular stands out as worthy of mention, the Ecumenical Society of the Blessed Virgin Mary. In view of the doctrinal controversies and still more the emotional passions that have been associated with the mother of Jesus in the history of the Church, the title of the Society might almost seem to be a contradiction in terms; I remember being sympathetically sceptical when, long before Vatican II, a Servite father told me at Oxford that he was convinced that a quite explicit stress on the place of Mary in the Christian dispensation would be a powerful force for Christian unity. Such was in any case the conviction of a remarkable Roman Catholic layman, a former Anglican deacon, Henry Martin Gillett, who founded the Society in 1966 and became its General Secretary. It was not perhaps surprising that he enlisted the support of leading Roman Catholic and Orthodox hierarchs, but he was successful also with Anglicans and Protestants. For Martin was not only naturally gifted with great powers of persistance and persuasion; he was also entirely devoted to this work. He lived in real poverty and worked no one knew how many hours a day, in spite of increasing ill health. Like many single-minded people he sometimes found it hard to understand that other people could be whole-hearted supporters of the Society but have other commitments as well, but he was always good-humoured about their weakness. When he died in 1980, after a sickness of rapidly increasing intensity which he bore with great fortitude and patience, he left behind him a remarkable organisation, with nine branches functioning in different parts of

Britain and a self-governing 'Chapter' in the United States. Four international conferences and a steady sequence of publications are the public signs of the Society's activity, while the facts that the Archbishop of Canterbury is one of its Presidents (the other being the Cardinal Archbishop of Westminster) and that the Society and its work were enthusiastically commended to the Methodist Conference in 1979 by the Conference's future President show that it is not to be dismissed as the fad of a handful of romantics and visionaries. It was a joy to all who were there that in the message which Pope John Paul II sent to the International Conference of the Society of 1979 he singled Martin out for special mention. Martin had already received a special medal and had been given the high distinction of a Knight Commander of the Order of St Gregory. I like, however, to remember him as the stocky little white-haired man with a slight limp who would arrive on the doorstep clutching his plastic shopping-bag and would have tea with me while he explained his theories about the Marian mosaics of the monastery of St Catherine on Mount Sinai and told me about some great opportunity that had just opened up for the Society.

The *cacoethes scribendi* which had got a firm grip on me at Oxford found London a congenial climate. In my inaugural lecture I had expounded the view that the primary fact about the Christian theologian is that he is a member of the Body of Christ and, within that Body, a member of the great historical tradition of Christian thinkers. Therefore, I asserted, *theologizandum est in fide*. 'The theologian's motto should *not* be "It all depends on me." He is not committed to "beginning all over again"; rather he is "in a great tradition."' In saying this I had in mind particularly the volume which had just come out in Cambridge under Alec Vidler's editorship with the title *Soundings*. It seemed to me to evince such a timidity and tentativeness in the face of contemporary secularism as to amount for most of its contributors to an abdication from Christian theology altogether. I therefore decided to accept its editor's own open invitation for criticism and gave a brief but systematic examination of it in a small work which, in line with its own metaphorical self-description, I called *Up and Down in Adria*. (I heard of two Biblical scholars who were so unacquainted with the Authorised Version of the Scriptures that they were baffled by this title.) I was, needless to say, influenced by the title *Some Loose Stones* which Ronald Knox had given to his reply to an earlier work of liberal theology, *Foundations*. I must also also admit that I got a good deal of pleasure out of writing it, though whether that pleasure was entirely innocent I am not sure. Certainly the chosen idiom gave me some good headings for my chapters: 'No Bottom Yet', 'Setting the Course', 'Pumping out the Bilge', 'Soundings by Hand', 'New Leads for Old' and 'Undergirding the Ship'. But I was in deadly earnest in my criticism, for it seemed to me that fundamentally what was at stake was whether the Christian religion is something given to us by God or something invented by us for ourselves. It was a joy when the one 'leadsman' with whose navigation I had found no fault — George Woods — joined us at King's in 1964 and became a most constructive and supportive colleague until he was suddenly taken from us almost overnight by an unheralded and fatal illness.

Soundings was soon forgotten in the excitement caused by John A. T. Robinson's supernova *Honest to God* and Paul M. van Buren's *Secular Meaning of the Gospel* in 1963, and the various works of secularised theology which followed them. Mainly for my own satisfaction, I made a careful analysis and critique of these two books and this was the basis of my own book *The Secularisation of Christianity*, which appeared in 1965. I was conscious that there might appear to be something unbalanced and indeed unchivalrous in subjecting to detailed analytical scrutiny books that were written for the general public and not for trained scholars, I was quite impenitent about this, for it seemed to me to be even more of a duty to avoid vagueness and ambiguity in a popular work than in a learned treatise, since the readers, being less skilled in the subject, were less able to correct for themselves any mistakes into which the writers might have fallen. I realised, however, that I was in danger of appearing as merely a demolition-agent, and when the Bishop of London invited me to give the Boyle Lectures in 1965 I took the opportunity of being more constructive and gave a straightforward reasoned account of the Faith which was published under the title of *The Christian Universe*. I had been slightly taken aback by discovering that, when the Honourable Robert Boyle founded the Lectureship in 1691, he charged the lecturer, among other things, to combat the error of Theism, and I wondered whether I should have to fall back on the second meaning of 'theism' in the O.E.D. as 'a morbid condition characterised by headache, sleeplessness, and palpitation of the heart, caused by excessive tea-drinking.' At this point, however, I was fortunate to discover that in Boyle's time 'theism' commonly meant what is now called 'deism', namely belief in God combined with disbelief in revelation; and so I breathed freely again. I was, however, both amused and irritated when, having concluded the course, I received a letter from a legal gentleman asking me to pay him a fee for certifying to the Trustees that I had in fact given the lectures and for what he described as 'obtaining' the stipend from them for me. I had never received any such request in connection with any other endowed lectures that I had given and I had moral scruples about paying him to make a statement whose truth he had not apparently personally verified. Furthermore, Boyle Lectures were frequently given by badly paid parish priests who could not afford to scatter unnecessary largesse. So I wrote to the Bishop explaining the matter, and I received the stipend without further formalities. Recalling the great saga of Gregory Dix, who at the time of his ordination had defeated the attempts of the legal officials of two dioceses to extract from him fees to which he succeeded in proving that they were not entitled, I felt that I had played my own tiny part in weakening the hold of the lawyers over the Church.

Two small books, *Theology and the Future* and *Nature and Supernature*, contained lectures given in the United States, at Catholic University, Washington, D.C., in 1968, and at Gonzaga University, Spokane, in 1973, respectively. Ever since leaving Oxford I had become more and more concerned with dogmatic theology and less with philosophy, not least because of the growing number of urgent problems in the former field and the lamentably small number of Anglicans prepared to interest themselves in it. I was therefore agreeably surprised, as well as slightly alarmed, to be invited to give the Gifford Lectures at Edinburgh in 1970–71. While paying only the necessary minimum of attention to the now rather wearied attacks on natural theology from the logical analysts on the one flank and the extreme revelationists on the other, I decided to devote a large amount of my time to the less familiar work of the transcendental Thomists before attempting to re-state a viable natural theology. The title which I gave to the published text, *The Openness of Being*, expressed my conviction that a traditionally based natural theology is not, as is often supposed, static and sterile but dynamic and fertile; and by adding four long appendices I was able to embrace a number of topics which considerations of time of appropriateness had excluded from the spoken version. I much enjoyed my visits to Edinburgh as Gifford Lecturer in spite of the climatic severity of November and February; I already had friends in the predominantly Presbyterian theological faculty there, as I was nearing the end of a four-year stint as external examiner at the time. My later books, *Theology and the Gospel of Christ* (1977) and *Whatever Happened to the Human Mind?*, were both written after my retirement. Possibly through an unconscious motive of defence I have always enjoyed reviewing other people's books as well as writing my own, and I wrote an inordinate number of reviews for a large number of periodicals, of many of which I have culpably failed to keep any record. I was popular with editors, for I possessed what was for them a more important virtue than excellence of material; I almost always produced my stuff on time. I thus acquired a large number of books which cost me nothing, but it is a melancholy fact that, now that the appalling price of books has made free copies more attractive, they are much less plentiful for the simple reason that far fewer religious periodical now exist.

Mention of Scotland reminds me that in 1967 the University of St Andrews made me an honorary D.D. In these secularised days universities are on the whole reluctant to honour theologians; when I was Dean of Divinity I discovered that London had only ever given three honorary D.D.s on primarily academic grounds, the most recent of which was in 1952; and all my efforts to extract another were rejected, though several D.Lit.s and D.Sc.s were given every year. St Andrews, however, was an exception in its readiness to honour theologians, and two of my colleagues at King's already possessed its degree. In June 1967 it gave no less than five, and those honoured included the Roman Catholic Archbishop of St Andrews and Edinburgh (the future Cardinal Gordon Gray and a former alumnus) and my much loved Dean of Christ Church, Cuthbert Simpson. (No corrupt practice is to be inferred from the fact that the Vice-Chancellor, Steven Watson, was formerly a history tutor at Christ Church!) St Andrews is a quite delightful town and, except for its location by the sea, preserves much of what one imagines must have been the atmosphere of Oxford and Cambridge in the last century. It has, however, two disadvantages: exposed to the winds of the north and the east, it is cold even in June, and the sun-bathing terraces on the sea-front seemed to me to be a fine example of the triumph of hope over experience; and it is a long way away, though I agree that the unanswerable answer to the latter complaint is provided by the question 'A long way from where?' I was intrigued to detect in the wording of the diploma which was given me a survival of the medieval concept of the University, going back to its foundation by the Antipope Benedict XIII in 1413. For, although the Professor who presented me simply asked that I should be made a doctor of the University of St Andrews, the Latin diploma plainly claimed for the University a higher power and for its doctors a wider scope. It began by affirming its right, recognised from antiquity, to confer the highest academic honours in every faculty, and then decreed that I was created a Doctor of Sacred Theology, adorned with all the ornaments and privileges which true doctors are allowed by all peoples (*usquam gentium*), finally declaring its will that I should be called a Doctor of Sacred Theology everywhere (*apud omnes*). In other words, the University of St Andrews was exercising its undoubted right as a *studium generale* to confer the *jus ubique docendi*, valid throughout the commonwealth of learning. This is the medieval idea of a university as the local expression and mani-festation of a universal fellowship of scholars, in contrast with the modern idea of a university as a self-contained and self-sufficient entity having no necessary connection with any other. I found this a more impressive sign of respect for tradition than the fact that I was tapped on the head with a scrap of fabric which the pious believe to be the remains of the doctoral cap of John Knox.

While I was at Oxford I had never seen any reason to belong to a London club, but on coming back to London I was glad to accept the offer of various friends to propose me for membership of the Athenaeum; my principal sponsors were, rather inappropriately, both doctors of music. Being neither a bishop nor an ambassador, I had to wait several years for election, so I joined, as a non-political member, the National Liberal Club, which had no waiting list, a low subscription and very good amenities. The terrace, overlooking the Embankment Gardens towards the River, was as pleasant a place as any in London to take friends for dinner in the summer, and the food was good and inexpensive. The building was redolent of the great days of the Liberal Party; there were more than twenty representations of the great Gladstone, ranging from the full-length marble statue in the dining-room with the large piece chipped off its frock-coat to the bust in the porch bearing in letters of gold the declaration, from a 'Speech in Chester', that 'the principle of Toryism is distrust of the people, qualified by fear; the principle of Liberalism is trust of the people, qualified by prudence'. (Fancy a present-day political leader announcing that his party believed in trusting the people, but not too much!) But with the decline of the Liberal Party the N.L.C. was suffering from economic difficulties more than most London clubs; its vast building and its host of bedrooms were both an asset and a liability. It offered housing to a number of smaller clubs and to a masonic temple; its membership spread from the political into the business world, and the splendid Gladstone Library was less and less used. I kept up my membership for several years after I was elected to the Athenaeum, for its location by the river made it extremely convenient for King's. But after I retired it was an unnecessary extravagance, and I resigned just at the time when the N.L.C. suffered its abortive takeover by a mysterious Canadian businessman. The final change in its character was marked by the transfer of the Gladstone Library to Bristol University in 1977.

The Athenaeum had a long-standing reputation for high thinking and low living and it was alleged that 'all the arts and sciences are understood there, except gastronomy'. However, while its *cordon* cannot be described as *bleu*, its food has certainly very much improved in recent years. How much this is due to the fact that lady guests are now admitted in the evening to the main dining room (called 'the coffee-room' on the *lucus a non lucendo* principle), instead of being relegated to a pleasant but characterless underground annexe, I cannot say, but, although the predominantly senior character of the membership preserves it from any suggestion of the discotheque, there is now a cheerful sociability about the atmosphere that is in marked contrast with the traditional image of a few scattered septuagenarians glowering fiercely at their mutton chops. It cannot compete with the opulence of, say, the Petroleum Club, on the top three floors of the fifty-storey Exxon Building at Houston, Texas, but it has an unassuming friendliness that is all its own. I have much enjoyed and valued belonging to a little group of about a dozen members, of extremely varied backgrounds and interests, who meet informally — so informally indeed that we have never been able to decide on a name for it — for dinner and discussion together; I am its only cleric. The Athenaeum is no longer, as it once was, heavily weighted with the episcopate — it is alleged that the cab-drivers knew it as 'Bishopsgate' —, largely, I think, because its bedroom accomodation is limited and bishops tend to swarm in London at the time of the General Synod. And, as most of its members are men who work, or at any rate have worked, for their living, it has never given the impression which another West-End club made on a visitor, of being like the mansion of a Duke — with the Duke lying dead upstairs.

I retired from King's College in 1973, but have found my time well occupied. If one lives in London, most of one's friends seem to turn up at some time or another. Pastoral contacts are frequent, and I have specially enjoyed being asked to supervise the studies of some of the more intelligent of the younger clergy. In 1974 the Bishop of Truro, Graham Leonard, who had made me one of his Examining Chaplains when he was a suffragan in the London diocese, asked me to become an honorary canon of Truro with the function of Canon Theologian. The statutory duties of the canonry are minimal, merely involving the preaching of an annual sermon in the cathedral, but it is understood that I am available as a kind of theological consultant, both by correspondence and, when I visit the diocese, in person. Cornwall is a beautiful county with a unique and fascinating character, and the diocese of Truro, which is congruent with it, has a sparkle and vigour not too common in rural dioceses. Distance makes me a less frequent visitor than I could wish, and I took the opportunity of dedicating my book *Theology and the Gospel of Christ* to the Clergy and Laity of the Diocese with the motto, taken from a hymn of St Hildebert, *De longinquo te saluto*. I was elected a Fellow of the British Academy in 1974, but my Truro canonry is the only ecclesiastical recognition that I have ever received, and I value it correspondingly; I take added pleasure in the fact that the light-blue *mozzetta* which I wear as a canon derives from the dedication of the cathedral to our Lady.

One other activity for which retirement has given me increased opportunities is that of foreign travel. I shall leave it to the following chapter.

Notes

1. *King's College London 1828–1978* (privately published by the College in 1978).
2. Headlam was a ruthless and brilliant administrator; he engineered the transformed constitution of 1908, which lasted for the next seventy years, and also made a variety of other reforms. At Oxford he raised the requirements for the D.D. from the level of a mere formality to that of substantial academic attainment. From 1923 to 1945 he was Bishop of Gloucester. He had a grim appearance and some disconcerting mannerisms, which included a habit of repeatedly performing a half-knee-bend while speaking. Shortly before his death, which was in 1947, he dined one evening in the Christ Church common-room. He suddenly remarked in a rasping voice, 'I sometimes wonder whether I was wise to become Bishop of Gloucester.' No one ventured to comment, and he continued, 'You see, I might still have been Regius Professor of Divinity here.' As two of his successors in that office had died and the third, who was about to retire, was sitting next to him, a noticeable *frisson* passed round the table. But he could be remarkably and unexpectedly flexible, as when he allowed my Vicar, Ernest St John, to go forward to ordination in spite of his examination failures.
3. Associate of King's College.
4. And I did in fact lecture for a short period on dogmatic theology in the admirable Southwark Ordination Course.
5. 'Reggie', the College mascot, a large plaster beast, originally adorning a Red Lion public house.

Chapter Twelve

Journeys Academic
and Ecumenical

(1958–1981)

It is a strange madness, this desire to be for ever sleeping in a strange bed.

— Petrarch to his secretary.

I have always been entirely unenterprising in the matter of holidays. The difficulty of deciding to go to one place rather than another has usually resulted in going nowhere at all; and, while I have almost always enjoyed doing some particular task for which I have been invited, I find doing nothing, even in pleasant surroundings, intensely boring. (I do not consider making my annual retreat 'doing nothing'.) Apart from the brief visit to Ireland which I have already described, I had not been abroad since before the War until I was asked to give the Bampton Lectures at Columbia University, New York City, in 1958; and I had no suspicion that this was to be the first of a succession of journeys across the Atlantic. The later journeys were all by air, but on this first occasion I travelled both ways on the *Queen Mary* (first class, paid for by the Bampton Trustees). I found the five-and-a-half days' voyage very tedious and the setting irritatingly opulent and ostentatious; the ship's newspaper seemed chiefly concerned to persuade one to have a spending spree in Fifth Avenue. There was a beautiful chapel, which had been splendidly furnished by the Society for the Propagation of the Gospel; but it had been mysteriously handed over to the Roman Catholics, and when I said mass, which I did each morning, I had to make use of the Library. Arriving by sea brought one great bonus, the quite magnificent view of New York from the Hudson River. This is one of the very few cases I know in which the reality is even more impressive than the photographs. I arrived in hot and sunny April weather, rather like what we hope

301

for in an English summer, and, coming from a particularly cold and wet English spring, I found New York enchanting. I must in honesty add that subsequent visits have modified this impression. Happy as I have been with the friends I have made there and appreciative as I am of the wonderful American hospitality, New York seems to me to have become more noisy, dirty and dangerous every time I have gone there; the pot-holes in its main thoroughfares have to be experienced from inside a taxi to be properly appreciated. And the underground railway (the 'Subway') might well have provided inspiration for the less restful parts of Dante's Inferno. Cuthbert Simpson had been Professor of the Old Testament at the General Theological Seminary in Chelsea Square and on his introduction I was generously invited to stay there. Chelsea Square a century earlier had been a wealthy residential suburb, from which tycoons drove up to Wall Street in their carriages every morning (compare Clapham and Mr Spenlow in *David Copperfield*), but it had descended far in the social scale and was mainly inhabited by negroes and Porto-Ricans; St Peter's Church, where I often said mass, had many of its services in Spanish, but I was interested to see on its walls memorial tablets of an earlier and wealthier period, including one to a former rector, who, it recorded, one Sunday morning 'in the course of Divine Service suddenly ceased to be mortal'. 'General', as the leading seminary of the Episcopal Church,[1] was lavishly endowed with both plant and personnel, but it could not compare for resources with the great undenominational Union Theological Seminary further up town, which had the prestigious name of Paul Tillich on its books.

Though my lectures kept me pretty much in New York City I was able to make brief excursions to some other places. I preached on the Sunday after Ascension Day in the cathedral at Garden City, Long Island, a fine modern gothic building surprisingly and ingeniously built of red stone outside and white stone within. I spent a few days with the Cowley Fathers at Poston, Mass., where I renewed my friendship with Fr George Florovsky and got a brief glimpse of Harvard University; on the way I had broken my journey at New Haven and got an even briefer glimpse of Yale. I had a refreshing break from these urban environments when I went to visit the Sisterhood of St Mary at Peekskill and the Holy Cross Fathers at Poughkeepsie; but for this I should not have realised how beautiful the hinterland of New York City is. I finished my time by flying to Chicago to stay with a friend who was chaplain to the great Medical Centre there. I was quite new to air-travel and the view of New York by night when we took-off from La

Guardia airport quite took my breath away. There was first of all the view of the city as an illuminated map alive with the moving traffic; then the whole visual expanse heeled over vertiginously as the plane swung round; then we plunged into the darkness of the clouds, from which we emerged into a new world of stillness, with the moon and the stars above and no sound but the steady hum of the engines. Later journeys by air have made me somewhat blasé to the joy of take-off, but I have never forgotten the sheer unexpected beauty of this first experience. The Chicago Medical Centre covered no less than fifteen blocks, and, according to legend, the famous gangster Al Capone, seeing that the medical facilities of the city were inadequate, exercised his not inconsiderable powers of persuasion to have them improved – and then sold the municipality the site for their reconstruction. Whether this is strictly true or not, the Centre certainly was a gigantic complex; and the chaplaincy, where I stayed, was only a stone's throw from the site of Capone's headquarters. I preached in the cathedral, gave a lecture and visited the Seabury Western Seminary. But my ineradicable memory of Chicago is of being driven by my host to the suburb of Wilmette with no other information than that I was to be given a surprise; and this I certainly was. For suddenly, on the shore of Lake Michigan, we were confronted by an enormous domed polygonal building of white stone, dazzling in the sunlight and surrounded by green lawns and beds of azaleas. This, it was divulged in reply to my astonished enquiry, was the Bahá'í House of Religion, dedicated in 1953 and built at a total cost of over 2½ million dollars contributed from all over the world. In spite of disparaging comparisons with a lemon-squeezer, it is undoutedly a beautiful object, and its style, which was deliberately devised to accord with the syncretic nature of the Bahá'í faith, has the added merit of originality.

I expected never to visit the United States again, so, as far as my time in New York allowed, I did all the proper things. I went up the Empire State Building and discovered that one journey up in the lift was more successful in clearing a blocked ear than a course of treatment by a specialist in Oxford. I went to the Cloisters in Fort Tryon Park, where a great mass of medieval buildings, transported from Europe, have been skilfully assembled into one great edifice. I went to the Metropolitan Museum of Art, where a lady urgently enquired whether I thought it was right that a painting of Christ should be in the same gallery as 'all those nudes'. I went to a number of the other galleries in which New York is so plentiful, largely owing to the propensity of American tycoons of the last century to expend their dubious gains on works of art which they later bestowed on the public. I felt unadventurous in not managing somehow to get to the Pacific coast, until I realised that most of the people who live in New York have not been there either, and that New York is just about as far from Los Angeles as it is from London. I returned to England with two convictions that subsequent visits to the States have only intensified. One is of the extraordinary kindness and hospitality of Americans in general, the other is of the warmth and appreicativeness of American audiences. For the chief difference between an American and an English audience is that, rightly or wrongly, an American audience assumes that the lecturer has done it a favour in coming to address it, while an English audience assumes that it has done the lecturer a favour in coming to hear him.

It was in fact just ten years later that I was to see New York again, but in August 1967 I was invited to Toronto, to be one of the speakers at the imposing Congress on the Theology of the Renewal of the Church which was held under Roman Catholic auspices to celebrate the centenary of the Dominion of Canada. I had earlier in that year made, also under Roman Catholic auspices, a lecture-tour in Ireland which I had found extremely stimulating and refreshing. It was the idea of two young priests, a White Father and a Jesuit respectively, who had been caught by the ecumenical and evangelistic spirit of Vatican II, and was organised with remarkable efficiency. It involved a most elaborate system of journeys by car and train, and, with the Englishman's traditional view of all things Irish, I fully expected to find myself in Cork when I ought to be in Belfast; in fact everything went without a hitch. It was considered prudent that my lectures should officially be philosophical rather than theological and, as it was the time when concern with Teilhard de Chardin was in the ascendant, I took his thought largely as my topic. But discussion was wide-ranging and uninhibited and some of the most interesting discussions took place in the evenings with the aid of a bottle of Irish whiskey. My programme took me to the White Fathers at Blacklion, the Divine Word Fathers . at Donamon Castle and both the Jesuits and the Vincentians in Dublin. I also spoke in the great seminary for secular priests at Maynooth and the smaller one at Carlow. This, with lectures at the University Colleges in Dublin and Cork and at Queen's University, Belfast, together with papers to two learned societies, filled up a fortnight that was full of surprises, almost all of them pleasant. The greatest surprise was to find that those among whom I found myself seemed little concerned with the traditional woes of Ireland but very much with the problems of the Third World; this was of course not unconnected with their involvement in missionary activity. I often felt myself to be moving in a wider climate of thought than when I was at home. Almost as great a surprise was the very cordial relationship almost everywhere between Roman Catholics and Anglicans; I was mildly surprised when the superior of a religious house in Dublin who had driven me to lunch with the Anglican Archbishop (George Simms, my colleague of Lincoln days) knelt and kissed the archiepiscopal ring. Of different nature was the surprise which I received when, on arriving on a Saturday morning at the White Fathers' house at Blacklion at the extreme north of the Republic, I was immediately sold a ticket in a sweepstake. For it was the day of the Grand National Steeplechase and if there is one thing that really excites the Irish it is of course horses. The whole community settled down after lunch to watch the race on television and continued with the Eurovision Song Contest. (It was the memorable occasion when almost all the horses fell on top of one another just before the end of the course and the race was won by a complete outsider who was so far behind as to avoid the *mêlé*.) Ecumenism has advanced a good deal in Ireland and there is now a flourishing ecumenical school in Dublin itself, but I am happy to have been involved in this brief contribution to the cause. As in subsequent years I have spent a good deal of time flying about the vast North American continent, it is good to have my springtime memories of the Emerald Isle, which can be crossed by car from East to West in a morning. But now, the Congress at Toronto.

Everything possible had been done to make it impressive. There were five cardinals, including the aged Dominican Cardinal Browne, who had come as special envoy of the Pope; there were archbishops and bishops innumerable; there were speakers from both sides of the Atlantic and from a variety of denomination, though predominantly Roman Catholic. There were four plenary sessions, and five sections met in parallel for the more specialised topics. Everything had to be printed in English and French, regardless of cost, and I was told that at the opening session Cardinal Léger, the Archbishop of Montreal, offended many of his flock by switching over from French to English early in his speech for what seemed to them the insufficient reason that it was being broadcast on radio. Of all the galaxy of prelates on the platform I could discern only two whose dignity was not concealed by simple clerical black; and when I asked my neighbour who the two Anglican bishops were he replied that one of the *porporati* was unknown to him but the other was the Moderator of the United Church of Canada!

A note of distinction and graciousness was provided by the opening address, which was delivered tactfully in alternate paragraphs of English and French by the wife of the Governor General of the Dominion, Dr Norah Willis Michener, herself a graduate of the University of Toronto and of the Pontifical Institute of Medieval Studies. There was a splendid mass in the cathedral, concelebrated by Cardinal Browne and ten archbishops, with several cardinals sitting in choir; its dignity was only marred by the inability of the public address system to cope with the famous Irish accent of the principal celebrant. I was housed in a modern and extremely luxurious hotel, but there was a disquieting incident when we were plunged in total darkness for several hours by a power failure and it was revealed that neither its modernity nor its luxuriousness had included the provision of emergency lighting. I fumbled my way up a spiral service-staircase and indentified my bedroom by feeling for the embossed numbers on the doors. I tremble to think what might have happened in a fire! My power of concentration at the meetings was impaired by the temperature, which was in the nineties; but I have rarely derived much profit from the addresses at vast gatherings. The two large volumes of papers (published bilingually of course) testify to the distinction of the speakers: Lonergan, Congar, Thurian, Schillebeeckx, Chenu, Rahner, de Lubac, Gilson; Pegis, Pelikan, Gilkey and Ricoeur, to name only a selection. I much valued the opportunity of making the personal acquaintance of scholars whom I had admired from their writings, such as Henri de Lubac and Bernard Lonergan, and most of all the aged philosopher Étienne Gilson. (I asked Gilson for his views on the dialogue between Christians and Marxists but the old man was not to be drawn. For me', he replied with a mischievous twinkle, 'the only dialogues are the Dialogues of Plato.') There had been an unscheduled and rather aggressive comment at the opening session by Marshall McLuhan, who was then at the height of his notoriety, but nothing more was seen of him. A mildly distracting element was provided by a background of hippies, who were having their kind of congress at the same time as ours. For me a quite unexpected pleasure was provided by running into a colleague from King's who was on sabbatical leave and who took me off to lunch. He was an eccentric figure, a teacher of English, who was alleged to have once been the boxing critic of a New-York newspaper. He would have fitted well into an Oxbridge common room but was something of a misfit in a modern university. I always found him agreeable and amusing but he had a reputation for awkwardness. He was alleged to have sent to a colleague a picture-postcard from a holiday resort, on which he had written 'Wish you were here' – and crossed the words out! His words as we parted in Toronto were characteristic – 'Remember me to A and B and C', mentioning colleagues at King's, 'and disremember me to X and Y and Z.'

From Toronto four of us went on to a smaller Conference on the Theology of Renewal at Dayton, Ohio, in the United States. Dayton is best known as the Home of Aviation, where the brothers Wilbur and Orville Wright made their first successful flying machine in 1905. It is less known as having, under the care of the Marianist Fathers, one of the largest Mariological libraries in the world. In 1966 the Fathers opened, under the title of Bergamo, a new Centre of Christian Renewal, of which our conference was one of the first activities. The four of us were a varied group, though all except myself were in full communion with the Pope. I use that precise description because one was the Melchite Archbishop George Hakim, soon to become the Patriarch Maximos V and a firm contendor for the position that his church was not part of the Roman Patriarchate. There was Mgr Charles Moeller, Professor of Literature at Louvain and writer on apologetics; he was later to become Secretary of the Secretariate for Christian Unity in Rome. And there was the Redemptorist Fr Bernard Häring, who has become the most distinguished moral theologian in the post-conciliar Church. The rest of the personnel was even more varied, going so far as to include several Jews. The Centre was clearly still feeling its way; the chapel was called 'the assembly' and the ante-chapel 'the baptistry', though it contained no evidence of the sacrament of baptism and was in fact a square room, carpeted from wall to wall, and descending by steps from each side to an empty space in the centre. When I got home I received a questionnaire inquiring whether, and in what respect, I thought we had achieved *metanoia*. The Conference itself, which included a large public meeting in the University, was well designed and useful, and the high-light liturgically was a concelebrated Eucharist in the Byzantine rite, celebrated in the spacious and dignified chapel of the Mariological Institute by Archbishop Hakim.

In the following year I was asked to deliver the Hart Memorial Lectures at the end of March at Catholic University, Washington, D.C. This gave me the opportunity to make use also of invitations to other places of learning, and in particular to visit Windsor, Ontario, where Frederick Temple Kingston, my one and only D. Phil. student at Oxford, was now Professor of Philosophy and Warden of the Anglican hall of residence. Most people are surprised to be told that part of Canada is south of the United

States, but so it is; and standing in Windsor one looks north across the Detroit River to the city of Detroit. The two cities are connected by the Ambassador Bridge, a monstrous erection raised high to clear the traffic in the waterway below, and by an underpass which is mercifully invisible. Detroit is the airport for the region and I was met there by Temple in his car. I passed to and fro several times during my stay and I was mildly nettled by the fact that, whereas United States citizens could pass freely into Canada without any formality whatever, I, who owed allegiance to the same sovereign as the Canadians, had to produce my passport and explain my business on each transit. I was in Windsor for just a week, but snatched twenty-four hours to fly down to Cincinnati for a lecture at the Roman Catholic seminary there. Windsor was well below freezing, with snow hard on the ground and great blocks of ice thundering down the River from the ice-breakers on Lake St Clair, and I felt I was inviting pneumonia by this brief immersion in the heat of southern Ohio. I went on from Windsor by train to Hamilton, where I broke my journey to give a lecture at McMaster University before going on to Trinity College, Toronto. In contrast with my former visit, Toronto was in the grip of frost and under deep snow. One thing that I discovered in Toronto was that it was not sufficient to say that I came from London, unless I added the qualifier 'England'; for Ontario has a city named London and, to make things more difficult, it is on the River Thames and its cathedral is St Paul's.

I flew down to Washington, where I stayed for a week at the Theological College run by the Sulpician Fathers just opposite the stupendous National Shrine of the Immaculate Conception. The Shrine is a gigantic white stone edifice, crowned by a blue and gold dome; it is not, I think, quite satisfactory in its proportions, but dazzling in the sunshine it is quite overwhelming. It has innumerable chapels, splendid with marble and mosaic, many of them the gifts of immigrant national groups and intensely moving in their associations; I remember in particular a mosaic of a mass being celebrated in a labour-camp. Among the Shrine's treasures are the stole worn by Pope John XXIII at the opening of the Vatican Council and the tiara sent by Pope Paul VI to raise funds for the Third World. It is easy to dismiss the Shrine as ostentatious, triumphalist and everything that is now unpopular in progressive circles, but it seems to me to be a more natural and uninhibited expression of American Christianity than the self-styled National Cathedral, that sandstone imitation of an English cathedral which, with all the accompaniments that in England itself are already obsolescent, the Episcopal Church, in apparent forgetfulness of its extremely minority status, has erected on a neighbouring hill.

I lectured each afternoon at 3 p.m. and had a surprisingly good attendance; the lectures were afterwards published with the title *Theology and the Future*. But what quite astonished me was to have an audience of nearly three hundred for a more popular lecture at two o'clock on the Sunday afternoon, which in England at least would have been the most impossible time in the whole week. The organisers themselves were surprised and had warned me that it was something of an experiment; it confirmed my conviction of the ineradicable passion of Americans for beings lectured to. Next door to the Theological College was the Dominican house of residence, which was *inter alia* an important publishing centre; its periodical *The Thomist* had a world-wide reputation and I had reviewed in it. Also I was systematically reviewing, for the English Dominican journal *New Blackfriars*, the successive volumes of the sixty-volume bilingual edition of the *Summa Theologiae*, so it was pleasant to meet these American Dominicans, with some of whom I had already corresponded; and I was asked to talk to their students. I did not entirely neglect my fellow-Anglicans; I preached at the long-established church of St Paul and I addressed the clerical society of the diocese. So, with a brief overnight visit to Baltimore, where two of my Oratory confreres were working, my week in Washington was well filled. I was allowed the use of an altar for mass at the Theological College each morning; I have almost always received this privilege in Roman Catholic institutions in the United States. When I left by air for New York the stands were already being erected for the Cherry Blossom Festival, which is the great spring celebration in Washington.

I was met at Kennedy Airport by John Macquarrie, who was then a Professor at Union Theological Seminary, where I was to stay; this was the beginning of a continuing friendship. I gave a lecture at Union and also preached in the Cathedral of St John the Divine, which had not then opened its doors to the more off-beat and esoteric religious cults. Ian (for that is how he is known to his friends) and I conducted a dialogue at St Mary the Virgin, the famous Anglo-Catholic church near Times Square; the audience got some amusement from our different foreign idioms, his Scots and mine English, especially when I had to ask him to repeat a remark which I had not understood. I also conducted a discussion at Trinity Institute. (Trinity Institute, it may be explained, was the latest of the projects financed by the incredibly wealthy parish of Trinity Church, which, having secured a vacant site in the early

days of New York City, now finds itself owning a large slice
of the most valuable Wall-Street area and is alleged to support,
among other good works, half the missionary activity of the
Episcopal Church.) Ian had arranged for me to finish with two
nights at Stamford, Connecticut, a very pleasant residential town
on Long Island Sound. The Rector, Norman Catir, and his wife
Zulie have become close friends; their names will recur, as will
that of Geddes MacGregor, who was there on vacation from the
University of Southern California at Los Angeles. Both he and
Ian Macquarrie had begun as ministers of the Church of Scotland,
had become professors in the United States and had there become
Anglicans of a firmly Catholic type.

I flew back to London by night and on arriving at Heathrow
heard that the Cherry Blossom Festival was cancelled. For, shortly
before I had left Kennedy Airport, Martin Luther King had been
assassinated in Washington.

1969 was for me a year of considerable mobility. At the beginning
of March I made a three-day visit to Belgium at the invitation of
Canon Dessain of Malines, the Ecumenical Officer to Cardinal
Suenens, the Archbishop of Malines and Brussels. Ever since
the famous but abortive Malines Conferences of 1921 to 1926
the word 'Malines' was remembered with pride at St Mary's,
Bourne Street, for Viscount Halifax, whose brain-child they were,
had been churchwarden at St Mary's and there was a splendid
memorial tablet to him in the church. And Canon Dessain's
uncle had been secretary to the great Cardinal Mercier, who
was Halifax's close ally. I stayed two nights with the Canon in
his family mansion, where he lived alone in complete simplicity
surrounded by exquisite furniture and ornaments, for the Dessain
family was of great note in Malines; an inscription recorded that
King Albert had resided there during the First World War. We
served each other at mass in his private chapel each morning. I
was invited to lunch by the Cardinal, who at that time was the
acknowledged leader of responsible progressive thought after the
Vatican Council; he had expressed his position in the term 'The
Extreme Centre'. We were alone and talked together for more than
two hours. Dessain took me to see the diocesan archives, which he
had tried to reduce to some kind of order from complete neglect;
and he was much excited to have found documentary proof that
the Malines Conversations had had the deliberate encouragement
of Pope Pius XI. He took me to lunch at the Diocesan Seminary
and I was impressed by both the institution and its staff; I found
it difficult to drag myself away from the library, where, neatly

bound up in separate volumes, were the sheets brought back from successive conclaves by the Cardinal Archbishops, one sheet for each ballot. Naturally the volumes varied greatly in thickness, and I just had time to observe how Sarto gradually won the tiara from Rampolla in 1903. From Malines I was taken to Louvain and then on to Brussels, but time was too short to do justice to either. At Brussels we did, however, drop in on the Bollandists, the Jesuit fathers who still work perseveringly on the great work on the lives of the Saints which their predecessors began in the sixteenth century. They occupied part, totally unheated, of one side of a great square building, most of which was a boys' school. We met four or five of them, all elderly, muffled up to the eyes, patient and courteous, and I could not help feeling ashamed of the comfort in which we Anglo-Saxon scholars work. We were joined by a younger priest, who excitedly quoted floods of statistics; but I could not follow his torrential French and I had no idea what it was about. Canon Dessain afterwards made the typical Belgian remark, 'He was a Frenchman.'

Less than a month later I was off to the United States for an intensive tour, starting and ending at New York and taking me for the first time to the Pacific Coast. I began at Fordham, the Jesuit university in the Bronx, where my contact was with Fr Christopher Mooney, one of the soundest interpreters of Teilhard de Chardin, and moved on from there to St Mary the Virgin, where the Rector, Fr Donald Garfield, had asked me to give the addresses in Holy Week. From here I flew down to West Palm Beach in Florida to lecture at an Easter-Week gathering near Boca Raton some thirty miles to the south. This had been arranged by a recently started institution giving itself the rather inflated title of the World Center for Liturgical Studies; it occupied one wing of an attractive and comfortable Vincentian seminary, some way inland. Florida is, of course, quite flat, but the climate is delightful and palm trees abound. The chapel, a large free-standing modern building, was thoroughly in keeping with its setting; it was surrounded by a small moat, and the windows, by a leading Parisian designer, were of large lumps of coloured glass set in a framework of concrete. From here I went to Los Angeles, and on crossing the southern end of the Rocky Mountains had my first and only experience of flying through a thunderstorm. We were assured that there was no danger, though there was most unpleasant turbulence and some of the passengers were quite alarmed; visually it was spectacular. (I might remark here that I am never the least bit nervous when flying; this has nothing to do with courage; I am not at all a brave person, and I have friends whom I know to be really courageous who suffer agonies in an aircraft whenever it takes off or lands.) Los Angeles has well been described as twenty suburbs looking for a city, and the main impression on a visitor is that he never knows in what part of it he is. Even in the rapidly growing American cities one can usually discern a centre and round it identifiable commercial, industrial, entertainment, university and residential zones, but in L. A. one seems always to be re-entering the place one has just left, even if in fact one has been hurtling away from it along one of the great elevated freeways by which the city is intersected. However, somewhere I ran to earth Geddes MacGregor, who was enjoying the enviable American status of Distinguished Professor, and I was delightfully entertained by him and his wife Betty. My engagement was to give four lectures and preach in the suburb of Pasadena in connection with Bloy House, a seminary for older ordinands in the Episcopal Church; it is typical of the American attitude to distance that it was decided to change the *venue* to Pomona University, at Claremont thirty miles away, and motor me there and back each evening! From Los Angeles I flew to San Francisco, and I must admit that as we came down there I was glad that I never feel nervous in the air. For we appeared to be plunging straight into the water of the Bay, and it was only when the splash seemed inevitable and imminent that the end of the runway appeared under the nose of the plane.

Placed as it is on the southern horn of a superb bay, San Francisco is, I think, the most beautifully located city I have ever seen. I had one lecturing engagement in the city itself, but I was to stay at the Church Divinity School of the Pacific, at Berkeley on the other side of the Bay, and to reach this involved crossing the six-mile-long Bay Bridge, which is as impressive, though in a totally different way, as the better-known bridge across the Golden Gate; half way across it changes for a spell from a bridge into a tunnel and burrows through the Yerba Buena Island. I had a pleasant and unexpected interlude when a former pupil of mine from King's College turned up in a pick-up car to take me to see his parish at Morgan Hill, forty miles south-east of San Francisco. It was farming country and quite unspoilt by urbanisation. We went straight off to a farm where an old couple were celebrating their golden wedding; apart from the swimming-pool in the middle of the farmyard, it was exactly like one of the Mary-Pickford films of my childhood, one of the guests even arriving in a buggy; and, after air-lines and motorways, it was delightful to be given a ride behind a horse. And three final notes on San Francisco: (1) it must have the steepest streets in its main business area of any city in the world; (2) to eat a fish meal on the Fishermen's Wharf is an experience not to be missed; (3) remembering that the city is immediately over the San Andreas Fault, the tactful visitor will refrain from talking about earthquakes and will refer to the catastrophe of 1906 simply as 'the Fire'. I flew to Dayton, Ohio, for a lecture at the Bergamo Institute and thence back to England via New York. On the flight to Dayton my neighbour on the plane suddenly asked me if I had ever seen the Grand Canyon. When I replied that I had not, he said, 'Well, if you look out of the window you'll see it now.' I did, and it was an impressive sight, though of course from the air one could not get any impression of its real size.

At the beginning of August I left for a six-week visit to South Africa at the invitation of the Anglican Church, to give lectures, sermons and a retreat. I flew on a British plane via Zurich and Nairobi to Johannesburg, and thence to East London. Here I got my first taste of Apartheid when, after walking across the tarmac to the airport building, I was confronted with two doors labelled respectively 'Whites' and 'Non-Whites', with the equivalent in Afrikaans. I will not attempt to describe my impressions of the racial situation, which were not substantially different from those of any other reasonably perceptive and cultured visitor, but I could see how an opulent and insensitive tourist could drift into the assumption that South Africa was a nation of privileged and deserving whites, with a vaguely defined background of blacks unobtrusively ministering to their comfort. Even those people whom I met to whom the Government's racial policy was most abhorrent seemed to have no doubt about its ability to suppress any stirrings of protest; they must have come to a very different opinion a few years later. I was driven by Fr Mark Tweedy, a Mirfield father whom I had known for many years, to Alice, where his community ran the Anglican section of the quadripartite Federal Theological Seminary, which has since been dispersed for its failure to conform to apartheid.[2] There I renewed a number of former friendships, with two former pupils from King's, Theodore Simpson, C. R., and Desmond Tutu (now Archbishop Tutu and of some fame for his conflicts with the South-African Government), a former pupil from Oxford, Donald Cragg, and, to my amazement, a former colleague from Bablake School, Coventry, David Bandey, who taught science there when I taught mathematics; both the last two were on the staff of the Methodist College. One of my memories of Alice is of looking out of my bedroom window and seeing a flock of white egrets on the lawn, no doubt a common enough sight there but

nevertheless one of great beauty. Fort Hare, the famous college
for blacks was close at hand, but in view of the delicate situation
it was thought best not to visit it.[3] Having given my lectures
at Alice, I was motored the sixty miles to Grahamstown to stay
at the (white) seminary, St Paul's College, to talk to clergy and
laity there.

Grahamstown was a surprise. In many ways it reminded me of
England before 1914, but I found it very hard to say why. One
felt it was very conscious of the fact that it had been the bastion
of the English (or at least the British) settlers against the Zulus.
(And when one is tempted to think of South Africa in terms of
blacks and whites one should not forget the difference between
those whites whose origin is British, and their natural language
English, and those whites whose origin is Dutch, and their natural
language Afrikaans.) From there I was driven to the airport at
Port Elizabeth, where I caught the plane to Cape Town to spend
a fortnight with the Archbishop, Robert Selby Taylor, who is a
fellow-member of the Oratory of the Good Shepherd and who had
asked me to be one of his commissaries.

I had a crowed time at Cape Town, with lectures, interviews
and the like. I celebrated mass one Sunday in a church on the
Cape Flats with a congregation of about eight hundred. I received
a good cross-sectional picture of church-life from the services to
which I accompanied the Archbishop. I remember in particular
a confirmation in a very poor district, when the church was full
of madonna-lilies. (These, locally known as 'pig lilies', are one of
the commonest wild flowers in the Cape Province, and there is a
sad story of a wealthy Englishman who, not knowing this, sent a
large number of them out in a refrigerated plane for the wedding
of a friend's daughter.) And I was much impressed to see, in the
lobby of the library of the University of Cape Town, the bronze
plaque which, in the words of the University Calendar, 'records
the removal of our academic freedom in the year 1960 and leaves
a space blank for the insertion of the date when our freedom is
restored to us.' It reads:

MONUMENTUM HOC AENEUM
DEDICAVIT CANCELLARIUS
EREPTAE LIBERTATIS ACADEMICAE
QUAE DEFECIT ANNO MCMLX
REDIIT ANNO –

My fortnight in Cape Town was not entirely given to work.

One day three of us – all members of the Oratory – went up Table Mountain by the cable-car and picnicked on the summit. One evening the Archbishop took me to dine at a delightful fish-restaurant in the remotest corner of the harbour, which I could never possibly have discovered for myself. On another evening we went to the ballet and on another to see, of all things, Oscar Wilde's play *An Ideal Husband*! A different form of entertainment was to meet a family of monkeys – grandfather, parents and children – out on a country walk and anxious to take a lift on the bonnet of the car. But harmless as they seemed, it was important, I gathered, not to leave the car with the window open, or one might find every bit of upholstery stripped off when one returned.

From Cape Town the Archbishop took me with him to Modderpoort in the Orange Free State, on the border of Lesotho, where the Kelham Fathers were to celebrate the centenary of the Mission which they had taken over in 1902. This involved a two-day drive across the Great Karoo Desert, and it was very noticeable that on crossing the coastal mountains one entered an entirely different climatic zone. The hot season was only about to begin and there was nothing visible but some scrub and an occasional sheep or ostrich. Once my attention was drawn to an ibis, a bird which, I imagine like most of my countrymen, I had thought was found only in Egypt. As I viewed the superb range of distant mountains, I had to abandon one of the dogmas with which I had been indoctrinated at Belvedere College, namely that Table Mountain was the only mountain in the world that was flat on top. Needless to say, the road was ideal for motoring, for there had been no lack of cheap labour for its construction; the difference was painful if one got on to the corrugated surface of one of the older roads. One sign of the march of civilisation – if that is how one should describe it – was the number of places, apparently remote from human habitation, where it was possible to obtain coca-cola and Lyon's ice-cream. We broke our journey for the night at a hotel at Beaufort West and went on to Modderpoort the following day. Modderpoort has some interesting prehistoric remains but I had little time to see them; I did however say mass in the tiny cave-chapel in which the Mission had begun. The great occasion was the centenary High Mass, which was celebrated by the diocesan, the Bishop of Bloemfontein, and at which the Archbishop preached. There was an enormous congregation, black, white and coloured, and the Administrator of the Orange Free State was present. The Archbishop preached in English, wearing a cope and mitre and precariously balanced on a bale of lucerne, and he was interpreted by an African who was balanced on a similar bale, whose version, enthusiastically delivered with the assistance of an umbrella, seemed very much longer than his Grace's original. Such exuberance I gathered was not uncommon and indeed was expected, and the celebration, held in the open air, was eucharistic in the most literal sense. It was followed by a great *al fresco* meal.

The following day I was handed over to the Bishop of Bloemfontein, Frederick Amoore, who took me back to lunch with him and then put me on the plane for Johannesburg. Johannesburg and Pretoria are only thirty-five miles apart and share the same airport, which was until recently the only international airport in the country. There I was met by Leslie Stradling, the Bishop, who took me to Rosettenville, where I was to conduct a retreat for clergy, black, white and coloured. (Rosettenville will be remembered by Trevor Huddleston's readers as one of those places where the Mirfield Fathers' work was put an end to by the Government.) After this I stayed for several days in the Bishop's house, where I woke each morning with the scent of jasmine coming from the bush beneath my open window, that lovely plant not having lost its fragance in Africa as it has in England. I said mass and preached in the cathedral, which has the rare privilege of a really mixed congregation, standing as it does where a black and a white area overlap. I also visited the university chaplaincy, which was admirably committed to Christian witness but which had a slovenly avant-garde Eucharist which I chiefly remember for the excessive length and inaudibility of the intercessions. Of a less directly religious character was the performance of Puccini's *Madame Butterfly* to which the Bishop took me.

A short journey took me to Pretoria, where the Bishop, Edward Knapp-Fisher, was an old friend, having been Principal of Cuddesdon Theological College when I was at Oxford. Each morning we went down from his house to the very convenient lecture-rooms next to the cathedral and it was warm enough for many of the proceedings, including the meals, to take place in the open air. The cathedral is in the busiest part of the city and a large notice outside defiantly announced that it was open to all without discrimination of colour or race. But I think I received some insight into the Afrikaner mentality when I was taken to see the Voortrekker Monument, which crowns a high hill outside the city. It is surrounded by a circular stone wall, carved to represent waggons arranged to form a defensive rampart round a camp at night, and itself consists of a gigantic brown stone cube, 130 feet in height, almost entirely empty but bearing on the front a great carved figure of a Boer woman. It is adorned with scenes from the voortrekkers' history and particularly their wars with the blacks. I remember especially a carving depicting the women sending their husbands back to fight when they have returned from being defeated by the Zulus; the men are sitting in dejection with their heads between their hands while their unsympathetic spouses are standing with their arms extended ordering them to return to the war. One was given the impression that it was the women who were the real tough guys in those days.

The work that I had come to do was now really finished but some enjoyment remained. John Ruston, a member of the Oratory, was chaplain to the Jane Furse Hospital in Sekukhuniland in the northern part of the Transvaal and had asked me to visit him there. This was virtually unspoilt Africa and permission had to be obtained for a white person to enter it. So it was arranged that Edward would take me to be met by him half way, and we all lunched together before John took me on. The Hospital was unlike anything that a European would expect a hospital to be. It looked simply like a large African village in a quite lovely setting, but on entering any of the huts one might find it equipped with the latest clinical apparatus. The medical superintendent was a white man but practically all the medical and nursing staff were black or coloured, as of course were all the patients, whose friends and relations could be found camping all over the place. The altitude was high and the latitude low, so the transition from day to night was extreme. The day was blazingly hot, but when the sun set, which it did rapidly and almost vertically, the temperature tumbled down, one rushed for extra clothing and by midnight it was freezing. The night sky was splendid, but in this respect the southern hemisphere cannot compare with the northern, and I do not think I am alone in finding the one easily recognisable feature, the Southern Cross, much smaller than one expected. On the last evening we dined with the medical superindentent, Dr Davies, and his wife, and the following morning John drove me to Lydenberg to hand me back to Edward and his wife Joan, who were taking me to spend my last three days in Africa in the Kruger National Park.

The Kruger Park, which is by far the largest of the nine national game-parks maintained by the Republic, stretches for more than two hundred miles from north to south along the border of Mozambique and is fitted in somehow by nature between the most overpowering mountain ranges. Time limited us to the southern end of the Park and we slept in the chief camp at Skukuza, where there were facilities from do-it-yourself open-air cooking to well-appointed restaurants and the sleeping was in comfortable rondavels. Edward had brought with him the necessaries for mass each morning. The lions had all migrated to the north and, being limited in speed to 25 m. p. h., we had not time to go in search of them. But we saw everything else: elephants in abundance (and it is surprising how even a herd of those great beasts can melt unobtrusively into a forest background); giraffes, frequently standing immobile by the road like lamp-standards but ready to launch out with deadly force if attacked by an enemy from the rear; hippos in their pool and apparently not there at all until what you had taken to be a large black boulder suddenly opened in a gigantic yawn, revealing rows of teeth and a vast gullet; and now and then, leaping across the landscape, a string of antelopes, *impala*, which must surely be the most graceful things in creation. I must confess, however, to a less agreeable impression when we stood on the Orpen Dam and watched the crocodiles enjoying their mid-day siesta on the sun-baked sand below. I felt quite revolted when one great monster, swollen almost to bursting with his meal, slowly dragged himself out of the lake and collapsed exhausted on the shore. No doubt there are beauties in the works of God to which I am blind, but, lest, improbably, anyone is tempted to write me off as a mere aesthete, may I testify that I can never recall without delight the wart-hogs, which, as far as appearance goes, must be the supreme example of unco-ordinated design in the animal kingdom. With his great head covered with lumps, his protruding jaw and tusks, totally out of proportion, his lumpy body and straggly hair and then, to conclude this catalogue of incoherence, his tail like a piece of string, which, far from concealing it in shame, he elevates to a vertical position when he runs, as if it were the aerial on a motor car, surely it is the wart-hog (*vlakvark* in Afrikaans) who, rather than the camel, fulfils the famous definition of an animal designed by a committee. Be that as it may, the impala and the wart-hog are the memories that I treasure most from the Kruger National Park. Edward and Joan motored me back to Johannesburgh to catch the plane back to England. It was a South African plane and therefore could not touch down in any black republic; it stopped at Luanda, which then was still Portuguese, and then at Las Palmas and Paris, and this put several hours on to the flight. What contribution I had made to the Church in South Africa it is not for me to say, still less for me on the strength of a brief visit to pass judgment on its success in struggling with a terribly difficult situation. South Africa is a country which has been blessed with wonderful beauty and every conceivable natural advantage and in which these have been tragically frustrated by human selfishness and stupidity. 'Where every prospect pleases and only man is vile' – indeed, as long as it is remembered that it is *'every* man' and the vileness is not total; otherwise there would be no place for hope or for the Christian Church. My most valued memento of my South African tour is a beautifully made folding conical straw hat of native design, given to me by a black priest in Pretoria.

In 1970 I realised a long contemplated plan of having a holiday in Rome, but, as this turned out to be only the first of seven visits, I will describe them together later on. In the following year I was twice invited behind the Iron curtain, and, although both of these visits were quite brief, I think they were sufficiently interesting to record. The first was to Rumania, and I have already described my eight crowded days there with Christopher Waddams in 1937[4]. Since then many changes had taken place; the country had been overrun first by the Germans and then by the Russians in the Second War, the quasi-Fascist government under the disreputable monarch Carol II had been superseded by the socialist regime of M. Ceausescu, and both Bessarabia and the Bukovina had been absorbed into the Soviet Union, so Chisinău and Cernăuti were now inaccessible. The signs of material progress were obvious; the main roads were first-class, whereas in 1937 even the most important were deep in dust in summer and in mud in winter, in town and village apartment-blocks and houses were being built in vast quantities though even to a casual glance, the bricks looked extremely inferior. It was astonishing in an avowedly communist country to find the Orthodox Church not only tolerated but accepted and encouraged as one of the great – indeed the greatest – historical institutions of the nation. No doubt much was to be attributed to the skill and tact of the impressive Patriarch, Justinian Marina, who, formerly a married parish-priest, became a monk after the death of his wife and was elected to the highest office in the Church in 1948. Much also was to be attributed to the realism of President Ceausescu, for anyone who has met Rumanians knows that, whatever may be the political regime under which they live, what really inspires them is a romantic nationalism; does not the very name of their country, *România*, testify that it is the true successor of imperial Rome? There are a number of seminaries and two theological institutes, at Bucharest and Sibiu; with the aid of interpreters I gave lectures at both of these, and I would commend to other countries the Rumanian custom by which, both before and after, the students burst into song. This both encourages the lecturer and relaxes the audience.

The hospitality was lavish; at Bucharest I was given the guest suite in the patriarchal palace; at Sibiu I stayed in the metropolitanate and was entertained by the Metropolitan-Archbishop himself. I had a converstion with the Patriarch and several meetings with his auxiliaries, Bishops Antim Nica and Antonie Plămădeala; the latter studied for his doctorate with the Jesuits at Heythrop College and I was later asked to be one of the examiners of his thesis — an interesting example of ecumenism. The day after my arrival was the Feast of the Annunciation and I attended a splendid liturgy celebrated by the Patriarch in his cathedral. During the next few days I was taken to see the Church's publishing and printing works and the factories of vestments and other church requisites. On the Saturday afternoon I went with Bishop Antonie to Cernica, which I had visited in 1937; I understood that the monastery had survived by the simple expedient of becoming an agricultural collective. Among its more aged monks was Bishop Tit Simedrea, who had come to St Andrew's, Stockwell, when I was a deacon; I did not see him in person, but I was taken to see his tombstone, which, according to the Rumanian custom, had been already prepared, with a blank space for the date. On the Sunday I said mass in the Anglican church and then travelled by train overnight to Sibiu with Dr Chitescu, Theological Institute, Fr Todoran, and were taken to the Metropolitanate for a welcome bath and breakfast. (One thing that had not improved since 1937 was the sleeping cars on the trains, which no longer included washing accomodation.) Sibiu, in Transylvania (the Ardeal) is the former Hermannstadt and shows many traces of its former German-Austrian dominance. In contrast to Walachia, where the houses were almost invariably open to view and even the smallest had delightful verandahs, the houses in Transylvania had high walls, with wide, and almost always closed, gateways. The Metropolitan, Nicolae Mladin, was young and vigorous; he was a moral theologian and had a great reputation as a spiritual force. With his piercing dark eyes his appearance could be forbidding, but his manner was gracious and friendly and he invited me to share his relaxation of watching the children's television programme. The splendid bedroom which was assigned to me had once been the personal chamber of the celebrated Metropolitan Saguna.

On the Wednesday morning Metropolitan Nicolae took me to the Lenten Liturgy of the Presanctified in his great cathedral; it lasted a good two hours and the singing of the choir was superb. At the end I was asked to say a few words, which I did in French with an interpreter. (Most of my conversation in Rumania had to be in French, a language which I can speak intelligibly but far from correctly.) Even more impressive was the evening service the same day, in which the large cathedral choir in the gallery was supplemented by over two hundred students in the body of the church, and the effect was both unforgettable and undescribable. There was a very large congregation and the silent devotion with which they stood or knelt, apparently unconscious of the passage of time, put the poor Western visitor to shame. One afternoon the Metropolitan took me in his car to the monastery to which he himself had belonged, an exquisite place under the Carpathians, Brancoveanu at Sîmbata de Sus. One of its specialities is the painting of icons on glass and I was given a very beautiful example of this work. It hangs now in my sitting room and I find it growing more and more upon me, for, in an obviously peasant idiom, it has an amazing restraint and tenderness as it depicts the Mother of God closely holding to her the divine Child. Another day I was taken to the village of Rasinari, the former residence of the Metropolitans; it had two churches, one glowing with ancient frescos, the other resplendent with modern work in the neo-Byzantine style, which, imitative as it admittedly is, is a great improvement on the sentimental work of the nineteenth century. In addition to my lectures I had some interesting discussions with the staff of the faculty. They were not as worried as I had expected by the Anglican adherence to the *Filioque*,[5] but were insistent that the Western Church taught a quite abhorrent doctrine that the grace of God was a purely created entity. When I suggested that, since grace united the creature to the Creator, it must have both a created and an uncreated aspect, they seemed astonished at the novelty of the notion and unsure what to make of it. I was told that Rumanian theology was the true Latin theology, but when I innocently enquired whether that meant that it was like that of Roman Catholicism I met with an indignant denial. When I asked how, then, it differed from Greek and Slav theology, I received the delightful reply that it was not so rationalistic as the Greek and not so confused as the Slav! It was added that the Rumanian Church was, contrary to common belief, the only Orthodox church in Europe with a vernacular liturgy, since the Greeks used patristic Greek and the Slavs used Old Slavonic. In spite of a certain inward-lookingness, Rumanian theology gave me the impression of real creative power, and this has been confirmed by the recently translated work by Fr Dumitru Staniloae, *Theology and the Church*, which, for example, on the traditionally polemical theme of the *Filioque* is thoroughly irenical and constructive.

From Sibiu I was driven through the valley of the river Olt, which cuts through the Carpathians from north to south and provides the most entrancing mountain scenery. Our destination was the town of

Rîmnicul Vulcea, whose bishop, like the Patriarch a widower, was the father of Fr. Lucian Gafton, the Rumanian priest in London and a former pupil of mine at King's. Bishop Josef was a magnificent white-bearded figure of seventy-five, full of vigour and enthusiasm. He had set up a splendidly equipped hostel for visiting priests and their families; his own residence, through which we were conducted, had been furnished with every conceivable variety of lock and safety-device by a predecessor who had had a pathological fear of assassination. I left with a pile of presents, which included a beautifully carved bishop's hand-cross and a rug of the typically Rumanian floral design which is now on my sitting-room floor. On the way to Rîmnic we had stopped at the monastery of Cozia, which overhung the river and furnished an exquisite view; its chief work was running a hospital for liver and kidney disease.

From Rîmnic I was driven to Curtea de Arges, one of the early capitals of Walachia. The church was built in the early sixteenth century by Prince Neagoe Basarab and contains the graves of a number of princes. Architecturally it is a perfect gem, not very large but perfectly proportioned, ornamented with a variety of different but harmonishing carvings and with the most elaborate columns ingeniously and fascinatingly disposed. Of even greater historical interest is the older royal church some distance away, which had become ruinous but was now being restored; the director of the restoration showed us, covered with a glass sheet, the open tomb containing the vested and crowned skeleton of one of the early princes. Altogether I found Curtea de Arges a most delightful town, which had preserved its ancient atmosphere most remarkably. I was all the more surprised to find that the former royal palace had been handed over by the Government to the Church as a seminary for late vocations. There I was met by Bishop Antonie, who had motored over from Bucurest that morning. And on the way back he took me to see three most interesting places. The first was Tirgoviste, another of the ancient capitals, where there are ruins of an enormous castle with cavernous dungeons, now converted into a museum. The second was Dealu, a monastery far up in the hills which had been made into a home for old and ailing monks and priests; the third was Viforita, which had been made into a similar home for nuns and priests' widows. Both these institutions were due to the initiative of Patriarch Justinian. They were staffed by nuns who were qualified nurses and the arrangements in both seemed admirable. The rooms were well heated and cheerfully furnished, with such modern conveniences as television. It was moving to hear the quavering voices of the old men greeting the bishop with the same melodies that, a few hours earlier, I had heard from the powerful lungs of more than a hundred seminarians at Arges.

We arrived at Bucharest late on Saturday night. The following day Bishop Antonie took me to the convent of Tiganesti some miles from the city. This was his first visit since his consecration and he celebrated the Liturgy for the community, though people came in from far around. The added ceremonial for a bishop and the long slow hymns of the monastic rite stretched out the Liturgy for more than three hours, but after the first hour I was almost unconscious of the flow of time as the other-worldly atmosphere of the rite took hold of me. There were two sermons, one by the nuns' chaplain after the Gospel and the other by the Bishop at the end of the Liturgy and both, as far as I could gather, virtually identical. The Bishop concluded his discourse with some kind words about me, to which I made, I hope, an appropriate reply. After lunch and a brief, but very welcome siesta, we went on to the monastery of Căldărusani several miles away.

In some respects Căldărusani struck me as the most beautiful of the monasteries which I visited. The sense of peace was extraordinarily intense; it must be a wonderful place for a retreat. Like Cernica it is by the side of a lake, and indeed a very large lake which almost encircles it and was, I was told, replete with fish, an important amenity for a monastery. The museum contains treasures that are priceless. Altogether, Căldărusani formed a perfect climax to my tour. The following morning, after a morning's shopping and a final visit to Bishop Antonie, I returned to England from Otopeni airport in a Trident Three of B.E.A.

An adequate description of the impressions which I received from my second visit to Rumania would need a more subtle and evocative pen than mine. The exquisite beauty of much of the countryside and of the villages and monasteries nestling among the trees and in the folds of the hills, the unrestrained welcome which I received from the Patriarch downwards, in episcopal places, monasteries and the homes of married parish-priests alike, the evidences of the practical efficiency with which the Orthodox Church was tackling the pastoral problems of the new housing-areas on the outskirts of the rapidly expanding industrial cities — all these gave the impression of a church which, while firmly rooted in the past and in the history of the people, was deeply conscious of the needs and challenges of the modern world and, in spite of its enclosed geographical situation, was eager to meet Christians and sincerely concerned with Christendom as a whole. Two things in particular impressed me. The first was the way in which the Rumanian monasteries and convents were caring for the active and contemplative aspects of the religious life, without any sense of conflict between them; partly, no doubt, this was due to the fact that, in the Orthodox Church, there is not the differentiation of religious communities and orders to which we are accustomed in the West, but simply one tradition of the religious life which is infinitely adaptable to the gifts and vocation of each individual. The second was the astonishing way (though perhaps it ought not to astonish us!) in which the Rumanian Church, like other Orthodox churches, combines great splendour and dignity in its worship with complete naturalness and informality on the part of all concerned in it; this is not entirely absent in the West, but it does not come at all easily to English people. And yet, in spite of the crowded churches, the bursting seminaries and the favours so lavishly granted by the State to the greatest national institution, one could not but be conscious that all this was bought at the price of total acquiescence in the social and political field under what has been described as one of the most repressive regimes in Europe. I mildly enquired of a highly placed prelate whether there was any dialogue in Rumania between Christians and Marxists. He stiffened immediately. 'Dialogue?' he replied, 'What dialogue could there be? We are good Christians and we are good Rumanians.' And at that I had to leave it.

After the experience of Rumania it was not such a surprise to find oneself taking part in an international Christian gathering in another communist country, namely Yugoslavia. Rumania is, of course, almost monolithically Eastern Orthodox in religion; in Yugoslavia the matter is more complicated. Croatia in the north is predominantly Roman Catholic, Serbia in the south is predominantly Orthodox, and there is a bewildering patchwork of Christian confessions in between. A large number of religious bodies are recognised by the state, including Jehovah's Witnesses and two minute but distinct groups of Old Catholics. There is, however, no religious teaching in the schools and, while existing churches are open and functioning without interference, it is, as in Rumania, extremely difficult to build any new ones. Thus, to take as an example the city of Zagreb, whose population increased from 160,000 at the end of the War to over 600,000 by 1971, the old city was well provided with churches of historic interest in which the sacraments were regularly celebrated, while in the whole of the uniform and depressively repetitive new area stretching for mile after mile on the south side of the River Save, the only place of religious activity was a minute but impressive chapel in the ground-floor flat occupied by a worker-priest. There was however no concealment, and clergy and religious in their habits were a familiar sight in the streets, though many of the clergy preferred to wear civilian suits with or without a clerical collar. My reason for being there was that I was attending the Sixth International Mariological Congress as one of three representatives of the Ecumenical Society of the Blessed Virgin Mary; the others were Martin Gillett, the secretary of the Society, and Neville Ward, the Methodist author of a widely read book on the Rosary. These Congresses had been organised at five-year intervals by the Pontifical International Marian Academy; its director, Fr Charles Balić, a Franciscan friar and himself a Croat, was realising a long cherished ambition to hold a Congress in his native country. I was the only Anglican present; there were two Orthodox, four German Lutherans and a Swiss Calvinist. There were Roman Catholics from all over the world, including an impressive contingent from the United States. We three Englishmen, together with eight French Catholics and the Swiss pastor, were given hospitality in a very modern guest-house run by a charming and most helpful community of Croatian nuns. Both the guest-house and the conference-centre were in the higher part of the city and got what breeze there was; a very welcome fact, especially during the first three days when the temperature was in the upper nineties. The eight French priests concelebrated in the convent chapel each morning, and on the Sunday the Archbishop of Zagreb, Mgr Franjo Kuharić, a most friendly and delightful prelate, gave me permission to say mass in the chapel, to give communion to two Wantage sisters who were passing through the city on their way to an Orthodox convent in Serbia.

I addressed one of the plenary sessions on the Place of Mariology in Christian Theology; there was an elaborate system of simultaneous translation which almost entirely failed to work. Apart from the academic activities several high lights remain in my memory. When an atheistic regime recognises a religious activity it can be relied on to do it properly, and the motto of the Congress, *Maria, mundi melioris origo*, could no doubt be given a tolerable interpretation. One evening we were given an official reception, which included a lavish buffet supper, by the Mayor of Zagreb. On the Sunday afternoon we were taken in motor-coaches to the Croatian national sanctuary of Marija Bistrica, which is about ten miles to the north-east of Zagreb as the crow flies but about thirty miles by road as the coach circles round the mountains. Bistrica is a charming place, dominated by the great basllica of our Lady, into which our whole party, over a hundred in all, marched singing the *Salve regina*. We drove away as dusk and rain were both beginning to fall, in order to dine in the country on the way back. After an hour and a half we dismounted, but not to dine. We found ourselves standing in a drizzle of rain, in pitch darkness lit only by the headlamps of the coaches. Before us was a large cottage entirely lost in the shadows; we heard afterwards that the whole region had been struck by a power-failure and this increased the effect of desolation. Word was passed round that we were in fact at Marshal Tito's birthplace and most of us observed a respectful and diplomatic silence. One German priest next to me was, however, moved to oral comment. 'Why we come to Tito birthplace?' he said to me, 'Tito not even Christian!'. After another hour in the coaches we stopped at a large road-house picturesquely lit by candles, as we were still in the power-failure area. Here we did dine and extremely well, getting back finally to Zagreb well towards midnight. Another evening we were entertained to dinner at the large and luxurious Inter-continental Esplanade Hotel, and were regaled not only by food and drink but also by a splendid performance of folk song and dance; we had happily coincided with a national song-and-dance festival, whose members generously allowed us to enjoy a quite delightful programme which they put on for us.

Most inspiring of all the events was the concelebrated High Mass in the Cathedral which concluded the Congress and in which four cardinals took part. These were Cardinal Suenens of Malines and Brussels, who was head of the international Marian organisation; Cardinal Oddy, a former Apostolic Delegate to Yugoslavia; Cardinal Carberry from the United States; and Cardinal Seper, who had become President of the Congregation of the Doctrine of the Faith in Rome. Cardinal Seper was formerly Archbishop of Zagreb and was paying his first return visit since his transfer to Rome; he gave the last and longest of the addresses before the Mass (there were five in all!), and was received with an ovation which I can only compare with that which Archbishop Michael Ramsey of Canterbury was given when he preached in Westminster Cathedral. During most of the mass I was in one of the stalls in the apse behind the altar. Between the stalls was the grave of Cardinal Stepinac, who was venerated both as a spiritual leader and as a national hero; the grave was continually piled up with flowers and with papers and tablets inscribed with prayers; it was constantly visited by the faithful, who knelt by it in devotion. There was in fact a quite spontaneous popular cultus of the great cardinal, but, if one wondered when it was likely to issue in formal canonisation, one had to recall the tragic story of post-War Yugoslavia, with the mutual killings of Catholic Croats and Orthodox Serbs, to see that the presence of even two Serbs at the Congress was significant.[6]

As the service ended, a thunderstorm began — and such a thunderstorm! When I left for the airport after lunch floods were everywhere, and half way to the airport they invaded the engine of the car in which a kindly French Dominican was acting as my chauffeur. I was providentially rescued by a passing taxi and returned to London without further mishap, sharing the aeroplane with — of all improbable companions — a party of Canadian Red Indians who were travelling to London from Bucharest. I was only sorry that I could not stay for the less academic and more popular Marian Congress which immediately followed the Mariological Congress. This culminated in a pilgrimage to Marija Bistrica on the following Sunday, the Feast of the Assumption, at which the number of pilgrims was variously estimated at from 100,000 to 250,000. Compared with this, our pilgrimages to Walsingham, inspiring as they are, seem less impressive. However, as we sometimes like to remind ourselves, numbers are not everything.

I may seem to have devoted inordinate space to two visits which, in the aggregate, amounted only to three weeks, but I found them intensely educative. It may seem anomalous for the Church to be tolerated and even encouraged in a professedly secularist and atheist country, but I wonder whether it is not as anomalous for it to be treated as a harmless and picturesque antiquity in a country where it is a constituent element in the constitution. I certainly felt that I had come to understand better the situation of the Church in the Roman Empire in, say, the third century, with the authorities of the state never being quite able to decide what to do with this uncomfortable unassimilable element in the community. Rumania, the only Latin Orthodox nation, and Croatia, one of the few Slavonic Catholic ones, were very different in many ways but in one they were surprisingly alike. Neither of them was suffering from any lack of vocations either to the priesthood or to the religious life. At a time when in the free democracies our blood is regularly curdled with stories of half-empty or closing seminaries and of priests and religious walking out of their jobs there may be a lesson for us to learn.

But now back to the United States. I was invited by the Jesuit Fathers at Gonzaga University, Spokane[7], in the state of Washington in the far north-west, to take part in 1973 in an interesting academic and ecumenical experiment; this was nothing less than a series of lecture-triads to be given by visiting scholars, seven in all at annual intervals, each lecturer being expected to pick up where the previous one had left off. The series had been inaugurated the previous year by the celebrated Jesuit philosopher and theologian Bernard Lonergan, and, as I had a great but not unquestioning admiration for his work, I accepted the invitation eagerly. (Eight years later I received a copy of the final triad, which had been delivered in 1979 by one of Lonergan's most faithful students, Frederick Crowe, S. J., and was a mature assessment of his work; so the wheel had come full circle.) I took the opportunity to plan this as part of an extensive lecture-tour, beginning at Windsor, Ontario, where I had been five years before and where I received a fine welcome from Frederick Temple, though the whole of my programme was nearly nipped in the bud at Detroit Airport through a mistake in my visa made by the American Embassy in London. This got sorted out while I was at Windsor and I was able to fly on from Detroit free from the dreadful suspicion of being an unlawful immigrant. (In passing, I always find the American epithet 'unlawful' much more daunting than our British 'illegal'.) We touched down at Chicago, which was bedlam, and at Billings, Montana, which was desolate; one solitary passenger, dressed as for a western film, came on at the latter airport and I could not help wondering whether he was hired by the management to provide local colour.

Spokane I found most enjoyable, intellectually, socially and geographically. It lies between the Rockies and the Cascade Mountains, and in late autumn, when the leaves of the maple trees were turning to scarlet and gold, the scenery was magnificent. Just outside the city is a beautiful long straggling lake with the intriguing name Coeur d'Alene; I was taken for a delightful drive round it one afternoon. In earlier days the Jesuits had done outstanding missionary and cultural work among the Indians[8] in the neighbourhood; many signs of it remained and indeed in a new form it continued. Their unique Indian museum was being rehoused and reorganised while I was there and I spent some hours being shown some of its treasures by its devoted director Fr Wilfred Schoenberg. I provoked a revealing reaction when I remarked to him that I had once been to the American Indian Museum in New York City, where all the exhibits are arranged in the most scientific and systematic way. 'Yes,' he said with a snort, 'everything there is dead. My museum is alive.' The University was in fact engaged on a large programme of expansion and was looking forward to an official visit from President Nixon; this was of course before Watergate! The fine library building was a benefaction of the film actor Bing Crosby, who was a devout Roman Catholic. I left Spokane with happy memories and some interesting literature about the Indians, including a translation of the Catechism into Flathead, a language of which I cannot claim any command.

My next engagements were at Dallas in Texas, where I was to

lecture at the University of Dallas, which is in fact at Irving near by, and to give a talk at an ecumenical meeting at the Anglican Cathedral Centre. I had to change planes at Denver, Colorado, where the Airport considerately relieved the tedium of a three-hour wait by a free cinema show; the flight was over some of the most aridly desolate land I have ever seen. If it did nothing else for one, air-travel in the States would at least impress upon one the astonishing variety of the surface of that gigantic country. Proverbially, everything in Texas is twice the size that it is everywhere else and immediate observation seems to bear out that estimate. The new Airport of Dallas/Fort-Waine, alleged to cover an area equal to that of Manhattan Island, had been completed but was not yet in use; I saw it towering in the distant mist.

I stayed with the Dominican Fathers, whose house was on the university campus; the chairman of the Theology Department was, rather to my surprise, a Cistercian monk. My next academic fixture being at Boston, Massachusetts, I spent several days in New York on the way; apart from a sermon at St Mary the Virgin on the Sunday morning, my engagements were entirely social, and, although I do not look upon New York as the most agreeable of cities, the fact that I have a number of friends there made the break very enjoyable. And let me tell one story which I could wish to see written in letters of gold and scarlet and told to the sound of trumpets. Walking near Central Park I found to my horror that my wallet, which contained much more money than I would ever carry at home, was missing from my pocket. Either I had been robbed or I had left it in a drug-store where I had bought some shaving cream. Feeling both anxious and foolish I returned to the drug-store, fully expecting to be met with protestations of ignorance. In fact, the assistant removed it from the safe where he had placed it for security and handed it to me intact, simply remarking 'Quite a lot of money, isn't it, Father?' One evening Fr Garfield, with whom I was staying, took me to Radio City Music Hall in the Rockefeller Center, and I can only describe the whole thing in Damon Runyon's phrase as More than Somewhat.

Both the stage and the auditorium must, I suppose, be the largest in the world, and the entertainment was on a scale to correspond. It consisted of a full-length film and a stage-show. The latter had a Cowboys-and-Indians theme, the numbers taking part were immense, the technique was of course first-class and there was nothing which were immense, the technique was of course first-class and there was nothing which could bring a blush to even the most sensitive cheek, for Radio City is very definitely a family house. But the film came to me, as a visitor from London, with a shock that was almost traumatic; for it was a Peter-Sellers tear-jerker, set in the East End of London, about an old man and a boy and his mongrel-dog pet, and the sentiment was laid on with a trowel. How it affected an American audience I cannot imagine, but it was the last thing that I expected to meet in Manhattan! My invitation to Boston had come from Peter Bertocci, Professor of Philosophy at Boston University; we had met in London when he was in England on sabbatical leave and had found ourselves to be very much in sympathy in our general philosophical orientation. He arranged for me to give a formal lecture and also to meet a student seminar. I stayed in a very conveniently located hotel, and an unexpected pleasure was to see from my bedroom-window numbers of small yachts with white sails sailing in the sunshine on the Charles River.

The hotel was within easy walking distance of the Museum of Fine Arts and, having a few hours to spare, I decided to use them in seeing the collection of French impressionists for which the Museum is famous. I was not disappointed. On ascending a staircase to the centre of a semicircular gallery I found Monet landscapes extending to either side. And there was the repeated joy of having one's eye caught by a picture which one had long known from its frequent reproductions. Thus, glancing along a narrow corridor I suddenly saw at the end of it Renoir's *Le Bal à Bougival*, one of the most *rhythmic* paintings that I know; it was actually hanging at one end of the side wall of a gallery into the opposite end of which the corridor debouched and would, I think, have been quite inconspicuous from any other viewpoint. On my previous visit to Boston in 1958 I left having paid for a fragment (I think it was a square second of arc) of the firmament of the Planetarium and purchased at the Science Museum a small portion of silly putty[9]; this time I returned with books of reproductions of impressionist paintings to give to my friends. I left from Logan International Airport and arrived at Heathrow without incident.

The following autumn I went twice to the States. The first time was to speak about secularisation to an association of women religious called *Consortium Perfectae Caritatis*. It had been in existence nearly a decade and I had been asked to address them some years previously in Rome but had been unable to do so. They were all Roman Catholics and were looked upon by some people as being reactionary and obscurantist, but this judgment seemed to me unfair. They took their vows seriously and retained the religious habit, and they were obviously distressed by the number who had been ready to abandon both. But their minds seemed to be vigorous and open, and if they had been obscurantist in outlook they and those who advised them would hardly have been willing to have an outsider like myself as one of their principal speakers. What I did find a little surprising was their meeting in an extremely opulent hotel, the Huntington-Sheraton at Los Angeles, but this seems to be a *sine qua non* of all gatherings in the United States, religious or secular.

I flew by Pan Am ten hours non-stop from from Heathrow to Los Angeles by great-circle route. This is described, inaccurately, as the Polar Service; it goes nowhere near the North Pole, though it does go over Greenland and Hudson Bay. Through the kindness of friends with cars – and in any case the almost complete absence of public transport in Los Angeles makes cars essential – I was able to squeeze in several bits of sight-seeing. I had a distant view of the *Queen Mary*, tied up at Long Beach and looking a very forlorn relic of the ostentatious vessel on which I made my first crossing of the Atlantic. I was taken to see the Greek Orthodox cathedral, which was built at the expense of two wealthy brothers in the film industry. The sumptuous brochure admits that it 'does not follow too closely the rigid Byzantine tradition'; I think it can best be described as Orthodoxy in the idiom of Hollywood. Fourteen great crystal chandeliers are suspended down the nave and in addition three chandeliers of immense proportions hang from the transept arches and the choir vault. And – this would, I fear, shock most of my Orthodox friends to the core – the whole building is seated with comfortable pews, except for a small number of tip-up seats for the family of the founders. I was told that, when it was proposed to build the present splendid edifice – it was actually consecrated in September 1952 – the priest who was in charge of the humbler building which it replaced pleaded that a scriptural text chosen by him should be inscribed in English across the interior of the west wall, so that all the faithful would be confronted with it as they left the church after the Liturgy. And there it is: 'For what shall it profit a man if he shall gain the whole world and lose his own soul.'

There were two other places in Los Angeles which I wanted to see, but time was running short and I had to choose between them. One was Disneyland and the other was one of the Forest Lawn Memorial Parks. It was a difficult choice, and the friend who had put himself and his car at my service made no attempt to influence me. The Memorial Park won and any implications of the morbid and the macabre must attach entirely to me. The truth simply was that, having read Evelyn Waugh's novel *The Loved One* and Jessica Mitford's serious research-report *The American Way of Death*, I felt a consuming curiosity to know what these places were really like. There are four of them; we visited the one at Covina Hills. The setting was undoubtedly beautiful, 'towering trees, sweeping lawns, splashing fountains, singing birds', as the prospectus says, but the 'beautiful statuary' and 'noble memorial architecture' of which it goes on to speak is almost entirely imitative or sentimental and trivial.

Thus one passes from Michelangelo's David and the Venus of Milo to a little group labelled 'Baby's Bath'. There are careful reproductions of churches which it is supposed patrons may have come across in their reading: 'the Little Church of the Flowers' is Stoke Poges, for Gray's *Elegy*; 'the Wee Kirk o' the Heather' is Glencairn, where Annie Laurie worshipped, and 'contains many historical mementos of Annie and her romantic love story'; 'the Church of the Recessional' is Kipling's Rottingdean, but on the wall outside there is inscribed not the poem of judgment whose name it bears but the author's more bracing product 'IF ...' 'The Church of the Hills' and 'the Old North Church' evoke New England, and Longfellow and Paul Revere respectively. And all are carpeted from wall to wall and have a glazed-in aisle full of brilliantly illuminated flowers — whether real or artificial I could not tell! All shades of religion or non-religion are catered for, from a sentimental religiosity to an ethical idealism strongly emphasising the American ideal of freedom and democracy.

I found something very revealing in a minor regulation concerning the Memorial Court of Honor. This is a Gothic hall in which the resting-places are restricted to 'men and women who contribute a service to humanity so outstanding that future generations will recognise its worth', a criterion whose application would seem to need the gift of prophecy but which has admitted, among others, the sculptor Gutzon Borglum, the song-writer Carrie Jacobs-Bond, the scientist Robert Millikan and, not surprisingly, Dr Hubert Easton, the founder of Forest Lawn. The end of the hall is occupied by a reproduction of Leonardo da Vinci's *Last Supper* as a stained glass window, and at intervals visitors are admitted to view it and to hear a recorded description. The Californian climate is, however, hot and many of the visitors, both male and female, are liable to have bare arms and/or legs. For reasons of reverence these are therefore required to put on disposable paper dressing gowns, provided by the management, before entering the Court of Honor! But, strangely, no such concession to propriety is demanded on entering the Hall of the Crucifixion-Resurrection, where one is privileged to see what I can well believe to be, as is claimed, the largest oil-painting in the world. Slightly to my surprise, my companion took me to the administration building and introduced me to a courteous but, I suspected, slightly reluctant official as a priest from England who had a special interest in funeral matters and wished to see how things were done at Forest Lawn. We were taken to the casket showroom and given a good deal of information about the different facilities offered and their cost, and I was fascinated to see the rudimentary garment in which the front of the top half of a loved one who was being disposed of at the cheapest rate was adorned in order to give a nattily tailored appearance. I was rather relieved that we were not admitted any further into the cosmetic aspect of the industry. On the whole I was glad to have seen Forest Lawn for myself. It was impossible not to admire the skill with which business method and sentimentality have combined to instil an attitude to death that is neither realistic nor Christian, while subtly claiming to be both. Miss Mitford's researches showed the extent to which the 'Dream' or 'Vision' (both terms are used) of 'the Builder', Dr Hubert Easton, had solid commercial results. I wonder whether I should not have done better in Disneyland after all.

I spent a night in New York with the Catirs on the way back and for the following week suffered the worst attack of jet-lag that I have ever had, presumably due to the effect on my bodily rhythms of restoring the eight-hour shift before I had become adjusted to the original displacement. I have often wondered how our modern jet-propelled diplomats manage to retain their sanity; no doubt a cynic would be tempted to make a slightly different comment!

Less than a month later I was back again in the States. 1974 was the seventh centenary of the death of the two great theologian-saints of the two great orders of Friars, St Thomas Aquinas of the Dominicans and St Bonaventure of the Franciscans. The Franciscans, with characteristic humility, kept their celebrations in a low key; the Dominicans, as befitted the Order of Preachers, made more public stir. An ambitious celebration was arranged to take place partly in Rome and partly near Naples, in the vicinity of St Thomas's birthplace; I had been invited but was unable to go. I had also written articles for several learned publications, including a two-volume symposium arranged by the Pontifical Institute of Medieval Studies at Toronto. But the three American Dominican Provinces, with the collaboration of the Franciscan School of Theology at Berkeley, California, had arranged a three-day programme at Berkeley and Oakland, on the north side of the San Francisco Bay, and I was asked to be one of the principal speakers at this. I was also asked to break my journey at Washington, D.C., to give a lecture at the Dominican House of

Studies and to meet with the members of the interdenominational Washington Theological Consortium.

In contrast with the old Washington Airport, situated conveniently in the centre of the city but now demoted to merely domestic status, the new Dulles Airport is about forty miles to the west of the city. But with typical American hospitality I was met there by my Dominican hosts and conveyed to the familiar setting of their house just opposite the National Shrine. This house is in fact the chief centre of Thomist studies in the United States and I was given a wonderful welcome; I was provided with an altar for mass each day as a matter of course. The Theological consortium met seventy miles away at the Lutheran Seminary in the historic town of Gettysburg; in the afternoon we were taken on a brilliantly organised tour of the historic battlefield, which received added piquancy from the fact that the guide was a southerner and made no attempt to conceal his sympathies. No doubt this was a crude and ignorant reaction, but I was quite amazed at the smallness of the area involved and the fact that the crucial engagement covered a space of little more than a mile. On the Sunday morning I preached at the Anglican church of St Paul and in the evening I delivered my lecture in the Dominican house, but in the afternoon, wandering across to the National Shrine, I was astonished to hear the strains of the Byzantine liturgy and to find the building crammed to the doors. The explanation was that a new Byzantine chapel was being consecrated in the crypt and that uniates (that is, Christians of Eastern rite in communion with Rome), including half a dozen bishops, from all over the country had come for the ceremony. This provided a striking example of the racial diversity of the United States, and a quite unexpected one at that. On the following day I spent a few hours at the Anglican seminary at Alexandria, just over the border in Virginia. It is an institution of evangelical tradition, strong on scholarship and liberal in sympathy; but I must confess that what most impressed me on a very brief visit was the beauty and lavishness of its setting, for its buildings are scattered over a broad and wooded parkland well insulated from the more painful aspects of the modern world.

Several of the Dominican fathers at Washington were going to the celebrations in California and invited me to travel with them. Situated as we were on the east side of the city, it was far more convenient to fly from Baltimore airport, which lies between the two cities at the pleasantly named site of Friendship, than to drive back through the centre of Washington and out again to Dulles. The programme at Oakland covered three days; it was, sensibly, planned much more to bring the insights of St Thomas and St Bonaventure to bear upon the problems, theological and philosophical, of the present day than to investigate historical and biographical questions; it culminated with a great concelebrated mass in Oakland cathedral, of which the impressiveness was unfortunately lessened by the illness and absence of the Bishop. I stayed in the Dominican Fathers' house and had some illuminating informal discussion; there was also time for some sightseeing and other relaxations. I was tremendously impressed with the new Roman Catholic cathedral in San Francisco, in which the most imaginative and attractive use had been made of modern materials and technology (though I must confess some puzzlement at the incorporation of large amounts of travertine stone from Italy). I made up for an omission on my previous visit by having a ride on one of the famous cable-cars. These are obsolescent, very uncomfortable, noisy, bumpy and great fun, and it will be a great pity when they finally wear out; I put them in the same class of precious anachronisms as Volk's Electric Railway on the sea-front at Brighton in Sussex. Most memorably, I was taken one day across the Golden Gate Bridge to Sausalito, to have lunch in the open air overlooking the Bay. As we arrived at the restaurant we were unobtrusively relieved not only of our coats but also of the automobile and they were returned together at the end of the meal. The view of the Bay in the sunlight was breathtaking. Eight miles away over the water was Oakland; in between were Alcatraz, the now disused convict island from which it was alleged that no prisoner ever escaped, and Treasure Island and Yerba Buena, with the Bay Bridge running through it. I would dearly have like to spend longer in the country of northern California, and in particular to spend some time in the Yosemite Park, but I had to tear myself away to preach at St Mary the Virgin, New York, on the other side of the continent. I have already mentioned Fr Donald Garfield, the Rector, as an old friend, and he provided this trip to the States with an interesting and delightful conclusion. It was now the middle of October, the season when the maple-trees with which the New-England mountains are clothed change the colour of their foliage from green to brilliant scarlet. Donald is himself a New-Englander and has so many connections there that I have sometimes had the impression that New England must be entirely populated by his cousins! (New-Englanders, like Scots, have a wonderful memory for family relationships.) He had arranged that we should spend three successive nights with three different friends of his in three different places.

In one respect we had a mild disappointment; the weather

was dull and showery, so the trees did not display themselves in their full autumn splendour. But in every other way it was delightful. I was astonished at the extent to which many of the small towns in Vermont, New Hampshire and Massachusetts have retained the flavour and in many cases the buildings of the colonial days; time after time one saw rows or whole streets of seventeenth- and eighteenth-century houses of the kind of which in England one finds scattered or isolated examples. One such house would be the town museum, with its farm and kitchen implements and household furniture. Many of the New-England localities are famous for their part in the struggle for American independence − Lexington and Concord, for instance, not to mention Boston and the 'teaparty' − and the incidents associated with them are briefly described on attractively designed monuments at the various sites; some ingenuity had been expended in reconciling sober history with romantic legend in the case of Paul Revere. An attractive spot is the hamlet of Plymouth Notch, Vermont, the birthplace − and burial-place − of that not very impressive President of the United States, Calvin Coolidge, who in 1923 succeeded automatically to the supreme office from what was in those days the totally obscure position of Vice-President on the sudden death of the outstandingly incompetent and corrupt Warren Gamaliel Harding. There one is shown the room in the family farmhouse where Coolidge, who was on vacation at the time, was administered the presidential oath by his father, a local notary public. He had the reputation of being the least loquacious of all American presidents and some good stories, many no doubt embroidered, are told of his taciturnity. One is that someone said to him at a social gathering, 'Mr President, I have made a bet that you will say at least three words this evening.' 'You lose,' he replied. He certainly appears to have been the opposite of the politician of whom it was said that he could set his face talking and go away and leave it; but the notion that he was simply an uneducated yokel is clearly false. He had had a university education and was a successful local lawyer and politician. But he was clearly not ambitious of presidential office, especially as Harding had left it, and his recorded reply at the next election, 'I do not choose to run', no doubt expressed his true feeling. Plymouth Notch was a delightful little spot and carefully preserved from tourist exploitation. But I was saddened by the following paragraph from the official leaflet, referring to the little congregational church:

In 1890 the church needed repairs, and the ladies, led by Carrie

Brown Coolidge, stepmother of the President, put on strawberry sociables and baked bean suppers to raise money for a more up-to-date interior. The church had box pews.

And now, alas, it has hard pine benches and there is nothing to differentiate the seat which the President occupied at the end of a row but the union flag which stands in it.

We finished our trip with an afternoon by the seaside at Salem, which is of course celebrated for the novels of Nathaniel Hawthorne and for the witch-trials at the end of the seventeenth century, though the Salem of the latter was Salem Village, several miles inland, and has been renamed Danvers. The Hawthorne associations have been carefully preserved and the House of the Seven Gables is identified; indeed the atmosphere in general is one of remarkably little development and modernisation. Boston, only fifteen miles to the south, would seem to have happily had more than its share of commercial and maritime expansion, leaving Salem out of the rat-race and free to remain its own peaceful self. Or is this just the delusion of a guileless and impressionable tourist on a pleasant autumn afternoon with his defences down? In any case I was to experience both the *grandeur* and the *misère* of our technological age after Donald deposited me at Boston Airport for my night journey back to England. For the plane left Logan dead on time and arrived at Heathrow dead on time, only to be unable to descend on account of dense fog. After circling around helplessly and being refused entry to other airports which were full up, we were flown to Prestwick in Scotland and dumped on the tarmac without food or information for three hours, during which time we were filled up by other bewildered travellers from somewhere in Asia. Finally, the fog cleared and we were taken back to Heathrow, where we were landed just eight hours after our original arrival. No doubt these tribulations were mild compared with those of crashes and hi-jackings, neither of which I have been unlucky enough to experience, or even with the hazards of snow-drifts and highwaymen in the seventeenth century, but I have all the same sometimes wondered whether our modern craze to travel faster and faster might not be described as flying in the face of Providence.

Nearly three years were to elapse before I was in the United States again, and this time for a longer and less mobile visit. This invitation, which was to spend ten weeks in the early part of 1977 at the Pontifical College Josephinum at Columbus, Ohio, came to me by telephone over a year before, when I was on one

of my periodical visits to Truro, and its source was the Dean of the
Faculty, the Capuchin Franciscan Father Ronald Lawler, whom I
had met more than once in England. This was my first long visit to
the state of Ohio and, although people from more famously scenic
parts of the country write it off as flat and uninteresting, I found
it very pleasant. It is agreeably undulating, it is well wooded and,
largely through the damming of rivers to make artificial reservoirs,
it has quite beautiful lakes. The Josephinum is on the outskirts
of the state capital, Columbus, in the suburb of Worthington. It
occupies an enormous area, to which it moved in 1931; the original
foundation was made in the heart of the city in 1888. The present
buildings are in a striking brick and stone American Gothic style.
They stand in an extensive parkland, behind which woods, replete
with wildlife (including, I was told, stags, though I did not see
these myself) stretch for well over a mile down to the Olentangy
river. The impression of unlimited space which every British visitor
to the United States receives was certainly emphatic here.

The College has an interesting and unique history. Unlike virtually all the Roman Catholic seminaries for diocesan priests in
the States, it was founded not for one particular diocese but for
the whole country, and its purpose was to train German-speaking
priests for the masses of German immigrants, many of whom spoke
little or no English. Hence it was put not under the local bishop
but under the Apostolic Delegate, as he Pope's representative, and
hence the world 'Pontifical' in its title. The particular linguistic
problem has now vanished and all the teaching is now in English,
but it has retained its nation-wide reference; there were students
from as far apart as Maine and California, Montana and Florida.
Originally the College was divided according to the traditional
post-Tragentine pattern into Minor and Major Seminaries but now,
in accordance with Modern American educational practice and with
the recognition that some mature experience of the wider world is
desirable before consciousness of vocation can be demanded, the
two sections have become a Liberal Arts College and a Seminary
in the strict sense. My special commitment was to be responsible
for the course on Christology in the Seminary, and it says a lot
for the ecumenical outlook of the faculty that they were prepared
to confide such a very central doctrinal theme to an Anglican. But
in fact for some time, without any loosening of its Catholic loyalty,
the Josephinum had developed a very outward-looking stance; it
had formed a 'Cluster of Theological Schools' with the Lutheran
and Methodist seminaries in the area, and my invitation had in
addition the support of the local Jewish foundation. Of the thirty

or so students in my class, nearly ten were Methodists and were very appreciative and responsive ones.

The liturgical life of the Josephinum centred, of course, in the liturgy of the mass, which was normally concelebrated each day by all the priests, with the exception of a few older ones who preferred to say mass privately (indeed very privately, without even a server!). The emphasis was on informality rather than ridigity, more so, I felt, than in the other two seminaries which I visited, at Cleveland and Cincinnati. Communion was invariably given in both kinds, and I was both delighted and deeply moved to be invited, with the permission of the bishop,[10] to receive communion whenever I wished. I was also allowed to celebrate mass myself and was provided with vessels, vestments and a server as desired. Indeed the only restriction of sacramental intercommunion was that I could not be invited to concelebrate, and this of course I thoroughly understood. I had many opportunities, through the never-failing thoughtfulness and hospitality of my hosts and friends, of seeing aspects of church life outside the Josephinum. Both in Cleveland and in Cincinnati I gave lectures and seminars, and in Cincinnati as well as in Columbus itself I talked to joint meetings of Roman Catholic and Anglican clergy about the recently published statement of the International Commission on Authority in the Church; this gave me the opportunity of saying some not universally welcome things about recent events in the American Episcopal Church. One of the trips which I personally found most enjoyable was to Wichita, Kansas, at the invitation of the Roman Catholic bishop. Bishop David Maloney, whom I had twice met in Rome when he was staying there with his friend Cardinal John Wright, had assured me of his desire that I should visit his see-city, which is geographically the central spot of The United States, and I was delighted when this became possible. If anyone, with memories of television westerns, should suppose that Wichita, Kansas, consists of one long street of saloons and general stores, with horses tied up outside and cowboys with six-shooters tucked into their fur trousers, let me say that it is an important city of well over 100,000 inhabitants in a prosperous farming and industrial area. One delightful touch is that, to reduce disturbance by noise, the actual landing area in Wichita Mid-continental Airport is quite a long way from the terminal building, so that one has the impression of taxi-ing in through cornfields. The cathedral is a perfectly charming medium-sized modern building in restrained but joyful Baroque style, so well adapted to the modern liturgical ways that it might have been, though it was not, made for them.

One unforeseen engagement was to address for the second time the association of nuns called *Consortium Perfectae Caritatis*, who were meeting this time at St Louis, Missouri. The organisers only discovered my presence in the country after the programmes had been printed and by then my only vacant time was that of the opening session. It says a lot for their anxiety to have a speaker who was Anglican and English that in spite of this they reshuffled the arrangements, so that the formal proceedings began with a lecture by myself in the presence of Cardinal Carberry and several bishops. Still more unforeseen, and the only really traumatic experience of my stay, was the occasion when I discovered towards the end of one morning at the Josephinum that I was expected that day to speak to a specially arranged lunch-time meeting of Roman Catholic and Anglican clergy, about which, by some administrative oversight, everyone had been informed except myself! An added complication was that I was booked that afternoon for a gastric X-ray for which I was under a strict twenty-four-hour fast. So, at practically no notice, I found myself seated with two Roman Catholic bishops on one side of me and the Anglican Bishop of Southern Ohio on the other, with an audience consuming delectable food and drink which I had firmly to refuse, while I spoke off the cuff on the Agreed Statement on Authority, before being whisked away to the radiology-clinic to consume large quantities of barium! The audience was most understanding and appreciative, as American audiences always are, but I was glad that I did not have to repeat this experience.

The academic staff at the Josephinum was even more varied in background than the student body. Most were, of course, Americans, but there were three Hungarians, two Spaniards and an Italian. Nearly all were secular clergy, with a heavy weighting of Monsignori, though the title was rarely used. (Incidentally my title of Canon was intriguing and I was told that the students knew me onomatopoeically as 'Boom-boom'.) A few were Salesians, from a large house of the Order in a poor part of the city, where they were doing fine work among boys and young men. One, a warm-hearted giant of a man, was a Dominican, Fr Terence O'Shaughnessy; he drove an enormous car with the appropriate licence-plate 'TOS OP'. The Rector, Mgr Frank Mouch, whose authority covered both sections of the Josephinum, was, I think, the only member of the staff who was a qualified air-pilot. Two much-loved residents were retired members of the staff, Mgr Hofer, who was devoting much care to a not very responsive little garden, and Mgr Undreiner, who went every summer to help in a poor parish in New Jersey. The latter celebrated the golden jubilee of his priesthood while I was there. He was the principal celebrant at a great mass at which the other con-celebrants included a great throng of his former pupils, among whom were, I think, five bishops, including the bishop of the diocese, who modestly subdued his liturgical predominance for the occasion. I suspect this was Mgr Undreiner's first participation in a concelebration, as one used to see him each morning toddling off to a side chapel for his private mass.

Universities and colleges in the United States are innumerable, and they vary in every respect: size, range of interest, degree of independence and, not least important, quality. Some are very good indeed, others – well, not so good. The gigantic State University of Ohio occupies a very large area of Columbus; it has a colossal sports stadium, holding 20,000 people, and magnificent equipment. Not surprisingly one heard the complaint that individuals frequently felt lonely and lost in it; in 1977 it was engaging in vigorous competition with a comparable institution for a potential undergraduate who was a nationally famous athelete. I was interested to see on the campus a sinister-looking vehicle with the inscription 'State University of Ohio Police' and I reflected on the contrast with the Cambridge 'bulldogs', armed with their halberd and butter-measure. In contrast, I was taken one afternoon to the small but distinguished Denison University, a community of rather over 2,000, in an idyllic setting (apart from the fact that it rained all the time that I was there) at Granville in the foothills of the Allegheny Mountains.

I saw little of my fellow-Anglicans on this visit, as I was very much integrated into the life of the Josephinum. But I spent Holy Week in New York City at the Church of the Transfiguration, which is better known as 'the Little Church around the Corner'. It derives this affectionate nickname from the fact that in 1870, when there was a strong prejudice against the theatre among churchpeople, an actor who was trying to arrange the funeral of a deceased colleague was told by a mid-town rector that 'there was a little church around the corner where they did that kind of thing.' Ever since then it has been closely connected with the theatrical profession and the Episcopal Actors Guild has its headquarters there. Both in lay-out and in execution it is out of the ordinary. One suddenly comes across it, a pagoda-like quasi-gothic structure with a lych-gate, occupying, with the rectory and social rooms, a neat and cheerful garden plot just off Fifth Avenue in a sleazy and run-down area, towered over by shabby buildings of less than skyscraper quality. Inside it gives a quite accurate impression of having been built in bits, and, as the official leaflet tactfully puts it, 'the many additions and alterations have added an eccentric and personal charm to the building'. But it has done, and continues to do, a great work for a highly diversified and widely scattered congregation and there is nowhere quite like it. I was invited there by Fr Norman Catir, who had moved there with his wife Zulie from Stamford, Connecticut, where I had stayed with them in 1968. The liturgy of the season was beautifully performed. I gave addresses in the course of the ceremonies on Good Friday, concelebrated with a black bishop on Easter Eve, and had the unusual experience of preaching to a congregation of seven hundred on Easter Day. The temperature considerately dropped from the upper eighties to the thirties as I arrived, and returned to nearly ninety when I left; in between I shivered in a thin raincoat, as I had trustingly left my heavy overcoat at Columbus. As always in New York, I spent as much time as I could in the Metropolitan Museum of Art. I also made the acquaintance of the quite amazing Frick collection, which must be one of the finest privately gathered assemblies of paintings in the world. On entering I was deferentially received by someone who might well have been the butler to a duke and who refused to accept any admission-fee from a recognisable cleric. Then, in the central room of the mansion, I was confronted by El Greco's St Jerome, hanging between Holbeins of St Thomas More and Thomas Cromwell. After this, I was prepared for anything – and got it! Gainsborough, Romney, Rembrandt, Titian, Turner, Van Dyck, Goya, to mention but a few, and finally one room completely hung with canvases by Fragonard and another completely panelled by Boucher. Most astonishing of all, however, was it to discover the story of Henry Frick himself, who made the collection, built the house and left both to posterity. He was one of the most ruthless of the 'Robber Barons', the great Pittsburgh coke and steel industrialist, who used Hungarian immigrants to break a strike of his workers and later, when the Hungarians had found their feet, hired Italians to break a strike of the Hungarians; whose family tried unsuccessfully to suppress his biography.[11] Back at Columbus, I preached on Whitsunday at a pleasant little church at Worthington. It claimed to be the first Anglican church to have been built west of the Alleghenies and had established a prescriptive right, which I was able to share, of picknicking on the green at the cross-roads outside.

I left Columbus Airport on Tuesday June 7th, taking with me a beautiful inscribed tray which the staff and students of the Josephinum had given me as a memento of my stay. It was the day of our Queen's Jubilee visit to St Paul's Cathedral and the Guildhall, and owing to the five-hour time-difference I was able to see the recorded television of her ride in the gold state-coach before I left the College. The extraordinary interest and indeed enthusiasm which the Jubilee aroused in the United States was shown by the fact that it had already been broadcast live across the nation, which meant from 5.50 am in Ohio and from 2.30 am in California. This concern was certainly not confined to the one day; it had for example been shown earlier at the time of President Carter's visit to England; and the contrast between different images of a head of state was painfully emphasised by David Frost's television interviews with ex-President Nixon. The implications for comparative national psychology, American and British, might make an interesting study, but I shall not attempt it here. I will only record two reflections. The first is that there are advantages in *not* combining the offices of head of state and head of government in the same person. The second, which I owe to an American friend, is that it is providential that the American constitution includes provision for impeachment, as otherwise the only means of removing a corrupt President would be assassination or revolution.

My ninth, and to date my final visit to the States took place in the beginning of 1981. It was to Houston in Texas, and was at the invitation of Fr Ronald Lawler, who had been given charge of a new Center for Thomistic Studies which was being set up in the University of St Thomas. Houston[12] is fifty miles from the sea and fifty feet above it, and owes its prosperity to the exploitation of the oil beneath this desolate coastland at the beginning of the century; skyscrapers, petroleum installations and multiple highways are the most prominent features of the landscape. It also contains the most enormous medical centre, probably the largest in the world and virtually a city in itself. I was astonished to find that, at a time of universal commercial depression, Houston appeared to be entirely confident and expansive in every respect, with the population increasing faster than in any other city in the country, new buildings going up everywhere and, I was assured, virtually no unemployment. Could such optimism possibly be justified, even in Texas, I kept on wondering; how long could it all go on? Education is on the expected Texan scale, with several immense universities, both public and private, but the University of St Thomas is a small coeducational liberal arts college, founded in 1947 by the Basilian Fathers[13]. It is entirely open in its membership but, to use its own phrase, it functions 'in the framework of a Catholic religious commitment'. It 'exists to cultivate the intellectual virtues' by 'giving primacy in the curriculum to the sciences of theology and philosophy'. It seemed to be a very appropriate home for a small but academically respectable centre for the furtherance of the principles of Thomistic thought. This had been encouraged by the Institute of Medieval Studies in Toronto, which had given it its first Director, the distinguished Thomist scholar Anton C. Pegis, but its emphasis was rather different, being less on historical research and more on contemporary applications. I stayed in the Basilian Fathers' residence, a pleasant house with the bedrooms opening from a verandah round a central green space with the inevitable swimming-pool; they were about twenty in number and were almost all engaged in teaching in the University. To one solicitous father, who occupied the next room to mine, I owe my introduction to the works of the delightful Georgian[14] novelist Flannery O'Connor. And I found an old friend in the person of Henry Veatch, who had recently retired from his chair at the Jesuit University of Georgetown at Washington and had come to do a brief spell teaching philosophy. He is a keen Anglican layman and formed my congregation at mass.

Anglicanism is not very flourishing in southern Texas, and what there is mainly of a liberal and low-church type. But I was sought out by the Rector of one of the few Anglo-Catholic parishes, who had made the acquaintance of one of my Oratorian brethren in Winchester Cathedral, and he entertained me lavishly, both in his rectory and at the fabulous Petroleum Club. The latter, as its name suggests, is based almost literally on the local oil industry; for it occupies the top three floors of the fifty-storey Exxon[15] Building and is on an enormous and opulent scale. In typically American fashion it has a quota of members who are ministers of religion and my host was one of these. He arranged a luncheon-party, at which all but he and I were laymen and most had ecclesiastical or academic connections. There was one extremely aged participant, who was very carefully taken home by his secretary at the end of the meal; I was told he was the son of the founder of Exxon and I presume he was the owner of the building! Fr Lawler took me one day to Galveston, on the sea-coast; it has been overtaken in importance by Houston but has some attractive houses in Mexican-Spanish style, going back to the days before air-conditioning, when the opulent of Houston would flee to Galveston from the intolerable summer heat and humidity. (Houston claims to beat even New York and Washington, D. C., for its lethal summer climate; in February it was pleasant enough in the eighties, with the exception of a sudden cold snap, when the temperature dropped overnight from ninety to somewhere in the twenties.) The neighbouring small town of La Porte must surely be unique in one respect. The attractive modern Roman Catholic church has twelve stained-glass windows representing the twelve Apostles; and the twelfth place is held, not by either St Matthias or St Paul, but by its original tenant Judas Iscariot, who is appropriately represented by a money-bag and a coil of rope.

As I look back on my nine visits to the United States my deepest impression is that of having received a great privilege. I have been, even if in some cases very briefly, in almost all parts of that great country, far more indeed than have most Americans themselves, and the only part which I regret having missed is the real traditional South. But I am certainly not going to set myself up as an authority on the strength of this or to emulate the legendary traveller who boarded the train at Leningrad and emerged at Vladivostok several days later with the manuscript of an authoritative work on Siberia, which he had written on the journey. For the United States, by its sheer size and even more by the diversity of the national and racial groups which make up its population, defeats any attempt at simple generalisations and owes much of its charm to this diversity. But certain characteristics stand out. One, on which I have more than once commented, is the generosity and hospitality with which the visitor is entertained; and, going with this, is a courtesy and what I can only describe as a kind of informal ceremoniousness which surprises the Englishman who has derived his expectation of American manners and speech from paper-backs and movies. The Englishman often gives the impression that if he is never going to meet someone again it is hardly worth while getting to know him; the American in the same situation gives the impression of wanting to make the best use that he can of his brief contact, and this is reflected in the little speech in which he assures one on being introduced that he is real glad to make one's acquaintance and that in which, on taking leave, he thanks one for the privilege of the interesting conversation which he has enjoyed. The astonishing achievement of welding into one nation in barely two centuries the welter of human groupings that have spread from New England to California is breath-taking almost beyond belief; and, if it has been accompanied by the uglier manifestations of industrial capitalism, it is at least true that many Americans are themselves vocally conscious of the ambiguities of their own situation. The fact that a system, however carefully designed, can never be immune from the

moral weakness of the human beings who compose and operate it is
startlingly evident when one compares the method which the fathers
of the Constitution devised for the selection of the President, by
electors of the highest integrity and disinterestedness, meeting in
an atmosphere approximating to that of a religious retreat, with
the actual conduct of the Conventions of the Democratic and
Republican Parties and all that goes on both before and after.
And there is the paradox by which time after time the nation
which above all others has gloried in its respect for freedom and
the rights of man has been committed by its government to the
support of odious and tyrannical regimes in other countries, under
pressure from big business and under the specious pretext that any
party that declares its opposition to communism must be a model
of social justice and enlightenment. It is much to the credit of the
Roman Catholic bishops in the United States to have expressed
their misgivings at President Reagan's support of the brutal and
repressive government of El Salvador.

One of my pleasures in the States has been my enjoyment of
the American language, whether written or spoken; perhaps one
should speak in the plural and say 'the American languages', for
there is a marked contrast between, say, the fastidious accents of
Boston, Mass., and the Southern drawl of Houston, Texas. If I
say that I first came to appreciate it through reading the works of
Damon Runyon, I am not ignorant that many authorities maintain
that his idiom was his own invention and that no one in fact ever
spoke like Harry the Horse and Little Isadore. If it comes to that, I
do not believe anyone ever spoke like Mrs Gamp and Sam Weller,
but I am sure that they could only have been conceived in Victorian
London and I am sure that Runyon's guys and dolls could only
have come to birth in New York in the days of Prohibition. And,
whether he recorded it or invented it, I endorse with enthusiasm
E. C. Bentley's judgment, 'There is a sort of ungrammatical purity
about it, an almost religious exactitude, that to me, at least, has
the strongest appeal.' My only cavil with this judgment is with the
word 'ungrammatical'; for it seems to me to have a very definite
grammar, a grammar of its own. And it rises at times to the level
of the sublime, as in the following passage, which is worthy of a
place in Dante's *Vita Nuova*: 'She has a smile that starts slow and
easy on her lips and in her eyes and seems to sort of flow over
the rest of her face until any male characters observing same are
wishing there is a murder handy they can commit for her.' But,
to descend from the sublime to the commonplace, I am always
fascinated simply by the ordinary differences of vocabulary and

idiom between British and American English. Some are of practical importance; an Englishman must be careful of the terms in which he tells an American lady that he is sorry she has been unwell; and if an American promises to call in the morning he means that he will telephone, not that he will appear in person. Even the most luxuriously appointed receptacle for the ablutions of a film-star or a tycoon has the humble name of a 'bath-tub'; a bath is what she or he takes in it. A sweet is a dessert, sweets are candies, biscuits are crackers; and if you ask for a ham-sandwich you are likely to be given a hot gammon-rasher on a thick-slice of buttered toast. And any meal which is at all formal is a banquet. I have always been delighted to receive the kindly message 'We are arranging for your transportation', which calls up for me the vision of being sent off in chains with a gang of convicts to Botany Bay. Many Americanisms are, of course, English forms which we have abandoned, such as closet for cupboard and faucet for tap; others are new inventions, some of which we are happily or less happily borrowing, such as the novel use of 'hopefully'.[16] And some, like the verb 'to contact', are perfectly correct formations of which the language is badly in need. And Americans, like Italians, have the courteous habit of thanking you for thanking them, 'You're welcome' being their equivalent of *Prego*; this is so much better than our awkward silence or our mumbled 'It's all right'. And it is cheering to be sent off with the exhortation to 'Have a good day':

At this point, with affection and gratitude to my American friends for the many good days which they have given me, I must turn from their vast and youthful continent to the little Italian peninsula and the eternal city of Rome.

Notes

1. The official name of the Anglican Church is 'The Episcopal Church in the U.S.A.', frequently abbreviated to ECUSA, with the corresponding adjective 'Episcopal'. Laypeople will inform one 'We're Episcopal' and one will meet a cleric with the tautologous description 'the Episcopal Bishop of N.'.
2. Racial, not denominational!
3. There are three main categories in South Africa, 'white', 'black' and 'coloured', the last meaning those of mixed descent. But the various gradings and the consequent disabilities are quite baffling. Thus Japanese, but not Chinese, count as white because the South Africans want Japanese cars and machinery.
4. See pp. 89–95 above.

5. The addition by the Western Church of the words 'and from the Son' to the formula in the Creed expressing the procession of the Holy Spirit from God the Father, a long-standing bone of contention between Eastern and Western Christendom.
6. See Trevor Beeson, *Discretion and Valour* (1974), pp. 257ff.
7. Pronounced by those who live there with a short 'a'; and the state of Washington should not be confused with the federal capital of Washington in the District of Columbia, the two being almost as far apart as is possible in the U.S.A.
8. That is, what we call 'Red Indians', not natives of India.
9. This is an interesting substance which yields to gentle pressure like ordinary putty but to a sudden blow either rebounds like steel or fragments like glass.
10. Mgr Hermann, a most friendly prelate, in appearance the exact double of Dr Coggan, the then Archbishop of Canterbury.
11. See Alistair Cooke, *America*, pp. 293, 296.
12. The local pronunciation is like 'Euston', preceded by an 'h'.
13. Not to be confused with the Basilian monks of the Byzantine rite. They are a modern congregation, founded in France, and are much involved in the Pontifical Institute of Medieval Studies in Toronto, Canada.
14. That is, of the state of Georgia in the U.S.A., not of the Soviet republic of Georgia in the Caucasus.
15. Exxon is the petroleum corporation which in England is, and in the U.S.A. was, known as Esso.
16. Though, if we can say 'I shall probably come', meaning not 'I shall come in a probable manner' but 'It is probable that I shall come', I do not see why we should not say 'I shall hopefully come', meaning not 'I shall come in a hopeful manner' but 'It is hoped that I shall come'.

Chapter Thirteen

And Now Rome

(1968–1976)

I am more an antique Roman than a Dane.
> – Shakespeare, *Hamlet*, V, ii.

*O Roma nobilis, orbis et domina ... te benedicimus – salve
per saecula!*
> – anon., saec. ix.

I have already remarked on my extreme lack of initiative in the
matter of holidays, but I can point to one exception which had
considerable consequences for me. Largely as a result of the
increased contacts which I had formed with Roman Catholic
theologians and ecclesiastics after the Second Vatican Council, I
came to feel a strong desire to see the Eternal City for myself and
I planned a visit for a fortnight in September 1968. This, however,
had to be cancelled at short notice, when I went into hospital for
an operation of the type common to ageing males, and it was not
until just two years later that I found myself almost literally in the
shadow of St Peter's. I took advantage of this postponement to
acquire the rudiments of Italian, and I found this very useful later
on, not so much for conversational purposes (for which indeed it
was very rarely needed) as for reading theological books, of which,
with the virtual abandonment of Latin in the Roman Colleges, more
and more are being published in that language. Earlier tourists have
described the thrill that they experienced when, as they approached
from the north, their coachman would bring his vehicle to a stop
on a hilltop and, pointing with his whip to a distant view, would
cry *Ecco Roma!* Arriving at Fiumicino at the Leonardo da Vinci
Airport and then taking the bus through the dingy southern suburbs
is less dramatic; nevertheless, when after the long stretch of the Via
Ostiense one is suddenly confronted by the Porta San Paolo and
the Pyramid of Caius Cestius and shortly afterwards skirts the

towering mass of the Colosseum, one certainly feels a thrill. I wonder whether I am alone when I record that my first surprise was to discover that the predominant colour of the ancient Roman buildings was not white, as in my ignorance I had expected, but a warm and mellow ochre.

Rome is an ideal place for sightseeing, not only in the quality and quantity of what it offers but in the fact that, with the not inconsiderable exception of the great extra-mural basilicas and the catacombs, almost everything that one wishes to see lies within an area less than two miles in any direction; from notes that I made in my copy of Fr S. G. A. Luff's admirable *Christian's Guide to Rome*, I see that in seven days I visited no less than fifty-three churches, in addition to climbing the dome of St Peter's, tramping the Vatican Galleries, rambling about the Forum and enjoying a walk in the sunshine along the Janiculum. Even so the time had been quite inadequate for even the briefest glimpse of all the buildings which I wanted to see, let alone a real enjoyment of their beauty or an assimilation of their various atmospheres, and I resolved to repeat my visit at the same time of the year in each of the following two years. For the sightseer in Rome the month of September is ideal; the weather is sunny and hot, though not unbearably so. One must be prepared for the occasional thunderstorm, and a Roman thunderstorm gives no half measures; there was one on my first evening, and, gazing at the dome of St Peter's from my hotel bedroom through the deluge, I felt forcefully reminded of the accounts of the famous storm of 1870 whose thunders drowned the voice of Pius IX decreeing his own infallibility. I stayed in three different houses in the course of these three visits, all of interest in their different ways. The first was the Hotel Columbus, in the Via della Conciliazione, very close to St Peter's; its rather cosmopolitan title conceals its identity as the palace of the Order of the Knights of the Holy Sepulchre. It is in fact run as an efficient modern tourist hotel, but is also the administrative centre of the Order. It contains a splendid council-chamber, with seats of state for the officers on a canopied dais; and one is served one's ossobuco or soglioglo on plates bearing the arms of the city of Jerusalem. The second is the Anglican Centre, of which I shall have much to say in a moment. The third is the Foyer Unitas; it is a hostel for non-Roman-Catholic Christians visiting Rome and is run by a religious community of Dutch ladies, who have dispensed with distinctive dress and distinctive titles but are perfectly orthodox in their beliefs. They were extraordinarily efficient in organising parties to visit sacred sites and attend ecclesiastical functions, and one sometimes heard the comment made, with a touch of envy, that it was easier for an Anglican to obtain a ticket for a papal audience than for a Roman Catholic, provided he applied through the Foyer Unitas. The Foyer occupies one large floor of a building in the Via S. Maria dell'Anima, backing on to the Piazza Navona; it is immediately over the Library and Centre of the American Franciscan Friars of Unity (the Graymoor Friars) and forms with them a focus of ecumenism. When I was staying with them, I was provided with a gratuitous and fortuitous piece of entertainment. It was late afternoon and I had just had a bath and changed my clothes after getting soaked to the skin in a thunderstorm which had suddenly burst when I was half-way from the Church of the Gesù. I was sitting at my window, which overlooked the Piazza, watching the lightning as it played on the flooded surface in the fading light, and waiting for the storm to slacken so that I could go out for dinner. Suddenly there was an explosion, deafening and momentary and quite unlike the normal roll of thunder; it sounded, in fact, exactly as if a bomb had gone off, not outside but in the room. There was also a vivid flash, simultaneous with the explosion. The building, we were told, had been struck by lightning, but, because of the very efficient lightning conductors, no serious harm had been done, though the electric supply and the telephones were out of order for some time.

Rome came up to all my expectations and I fell in love with the Eternal City as soon as I arrived. I shall not attempt to do the job of the guide-books, nor to perform the ungrateful task of remarking on the mistakes which I discovered from time to time in the excellent pair with which I equipped myself, Fr Luff's which I have already mentioned and Georgina Masson's invaluable *Companion Guide to Rome*.[1] But I will just mention some of the churches which I found most attractive, for they are not all of them the most celebrated or spectacular. First, St Peter in Montorio, which I lighted upon on my second day after walking in the sunshine along the Janiculum. There, high above the Tiber with the whole of the city spreading away on the other side of the river, a wedding-party was just celebrating, and the whole scene was so perfect that I quite forgot Bramante's Tempietto, which is what one comes there to see. Then down into the rabbit-warren of the Trastevere, with its great basilica of St Mary, of which I will only say that the splendid mosaic in the apse, which is puzzlingly the sole example of this design, presenting Christ enthroned as the central figure, with his Mother, robed and crowned, sharing his throne and embraced by his arm, seems to me the supreme iconographic depiction of a sound Mariology. Near at hand was the charming miniature basilica of St Benedict *a Piscinula*. St Cecilia's, also in the Trastevere, has an apse-mosaic of our Lord, in which the face expresses with an intensity that I have seen in no other mosaic the union of the Godhead and manhood in the one Christ; this is the more noteworthy because the faces are often the least satisfactory features in even the best mosaics. In the same church there is a Latin inscription, highly comforting to the clergy, describing how the location of the body of St Cecilia was revealed to Pope Paschal I in a dream when he had fallen asleep during the office in St Peter's; *sopore in aliquo corporis fragilitatem aggravante*. SS Cosmas and Damian, in the Forum, contains perhaps the most overpowering mosaic of all: Christ in robes of gold striding down on the clouds of heaven. Unfortunately, the floor of the church was raised at some time to avoid flooding, so it is impossible to look up at it as one should; the best one can do is to lie down on the floor and observe it at various angles. I am glad to have seen the ossuary under the Capuchin Church of the Immaculate Conception, with its tasteful and artistic arrangement of the mortal fragments of innumerable departed friars in what I can only describe as grottos, with here and there a complete skeleton in its brown habit hanging from the ceiling; it is an edifying spiritual exercise to compare it with the Forest Lawn Memorial Parks in Los Angeles, California: two attitudes to death! And deeply moving is the inscription in the church above over the tomb of Cardinal Antonio Barberini, a Capuchin friar who was the elder brother of the magnificent Pope Urban VIII. The plain slab does not even record his name, only the Latin epitaph *Hic jacet Pulvis, Cinis et Nihil*, 'Here lies Dust, Ashes and Nothing'. If I were to attempt the impossible task of deciding which of all the Roman churches is my favourite, I think I should have to answer 'Santa Prassede'. Prassede (Praxedes) was the sister of Pudentiana, whose much better known church is not far away from hers; but it is in the crypt of Santa Prassede that both of them are buried. Those who seek the church out — it is tucked away near the mighty Santa Maria Maggiore — usually do so for the sake of the exquisite little mosaic-studded chapel of St Zeno, erected by Pope Paschal I in honour of his mother and containing her portrait, inscribed *Theodora Episcopa* (which does not mean 'Lady Bishop'!). What I find most attractive, however, is the apse-mosaic, in which the majestic central figure of the standing Christ is flanked by the Apostles Peter and Paul, each of whom had one arm affectionately round one of the two sisters

Pudentiana and Praxedes. Or would I give pride of place to
Sant'Agata dei Goti, in the ancient Suburra, built in the fifth
century for Gothic immigrants, who were Arian heretics? With
its lovely little creeper-hung courtyard and its quiet interior, so
largely unspoilt, it breathes peace and recollection in the turbulent
modern city. One other impression I must record from these early
visits is of secular and not religious association. In the Forum, on
the merble pavement of the ruined Basilica Aemilia, one observes,
if one looks closely, small green circular patches about the size of
coins. That, in fact, is what they are, copper coins melted into the
stone by the heat of the fire when, on the night of August 23rd
A.D. 410, the Goths entered the city and sacked it. I can personally
confirm Georgina Masson's words when she writes:

> Nowhere else in the city is the scene brought so vividly before
> our eyes as by these few scattered coins. For six days the savage
> tribesmen sacked imperial Rome, the mistress of the world, and it
> must have seemed as if civilisation itself was crashing into ruins
> with the great basilica on that sultry August night.[2]

Part of my first visit, and most of my later ones, I spent
at the Anglican Centre as the guest of the Director, Dr Harry
Reynolds Smythe. The centre was founded in 1966 and blessed by
Archbishop Michael Ramsey on the occasion of his visit to Pope
Paul VI. Its function is to provide a permanent Anglican presence
in Rome, where contacts between the two communions can be
maintained and developed and where facilities can be given for
the study of Anglicanism in all its aspects. Of central importance,
therefore, is its library, which is small but of unique character, as
constituting the only place in Rome where a really representative
and virtually complete range of Anglican theological books and
periodicals can be consulted or read at leisure. Research into the
history and doctrine of Anglicanism has become a popular subject
for doctoral study in the Roman universities and I have had some
interesting and profitable conversations with people whom I have
met in the library of the Centre. The Centre is housed on the top
floor of one wing of the great Palazzo Doria, by the generosity of
Princess and Commander Doria-Pamphilj; the Dorias are one of
the few great Roman families who still occupy the *piano nobile*
of their eponymous mansion. With their two children, who were
at school in England, they set an admirable, and not superfluous,
example of Christian domestic life to the rest of the Italian nobility.
The Princess's parents were courageous and outstanding opponents

of Mussolini during the Fascist regime, which they spent partly
in hiding and partly in prison; her husband is an Englishman, a
commander of the Royal Navy, and they met during the Second
World War, when she was nursing in a hospital. The state rooms
of the Palazzo, which are open to the public regularly, are an
amazing treasure-house of furniture, pictures and tapestries, among
which the family live with truly Italian naturalness and simplicity.
Probably their most famous treasure is the portrait by Velasquez
of the Pamphilj pope, Innocent X, a very disconcerting pontiff
when one comes upon him, as one does, suddenly; but some of
the tapestries are overwhelming. To find oneself at luncheon, as
I did one day, with two married couples and their children, under
the tapestried panorama of the Battle of Lepanto (the great Admiral
Andrea Doria was, of course, one of the family), might have been
intimidating in a less informal atmosphere; as it was, it was wholly
delightful. The Palazzo, with its two hundred apartments, of all
sizes and uses, has something of the nature of a village concentrated
into one enormous building and planted in the centre of a great
city (for it is just at the bottom of the Corso and only a stone's
throw from the Piazza Venezia, where the Duce used to harangue
his supporters); and the concern which Donna Orietta and the
Commander Doria showed for its inhabitants and their welfare
reminded me of the rapidly vanishing family outlook traditional
of rural communities. But to return to the Anglican Centre on the
top floor of the south wing.

Next to the library there is a simply furnished but adequate
chapel, where the Blessed Sacrament was continuously reserved,
and on the other side is the Director's apartment, through which
there is access to the roof-garden (hence the advantage of being
on the top floor!), from which there is a quite superb view of
Rome, looking past the Gesù and over the Pantheon to St Peter's;
it provides a welcome refuge from the noise and petrol-fumes of
the city. The first Director, John Findlow, had been a pupil of
mine at Lincoln Theological College; he died in 1970. His widow,
Irina, a Russian Orthodox, continued to live in Rome for some
time after his death; she wrote his biography, in the Orthodox
idiom of an address to the deceased, under the title *Journey
into Unity*. He had had previous experience of Rome, first as
chaplain of the English Church from 1949 to 1956, and then
from 1964 as the Archbishop of Canterbury's representative to
the Vatican. His successor, Dr Harry Reynolds Smythe, a priest
from Australia, studied for his doctorate at Christ Church, Oxford,
when I was theology tutor there. After his establishment in Rome I

enjoyed his hospitality many times and we became close personal friends.

The work of the Centre has three main aspects. The first I have already mentioned, namely the facilities which it offers to scholars who wish to make a study of Anglicanism. The second consists of *ad hoc* gatherings for the discussion of particular topics or for lectures by visiting Anglicans who may happen to be available. But perhaps the most valuable activity – and it is one for which Harry Smythe showed himself to have a quite astonishing aptitude – is the establishment and development of contacts with important Roman Catholic personalities and with colleges and religious communities, not only in Rome but in many other parts of Italy and even abroad in places as distant as Innsbruck and Trier. At Harry's invitation I transferred myself from the Hotel Columbus to the Centre for the last week of my stay and for two days of this he took me to Assisi, where he had taken a charming little house opposite the Cathedral as a refuge from the urban turmoil of Rome. Assisi was all that I expected it to be and had preserved its serenity amazingly under the assault of tourism. It would be pointless to repeat what is to be found in all the guide-books; I will only remark on the beauty of the local stone, a shiny yellow with pink patches which I have seen nowhere else. The weather was torrid and when in the evening we walked down the hill outside the walls to see the town silhouetted against the sky the noise of the cicadas was quite deafening. Back in Rome we found a ticket awaiting us for a papal audience at Castel Gandolfo, the Pope's summer residence on the Alban Hills, and we decided to hire a car with a chauffeur and make this the occasion for a day in the country. Castel Gandolfo is a small and peaceful place, with the papal palace forming one side of the square. We drove across the Campagna and arrived in good time for the audience, which was at midday. Together with others who had come on the same mission we sat refreshing ourselves at a conveniently placed café until just before the appointed time, when we strolled across to the palace and showed our tickets. We were directed upstairs and found ourselves with a miscellaneous company of thirty or so, sitting round the wall of a largish hall. Noticeable was a little group of nuns carrying a parcel which looked as if it contained a very large teddy-bear but was presumably a statue for the Pontiff to bless. Pope Paul entered with the rapid walk which was normal with him before his later painful infirmities, waving both hands in a welcoming gesture; some of his attendants found it difficult to keep up with him. He first of all received a group of diplomats standing; then he sat down, and the rest of us were presented singly or in our groups. Harry and I came together. It seemed natural to kneel and kiss the Pope's ring; this was in no way enforced and four years later it was positively discouraged.[3] The arrangement for interpretation was brilliant; a young monsignor kept the conversation moving by murmuring in Italian and English and it was difficult to realise afterwards that more than one language had been used. The Pope had quite a lot to say to Harry, who had brought him a message of greetings from the Anglican Archbishop of Melbourne; his remarks to me were briefer but very kindly. One thing that puzzled me was the rather unmilitary bearing of the Swiss Guards and their obvious difficulty with their halberds; this was explained when it was revealed that they were not in fact Swiss Guards at all, but Swiss seminarists who were standing in for them while they were on holiday. We want on from Castel Gandolfo to Frascati, the Roman Tusculum, where we had lunch, and then to Tivoli, where we visited both the Villa D'Este, with its incredible fountains, and the equally incredible Hadrian's Villa. Altogether, this was quite a good programme for one day, but, though I was conscious of the number of things that we *didn't* see, I did not have any sense of haste.

On my second visit, in 1971, I was fortunate to see the excavations of the second-century necropolis under St Peter's, which were begun in 1940 and are generally held to have confirmed the traditional location of the grave of the Prince of the Apostles. Everything is done to make access possible and the only restriction is that imposed by space, which limits the size of parties to fifteen persons. I simply left my name and that of my hotel at the office of the *Scavi* in the Vatican City and on the following day I received a phone call telling me the time of the next English-language party. Apart from myself the party seemed to consist of Americans of very diverse ages and types; one, a priest, introduced himself to me with the explanation that he had heard me lecture in San Francisco! Our guide, who himself spoke excellent English, gave an admirable exposition, which would have been as informative to those who were ignorant of the story of the excavations as it was to me who had made a detailed study of the writings of Fr Engelbert Kirschbaum; altogether it took about an hour and a half and was a thoroughly scholarly exercise for us all. I found it fascinating to examine the street of mausolea, now deep beneath St Peter's, of which I had seen the photographs and plans and pored over the descriptions, but what gave me a real thrill was the sudden realisation that I was walking through

the foundations of the three massive walls which Constantine had
built to support the south side of his basilica. Controversy will no
doubt continue as long as their are scholars to indulge in it, but I
think a responsible judgment would be that the great church on the
Vatican Hill does enshrine the grave of St Peter, but one cannot
be so confident about his bones. Late on my last evening I found
at the hotel an unexpected phone message which initiated a very
pleasant and invigorating acquaintanceship; it was from Cardinal
John Wright, the Prefect of the Congregation for the Clergy and
a former Bishop of Pittsburgh, Pennsylvania. I had been urged to
make myself known to him by Fr Ronald Lawler, the Capuchin
friar whose name has already occurred in this story and who was
very anxious that we should meet. September is of course a bad time
for finding anyone except tourists in Rome, as most of the Vatican
departments and the colleges are virtually closed for the vacation,
but I had written to his office on the off chance of finding him. The
message was to say that he had just returned and to ask me to phone
him back. I did this, explaining that I had to leave at midday and
expected that he would be far too busy to see me. I was, however,
wrong; he sent his secretary, Mgr Donald Wuerl, to the hotel at nine
o'clock next morning to conduct me to his office and we spent the
best part of an hour together. I felt somewhat embarrassed by the
fact that I was dressed in shabby light clothes for travelling, which
hardly seemed appropriate for calling upon a Cardinal of the Holy
Roman Church, but I need not have worried. Cardinal Wright was
a most friendly and informal prelate. His manner and speech were
breezy and idiomatic; when in the following year he gave a lecture
in London he startled his audience by the downright vigour of his
American diction. 'In the Commonwealth of Pennsylvania, where
I was last Bishop, every teacher can be as ignorant as Paddy's pig
on the subject that she's teaching – but she must do a course in
methodology'; or this:

In the whole world of methodology and pedagogy there took place a
revolution which made approximately a million bucks for a professor
who was getting $7000 a year at the University of Toronto up till that
time. He discovered that we have undergone a great change. We have
changed from a reading civilisation into a visual and photographic
civilisation – so Fordham immediately hired him for $100,000 a
year to explain to the students that they like to look at pictures
better than they like to read books. The students hadn't discovered
that yet, you see, and therefore he gave lectures all over the world,
since he had made 'the most important discovery since the invention
of movable type'.

This was not the traditional *stylus curiae*, but it expressed the instinctive reaction of a warm-hearted and pastorally minded bishop whose impulsiveness more than once led him into diplomatic embarrassment. We sat talking in his room, which looked looked to St Peter's across the bottom end of the great colonnade, and, pointing to the name of the Chigi pontiff Alexander VII, he said, 'When I feel things are getting me down I look at that and think what he had to bear.' Twice on my later visits he came to lunch accompanied by his friend Bishop David Maloney; on the second occasion he was obviously a sick man and had difficulty in walking. But he was genial and charming, and congratulated Harry Smythe's housekeeper, Signora Claudia Conti, on her famous dish of *melanzane*. He was in hospital for the conclave of August 1978, which elected Pope John Paul I, but attended in a wheel-chair for the election of John Paul II the next month. He died in August of the following year.

I have said that September was a good time for sightseeing but a bad time academically and ecclesiastically, as the Colleges were closed and almost all the people I should have liked to meet were away. On my third visit Harry invited me to return for a week in December, when the institutions would have come to life. Brief as this was it made a number of contacts which I was able to develop later. I gave a lecture at the Beda College, once famous (and anathema to loyal Anglicans!) as a seminary for converts from the Church of England but now simply for English-speaking men with late vocations; its atmosphere was friendly and relaxed. The Anglican Centre was very near to the great Jesuit University, the Gregorian, and on December 12th several of the Fathers arranged a luncheon for me; I was able to disclose at the end of the meal that, unknowingly, they had given me a birthday-party. One evening we went to Grottaferrata in the Alban Hills, not to the famous Italo-Greek monastery there but to the very much more modern settlement − for it is difficult to know how else to describe it − set up by that remarkable movement the Focolari. It was a very multilingual gathering of, I suppose, well over two hundred people, and, with a lot of translation, the meeting lasted a very long time; it turned into a concelebrated mass, simple but very reverent and with no eccentricities. Then we were given supper with a small group and driven back to Rome. It had been an impressive experience and I felt that I had been in a thoroughly devout and practical community, free from self-consciousness and preciosity. But we were reminded of a sinister aspect of contemporary Rome on our return. It was getting on towards midnight and we had asked our driver to drop us in the Piazza Venezia, where it was easier for him to turn round than at the bottom of the Corso. The streets seemed unusually quiet and we suddenly noticed that they were lined with riot police equipped with enormous shields and standing in complete and ominous silence. Nothing whatever happened and we got to the Anglican Centre unmolested; so what I have recorded was really a non-event. But we heard next morning that it had been preceded by what was anything but a non-event; while we were out at Grottaferrata there had been an outbreak of rioting in Rome, in solidarity with students' upheavals elsewhere, and the police had intervened with violent and, it was said, fatal consequences. My parting memory of Rome in December, however, was of ochre buildings in the low beams of the winter sun, looking so much gentler and softer than they had been with their dazzling surfaces, hard outlines and narrow sharp shadow under the remorseless sky of the summer.

I retired from my chair at King's College, London, in July 1973 and was therefore free, in Maurice Bowra's memorable phrase, to enter upon a wider sphere of uselessness. People who have retired from professional appointments are often accused of salving their consciences by persuading themselves that they are busier than they were when doing full-time jobs. I shall not join that particular band of boasters, but I can truthfully say that the first fifteen months of my retirement were, if not busier, at least more mobile than any comparable period in my life. They included three trips to the United States, which I have already described, and also two to Italy. The first of these was in February 1974; I met Harry Smythe in Rome and spent the following night at the Centre. The following morning we took the train to Salerno, and went on from there by bus to Ravello, changing at Amalfi. The last stage of the journey, which was in a long bus and along a narrow and winding cliffside road, put rather a strain on one's nerves, especially when we performed a complicated reversing manoeuvre, largely, as it seemed, hanging over space, to negotiate a very sharp turn. Ravello is described as 'the most tranquil, solitary and silent city in the world'. So the official guide-book quotes Mario Stefanile; and even in February it was delightful. The chief hotels are the former palaces of the nobility, on the high ground away from the sea; ours was just opposite the church of San Giovanni del Toro — St John of the Bull — though what bull it was and what it did was not clear. The cathedral — for Ravello still officially has a cathedral though it has not had its own bishop since 1818 — contains a splendid cosmatesque pulpit, whose six supporting pillars stand on the most charming figures of small lions, which in fact look rather more like chubby pet dogs. It also contains a relic of the blood of its titular, St Pantaleone, which, in common with similar relics in the south of Italy, is accustomed to liquefy on expected occasions. But it is for its two beautiful villas, the Rufulo and the Cimbrone, that Ravello is most celebrated; both consist of rambling but imposing buildings set in glorious gardens, and the tip of the Cimbrone gardens hangs vertiginously over the sea. The Rufino claims to have inspired both Giovanni Boccaccio and Richard Wagner; the latter is recorded to have cried, in 'an impetus of triumphant joy', *Ecco il magnifico giardino di Klongsor!* Certainly one could feel a touch of eeerieness if not of witchcraft in the secluded corner which is known as 'the magic garden'. The Cimbrone owes its greater splendour to an English nobleman, the Hon. Ernest Beckett, afterwards Lord Grimthorpe, who fell in love with it at the end of the last century, acquired it in 1904 through the skill of an intermediary, Nicola Mansi, whom he had met when the latter was working as a waiter in London, spent a vast sum on its amplification, and arranged that after his death, which occurred in 1917, his ashes should be interred under the little Temple of Bacchus which he had built and had inscribed with some of the more respectable verses of Catullus. His religious views were presumably unlike those of the first Baron, who was president of the Protestant Churchmen's Alliance.

Mass on the Sunday morning at San Giovanni was vernacular but ill attended; it is only fair to note that this was in a thinly populated part of the city. It was surprising to hear the hymns vigorously sung in Italian to the melodies of Wales! On the following day we were due to leave, and we were given a kind but hair-raising lift in a small car to Sorrento by the coast road through Positano; after lunching at Sorrento we went to Naples on the pleasant light railway which rejoices in the title of the *Circumvesuviana*. Harry had been in Naples before but it was my first visit and I was to address some of the students at the Theological Institute of Southern Italy, which is high up on Capodimonte and just over the road from the archidiocesan seminary, with which it is closely associated. My own contact there was with a very able young professor, Fr Bruno Forte, who had stayed with us for a month at Bourne Street; his Archbishop, Cardinal Ursi, was giving him responsibilities for Ecumenism and had wished him to see something of a typical Anglican parish. He had in fact showed great initiative and had even included a trip to Edinburgh in his self-education. I was delighted to renew our friendship; his name will appear again later on. We returned to Rome the following day and I found waiting for me a ticket for a papal audience the day after.

Pope Paul was of course now back in the Vatican City, so I was received in the great new audience hall or, to be precise, in a smaller hall in the same building. In the ante-room where I waited one could watch on television a massive audience that was taking place in the main hall; one could also observe those who, like myself, were awaiting their turn to be received privately. We were a mixed body, about fifteen in all, several typical American males, three ladies of aristocratic appearance clad very correctly in long black dresses with mantillas, and an Italian woman of the working class in her Sunday-best accompanied by her teen-age daughter. When my turn came I was received very graciously by the Holy Father, who held my hands between his own while we talked for several minutes, mainly about his interest in Cardinal Newman; intermittent clicks in the background betrayed the presence of the photographer, from whom I later received five remarkable fine coloured specimens of his skill. I left with the pontifical blessing and a fine medallion, which I treasured with the one that I had received four years before at Castel Gandolfo, until they were both stolen one day from my flat. In view of current controversy there was a certain piqancy about the inscription which it bore, declaring that Holy Mother Church defends the gift of human life, *humanae vitae*. On leaving the presence I had just time to get in a taxi to the English College – the famous *Venerabile* – where I had been invited to lunch. There followed two quite crowded days, lunch at the Anglican Centre, with Cardinal Wright and his friend Bishop Maloney, and Fr Martin Molyneux from the Beda, then – as a frivolous relaxation – a visit to the Rome Opera to hear Donizetti's *Il Trionfo di Amore* (we sat in the gallery and had a quite exciting experience of what audience-participation means in Italy); the next day Canon William Purdy of the Secretariate for Unity came to lunch, and in the evening I dined at the English College and gave a talk about modern spirituality. (Here I may interject that the Venerable English College is the leading seminary in Rome for English candidates for the diocesan priesthood; its relations with Anglicanism have in recent years been extremely cordial, and it was there that Archbishop Michael Ramsey stayed when he made his historic visit to Pope Paul; Anglican theological students have been welcomed as guests; and its genial and hospitable Rector Mgr Cormac Murphy O'Connor has recently become better known to English people as Bishop of Arundel and Brighton.) In the two days that I had left I spoke at the Anglican Centre and at the Library of the Graymoor Friars, besides having a long conversation over lunch with Mgr Charles Moeller, whom I had met at Toronto in 1967; he had now become Secretary of the Secretariate for Christian Unity, and from his apartment in the Via dell'Erba one looked down into the battlemented passage along the top of the *corridoro* which, in more turbulent times, provided hard-pressed pontiffs with an escaperoute from the Vatican to the Castel Sant'Angelo. I was also entertained to dinner by three young English monks at Sant'Anselmo, the international Benedictine College on the Aventine Hill, one of the two spots in Rome where I felt real quiet and seclusion (the other is the garden of the Palazzo dei Conservatori, on the Capitol).

Returning to London, I found St Mary's, Bourne Street, in the full flood of preparation for the centenary celebrations which were to take place in the summer. These opened, on Sunday June 30th, with a pontifical mass, at which the celebrant and preacher was Dr Graham Leonard, the Bishop of Truro. He had formerly been a suffragan in the London diocese; what neither he nor anyone else of course knew was that seven years later he would become Bishop of London itself. Then the Blessed Sacrament was exposed for adoration and intercession for forty hours; prayer was kept continously and the church was ablaze with the light of candles; the sermon was preached by Eric Abbott, the former Dean of Westminster. On the following day, at the Centenary Mass, the preacher was the Archbishop of Canterbury Michael Ramsey, and it was pleasant for me to recall that, years ago, these two had been, the one my chief and the other my predecessor, at Lincoln Theological College. Other visitors during the Centenary were the Bishop of Exeter, Robert Mortimer, (my predecessor at Christ Church, Oxford) and Trevor Huddleston, then Bishop of Stepney but more famous for his championship of the negroes in South Africa and his disturbing book *Naught for your Comfort*. It was certainly a time of great joy and thankfulness, but it left one wondering what would be the condition of things in the year 2074 – and grateful that one simply did not know.

The beginning of December found me back in Rome. The weather was warm and sunny and, even with some austerity in lighting caused by a fuel-crisis, the preparations for Christmas were much in evidence. The stalls were being erected in the Piazza Navona and the streets off the Corso were delightful with Christmas trees and no wheeled traffic. I was staying as before at the Anglican Centre and I lectured there as well as the Gregorian University and the Beda. I was invited to a very enjoyable anniversary luncheon at the English College, where I met three students from King's College, London, who were there. From Rome Harry Smythe and I went by train to Florence, where he had arranged for me to deliver two lectures, one at the Archepiscopal Seminary and one at a public meeting at the Jesuit centre. This was my first – and much overdue – visit to Florence and in the three days that we were there I saw as much as I could – which was needless to say much less than I could have wished. We stayed at the famous and magnificent Abbey of San Miniato overlooking the city, and I was given the most splendid guest-suite I have ever occupied – two enormous rooms with gorgeously painted walls and ceilings and, through an almost invisible door, a fully equipped modern American bathroom! The monks, a quite small community of Olivetan Benedictines, wear white habits. The Abbot, Dom Vittorio Aldinucci, was the ecumenical officer of the diocese and a perfect host; he gave up a complete morning to show me round the Uffizi Gallery. We were allowed the use of an altar in the abbey church. I was deeply moved to be shown the grave of the Anglican Franciscan Father Peter, who had several times stayed with me in college at Oxford; he had died suddenly at San Miniato and and was buried in the monks' own cemetery. We managed to see the famous cathedral baptistry and also Santa Croce and San Lorenzo (with the fine tomb of the antipope John XXIII, or, as the inscription tactfully names him, *Johannes Quondam Papa*), but had time for nothing more. Having a sentimental attachment to the Stuarts, I was interested to locate in Santa Croce the tombs of Louise Stolberg, the wayward wife of the tragic Young Pretender (Charles III), and of her lover, the poet Alfieri, though in different chapels and without any indication of their connection! We were received by the Archbishop, Cardinal Ermenegildo Florit, who had a reputation at Vatican II for extreme conservatism but whom we found most friendly and fatherly; all the time we were with him I was reminded of Pope John XXIII (not the antipope this time!) and I treasure a book of pictures of the cathedral which he inscribed and gave to me when we left. My only unpleasant recollection of Florence was of the temperature, which was really bitter!

On leaving Florence we spent a night in Verona, with the Franciscans at San Bernardino. We had to leave early on the Sunday morning – it was the Feast of the Immaculate Conception – after attending mass in their chapel. We had time for only some brief informal conversations, but I was impressed by the simple and homely atmosphere which had somehow been preserved in this vast and, now alas, only partly inhabited monastery. I had a parting gift, from a brother who was a musical expert, of a record of Mozart's Requiem Mass; long afterwards, he – Frate Ireneo – sent me the announcement of his ordination to the priesthood.

From Verona we went on by train to Innsbruck over the Brenner Pass, moving roughly parallel with the motor-road and getting a sensational view of the great new road-bridge. Incidentally, I was interested to observe the extreme casualness of the passport and customs examination at both the Italian-Austrian and the Austrian-German frontiers since the advent of EEC. Memories of being turned out on the platform in the middle of a cold night at Aachen in the 1930s and of more recent complications with American officials at Detroit Airport made the casual glance through the carriage-window at Brenner and Kufstein extremely welcome.

Innsbruck is one of the great centres of Austrian baroque, as well as housing the finest collection of Tyrolean folk-art in existence. The fascinating museum of Christmas cribs, of every degree of simplicity and complexity and of every variety of style, has been maintained continuously down to the present day and contains some very striking contemporary examples. A very pleasing feature is the provision of several steps in front of each exhibit for the convenience of the more juvenile members of the public, who visit the gallery in large numbers. The Summer Palace witnesses to the Holy Roman Empire at its most opulent; the gigantic ball-room, whose walls incorporate separate full-length portraits of the Empress Maria-Teresa's sixteen children, advertises imperial family-planning on a heroic scale. But it is of course in the churches that Austrian baroque finds its most natural expression, and in comparison with it the baroque of Rome is almost puritanically restrained and austere. The imperial chapel contains, along the length of its nave, the great avenue of more than life-size bronze statues of medieval warriors, of which the best known to English people is the fine figure of King Arthur in late medieval armour. I must, however, confess that I was specially intrigued by one worthy, whose face, alone of the whole number, was concealed in a helmet of an oddly pointed shape, which gave him the appearance of some prehistoric bird or space-age visitant from another world; but his identity and the reason for this concealment I could not discover.

We stayed in Innsbruck at the Canesianum, an impressive international theological institute, run by the Jesuit fathers but containing many non-Jesuit students of over seventy nationalities. Lecturing was made easier for me by the fact that a very large number spoke English or at least understood it. The famous brothers Karl and Hugo Rahner had once been professors there. The chapel, a superbly ornate baroque edifice, had presented something of a problem to the reforming zeal of the avant-garde liturgists of the present day, especially because the building was protected by legislation as an ancient monument. However, with a heroic defiance of both aesthetic and economic considerations, the walls and the entrance to the sanctuary had been covered over by immense white plastic Venetian blinds, in front of the last of which a very functional altar was placed. By electrical means this blind could be raised in order to reveal the now abandoned high-altar for the benefit of nostalgic visitors. Beneath the ceiling a great convex cylindrical white plastic false roof was slung, higher at one side than at the other; this, we were rather anxiously assured, greatly improved he acoustics. Altogether this was the most thorough-going example I have seen of the conscientious application of a principle regardless of all other considerations. But I was much impressed by the intellectual vigour and the spirit of tolerance in this highly multi-national and multi-racial community; and the hospitality and consideration with which they entertained their Anglican visitors was delightful.

I had one quite unforgettable experience. One free afternoon the young Jesuit who was looking after us enquired whether we would like to go for a drive to the mountain-resort of Achenkirch. I accepted eagerly, as I had had a summer holiday there with Christopher Waddams over forty years ago. We set out in a small car. Innsbruck itself was rather misty, but as we want up the valley of the Inn the fog thickened considerably and when we turned off up the Achen valley it became denser and denser, until when we got well up into the mountains all we could see was snow piled up on either side of the road. By this time the expedition seemed to me to be thoroughly futile, as we could see nothing and looked like being stranded in the fog. However our driver was unconcerned and continued to drive quite fast, and I was fortunately sufficiently restrained to keep silent. Suddenly we came to a spot where it seemed to have become clearer, and he drove the car into a small parking-place facing up the slope of the mountain. 'We get out here for a moment,' he said, and so we did. Then he said, 'Now turn round,' and we obeyed. And there we were, just above the level of the fog and in front of us, stretching away on either side were the snow covered mountains, gleaming in the sun, with dazzling blue sky behind them. And then we drove on for another five or six miles in the brilliant sunshine by the side of the Achensee, before turning back to plunge again into the fog on our way back to the city of Innsbruck.

After this it is anti-climactic to say that two days later I caught the train from Innsbruck at 7.30 a.m. to get the plane at Munich Airport, and was back at Bourne Street soon after 3 p.m. with memories of eleven crowded and delightful days and a faint hope to have done something for the cause of Christian unity.

My latest, and as far as I can tell, my final visit to Italy took place more than a year later, in the spring of 1976. It arose out of an agreement between the Gregorian University and the Anglican Centre, generously backed by S.P.C.K., to have an annual course of lectures by a visiting Anglican theologian. The project was initiated by a brilliant course on Anglican Spirituality by Harry Smythe himself; I took as my subject 'The Unity of Christian Doctrine', with the sub-title 'An Anglican Presentation', and my intention, whether I was successful or not, was not so much to demonstrate an achieved and formulated position over against that of other Christian churches as to make an Anglican contribution to a developing and still fluid situation. I have already said something about the Anglican Centre; now for something about the Gregorian University.

'University', in the language of ecclesiastical Rome, has retained its original meaning, of a corporate body, especially one of academic type, and does not mean an organisation of universal scope that tries to teach everything under the sun. The ecclesiastical universities in Rome are all concerned with some aspect or aspects of theology, in the wide sense that the word 'theology' has come to have in Britain; in Rome, theology means what we would call systematic or dogmatic theology, and a great institution like the Gregorian is divided into faculties of theology, philosophy, church history, spirituality, sacred scripture, missiology, canon law and so forth, while a smaller one may have a more limited and specialised scope. Of the multi-faculty ecclesiastical universities, the Gregorian, with something like 300 teachers and 3,000 students, is the largest. It is under the direction of the Jesuit order. It began in 1552 (an ominous date for Anglicans!) and was refounded in 1582 by Pope Gregory XIII, from whom its takes its name, though its earlier title was simply the Collegium Romanum. Gregory's interest in scholarship is shown, among other things, by the reform of the Calendar which, like the University, bears his name. The Universities are purely teaching and research institutions; none of the students and only some of the teachers live in them. The students eat and sleep and get their social life either in the various national colleges or, if they are members of religious orders, in the houses of their respective orders, of which there are, of course, a vast number. The English College, in the Via Monserrato, the Beda, just by the Basilica of St Paul, and the Benedictine College of Sant' Anselmo, on the Aventine, became specially familiar to me. I lunched at Sant' Anselmo on the day after my arrival; on the previous day the future Cardinal Hume and I travelled together to Rome on the same plane and it had been expected that we should make contact, but by some strange chance we failed to do so. One consequence was a phone call in which I thought that I had been answered by a junior monk but in fact was talking to the Abbot Primate! But that sort of thing happens in Rome. The North American (i.e. U.S.A.) College, on the Janiculum, is a vast building with a splendid view over the city from its roof, but it was alas nothing like full. One satisfying fact for a visiting lecturer is that the students, having been specially chosen by their dioceses or orders, are of very high grade intellectually; only the best ones make the grade for Rome. A sad fact was that there were very few from the Latin American countries; the plight of their currencies, which was even worse than that of the lira, was the reason, and the Gregorian could no longer, as formerly, give its teaching free of charge. Two great changes since Vatican II are concerned with clothing and language. No longer are the streets of Rome made picturesque by the variegated garments of the national colleges and the religious orders. The students look much like students elsewhere, with open-necked shirts, anoraks and jeans; even those who are priests are often unrecognisable as such. Only the nuns − or some of them − preserve something like their old appearance, though they too have undergone *aggiornamento*. The language had also changed except; in the faculty of Canon Law, Latin was practically extinct; its place was almost entirely taken by Italian, as the language which anyone living in Rome was compelled to acquire, and more and more theological books were being published in that tongue. It is easy enough to acquire for reading purposes and my own belief is that theologians would be wise to learn it. My own lectures were perforce in English, which limited my class to English-speakers. English is, however, one of the most widely − possibly *the* most widely − spoken of languages today, and few of the twenty students who formed my class were United-Kingdom citizens. Ireland, the United States, Australia, and various countries of Africa and Asia contributed to its composition. Apart from this, and the fact that they were, as I have said, picked persons, they were very much like the more mature students in England. They were anxious to learn as much as they could about Anglicanism, the study of which was of course a non-compulsory subject for which they had deliberately opted, but were, I felt, chiefly concerned to get a grasp of the way that an Anglican theologian viewed the whole corpus of Christian belief and the manner in which his mind worked when he was theologising. They were eager to discuss, and were as laudably uninhibited as English students are in expressing their views; and they were grateful for any opportunities of personal contacts that their heavily loaded work-schedules made possible. Personally I found lecturing at the Gregorian an exhilarating and rewarding experience. And I very much enjoyed the conversations which I had with various students for higher degrees who dropped in to the Centre to talk about their work, which might be on some specific topic concerning Anglicanism (this was a quite popular field) or on some issue in philosophical or dogmatic theology which was up my street.

My contacts with the professors in the Faculty were cordial and theologically profitable. Fr René Latourelle, the Dean, a French Canadian and the author of books on Revelation, was as charming in person as his beautifully written letters in French had led me to expect. He and his Dutch assistant Fr Witte made me wonderfully welcome and arranged a dinner-party for me soon after my arrival. I was specially glad to make the acquaintance of Fr Jean Galot, who is a Belgian formerly teaching at Louvain and in my opinion is one of the best theologians alive today. Unfortunately, his books, which were written in either French or Italian, were little known in English-speaking circles and, unjustly in my opinion, neglected elsewhere; more recently they have begun to appear in English. We had several most interesting meetings and have corresponded with each other since.

Harry Smythe was, as always, a splendid host, but I did not spend all my time at the Centre. I paid two brief visits to Naples, where Bruno Forte had arranged for me to conduct a seminar at the Theological Institute; it is an impressive place of learning, in spite of the inevitable magnetic attraction of the great Roman colleges only a hundred miles to the north, and its journal, named *Asprenas* after the first Bishop of Naples, contains articles of high quality. Bruno, who must have been one of the youngest teachers on its staff, is also the youngest member of a family of eight, all of whom are engaged in professional pursuits, and it was a joy to meet his parents, who had an apartment of typically Neapolitan character not far from the sea-front. On one wall there hung a series of portraits, taken at some date in the past by a photographer friend; the last was of

a small boy with black hair and dark, flashing eyes, the youthful
Bruno. I stayed in the Archidiocesan Seminary on Capodimonte,
an imposing building just above the great domed church of Santa
Maria Immacolata and looking over the city to the sea. A friend of
Bruno's took us both one morning to Pompeii; it was, of course,
intensely interesting, but I laugh sardonically when I read how one
leans on a hot wall under the blazing sun, watching the lizards
scuttling into the shade; when I was there it was cold and cloudy,
with an intermittent drizzle, and any lizards had taken precautions
to scuttle away well in advance. (In fact on all my visits to Naples
the weather was cold and wet and quite unlike what the English
visitor expects in the south of Italy.) More interesting almost than
Pompeii was the catacomb of St Januarius (San Gennaro), just
under Capodimonte. It is entirely unlike the Roman catacombs
and consists not of passages but of two large caverns on different
levels; they are lavishly adorned with paintings, some of which are
dated back to the fifth century A.D. A puzzling feature is that one
of the painted figures, which is clearly labelled as St Januarius,
has on his nimbus the Alpha-Omega and Chi-Rho symbols which
are always indicative of Christ. The guide-book describes this as
'a sign of very special honour'; I wonder whether, as I have
suspected with some other anomalies, that the explanation may
be the simple one that the painter was hurried and distracted and
just made a mistake. Bruno took me on a rapid tour of some
of the other sights: the Cathedral, where is the blood of the
Saint which regularly liquefies, and the Dominican church which
houses the crucifix which spoke to St Thomas Aquinas. But also –
and this was much more impressive – I was shown something of
the evangelistic and educational work which the Church is doing,
especially among the young, and of the realistic and thoroughly
contemporary functioning of the Missionary Institute. This entirely
disposed of the common notion that mediterranean Catholicism is
superstitious, complacent and corrupt. Cardinal Corrado Ursi, the
Archbishop, whom I met twice, is a sensitive and inspiring leader;
he has twice been mentioned as a possible pope.

For most of this visit, which lasted just over ten weeks, I was
enjoying the long-suffering hospitality of Harry Smythe, but for
one week I accepted an invitation to stay at the Beda. Some years
ago the Beda moved out from the centre of Rome to a large
and convenient modern building near St Paul's-outside-the-Walls
in a growing and largely slummy district. Being a college for late
vocations, it draws from an astonishing variety of educational,
social and geographical backgrounds. As is appropriate with older

and mature men, there is a great deal of freedom and, with it, of individual responsibility, and it was most impressive to see how strong a sense of corporate life was evident in spite (or was it because?) of such a wide variety of personality and corporate experience. This is a great tribute to the wisdom and understanding of the Rector and the other members of the staff. One privilege which the Beda enjoyed was that of being not on Italian but on Vatican City territory, and this, I gathered, carried considerable advantages of a fiscal kind. Certainly, the catering, which was done by English nuns was excellent and one could even have on occasion what is unknown in Italy, a roast joint with vegetables!

Being at the Beda gave me the opportunity of seeing two places which I had previously missed, namely the Catacomb of Domitilla and the Monastery of Trefontane, and to each of these I was accompanied by Fr Martin Molyneux, who was most solicitous for my welfare. Domitilla is distinguished by the vast half-underground basilica which was cut out of the sloping hillside at the entrance. It is maintained by a German brotherhood and I presume it was one of these who acted as our guide, though he was in ordinary lay attire. He was most attentive and at the end of the circuit asked whether there was anything else we would like to know. I remembered having read that somewhere in Domitilla there was one of the very few mosaics to be found in any catacomb and I enquired about this. He was delighted and led us back along a maze of passages and finally up a long and narrow staircase, at the top of which was a small burial chamber containing the mosaic of Christ between St Peter and St Paul. I had previously seen the catacombs of Sebastian, Callixtus and Priscilla, but I think Domitilla is more interesting, though Priscilla, under the Via Salaria on the north side of Rome in the care of Benedictine nuns, runs it very close, containing among other fascinating paintings what is probably the earliest known representation of our Lady and the Holy Child. The famous Trappist abbey of the Trefontane, with the adjoining two churches, has all the austere tranquillity that the guide-books ascribe to it, but I was equally impressed with the encampment, for it is difficult to know how else to describe it, which the Little Sisters of Jesus, inspired by the teaching of Charles de Foucauld, have established for their novitiate on the slope of the hillside above. Everything is of the greatest simplicity, with the chapel made out of a cave. Fr Luff writes that 'the hutted novitiate is reminiscent of a Wild West town in the old style', but I find it hard to imagine a Wild West town so peaceful and contemplative.

But there is surely an object-lesson in the collocation of these two forms of contemplative spirituality, the Reformed Cistercians of the Stricter Observance and the Little Sisters going out each day to work in the world. My week at the Beda was a most delightful interlude; I will only add that there, as at Naples, it was taken for granted that I would celebrate mass each day, and I was given all facilities for doing so.

Holy Week gave me the opportunity to be present at the public celebration of the great liturgical ceremonies by Pope Paul. I am glad to have had this experience once in my lifetime, but, in spite of all that is done to ensure the essentials of reverence and order, Rome when it is full of tourists, many of whom have little or no understanding of the Catholic religion, is not the best place for devout participation in the mysteries of our redemption. On Palm Sunday and Good Friday the Pope celebrated in St Peter's; on Maundy Thursday, in his cathedral church of St John Lateran. On this last occasion one was made acutely conscious of the problems raised by the increased number of communicants in consequence of the recent relaxations of the Eucharistic fast. In St Peter's a number of priests holding ciboria stood before the altar and communicants lined up in front of each of them, so at least the minimum element of a deliberate decision to apply for the sacrament was preserved. At the Lateran, however, and I have seen this in other churches too, priests with ciboria walked about through the crowd standing in the nave and put hosts into the mouths of any who were willing to receive them. So perhaps I ought not to have been surprised when, on running after the mass into a young couple whom I had met in England and knew to be members of Dr Moon's Unification Church, one of them said to me, 'We thought it was so nice to take communion at the Pope's service'. I was left wondering what all the discussions on intercommunion were really about! On Easter Day Harry had obtained tickets for the Pope's mass in St Peter's Square; this was a tremendous and spectacular function, though hardly a devotional one. The weather, which had been dull and chilly all through Holy Week, suddenly cleared and the mass was celebrated in brilliant sunshine. Then at lunch-time the clouds returned and down came the rain. After Easter I realised a long-held desire, when we went for a few days to Ravenna and Venice. Ravenna came up to all my expectations, and, although we were there for little more than twenty-four hours, it is so compact that we managed to see enough to make all the pictures and accounts in the books a living reality. Sant'Apollinare in Classe and Sant'Apollinare Nuovo, San Vitale and Galla Placidia, the two Baptistries, all these, with their

glorious mosaics, live in my mind with a vividness shared, I think,
by no other places that I have seen. I will add only one brief
note to the descriptions in the guide-books. The church of San
Francesco, which dates in its present form from the ninth and
eleventh centuries, has, like many other churches of the period,
under the high-altar, a *confessio*, that is, a crypt reached by steps
from the nave and intended for the tomb or reliquary of a saint.
What, however, to one's surprise and delight, one finds at the
bottom of the steps in San Francesco is a lake with goldfish
swimming in it. The explanation is in fact simple. Ravenna is
built on a swamp, into which it has gradually sunk; and the crypt
of San Francesco has sunk no less than six feet. So the water was
an uninvited intruder into the resting-place of the saintly Bishop
Neon. But what a happy thought it was to add the goldfish! And
then Venice.

If I say that my predominant feeling towards the *Serenissima* is
one of dislike, I hope I shall not for that reason be condemned
as either a Philistine or a Vandal. There can be few lovelier
sights in Europe than that of Santa Maria della Salute or San
Giorgio, with their steps coming down to the canal. No means of
transport (in fine weather) can be more romantic than gliding in a
gondola or more fun than popping in a vaporetto. If I had more
knowledge of Renaissance painting than I have I should, I am
sure, have been intoxicated by a city in which Giorgiones, Titians
and Tintorettos confront one on every hand. Two of my favourite
composers are Monteverdi and Vivaldi. And, being fascinated by
mosaics, I could hardly drag myself away from San Marco, which
is just simply mosaics all over. It is a joy, and one that can be
experienced nowhere else, to walk about a city which is entirely
devoid of wheeled traffic. And I wish the Venetians all success in
their endeavours to save their unique achievement from vanishing
beneath the lagoon. What then is the ground for my repugnance?
Simply that the accumulation of all these wonders is the result of
a career, extending over centuries, of ostentation, greed and theft,
compounded by guile and deceit and almost unrelieved by any
nobler motive. The famous four bronze horses over the portal of
San Marco and the great gold reredos – the *Pala d'Oro* – are loot
from the sacking of Constantinople in 1204, that act of fratricidal
treachery within the Body of Christ which Eastern Christendom
has not to this day felt able to forgive. All cities and states have
strands of sin woven into even their finest accomplishments, but
Venice would appear to have made the lust of the flesh and the
lust of the eyes and the pride of life the all but explicit principle of

its being. Even the body of its patron saint was avowedly obtained
by theft. If its ultimate fate is to be engulphed by the waves,
perhaps our comment may best be given in those devastating words
by which the great Augustine demolished at one stroke all the
constructions of human vainglory – *acceperunt mercedem suam,
vani vanam*, they have received their reward, a reward as hollow
as they.

Our trip to Ravenna and Venice was in Easter-Week and was pure
relaxation, but shortly afterwards we made an excursion to Siena,
where we were to visit a Franciscan monastery on the outskirts of
the city. We arrived by train and waited long and fruitlessly at the
taxi-rank, until a kindly passer-by offered the explanation *sciopero*;
the word was all too familiar, strikes being as frequent in Italy
as in Britain and much more sudden and unheralded. We were
rescued by our hosts in response to a phone-call. The friars were
charming and hospitable, but the conditions were austere; although
the temperature was below freezing, there was no heating and the
windows were mostly wide open. With Harry's aid as interpreter I
gave a couple of talks, and we had what was to me a novel form of
Eucharistic celebration. Harry was the celebrant, using the 'Series
Two' of the Church of England, translated by himself into Italian,
with the friars all present and joining in the dialogue; and, then at
the time of communion, while Harry and I received the sacramental
elements which he had consecrated, the Franciscan superior fetched
the reserved Sacrament from an adjacent chapel and communicated
his brethren at the same time. This arrangement, which was the
nearest thing to full intercommunion that was compatible with the
existing regulations, had, we were told, the full approval of the
Archbishop. We went on from Siena to Assisi for two days and
were there for the local May-Day festival. The *Calendimaggio*, as it
is called, is a most colourful occasion. All the inhabitants of Assisi,
or at any rate the younger ones, male and female, put on medieval
costume and march in procession, bearing splendid banners, with
which they perform the most dazzling evolutions. And all this, of
course, takes place in the brilliant sunshine and lovely warm spring
weather – or so the books say.

On May-Day 1976 Assisi certainly had brilliant sunshine, but the
temperature never rose above freezing and the wind was biting. The
participants seemed quite undaunted, but I was glad to view most
of the proceedings through the window. On returning to Rome
I had ten days in which to tidy up my work at the Gregorian
before flying back to England. This would seem to be a suitable
place in which to gather up one or two impressions and memories

which have so far eluded my pen. There was lunch with Cardinal Sergio Pignedoli, the gracious and genial President of the Secretariate for Non-believers (among whom he clearly did not number us!) in the beautiful apartment which he occupied in the Vatican City immediately over the long-suffering Ukrainian quasi-patriarch Cardinal Slipyi. There was the shameful incident, for such an experienced traveller as myself, of having my wallet stolen in the standard location of a crowded No. 64 bus after High Mass at St Peter's on a Sunday. There was the joy of indulging my wholly amateur love of mosaics in the various Roman basilicas, or of finding some unexpected pre-Christian buildings that had been unearthed under a later church. And, although museums interested me less on the whole than churches, I spent several mornings in the Vatican Galleries, the Palazzo Barberini and the Villa Borghese on the Pincio, where it requires a strong will to refrain from ducking when you suddenly come upon Bernini's David about to lauch the stone at you from his sling. I spent some time tracing the footsteps of the Stuarts, starting from the Palazzo Muti (now called the Palazzo Balestra), which they occupied on the narrow north side of the Piazza dei SS. Apostoli. It is now split up and appallingly dilapidated, but a tablet in the archway announces in Italian that 'There once dwelt in this Palace Henry, Duke and afterwards Cardinal of York, who as sole surviving son of James III of England took the title of Henry IX and in whom the Dynasty of Stuart expired in the year 1807.' In fact James III himself and also his elder son Charles III lived there too, and James in his later years spent long hours in prayer in the neighbouring church of the Apostles; the heart of his wife, Clementina Sobieski, is enclosed in one of the pillars of the nave. There always seemed to me to be a remarkable atmosphere of peace in this church and during my time at the Gregorian I often made use of it for my prayers. The other two churches with Stuart associations were both at different times titular churches of Henry as Cardinal: Santa Maria in Campitelli, where prayers are still regularly said for the conversion of England, and Santa Maria in Trastevere; in both of these the Stuart armorials are in evidence. James, Clementina, Charles and Henry are all buried in the crypt of St Peter's. Clementina, who pre-deceased her husband by more than thirty years, has her own monument there and is one of the few women who has. James and his two sons have their famous monument by Canova in the south aisle, but it is not, I think, often noticed that the inscription is tactfully worded to take account of the fact that, while the Holy See recognised the regal title of James, it would never, in spite of repeated requests, recognise those of Charles and Henry, through its desire to avoid offending the Hanoverians.[4]

Finally, because this chronicle must have an end, I must mention the morning which Mgr Charles Burns, of the Vatican Archives, invited Harry Smythe and me to see some of the documents in his charge. We expected to be fascinated, but what we saw left us in such a daze that on returning to the Centre we sat down and independently made lists of the documents that we had seen, to convince ourselves that we were not suffering from hallucinations. First, a random list of some of the signatures we were shown: Henry VIII, Galileo, Mary Queen of Scots, Erasmus, Thomas Wolsey, Michel Angelo, St Teresa of Avila and Napoleon. Then again, at random, some documents of historical interest: the deed of union of the Greek and Latin Churches at the Council of Florence, sealed in lead by Pope Eugenius IV and in gold by the Emperor John Palaeologus; the dispensation for Henry VIII's marriage to Catharine of Aragon; a series of letters from Henry, backed by a petition from the nobles of England, headed by Wolsey and Wareham, for the annulment of the same marriage some years later; a letter from England reporting the execution of Bishop John Fisher; the formal excommunication of Martin Luther; the bull *Regnans in Eccelsis*, deposing Elizabeth I from her throne. Going back a little: the Register of Pope John VIII, c. 870; letters from the Pope to William the Conqueror and the Empress Matilda; the bull of Alexander VI dividing the New World between Spain and Portugal; and — an unofficial item this — a small collection of letters between the same Pope and his daughter Lucrezia Borgia. A long dark green scroll with gold Asiatic writing, which was a letter from the nephew of Genghis Khan. And, coming again to a later date, the instrument of abdication of Queen Christina of Sweden, witnessed by three hundred of her nobles, with their seals hanging on it by long strings. Some of these one had, of course, seen pictures of in books. But to me the most surprising, and perhaps the most moving, were two tiny letters, about six inches by three and folded three times each way, which had been written by our King Charles I to Pope Innocent X and secretly conveyed to Rome: *Beatissime Pater ... Sanctitatis Vestrae Humilimum et obedientissimum servum. Charles R. Apud Curiam nostram Oxoniae. Octob. 20. 1645.* There was nothing in itself compromising in the contents, which merely introduced the Earl of Glamorgan, but one can imagine what use could have been made of the mere fact of their existence. This was altogether a most memorable morning, and among the lighter moments was

Mgr Burn's story of the medieval abbot tapping the shoulder of a young monk in the scriptorium with the words 'Go easy on the gold-leaf, my son; it's a begging letter that you're writing.'

A cynic once remarked that, as far as he could see, the chief purpose of the Ecumenical Movement had been to provide free travel and hospitality for clergymen, and I suppose I have done a good deal to provide an excuse for that judgment. It is not for me to assess the value of any contribution that I have made in return. But I would just say this, and especially to those younger Christians who express exasperation at the slowness of the movement for unity: if your memory went back only thirty years, you would thank God in astonishment at the change that has taken place in that brief period. In 1950 Anglican and Roman Catholic priests hardly ever met, and if they did it was in an atmosphere of studied politeness or careful defensiveness which made any constructive discussion impossible; and the frank exploration of common problems and strategies was out of the question. The suggestion that the day would soon come when the Pope and the Archbishop of Canterbury would sign a joint statement in the Sistine Chapel, that Dr Randall Davidson's successor would preach in Westminster Cathedral and Cardinal Bourne's in St Paul's would have been received with the scandalised protest that even romantic fiction would bear some faint appearance of verisimilitude. But to my mind, quite as significant as these great public occasions, and even as the agreed statements of joint commissions, is the quiet and constructive way in which theologians of the different communions have been able to discuss the problems with which they are faced in the modern world both from within and from without their borders. I was amused to rediscover recently the following paragraph from *The Tablet* of September 28th 1963:

> The Congregation of Seminaries and Universities has refused permission to the faculty of theology of the Catholic University of Nijmegen, Holland, to grant an honorary doctorate to the Anglican theologian Dr E. L. Mascall. This decision, which has aroused concern among academic circles in Nijmegen, is said by the Dutch Catholic News agency KNP to have been based on the advice of the late Cardinal Godfrey: the Congregation held that an honorary degree would be inopportune both because of the position of Catholics in England and because of controversy within the Church of England over Dr Mascall's position.

It is perhaps a measure of the extent to which relations have changed in less than twenty years that I had entirely forgotten this incident. And it provides added ground for thankfulness that I have been able, under the hand of God, to make some small contribution to the great cause of Christian unity. *Eppur si muove.*

Notes

1. I must however record my surprise at the ommission, in so omniscient a work, of any reference, in text or plan, to the churches of St Alexis and St Sylvester *in Capite*, the latter, just by the General Post Office, being the centre for English Roman Catholics!
2. *The Companion Guide to Rome*, p. 50.
3. Even at liturgical services in St Peter's the Pope is now greeted only with a simple bow of the head.
4. It runs (in translation): 'To James III, the Son of King James II of Great Britain, and to Charles Edward and to Henry, Dean of the Cardinal Fathers, the Sons of James III, last of the Royal Line of Stuart. In the Year 1819'.

Epilogue

Je te salue, heureuse et profitable Mort

– Ronsard

Whatever this book may be, it is not an *apologia pro vita mea*, for as I look back on my life the one thing that is clear is that I have had very little say in designing it. There have been critical moments when it was not at all obvious what I was meant to do next; but this was not because I was faced with an embarrassing variety of alternatives between which to choose but because, as far as I could see, nobody was particularly anxious that I should do anything at all; and when the way opened up again it turned out to be quite different from anything that I had imagined. When I got a fairly good degree in mathematics at Cambridge, I hoped for an academic career, but not a single university post was offered me; and three years of teaching in a school convinced me that I was not meant to be a schoolmaster. When I became conscious of a call to the priesthood, I took this as meaning that I should be engaged in parish work for the rest of my working life; it was a complete surprise to be asked to assist in the training of ordinands at Lincoln. And when that came to an end, nothing could have seemed less likely than that I, whose sole academic training had been in mathematics at Cambridge, should be appointed to teach and research in theology at Oxford. Truly, God moves in a mysterious way his wonders to perform; but, while I am only too conscious of the handicap which I have suffered through a complete lack of the training which it had come to be assumed as proper and necessary for a future theologian to receive, I also discovered that the intellectual discipline in which I had been trained as a mathematician gave me an approach and an instrument of which theology was badly in need and which the accepted means of theological education not only did little to supply but, where some

378

faint traces of it existed, could even do something to destroy. Of course I did not see all this in a flash, but it gradually became more and more evident to me that most of what was taught in the academic faculties under the name of theology had little appeal or utility to those who were called to the Church's pastoral and evangelistic work. There seemed, in short, to be a theological task for even as untrained and unconventional a theologian as I, and I located it as lying in the distinct but related areas of philosophical and of dogmatic theology. The reception which my books have received suggests that I was not mistaken. It should at least be clear that I have never thought of myself as an academic who found it convenient to be in holy orders but as a priest who. to his surprise, found himself called to exercise his priesthood in the academic realm.

Does this imply that my freedom as a scholar has been cramped or stunted by my religious commitment? Not in the least, if there is truth in the adage that grace does not destroy nature but perfects it, for the Christian theologian is not merely someone who has been trained in a certain investigative method and then turned loose to practice it upon the documents and institutions of Christianity; he is − or should be − living and thinking and praying within a great tradition. To quote some words from my inaugural lecture at King's College, London, in 1962:

> As I see it, the task of the Christian theologian is that of theologising within the great historical Christian tradition; *theologizandum est in fide*. Even when he feels constrained to criticise adversely the contemporary expressions of the tradition, he will be conscious that he is bringing out from the depths of the tradition its latent and hitherto unrecognised contents; he is acting as its organ and its exponent. He will also offer his own contribution for it to digest and assimilate if it can. Like the good householder he will bring out of his treasure things new and old. But he will have no other gospel than that which he has received.[1]

There are, of course, many questions to which I do not profess to know the answers, about apparent contradictions between some elements in traditional Christianity and what are described as the assured results of modern scholarship; this does not seriously trouble me, as I have no particular right to expect answers to all my questions in this life; rather I am astonished to have been given answers to so many. What I am not prepared to do is to jettison the accumulated wisdom of the Christian ages in order to come to terms with what may well be a passing phase of critical scholarship.² And although establishments develop an infuriating capacity for blandly ignoring attacks that they cannot refute, there are at last ominous signs that the relativism and antisupernaturalism which have dominated the study of Christian origins for nearly a century are crumbling from within.³ Throughout my active lifetime, however, the Church, in all its branches, has been subjected to a widespread and many-faced process of erosion, of which its leaders have been largely unconscious and to which, even when they have been conscious of it, they have often helplessly capitulated. On the level of belief it consists of that relativistic view of truth and that naturalistic view of religion to which I have just referred; the extent to which it has gone is shown by the fact that, when recently an Anglican priest in an academic post, outstripping his colleagues who had denied the Trinity and the Incarnation, proposed to dispense with the existence of God, no formal rejection of his position ensued. On the practical level it is shown by the tendency to make decisions by reference not to the teaching of Christ or the insights and traditions of Christendom but to the pressures of contemporary secularised society; the decision of the Episcopal Church in the U.S.A. about the ordination of women and the attitudes of various Anglican churches about the marriage of divorced persons are examples of this. I sympathise deeply with my fellow Anglicans in the States in the catastrophe which has all but destroyed their church, and the more so because I believe they have simply been struck by the first wave of a storm which is breaking upon the Church as a whole, namely that of a radical relativism and naturalism. For the question which faces every Christian body to day and which underlies all individual practical issues is this: is the Christian religion something revealed by God in Christ, which therefore demands our grateful obedience, or is it something to be made up by ourselves to our own specification, according to our own immediate desires? When we assent, as I am convinced we must, to the first alternative, we must also insist that the second is not only false but bogus, and that our true fulfilment and happiness is not to be found by following our own whims but by giving ourselves to God in Christ, who has given himself for us. For, once again, grace does not destroy nature but fulfils it.

One bright feature in our present situation is the remarkable drawing together not only of Christians of liberal and undogmatic outlook – there is nothing surprising in that – but those of firm traditional allegiance, in bodies that have historically often been at daggers drawn. I recently discovered some quite prophetic remarks made as long ago as 1938 by an anonymous writer in the Quarterly

Review of St Mary's, Graham Street, a church which had acquired
some notoriety as one of the more extreme centres of Anglo-
Catholicism in London and certainly not suspected of sympathy
for Protestantism. The writer was reviewing the Report entitled
Doctrine in the Church of England, which had just been published,
after fifteen years of intensive work, by a very mixed commission
appointed by the two Archbishops in 1922. The reviewer remarked
that 'one of the most curious features of the document [was] the
way in which Catholics, Evangelicals, and professed Modernists
alike show[ed] themselves as tarred with the same brush', namely,
that 'the great problem seemed to be to bring Christianity into
step with the "march of mind", instead of ... to rescue it from
the flight from reason in which modern civilisation seems to be
more and more involving itself ... All alike come to the study of
doctrine with the same presuppositions, and their naïve surprise at
the measure of agreement they have found is in the circumstances
rather comic. What however is not comic but pathetic', the reviewer
continued, and it is here that he became prophetic 'is that there
does exist today, as perhaps never before, a basis upon which
Catholicism and Protestantism might find a point of departure
for agreement, namely a profound belief in revelation and the
supernatural; and this the Report hardly even considers.'[4] Over
forty years later those words have become strikingly true, in
many places and in many ways. The document *Growing into
Union*, produced in 1970 at the time of the Anglican-Methodist
scheme is one example; the close relations between the Conservative
Evangelical[5] theological college at Oak Hill and the Roman Catholic
Benedictine communities at Cockfosters is another; in the United
States the movement named 'Pastoral Renewal', based in Ann
Arbor, Michigan, has brought traditionally minded Catholics and
Protestants together over a vast area; and individual contacts are
widespread. In all this the key-words are 'Revelation' and 'the
supernatural'. There is of course plenty of theological liberalism
about, and when reading some recent professorial utterances I hear
not so much trumpet-calls for the world of the nineteen-eighties as
echoes of the Cambridge of the nineteen-twenties. This has been
reinforced by Roman Catholics, rejoicing in their post-conciliar
freedom not always very responsibly; both by them and by the
ecclesiastical authorities there has been a tendency to repeat, though
in a milder climate, the confusion which so bedevilled the Modernist
controversy at the beginning of the century and to lump together
the demand for a conscientiously exercised freedom of academic
research with a radical rejection of revelation and the supernatural.

This raises issues of tremendous practical importance at the present day, but I cannot discuss them here.

If the task of the Christian theologian is what I have suggested, the question inevitably arises not only whether it is being adequately performed in our academic institutions — I have rather firmly maintained that it is not — but whether, as the nature of those institutions is currently understood, it possibly can be. The very impressive Jesuit thinker Fr Bernard Lonergan has argued in his book *Method in Theology* that a necessary moment in the training of the Christian theologian is a costing and irrevocable conversion, which must take place on the intellectual, the moral and the religious plane. His authoritative interpreter Fr Frederick Crowe, S.J., in his book *The Lonergan Enterprise* presses the point home ruthlessly:

> Do I allow questions of ultimate concern to invade my consciousness, or do I brush them aside because they force me to take a stand on God? With such questions we are being forced to the roots of our own living, challenged to discover, declare, and, if need be, to abandon our horizon in favour of a new one in which our knowing is transformed and our values are transvalued. We are also abandoning the neutral position of an observer, and entering another phase of study altogether.[6]

Fr Crowe also insists that the required renewal of theology and philosophy cannot come about through our existing academic institutions:

> Can you even imagine, much less contemplate as a serious proposal, inviting your university colleagues to a discussion and informing them casually that the spirit of the meeting would be a prayerful one, and that a good part of the input would be the self-revelations of your interior spiritual life and theirs? ... In any case there would be the problem of a state-supported university in a secular state sponsoring such activities. Still negatively, the average theological congress will not be the vehicle for this theology — for the same reason that applies to the university, and for the additional reason that the average congress is described, with a degree of exaggeration but with a grain of truth, too, as a dialogue of deaf persons. One goes there to get off one's chest the ideas that no one back home will listen to; no one at the congress listens, either, but the speaker is not so acutely aware of it.[7]

Fr Crowe suggests that what is needed is a theological centre on the model of the retreat-house:

A theological centre modeled on that would be a place of prayerful and thoughtful quiet to which theologians could retire, not just for two days or a week, but for forty days of retreat from offices and deans' schedules and committee meetings on tenure. They could do theology together in a contemplative mood. Nor would I exclude congresses of shorter duration, provided they are not the 'average' type I just mentioned.[8]

This, it is stressed, still leaves the university with a vital theological role:

> In addition to providing the academic setting for critical scholarship, the first phase and its tasks, as it has been doing for some centuries, it will also be the ordinary vehicle for the interdisciplinary discussions which are a part of systematics and communications. These are discussions without which theology cannot mediate between a religion and a cultural matrix.[9]

Whether there is any real prospect of a radical renewal of the theological enterprise on these lines may indeed seem doubtful, as much perhaps on temperamental as on material grounds. But for myself I can only say this, that, while I am deeply sensible of the tolerance and sympathy which I have received from the academic faculties in which I have worked, the Christian Faith and the Christian Church have been the source from which my inspiration as a theologian has been drawn. I have used the phrase *Theologizandum est in Fide*, and I would now add the words *in Ecclesia, in Liturgia*. Finally, remembering that great master who declared shortly before the end of his earthly pilgrimage that he could write no more because that had been revealed to him compared with which all that he had written was as a straw, I look to the day when, in the words of a possibly even greater master, 'all our activity will be Amen and Alleluya'.

Notes

1. *Theology and History*,. p. 17.
2. Thus, for example, the proposal to abandon St John's Gospel as a source of Christian teaching because of the theory that it is a ghostic fiction is to my mind quite outrageous.
3. See, e.g., Patrick Henry, *New Directions in New Testament Study*, 1979.
4. *St Mary's Graham Street Quarterly Review*, spring 1938, p. 41.

5. I must put in a word of protest against the frequent dismissal of Conservative Evangelicals as 'fundamentalists', in the pejorative sense of that flexible term. Some no doubt are, but others are as certainly not.
6. *The Lonergan Enterprise*, p. 57.
7. ibid., p. 95.
8. ibid.
9. ibid., p. 96.

Index

Indexer's note: E L Mascall's own publications are included in the general index (rather than under his own entry) and are distinguished by an asterisk '*' after the date of publication.